Methods in
Experimental
Psychology

DAVID G. ELMES
Washington & Lee University

BARRY H. KANTOWITZ
Purdue University

HENRY L. ROEDIGER III
Purdue University

Methods in Experimental Psychology

HOUGHTON MIFFLIN COMPANY   BOSTON
Dallas   Geneva, Illinois   Hopewell, New Jersey
Palo Alto   London

Printed in the U.S.A.

Library of Congress Catalog Card Number: 80-50968

ISBN: 0-395-30798-8

This book is dedicated to the memory of

David A. Grant
William M. Hinton
L. Starling Reid

Contents

3 How to Read and Write a Research Report

4 Pitfalls in Conducting Research

5 Basic Experimentation

6   Descriptive Statistics

7   Correlational and Quasi-Experimental Research

To the Reader

This text is derived from an earlier book, *Experimental Psychology* by Kantowitz & Roediger. While the earlier book stressed an integrated approach to both methodology and content, many of our colleagues asked for a shorter text that emphasized methodology only. The book you are now holding is our response to this demand.

We wrote it to help you understand the methods of modern scientific psychology. Few of you will go on to become experimental psychologists, but all of you will be consumers of psychological research even if only through reports in newspapers and magazines. We hope this book will teach you how to evaluate the claims and uses of psychological research.

We have added special features to aid you in reaching this goal. The page facing each chapter presents a conceptual summary of that chapter's contents. Use it as an organizational aid before you start reading the chapter, and, later, use it when you are studying for tests or designing your own experiments. Each chapter has an overview as well as a summary to help you integrate the material it contains. The list of key terms at the end of each chapter is also a helpful review. Finally, try your hand at some of the exercises to make sure you really do understand the concepts that were presented. If a technical term is unclear, use the glossary at the end of the text to find its meaning.

We think experimental psychology is fun and exciting. If we have managed to communicate our feeling to you, then as authors we have achieved one of our most important goals. We dedicate this book to the memory of three outstanding individuals who have shared the fun and excitement of experimental psychology with us: David A. Grant, William M. Hinton, and L. Starling Reid. Each of them, in his own way, has encouraged students to engage in sound psychological science according to their own interests. We encourage you to do the same.

D.G.E.
B.H.K.
H.L.R. III

Methods in Experimental Psychology

THE FUNDAMENTAL QUESTION
Why do we think and act as we do?

Analytic Questions	Purposes	Procedures
What? How often? How much? ⟶	Description ⟶	Naturalistic observation, case studies, surveys, tests
What relates to what? ⟶	Prediction Selection ⟶	Correlation
When? Why? Under what conditions? ⟶	Explanation Finding causes ⟶	"Natural" experiments Laboratory experiments

Fixing Belief

Authority
A priori ⟶ Facts, opinions, stereotypes
Tenacity

Empirical observation
(self-correcting, ⟶ Data
deterministic,
lawful)

Methods of Science

Inductive ⟶ Emphasizes data
Deductive ⟶ Emphasizes theory

Theories

TYPES
inductive, deductive, ⟶ CRITERIA FOR SELECTION
functional, models   parsimony, precision, testability

Scientists

Motivated by curiosity
Follow rules
Recognize serendipity

Introduction to Scientific Psychology

1

Overview

What is scientific psychology all about? How does science differ from other modes of knowing? What are the assumptions underlying the scientific method? These questions will be pursued in this chapter. The answers to these questions provide a framework for the rest of the text, so be sure you understand what is meant by science and scientific psychology.

Purposes of Psychological Research

Psychological research has established the following:

1. Patients waiting to visit a dentist are more fidgety (i.e., they make more restless movements) than nonpatients who are also waiting (Barash, 1974).

2. Bachman and Johnston (1979) report that daily use of marijuana occurs about twice as often among high-school graduates not heading for college than among their college-bound peers.

3. When she started therapy, Ruth L., age 30, washed her hands at least four times each hour, she completely cleaned her small apartment two or more times a day, and she took six or seven extremely thorough showers every day (Leon, 1974).

4. There is little relationship between one's intelligence and one's memory for events that happened 12 years earlier (Squire and Slater, 1975).

5. The more often children choose to watch violent TV in the third grade, the more likely they are to be aggressive in their late teens (Eron et al., 1972).

6. Creating mental images can triple the number of unrelated words you can remember from a long list (Bower, 1972).

7. If an unborn rat is subjected to simulated airplane travel, its growth and behavioral development are retarded (Graessle, Ahbel, and Porges, 1978).

The Fundamental Question

Why do people think and act as they do?   This is the fundamental question scientific psychology attempts to answer. Science usually begins with analysis—the breaking down of a complex problem into its elements. So, scientific answers to our fundamental question involve three interrelated aspects of analysis: *description* of thought and behavior; *prediction* of thought and behavior; and *explanation* of thought and behavior. With regard to the research findings listed at the beginning of this section, we need to describe what *thoughts* and *behaviors* occur and in what *quantity* and *frequency*—waiting dental patients are fidgety, Ruth washes her hands four times an hour, and some of our youth turn on more than others.

As we progress toward answering the question why do people think and act as they do, we need to determine more than just descriptive evidence. We need to be able to specify what thoughts and behaviors go with other thoughts and behaviors. What is the relation between intelligence and remote memory? How does preference for violent TV as a youngster relate to later aggressive activity? Answers to these two questions involve correlation between observations and, therefore, go beyond simple description. *Correlations* between two behaviors allow us to make predictions about future behavior (e.g., predicting aggressiveness on the basis of TV preferences), and we can subsequently make selections on the basis of our correlations (e.g., we need to find some potentially nonaggressive people, so we select them on the basis of their dislike for violent TV programs). Ultimately we want to be able to explain thought and behavior—the causes of retarded growth and development and the conditions leading to improved memory.

These three types of analysis (description, prediction, and explanation) that allow us to break down our fundamental question coordinate with the three major classes of research techniques used in scientific psychology: *observation, correlation,* and *experimentation.* As outlined in Table 1–1, observational procedures include surveys, case studies, tests, and naturalistic observation. Ruth L.'s behavior was catalogued via a case study, which also obtained information about her childhood thoughts and activities. People in a dentist's waiting room were observed naturalistically; that is, they did not know that they were being watched. The observer counted various categories of behavior, such as tapping of feet and drumming of fingers. Surveys and tests are similar in that they both elicit a response from the subject on a particular topic. The 17,000 high school graduates surveyed in June of 1979 by Bachman and Johnston responded to a number of questions about such things as their life goals, money, marriage, politics, and drug use.

Very often the results from these observation procedures allow us to engage in further research. We might use a correlational technique

			Table 1-1
Examples of Questions, Purposes, and Procedures of Psychological Research			

Questions	Primary Purpose	Procedures	Examples
I. What?	Description	a. Naturalistic observation	Behavior in dentist's office
How often?		b. Surveys	Attitudes of high school graduates
How much?		c. Case study	Ruth's compulsive washing
		d. Tests	Measures of intelligence
II. What relates to what?	Prediction Selection	Correlation of two thoughts or behaviors	Relating TV preference to aggression
III. When? Why?	Explanation	a. "Natural" experiments	Determining what people remember from 12 years ago
Under what conditions?	Finding causes	b. Laboratory experiments	Studying the effects of imagery on memory

for the purposes of prediction or selection. Even though you may not have been aware of it, it is likely that you were selected by your college admissions office on the basis of the results of correlational research. A college admissions office correlates such things as high-school grades with freshman college grades so that they can predict who will succeed (at least in the freshman year). Thereafter students with certain high-school credentials are selected on the basis of the previous correlation, and the admissions office can then predict that the selected students have a particular chance of success.

Experimentation involves manipulating or changing some aspect of the situation and observing the effects on a particular thought or behavior. If we want to determine what causes excellent retention, we might vary how people try to remember something (e.g., creating mental images versus simple repetition of the material) and observe the differences in retention that result from these two memorizing procedures. What are the effects of air travel during gestation (i.e., when the baby is still in the mother's womb) on subsequent development? To find out, we subject some pregnant rat mothers to mild atmospheric decompressions and compare the development of their offspring to the development of other rats who were not subjected to decompression prior to birth.

All of these scientific procedures are designed to get information, or what scientists usually call *data* (data is the plural form of the word *datum*), about our fundamental question. The appropriate use of these techniques and the data that are obtained can lead to explanations of why we think and act as we do.

Cause: A note.   Lately it has become popular among scientists, due to the influence of some philosophers of science, not to use the terms "why" and "cause" because the philosophical implications of these terms become frightfully complicated. Thinking too long about the cause of even a very simple event leads to an infinite regress of causes for that event. Imagery causes better memory than simple repetition. Why? Because imagery results in more associations than does repetition. Why? Because more protein molecules in the brain become active when imagery is used. Why? Because. . . . In this book we muddle along using the term "cause" and asking the question "why" since their meanings are always limited; experiments lead to causal inferences because one factor is varied while others, in the ideal case, are held constant. Thus, we can say that whatever effect occurs in such cases was caused by the factor that varied. Instead of asking "why does lung cancer occur?" many prefer "under what conditions does lung cancer occur?" Likewise, instead of "cigarette smoking often causes lung cancer" some prefer to say "cigarette smoking may produce (is an antecedent condition of, determines, or directly affects) lung cancer." We will use the latter terms interchangeably with cause.

Psychology as a Science

Some students find it difficult to think of psychology as a science in the same sense that physics and chemistry are sciences. They believe that there are aspects of human experience, such as the arts, literature, and religion, that defy scientific analysis. Can the beauty of a Klee lithograph or a Beethoven sonata be reduced to cold scientific equations? Can the tender feelings of a first romance, the thrill of driving a sports car at 100 miles per hour, and the agony of a defeated football team be captured in the objective, disinterested fashion required by science?

A group of psychologists, known as humanists, would answer these questions in the negative. Humanists in psychology, most often clinical and counseling psychologists, claim that it is impossible to objectively evaluate and test much of human feelings and experience by traditional scientific methods. Even tough "brass-instrument" experimental psychologists concur that the domain of science is limited. We cannot establish or refute the existence of God by scientific means any more than we could test gravity by theological methods. Science operates where its tools are appropriate. This does not imply that knowledge cannot be gained wherever science fears to tread—that is, by nonscientific means. Many important fields of human endeavor have yet to benefit from extensive scientific analysis: ethics, morals, and law, to name a few.

However, most scientists would hold out the hope that scientific analysis eventually might be usefully applied to many such areas. Much of contemporary psychology was regarded the sole property of philosophy at one time. As psychological techniques improved, these aspects of human experience and behavior moved into the realm of science. And so most psychologists believe that virtually all facets of human experience are fair game for the science of psychology. Making fun of scientific progress in psychology, as did one United States senator who criticized the National Science Foundation for supporting research on romantic love, will not halt efforts to expand psychological knowledge. While concern for the proper and ethical use of such knowledge is valid and important, ignorance is no solution.

The research topics summarized at the beginning of this chapter may not be as earth-shattering as the scientific study of beauty or of morals; however, we think you will agree that those topics are neither completely bizarre nor esoteric. Remember, science nearly always begins with analysis, and it may take a while to apply psychological research techniques to extremely complex problems.

The Fixation of Belief

We think that science and scientific psychology in particular are valid ways to acquire knowledge about the world around us. What characteristics of the scientific approach make it a desirable way to learn and fix our beliefs about the nature of things? Perhaps the best way to answer this question is to contrast science with other modes of fixing belief, because science is only one way that beliefs are formed.

Over 100 years ago, the American philosopher, Charles Sanders Peirce (1877), contrasted the scientific way of knowing with three other methods of developing beliefs. He called these the methods of *authority, tenacity,* and *a priori.* According to Peirce, the simplest way of fixing belief is to take someone else's word on faith. A trusted *authority* tells you what is true and what is false. Young children believe what their parents tell them simply because Mommy and Daddy are always right. As they get older they may discover, unhappily, that Mommy and Daddy are big dummies when it comes to astrophysics, macroeconomics, computer technology, and other specialized fields of knowledge. While this may cause them to doubt some of their parents' earlier proclamations—for example, premarital sex is bad for you—it may not result in utter rejection of this method of fixing belief. Instead, some other authority may be sought. Religious beliefs are formed by the method of authority. Long after you have rejected your parents as the source of all knowledge, you may still believe that the pope is infallible insofar as religious doctrine is concerned. Believing the evening news means that you accept Walter Cronkite or some other news commentator as authority. You believe your professors because they are authorities. Since we lack the resources to investigate everything we learn, much of our knowledge and beliefs have been fixed by the method of authority. Provided nothing happens to raise doubts about the competence of authority setting your beliefs, this method offers the great advantages of minimum effort, comfort, and security. It is most pleasant in a troubled world to have complete faith in beliefs handed down to you.

Another method of fixing belief is one in which a person steadfastly refuses to alter acquired knowledge regardless of evidence to the contrary. The *method of tenacity,* as it was termed by Peirce, is commonly seen in racial bigots who rigidly cling to a stereotype even in the presence of a good counterexample. While this method of maintaining a belief may not be entirely rational, we cannot say it is always nonadaptive. Bigots are still around and somehow manage to find a few others to share their beliefs. The method of tenacity allows people to maintain a uniform and constant outlook on things, so it may relieve them from a certain amount of stress and psychological discomfort. For people who have difficulty handling stress, the method of tenacity may be a reasonable way to fix belief.

The third nonscientific method discussed by Peirce fixes belief *a priori.* The term *a priori* refers to something that is believed without prior study or examination. Propositions that seem reasonable are believed. In this instance we have an extension of the method of authority. While there is no one particular authority that is followed blindly in this method, the general cultural outlook is what seems to fix belief a priori. People once believed the world was flat; and it did seem reasonable to suppose that the sun revolved around the earth as does the moon. Indeed, the world does look flat if you are not in a spacecraft.

If we define scientific psychology (as well as science in general) as a self-correcting endeavor that seeks to understand phenomena on the basis of empirical observation, then we can see several serious drawbacks to the three methods of fixing belief outlined above. First, none of those methods relies upon data obtained by systematic observation. Stating this objection somewhat differently, we would say that there is no empirical basis for fixing belief. The word *empirical* is derived from an old Greek word meaning *experience.* So, having an empirical basis for our beliefs means that we rely on experience for our facts rather than on faith. Having one's beliefs fixed by authority carries no guarantee that the authority obtained data before forming an opinion. The method of tenacity by definition refuses to consider data, as does the *a priori* method. Where facts are considered in these other modes of fixing belief, they are not ordinarily obtained by systematic procedures. Casual observation led to the idea that the world was flat or that frogs spontaneously generated from the mud each spring, as the ancient philosopher Aristotle believed.

The second disadvantage of these methods is that none offers a procedure for establishing the superiority of one belief over the other.

Persons holding different beliefs will find it difficult to reconcile their opinions. Science overcomes this problem. In principle, anyone can make an empirical observation, which means that scientific data can be public and can be repeatedly obtained. Through public observations, new beliefs are compared with old beliefs, and old beliefs are discarded if they do not fit the empirical facts. This does not imply that each and every scientist instantaneously drops outmoded beliefs in favor of new opinions. Changing scientific beliefs is usually a slow process, but eventually incorrect ideas are weeded out. Empirical, public observations are the cornerstone of the scientific method, because they make science a *self-correcting* endeavor.

The fact that science seeks to understand and explain is often summarized as a belief in *determinism.* In the abstract, determinism means that there are reasons (causes or determinants) for a particular event. With regard to psychology, determinism refers to the idea that all thought and behavior results from the heredity and environment of the individual (Hebb, 1974). Other modes of fixing belief emphasize and rely upon traditional, indeterminate causes of thought and action, such as spirits, the spark of life, and human nature. Through our use of empirical methods, we can determine the publicly verifiable causes of thought and action.

The final two advantages of a scientific method over the other methods of fixing belief derive from an acceptance of the principle of determinism. If there are empirical determinants of thought and action, then the causes are *knowable* or *discoverable.* We may not know *all* of the determinants of good memory or adolescent attitudes, but we assume that there are actual, knowable causes that we can, in principle, discover. Discovery may have to wait for the development of scientific techniques and additional knowledge.

It also follows from the idea of determinism that the causes of retarded development in offspring or the determinants of restless behavior in the dentist's office are regular or *lawful.* How the causes of thought and action work follow rules or laws. Authority changes as does a priori reasonableness of something—the rules of equal opportunity or capitalistic economics can and have altered. However, we have to assume that custom or authority does not change the rules of how thought and behavior work.

Public Examination of Thought and Behavior

To summarize our argument so far, scientific psychology is a public, self-correcting enterprise that relies on systematic, empirical observation for its data.

It might have occurred to you that behavior is a public phenomenon capable of scientific analysis, but that thoughts and feelings, being private internal events, probably are not determinable, knowable phenomena. If these ideas did occur to you, you were partially correct, and you were in the mainstream of psychological theorizing.

The fundamental difficulty is how can we scientifically study thoughts as well as behaviors? The way that internal affairs become objects of scientific study is indirect. Thoughts, attitudes, and the like must be observed in behavior before they can be subjected to scientific analysis. We assume that many behaviors (e.g., restless activity in a dentist's waiting room) can reflect an underlying feeling, in this case "nervous tension." Furthermore, other public events, such as verbal reports (e.g., "Marijuana use should be legal") and physiological responses (e.g., brain waves), can correspond to important internal events.

Accordingly, psychology is, as stated in most introductory textbooks, the scientific study of behavior. However, behavior is examined to understand human action directly and human thought indirectly. Just because we study behavior, we should not be blind to the fact that behavior can reflect underlying processes that are not directly observable. The fundamental question is a valid one—thoughts are harder to study than behaviors. But complexity should not deter us. Therefore, even though psychology may be defined as the scientific study of behavior, its purpose is to unravel both the internal and external mysteries of human activity.

Science is not the only way to know; however, it is a very good way to fix belief. The remainder of this chapter considers some additional aspects of the scientific method.

Two Methods of Science: Inductive and Deductive

Certain basic elements are shared by all approaches to science. The most important of these are *data* (observations) and *theory* (explanation). Science needs and uses both data and theory. However, individual scientists often differ about which is more important and which comes first. Trying to decide this is a little like trying to decide whether the chicken or the egg came first. We shall not try to foist our own prejudices in this manner upon you. Important scientific achievements have been obtained by scientists who stress data and by scientists who stress theory. We shall call the scientist who starts with data and works up to theory an *inductive* scientist and one who starts with theory and works down to data a *deductive* scientist. Although we shall pretend that these two approaches are black and white with no shades of gray in order to emphasize their differences, it is easy to combine them, and many psychologists have used both approaches.

The Inductive Scientist: Emphasis on Data

The inductive scientist is primarily concerned with data. But what are data and where do they come from? What does the scientist do with data once they are obtained? Data (more than one) or a datum (singular) are technical terms that correspond to what the nonscientist means by the terms facts or fact. Thus, a datum is a piece of information resulting from a systematic observation. The difference between a fact (nontechnical term) and a datum (technical term) can be illustrated through the casual or systematic observation of a cow. Let's say you are driving by a farm and you see a solitary cow grazing. You might state that you know for a fact that the cow is black. However, a scientist would object to your statement on the grounds that your observation has not been systematic. In particular, you have only seen one side of the cow. Before the scientist would accept your fact as a datum he or she would insist upon viewing the other side of the cow to see if it also were black. Without this observation your fact would be only a plausible guess to the scientist. Perhaps you feel that this example is a bit farfetched, like quibbling over how many angels can crowd onto the head of a pin. But if you substitute the moon for the cow, the argument falls into proper perspective. Until a spacecraft actually made observations of the far side of the moon, no one really knew what was there. While it was plausible to assume that the far side of the moon was just like the visible side, no one knew for sure. There were no data. Useful data are thus obtained by systematic, rather than by haphazard or casual, observation. There are many systematic ways to make observations and these are discussed throughout this book. For now, merely note that observations must be made in some orderly (and usually predetermined) way before they can lead to data.

Data have many characteristics—variance, reliability, validity, to name a few you will encounter later on—that are of great importance to the scientist, and these facets of data are treated throughout this text. Before data can be useful, they must be checked to assure that they meet current standards. This is often accomplished by the use of statistics, although statistics by themselves do not guarantee that data will be useful. A large part of the craft of experimental psychology is establishing situations for obtaining data in such a manner as to make it quite likely that these data meet all necessary requirements. Thus it is essential that the scientist demonstrate that data exhibit proper characteristics; discussion of how this can be accomplished is deferred until following chapters.

After the scientist is satisfied that the data are in order and can be sensibly interpreted, the final step is communication. The data are published in a suitable journal for other scientists to read. Then the inductive scientist goes back to the laboratory to obtain additional data. It is here that the most dramatic distinction between inductive and deductive scientists occurs. The inductive scientist believes that if enough data are gathered, patterns of explanation will become obvious. For example, if I ask you to complete the series "2, 4, . . .," you might say "6" or "8," or you might reply "16." You do not have enough data for a pattern to emerge. If I give you an additional datum, say "16," you can now predict that the next number in the series should be 256. The pattern calls for squaring each number (multiplying it by itself) to obtain the next number. With sufficient data, the pattern became obvious. The inductive scientist is guided mostly by past data that tell what questions should be asked next. But the deductive scientist questions the value of this approach, claiming that data by themselves will never turn into explanation, regardless of how much data may be gathered.

Figure 1–1   Unlike Lucy's perfect theory, a good scientific theory can be rejected.

The Deductive Scientist: Emphasis on Theory

The deductive scientist emphasizes the importance of explanation. Data are useful only insofar as they directly bear upon the validity of some proposed explanation. In particular, data may permit the deductive scientist to decide which of two or more alternate explanations is correct. If, however, no explanations of some effect or phenomenon have been offered, then the deductive scientist has little interest in obtaining data. Instead, the scientist would devote time and energy to creating some explanation. The deductive scientist believes that data cannot be collected intelligently without the guiding framework of some explanation, even if this attempted explanation is far from complete. Many deductive scientists would have little interest in obtaining data if only one explanation were available. These scientists argue that explanations are discarded only when better explanations emerge. Data are most valuable when they can distinguish among competing explanations. While data that are inconsistent with a single explanation may eventually motivate new and better explanations, the deductive scientist would rather spend time thinking about explanations instead of gathering more data. The deductive scientist becomes enthusiastic about data only after the many details of some explanation have been worked out beforehand. Even then, the pure deductive scientist may not gather data if existing data, possibly obtained by an inductive scientist, can be located and borrowed.

It should be clear, then, that the deductive scientist is concerned primarily with ideas. Most effort goes into formulating a theoretical explanation. Once the explanation has been completed, the scientist deduces what should occur in some particular situation and is able to generate a prediction even though no other scientist may have studied this particular situation. You may never have seen a raw egg thrown into a rotating electric fan. Nevertheless, you probably can make an excellent prediction about the outcome of this particular situation. To do so you are making a deduction based upon your intuitive theoretical understanding of biology and physics. A physicist and a biologist could probably make more exact predictions than you, such as the precise dispersion pattern depending upon the size of the egg, the speed of the fan, etc. But even without this knowledge, you can still generate a reasonably accurate, although undetailed, prediction.

Comparing Inductive and Deductive Scientists

Portraits of inductive and deductive scientists have been constructed by Mitroff and Kilmann (1975). Here are portions of their descriptions:

> Type A [what we would call the inductive scientist] is the kind of scientist who first and foremost regards himself as a Hard Experimentalist. He takes extreme pride in his carefully designed and detailed experimental work. In general, he prefers hard data gathering to abstract theorizing. . . . He feels that one really doesn't understand something until he has collected some hard data on it. He feels that abstract theorists have a tendency to get lost in their abstractions for their own sake and hence to mistake them for reality. . . . He feels that theorizing and speculating are only warranted when the data are available that clearly support such activities. He is quick to master complicated and sophisticated experimental techniques.
>
> Type B [what we would call the deductive scientist] is the kind of scientist who first and foremost regards himself as an Abstract Theorizer. He takes extreme pride in his ability to construct formal, analytical models. . . . In general, he prefers building abstract theoretical models to experimental data gathering. He feels that one really doesn't understand something until he has built a general theory of it. He feels that hard data gatherers have a tendency to become so engrossed in collecting data for its own sake that they never get around to putting it all together in some systematic conceptual sense.

These portraits should give you some insight into the personalities of the two different types of scientists. We have been very careful to avoid stating which type of science is "better" because both are necessary. In the long run, both types of scientist have the same goal. They differ about the best tactics for reaching this goal. The inductive scientist starts with data and works up to (or induces) explanation. The deductive scientist starts with explanation and then uses data to verify or correct the abstract model. It is important to realize that neither the inductive nor deductive approach is an automatic formula for scientific success. Intuition and creativity play an important role that has only begun to be documented (Medawar, 1969).

Before concluding this section, we should remind you of the warning that preceded it. In order to distinguish clearly between inductive and deductive approaches to science, we have pretended that they are black and white. In psychology, this is seldom the case. While well-established sciences like astronomy can divide practitioners into those concerned almost entirely with explanation and theory (theoretical astronomers) and those concerned with data acquisition (observers) the dividing line in psychology is much more blurred. The same psychologist can often act like a deductive scientist one moment and an inductive scientist the next.

Theory Construction in Psychology

Being familiar with observation and data, you may have found it easier to understand the inductive scientist than the deductive scientist. Detailed discussion of the distinctions between types of common observation and scientific observation is left for later discussion. Now we focus upon theory and explanation. The concept of a theory is more difficult than the concept of an observation. There is more than one type of theorizing in science, and even a specific science, such as psychology, contains more than one kind of theoretical statement.

What Is a Theory?

A theory can be crudely defined as a set of related statements that explain a variety of occurrences. The more the occurrences, and the fewer the statements, the better the theory. The law of gravity explains falling apples, the behavior of roller coasters, and the position of bodies within the solar system. With a small number of statements about the mutual attraction of bodies, it explains a large number of events. It is therefore a powerful theory. (This does not necessarily mean it is a correct theory, since there are some events it cannot explain.)

Theory in psychology performs two major functions. First, it provides a framework for the systematic and orderly display of data—that is, it serves as a convenient way for the scientist to *organize* data. Even the most dedicated inductive scientist will eventually have difficulty remembering the outcomes of dozens of experiments. Theory can be used as a kind of filing system to help experimenters organize results. Second, it allows the scientist to generate *predictions* for situations where no data have been obtained. The greater the degree of agreement about these predictions, the better the theory. With the best of intentions, scientists who claim to be testing the same theory often derive from the theory different predictions about the same situation. This unfortunate circumstance is relatively more common in psychology, where many theories are stated in a loose verbal fashion, than in physics, where theories are more formal and better quantified. While psychologists are rapidly stating their theories more precisely through formal mechanisms like mathematics and computer simulations, it is still true that the typical psychological theory has nowhere near the elegance of theories in more established, older sciences.

Sometimes these two functions of theory—organization and prediction—are called *description* and *explanation* respectively. Unfortunately, formulating the roles of theory in this manner often leads to an argument about the relative superiority of deductive or inductive approaches to science—a discussion we have already dismissed as fruitless. According to the deductive scientist, the inductive scientist is concerned only with description. The inductive scientist defends against this charge by retorting that description is explanation—if we could correctly predict and control all behavior by referring to properly organized sets of results, then we could indeed also explain behavior. The argument is futile because both types of scientist are correct. *If* we already had all the data we needed properly organized, we could make predictions without recourse to a formal body of theoretical statements. Since we don't have all the data properly organized as yet, and perhaps never will, theories are required to bridge the gap between knowledge and ignorance. Remember, however, that our theories will never be complete because all the data will never be in. So, we have merely recast the argument between inductive and deductive scientists about which technique will more quickly and surely lead to an answer to our fundamental question.

Ultimately description and explanation may be equivalent, which is really saying that the two terms describe the path taken more than the eventual theoretical outcome. At this point you should reread Table 1–1. The systematic procedures for gathering data have slightly different purposes in the scientific scheme of things, but those procedures and the two general scientific approaches have one thing in common: determination of why people think and act as they do.

Four Kinds of Psychological Theory Construction

Just as there is more than one way to build a house, there also are several ways to build a theory. If we start with the foundation and work our way up to the roof, we have an *inductive* theory. If we alternate where we can between foundation and roof, putting in a wall here or there, then a basement window, then a chimney, we have a *functional* theory. If we build the roof first and have a crane hold it up while we insert the foundations under it, we have a *deductive* theory, once the crane is removed. If, on the other hand, we always need a crane to hold up the roof, we have a *model.*

These fanciful analogies with house construction are far from exact descriptions of the kinds of theory. Marx (1963) has more formally described these four modes of theory construction. They are illustrated in Figure 1–2. Two of them correspond quite closely to the style of the inductive and deductive scientists previously discussed. An *inductive theory* starts from the data base and organizes empirical relationships into theoretical principles. In psychology this type of theory construction is most often identified with the work of Skinner (1956) on reinforcement and learning.

Figure 1–2

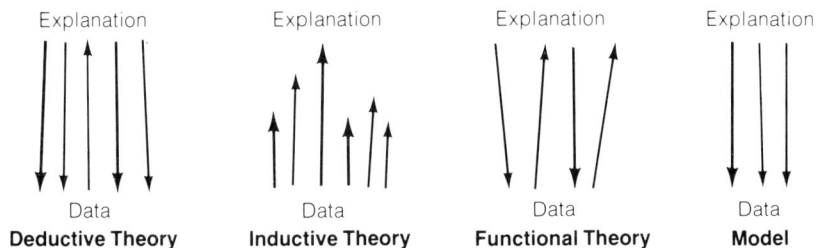

Four modes of theory construction in psychology. While all theories use both data and explanation, they differ in their emphases upon each and in how each modifies the other (adapted from Marx, 1963).

The *deductive theory* starts with explanation and then consults data to test predictions of (deductions from) the theory. If the data are not in agreement with predictions, the theory is modified and new predictions are generated. This process is continued repetitively until either the modifications to the theory become so unwieldy that a newer, more compact theory replaces it, or most psychologists lose interest in the issues the theory explains. The deductive theory is often referred to as the classical type of theory construction because it offers the greatest degree of formality and has been quite successfully employed in older sciences like physics and chemistry. Psychologists who favor the deductive theory argue that these past successes in other sciences make it the best choice. Clark Hull is the psychologist most often associated with deductive theory construction in the area of learning and motivation.

Hull's theory (1943) was an ambitious attempt to formally characterize a wide span of knowledge. This theory dominated work in this area for over a decade. Yet now it is considered outmoded, if not incorrect, by most psychologists in the area of learning, although psychologists in other areas such as social psychology still use constructs derived from Hull's theory.

The *functional theory* is a hybrid creature combining both inductive and deductive elements. It stresses data and explanation about equally. The name functional theory is derived from a school of psychology that was concerned with how organisms function in coping with their environment. As a compromise position it was, and still is, more typical of American psychological research than either the pure inductive or deductive mode. Some noted psychologists associated with functional theory are Benton Underwood (in the area of memory) and Leon Festinger (for his congitive-dissonance theory of attitude change in social psychology).

The *model* has become the theory of choice in recent times, particularly in cognitive psychology. The great popularity of information processing approaches to psychology with their accompanying "black box" diagrams has much to do with this change in the theoretical style of American psychology. The model has several unique features, not all of which can be schematically represented in Figure 1–2, that account for its current popularity. The model can tolerate large differences between its predictions and actual data. Figure 1–2 represents this by *not* showing any arrows leading from data back to model. This unusual theoretical feature arises because a model is really an *analogy.* Analogies in psychology are generally based upon physical, electronic, chemical, and computer technologies. Right now, computer analogies are most popular, but psychology has a long history of borrowing concepts from other sciences and adapting them to handle psychological issues. For example, Freud's model of the mind can be considered to derive from the hydraulic (fluid-flow) analogy, with the ego and superego acting like a valve controlling fluid pressure and flow (the force of the id).

Do not confuse this use of the term model with its use in phrases like "mathematical model" or "computer model." These are really formal deductive theories and not models in the technical sense of one of the four kinds of theory construction. Models are used to guide data collection and to serve as frameworks for more formal subsequent theoretical efforts. These latter efforts often are of the deductive type. From this perspective, models are initial stages of theoretical development rather than ultimate ends. As models are modified by data collection they become more and more like functional or deductive theories.

Since the model is such an important mode of theory, we will illustrate it with an example. The concept of feedback, originally used in engineering, has become important in psychology (Miller, Galanter, and Pribram, 1960; Annett, 1969; Welford, 1976). *Feedback* is defined as a flow of information (or energy) counter to the main flow. This is somewhat abstract, so we will take a concrete example, the thermostat in your house, to help explain it. You set your thermostat for the desired room temperature, say, 68° F. This value is called the input signal. A sensor inside the thermostat measures actual room temperature. Another device inside the thermostat, called a comparator, checks to see if the input signal and the actual temperature agree. If they do, no action is required. It they don't, the thermostat turns on the furnace (or air conditioner) to bring the two values into agreement. This sequence of events is depicted in Figure 1–3, where the role of feedback is shown. The main flow of information and energy is from left to right in the diagram. The loop going from the output of the furnace back to the thermostat is called a feedback loop. Information about room temperature is fed back from the output to the comparator inside your thermostat. As a result of this feedback information, the comparator decides, after checking the input signal, whether or not to turn on the furnace, or if the furnace is already on, whether or not to turn it off. So the thermostat is an example of a physical system that uses feedback.

What does this have to do with psychological systems and behavior? Many recent models of behavior assume that it is controlled, at least in part, by feedback information. Close your eyes and try to touch the tips of your index fingers together. You probably came very close. Feedback from your muscles allows you to estimate the positions of your fingers. Of course, you can do this much better with your eyes open. This tells us that visual feedback is a more important component of the positioning model than is muscle feedback. Other more complicated models based upon feedback could be given (Miller et al., 1960;

Figure 1–3

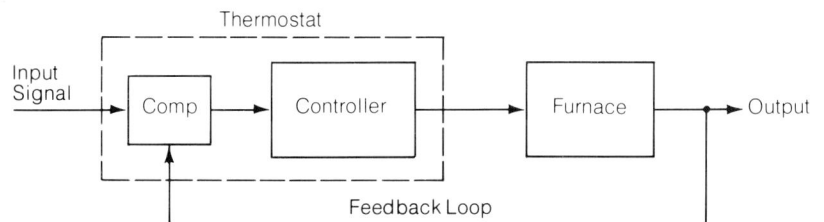

A feedback system. The input signal is the setting of your thermostat. The comparator (Comp) matches input and feedback. If they differ, the controller turns on the furnace. This increases room temperature and changes the feedback signal received by the comparator. When input and feedback signals match, the controller turns off the furnace.

Annett, 1969; Welford, 1976). The important point is that a concept derived from a physical model can and has been used to model human and animal behavior.

Never forget that a model is just an analogy. No one expects an analogy to be 100 percent accurate. We may not behave exactly like thermostats but this does not upset the model unduly. A model can tolerate discrepancies that would be fatal to a formal deductive theory. Why then are models useful if they can be so inaccurate? The model serves mainly to meet the organizational requirements of theory. It is less useful when precise predictions are made, although models do make predictions.

Another unique feature of the model as used in psychology is its limited scope. While classical theories like Hull's tried to encompass many different kinds of situations and events, current models are most typically tied to only a few specific types of situations. That is why models are sometimes referred to as "pocket theories" or "mini-theories." These limitations make it easier to make theoretical statements, since only a small amount of ground needs to be covered. However, the disadvantage of models is that it is difficult to tie several models together to explain several situations. Many psychologists feel that the extensive use of models has resulted in a patchwork theoretical structure and has caused the various subspecialties within experimental psychology to draw apart from each other. For better or worse, there is nothing on the theoretical horizon that will soon replace the model.

Evaluating Theories: When Explanations Collide

The sophisticated scientist does not try to determine if a particular theory is true or false in an absolute sense. There is no black and white approach to theory evaluation. A theory may be known to be incorrect in some portion and yet continue to be used. In modern physics, light is represented, according to the theory chosen, as either discrete particles called quanta or continuous waves. Logically, light cannot be both at the same time. Thus, you might think that at least one of these two theoretical views must necessarily be false. The physicist tolerates this ambiguity, perhaps not cheerfully, and uses whichever representation —quanta or wave—is more appropriate. Instead of flatly stating that a theory is true, the scientist is much more likely to state that it is supported substantially by data, thereby leaving open the possibility that new data may not support the theory. A theory can never be proved but only disproved. Data that are inconsistent with a theory can lead to its eventual rejection. Data that are only partially consistent with a theory cause it to be modified and to evolve. But data that support a theory only postpone its ultimate rejection. Although scientists do not state that a theory is true, they must often decide which of several theories is best. Although none of them may be true—that is, ultimately all may be rejected and replaced by others—the scientist still needs to decide which theory is best for now. In order to do so, there must be explicit criteria for evaluating a theory.

We have already hinted at one important criterion when we earlier stated the fewer the statements in a theory, the better the theory. This criterion is called *parsimony* or sometimes Occam's razor, after the English philosopher William of Occam. If a theory needs a separate statement for every result it must explain, clearly no economy has been gained by the theory. Theories gain power when they can explain many results with fewer explanatory concepts. Thus, if two theories have the same number of concepts, the one that can explain more results is a better theory. If two theories can explain the same number of results, the one with fewer explanatory concepts is preferred.

Precision is another important criterion, especially in psychology where it is often lacking. Theories that involve mathematical equations or computer programs are generally more precise, and hence better, than those that use loose verbal statements (all other things being equal, of course). Unless a theory is sufficiently precise so that different investigators can agree about its predictions, it is for all intents and purposes useless.

Testability goes beyond precision. A theory can be very precise and yet not able to be tested. For example, when Einstein proposed the equivalence of matter and energy ($E = MC^2$), nuclear technology was not able to directly test this relationship. Since theories can never be proved, but only disproved, the scientist places a very high value on the criterion of testability. A theory that cannot be tested can never be disproved (see Figure 1–1). At first you might think this would be a good quality since it would be impossible to demonstrate that such a theory was incorrect. The scientist takes the opposite view. For example, let's take ESP (extrasensory perception). Some believers in ESP claim that the presence of a disbeliever is sufficient to prevent a person gifted with ESP from performing, since the disbeliever puts out bad vibes that disrupt ESP. This means that ESP cannot be disproved, because only believers can be present when it is demonstrated. The scientist takes a dim view of this logic, and most scientists, especially psychologists, are skeptical about ESP. Unless a theory can potentially be disproved, it is not testable. Our belief in a theory increases as it survives tests that could reject it. Since it is logically possible that some future test may find a flaw, our belief in a theory is never absolute. If it is not logically possible to test a theory, it cannot be evaluated and hence is useless to the scientist. If it is logically possible but not yet technically feasible, as was once the case with Einstein's theory, then evaluation of a theory is deferred.

Remember what the functions of a theory are: to provide a summary of our data and to yield a scientific description or explanation of our data. We must be cautious about our theorizing. Unfortunately many scientists, regardless of their general approach, can get carried away with the value of a particular theory. All too often an attractive theory becomes a faddish explanation for all kinds of psychological phenomena, even though the theory or model was not intended to be so general. As long as our theories make contact with our data, there are few serious problems. If we forget the purposes of a theory and try to make the theory take on an existence independent of our data, difficulties arise. For example, suppose we account for the better retention that results from imagery by saying that imagery results in a more organized memory. This theoretical description fits with a lot of other data we have about memory, and the implications of an organized memory should be testable. There is a strong tendency, however, to then suppose that there is a thing (presumably in the brain) called *organization,* which implies that we could, conceivably, go inside a person and manipulate that structure called organization. When we think we can do that, we have incorrectly given a hypothetical concept a life of its own—just as Rip Van Winkle believed thunder to be caused by bowling matches in the sky. Making a concept real is called *reification,* and we can avoid this pitfall if we remember that theories are tentative ways of describing and explaining data. Any theoretical explanation must be testable, which means that it can stand the test of empirical evaluation—saying that a concept such as organization exists (it has empirical status) requires independent evidence for its existence. One of the purposes of a broad attack on an empirical problem is to converge upon a satisfactory explanation of the data (see Chapter 10 on converging operations).

Rules and Guidelines in Science

Most of this text is devoted to a presentation of procedures, methods, and rules for conducting and evaluating psychological research. Presentation of these rules and guidelines has an effect similar to the worn out "good news/bad news" jokes. The good news is that the rules and guidelines should permit you to do precise research, and they should provide you with an adequate framework from which you can consider the results presented by others. So, the rules of scientific procedure—the "Scientific Method"—can be viewed as means to help guarantee the self-correcting benefits of science: good science and good scientific evaluation will supplant errors and generate more good science. The bad news about rules and regulations is that they may stifle scientific curiosity and creativity (Hinton, 1966; Skinner, 1956).

Much of what we have said so far seems to indicate that the collection of data and subsequent theorizing is a neat, orderly process; and neat, orderly psychological research is what this book is all about.

However, two things should have forewarned you about the bad news. We have put the phrase scientific method in quotation marks, and we have emphasized the role of curiosity about people as a basis for scientific psychology. The quotation marks suggest that the phrase the *scientific method* may be misleading, and our concern with curiosity indicates that the orderly progression of science may depend upon a lucky by-product of research, what Hinton (1966) called a serendipitous pattern. "The creative scientist must learn to tolerate ambiguity, to be stimulated by it, and that it is essential that he avoid a compulsive passion for experimental design which might prevent the occurrence of the *serendipitous pattern*, that unexpected and anomalous finding which elicits and investigator's curiosity and conducts him along an unpremeditated by-path to a fresh hypothesis and new vistas" (p. 62, italics added).

When we follow the rules of scientific observation, we must realize that we may never come up with a finished product. Empirical observations are, in a sense, waiting to be refuted by the next empirical observation. This makes psychological research never-ending, exciting, and dependent upon curious and creative scientists. What *will* happen next? What will I find out in the future? We may chance upon a serendipitous finding in the course of our research, and we had better be in a position to drop everything else and follow up our interesting findings as Skinner (1956) has noted. However, we had better not leave everything to chance. Pasteur, the famous chemist and immunologist, is supposed to have said that, "chance favors the prepared mind." We would like to add that chance also favors the curious, creative mind.

Summary

Scientific psychology is a self-correcting search for knowledge that attempts to determine why we think and act as we do on the basis of systematic empirical observation. Other modes of fixing belief, authority, a priori reasonableness, and tenacity, do not have the important characteristics of the scientific method: empirical approach, self-correction, determinism, knowability, and lawfulness.

In trying to understand thought and behavior, some scientists emphasize data (inductive approach) and some scientists emphasize theory (deductive approach). Both approaches ultimately rely upon data obtained by empirical means: observation, correlation, and experimentation. Simple, precise, and testable theories, regardless of their particular form, help summarize and explain why we think and act as we do. We must not take our theories too seriously, however, and we should always be in a position to take advantage of serendipitous findings.

Exercises

1. Jot down several questions you may have pondered about why people think and act as they do. How would you go about trying to answer these questions? Which of the research techniques indicated in Table 1–1 seems most appropriate to use in answering each of your questions?

2. Suppose that astronauts in the year 3000 find a living organism on a distant planet whose behavior is markedly different from ours. This creature seems to respond to the presence of the astronauts in their silvery, shimmering spacesuits, but the new-found cousin does not appear to notice the red, white, and blue flag that is carried by the astronauts. What kinds of deductions do you make about the psychology and physiology of this creature? How would you go about demonstrating that your deductions are true?

3. Various models have played an important part in the development of scientific psychology. See how many different models of people you can think of that have been used as a starting point for psychological investigation. You might find it interesting that one of the first models, other than a spiritual one, that had a big impact on psychological thought was the robot or mechanical model proposed by Descartes, a French philosopher, in the middle of the seventeenth century! Apparently Descartes got his idea for a machine model from the intricate motor-driven statues and garden fountains that were common in France at that time.

4. Some psychologists view the effects of reinforcement on behavior as due to a theoretical effect inside the organism, such as the satisfaction of a biological drive like hunger. Others ignore such theories and simply point to the effectiveness of the reinforcing operation. Describe these two views from the standpoint of the deductive/inductive dichotomy. What are some of the values and drawbacks of each approach?

Key Concepts

fundamental question 2	cause 4
description 2	method of authority 5
prediction 2	method of tenacity 6
explanation 2	a priori method 6
correlation 2	empirical 6
observation 2	self-correcting nature of science 7
experimentation 3	determinism 7
data 3	knowability in science 7

Suggested Readings

Further information about the nature of science and scientific psychology may be found in *Experimental psychology: understanding behavioral research* by B. H. Kantowitz and H. L. Roediger III. Chapters 1–3, Chicago: Rand McNally, 1978.

Excellent discussions about the nature and importance of scientific psychology appear in these publications: Broadbent, D. E. *In defence of empirical psychology.* London: Methuen, 1973. Hebb, D. O. What psychology is about. *American Psychologist,* 1974, *29,* 71–79. Sidman, M. *Tactics of scientific research.* New York: Basic Books, 1960.

DATA

↓

Measurable attributes of thought and behavior

Measurement Scales:

Nominal
Ordinal
Interval
Ratio

Measurement Techniques:

Category ratings
  (indirect measurement)
Magnitude estimation
  (direct measurement)

Good data are: Reliable and Valid

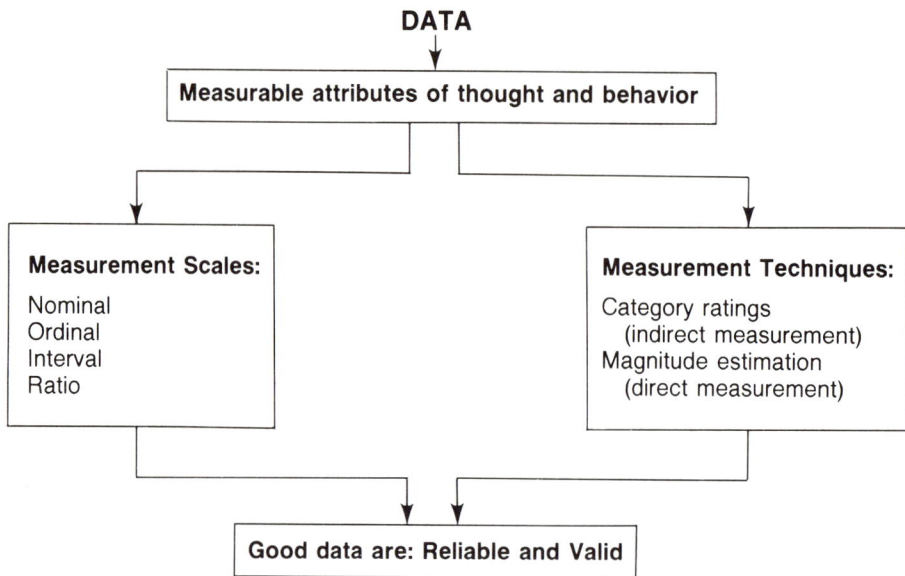

DATA COLLECTION PROCEDURES

For descriptive data: **Naturalistic observation**
                               must be unobtrusive

                               Case study
                               often uses deviant case analysis

                               Survey research
                               may use participant observer method

---

For predictive data: **Correlational approach**
                               measured by the correlation coefficient—causal statements are
                               difficult

For explanatory data: **Quasi-experiments**
                               ex post facto studies, which lack control

                               True experiments
                               since the independent variable is varied and other variables
                               controlled, causal statements about the dependent variable are
                               possible

Data and Data Collection in Psychology

2

What are data? In this chapter we follow up our discussion of scientific psychology by considering the nature of psychological data and data collection. We define data as the attributes of behavior that are measured by systematic observation. Direct and indirect measurement procedures and the primary data collection techniques—observation, correlation, and experimentation—are detailed.

Overview

In the previous chapter we distinguished between facts and data by noting that data are the result of scientific (systematic) observation, while facts derive from either casual observation or other modes of fixing belief. Since the purpose of scientific psychology is to understand why people think and act as they do, we need a data base upon which to theorize and try to explain thought and behavior. So, the starting point for you is an understanding of the nature of data and data collection in psychology.

Data: The Measurement of Behavior

Attributes of Thought and Behavior

Science, as we have said, begins with analysis. *Analysis* means to break something down into its components and then to examine each component. In turn, analysis and examination imply that we have the ability to describe the constituent parts in a systematic, scientific way. What does this abstract description of analysis have to do with psychology? Consider these two versions of the same (true) story.

Version I This girl in my dorm, Barbara, is totally messed up. She got so far behind in her assignments that she had to cheat on a lab test. She got caught and was suspended from school.

Version II This girl in my dorm, Barbara, is totally messed up. Instead of doing her assignments, she would goof off by reading science fiction and listening to her stereo. She got so far behind that she cheated on a lab test and got caught cheating. She was suspended from school.

The major difference between the two versions is that Version 2 specifies some aspects or attributes of Barbara's behavior; Version 1

25

does not. Simply stating that someone is "messed up," regardless of whether or not "messed up" is the appropriate technical jargon, is insufficient for a meaningful analysis. In order to try to understand Barbara's problems, we have to have some way to describe the attributes of her thought and behavior. What is she doing that makes her messed up? What activities and attitudes resulted in her eventual need to cheat on a lab exam? While the need for analytic description in this particular example may be obvious to you, what may not be so obvious is that the Version 2 description provides attributes that have the possibility of being measured. *Measurement* is a systematic way of assigning numbers to objects and their attributes. It is a dictum in psychology that anything that exists, be it the amount of time studied or attitudes toward science fiction novels, exists in some amount. And anything that exists in some amount can be measured. In order to analyze thought and behavior, we have to have some measure of the thoughts and behaviors themselves. We cannot attack a problem via scientific procedures until we have some way of measuring what is going on.

If you will reconsider the analytic breakdown of the fundamental question (why people think and act as they do) into observation, prediction, and explanation, you should now recognize that the procedures associated with that breakdown and the questions that go with them require *measurable data* before the procedures can be successful. With regard to Barbara, we need to know at least some of the following: What did she do instead of school work? When did she escape into science fiction? Under what conditions would she find it essential to cheat? What other attributes of her behavior help us understand why she is so reluctant to do her school work?

To summarize, data are the measurable attributes of behavior and thought that result from systematic application of scientific procedures. Now we must consider some of the characteristics of measurement.

Measurement of Thought and Behavior

Types of Measurement Scales. When we systematically assign numbers to objects or the attributes of objects, that is, when we measure them, we have gone a long way toward collecting data. However, not all measurement scales are equivalent. In particular, different *scales* result from different measurement operations. A scale type is mathematically defined (Suppes and Zinnes, 1963) by the kinds of transformations, such as adding a constant or multiplying by a constant and so forth, that can be performed without altering the unique properties of the scale. Psychologists are most concerned with four types of scales called *nominal, ordinal, interval,* and *ratio,* although other types exist. These four scale types have been listed here according to increasing power of measurement, with each successive scale type having the properties of preceding types plus new properties. One thing this means is that data obtained using a ratio scale could be statistically analyzed by methods appropriate to any of the three lesser scales, but statistics appropriate only for a ratio scale would not fit the other scales (see Chapter 9).

It is interesting that the simplest measurement operation—counting —produces the highest scale type—ratio. A *ratio scale* remains unique if all the scale numbers are multiplied by a constant. Any other arithmetic operation destroys the ratio properties of the scale. The easiest way for you to tell if a scale has ratio properties is to look for two characteristics. First, the scale has a real zero corresponding to no objects or none of the scale property. A physical scale that satisfies this condition is weight in grams. Zero grams truly means no weight. The second characteristic of the ratio scale, from which its name derives, is that ratios of scale values make sense. Thus, a ten gram weight has the same relationship to a five gram weight as a 24 gram weight has to a 12 gram weight, since the ratio of the two weights is 2.0 in both cases. A scale that satisfies these conditions for Barbara would be study time. Zero study time truly means no time spent in study. Also, three hours of study time has the same relation to one hour as does six hours of study to two hours, since the ratio of the two study periods is 3.0 in both instances.

An *interval scale* is unchanged if a constant is added or if scale values are multiplied by a constant. In an interval scale there is no real zero, and although distances between adjacent scale numbers are equal, ratios of pairs of scale values are not meaningful. Fahrenheit and Centigrade are interval scales. While the zero value will change depending upon whether Fahrenheit or Centigrade scale units are chosen, the distance between adjacent units is equal. A temperature increase from 34° to 35° produces the same change as an increase from 35° to 36° (on either scale). An interval scale of some attribute of Barbara could be her grade in a particular course. It is usually assumed (that is, the grading scales are so devised) that the intervals between *A*s and *B*s are about the same as the intervals between *B*s and *C*s and so on. However, on the typical letter-grade scale, there is little reason to assume that a person who received an *A* did twice as well as someone who did *C* work or that the *A* student is half-again better than the *B* student.

In fact, most grading schemes and most intelligence tests are best viewed as examples of ordinal scales. An *ordinal scale* is unchanged by any monotonic (steadily increasing or decreasing) operation, such as taking the square root, adding or multiplying by a constant, or taking a logarithm. It lacks an absolute zero, and the distances between adjacent scale values are unequal. This scale type is achieved most often by asking people to rank order a set of objects, for example, to list all your friends of the opposite sex according to attractiveness. If Person$_1$ is the

28

most attractive, Person$_2$ the next most, and so on, the difference in attractiveness between adjacent persons changes as you go down your list. So, without making some questionable assumptions it might be impossible to say that Barbara's I.Q. score of 120 represents the same difference in I.Q. to a score of 110 as does the difference between scores of 85 and 95. All we can usually say is that 120 represents greater intelligence than does 110, and, in turn, 95 represents more intelligence than does 85.

A *nominal scale* is the weakest type of measurement since it merely sorts objects into different categories. Just about any arithmetic transformation can be used without changing the scale properties; so long as objects are not pulled out of one bin and pushed into another. Numbers on an athlete's jersey represent nominal measurement since all they do is identify particular individuals without telling you anything about them. (For that you need a scorecard.) It would be silly to add the numbers that two different athletes are wearing and expect the result to be meaningful. Sex is also a nominal measurement since almost all individuals can be classified into one of two categories: male or female. Calling a person by a particular name or label merely categorizes them and does not necessarily tell us anything about them as individuals. Barbara is female and also a college freshman—pieces of information that help us to identify her but do not assist us in measuring her attributes with any depth.

Importance of Measurement Scales. Some of our discussion of scales may have seemed too abstract to you to be pertinent to an understanding of why people think and act as they do. The examples we included about the different measures of Barbara's behavior should have indicated that the different scales provide different kinds of information. Since a ratio scale represents the most powerful form of measurement, psychologists should always strive for ratio measurement of thought and action. Unfortunately this is easier said than done. It turns out to be the case that the majority of psychological measurement is at the ordinal and interval level. What does that mean to you? One thing it means is that when you evaluate the assertions of a researcher, you should be able to identify the measurement scale underlying the assertions. You should recognize that it is invalid to say that "Barbara is twice as lazy as Tom," unless your measure of laziness is at the level of a ratio scale. Scale type will also play an important part in your own research. If you know that Barbara is lazier than Tom but not how much more (an ordinal scale), then you are constrained as to what you can say about the differences between Barbara and Tom. You are even further constrained if all you know is that Barbara is lazy and Tom is not (a nominal scale).

Measuring Friendliness

The type of measurement scale on which a psychological attribute is measured plays an important role in determining the kinds of conclusions we can reach. Since we feel it is crucial that you understand the importance of measurement scales, we will examine two different types of scaling procedures that might help us understand more about Barbara. Necessarily, our discussion of measurement is limited. If you desire additional information, we recommend Gescheider (1976) as a more detailed source on measurement.

Among the most common form of psychological measurement is a variant of the *rating technique.* Everything from students' grades to the intensities of lights has been measured by this technique. Generally, what a person does in a rating task is to arrange the attributes in question into groups or categories that lie along some continuum. So, an observer might be shown lights of differing intensities and asked to place the dimmest appearing light in Category 1 and the brightest appearing light in Category 7. Lights of intermediate intensities are to be assigned values between 1 and 7, according to their relative perceived brightness. At the very least, therefore, a rating scale should yield an ordinal scale of measurement: lights rated 5, 6, or 7 appear brighter than those rated 1, 2, 3, or 4. Likewise, 4 appears brighter than 3 and so on. If we have devised a good category scale and if we have some knowledge of the underlying physical scale (e.g., some measure of the physical intensity of light), then it may be the case that our rating procedure has yielded an interval scale.

How might we apply the rating technique to Barbara? Let us suppose that we think Barbara's lack of academic motivation stems from the fact that she is lonely and unhappy. Barbara does not get along well with her peers, so we decide to measure her friendliness as compared to the friendliness of other freshmen in her dormitory. Our procedure will be like this: we will develop a rating scale, then we will have 20 sophomores who know our 11 stimuli (Barbara and the other 10 freshmen) sort them into the categories. Finally, we will determine the average rating for each student. Let us assume that we have developed the following seven-category rating scale:

1. a mean, nasty person who goes out of the way to be unfriendly
2. mean and unfriendly, but not as aggressive about it as category 1
3. not as friendly as most people, doesn't get along well
4. typical person, neither overly friendly nor unfriendly
5. more friendly than average, pleasant to be with
6. a very friendly person, enjoyable to be with
7. extremely friendly, goes out of the way to be nice to others

Our observers' task is to sort the 11 people into these categories. Typically there is no restriction on the repeated use of a particular category (some observer might perceive our stimuli all as *4*s) or on which categories should be used, except, of course, that the rating follow the observer's perceptions of the stimuli.

The results of our rating procedure might look something like that shown in Table 2–1. Here we have the number of times each of the freshmen was rated in each of the categories. Also shown is the mean (average) rating for each freshman. The mean (usually abbreviated M or $\bar{X}$) is calculated by dividing the total score by the number of scores that yielded the total (in this case the total rating was divided by 20, the number of sophomores who made the ratings). Barbara's mean rating ($M = 2.0$) indicates that she is the least friendly according to the sophomore raters. Student *9* is the most friendly with a mean rating of 6.05. Note that the extreme values of the scale (Categories 1 and 7) were not used very often; nevertheless, there was pretty good agreement in assignment to categories—only in one case (Student 4) was there any obvious disagreement.

There are a couple of things that may have bothered you about our rating procedure. In the first place, the rating task is an *indirect measuring technique.* Indirect measurement scales force the observer to limit judg-

Table 2-1   Fictional Frequency of Friendliness Ratings

				Category				
Freshman	1	2	3	4	5	6	7	Mean
1 (Barbara)	2	17	0	1	0	0	0	2.0
2	0	0	4	11	5	0	0	4.05
3	1	1	2	15	1	0	0	3.70
4	0	2	1	11	3	2	1	4.25
5	0	0	0	17	3	0	0	4.15
6	0	0	2	15	3	0	0	4.05
7	0	1	5	14	0	0	0	3.65
8	0	0	3	15	1	1	0	4.00
9	0	0	0	0	2	15	3	6.05
10	0	1	1	18	0	0	0	3.85
11	0	0	1	14	4	1	0	4.25

Note. In the body of the table are the frequencies with which each freshman was assigned to each friendliness category. For example, 17 of the observers rated Barbara as a *2* in friendliness, two observers rated her as a *1*, and one observer rated her as a *4*. The mean rating in the right-hand column is derived from dividing the sum of the ratings by the number of observers (there were 20 observers). To calculate the mean rating for Barbara, we add 2 (2 × 1—two observers gave a *1* rating), 34 (17 × 2—17 observers gave a *2* rating), and 4 (1 × 4—one observer gave a *4* rating). Then divide this sum, which is 40, by 20, the number of observers. The result is a mean = 2. Barbara received the lowest mean rating, and freshman 9 received the highest mean rating (6.05).

ments to a small set of categories, and from this limited set the observer is supposed to develop a scale appropriate to the attributes in question. A second problem has to do with the metric that is supposed to underlie our scale. Is category 1 as different from category 2 as is category 6 from category 7? In order to have an interval scale we would have answer that question in the affirmative, but in this instance we have no way of doing so. A third, related problem, has to do with the categories themselves. Suppose you tried rating some of your friends on this scale. We bet that one thing you would find is that it would be difficult to pigeonhole some of your friends exactly. You might, just for the sake of argument, have two average friends, so you would have to rate them both as *4*s on our scale. Suppose, however, that one of the friends is just a little friendlier than the other. How do you rate them? Does one friend receive a *4* and the other a *3*? Or do you rate the more friendly one as a *5* and the less friendly one as a *4*? You may want to give one friend a *4* and the other a *4.5*, but in this rating scheme you can't.

What we need is a procedure for direct measurements that will give us some flexibility in assigning judgments at the interval or ratio level of measurement. Such a scaling procedure exists; it is called the *method of magnitude estimation.* As the name implies, observers assign numbers (magnitudes) to the attributes in question, usually without any particular restriction except that the numbers are assigned proportionately to the judged magnitude of the attributes. What this means is that if something has a value twice as large as another, then the larger receives a magnitude estimate twice as great as the other. In contrast to the rating procedure, magnitude estimation allows the observer to use his or her own scale and also permits considerable flexibility in the assignment of numbers. Sometimes an anchor point or *modulus* is used in magnitude estimation so that the observers use roughly equivalent numbers. In the case of estimating the magnitude of friendliness, there might be instructions to the effect that 50 (or 100 or 136.2) represents average friendliness and all other estimations are to be based on that anchor point. Since we want to provide flexibility and also have observers directly scale attributes, we probably would not want to provide a modulus that might artificially limit the range of estimations.

To generate a friendliness scale by means of magnitude estimation, we could instruct our observers to assign the lowest possible scores to the nastiest, least friendly people and the highest estimates to the nicest, friendliest people. People who fall between the extremes receive proportional estimates such that someone twice as friendly as another would receive twice the magnitude estimate. Fictitious results of magnitude estimation for our 11 freshmen (including Barbara) are in Table 2–2. The results agree with the rating data shown in Table 2–1: students high on one scale received high scores on the other and vice versa. Note, however, that there is a much greater range of estimates than possible ratings, which has the effect of spreading out our scale. Quite likely, therefore, we can observe finer differences using magnitude estimation than would be the case using a rating procedure. A comparison of the two tables also indicates that there are somewhat greater differences among our average people according to the magnitude estimates than according to the ratings. Again, this result suggests that magnitude estimation is more sensitive than the rating technique.

If magnitude estimation yields a higher scale than does rating (i.e., a ratio scale instead of, at best, an interval scale), and if the technique is more direct and flexible than rating, why is it that the rating (and other less powerful) techniques are used at all? One reason is the controversy over *what* the magnitude estimation procedure actually measures (Natsoulas, 1967). The relative freedom of this procedure could lead observers astray. The controversy centers on whether observers report the magnitude of their judgments or instead report falsely on the basis of some confounded attribute that is somehow linked to the stimulus. So, for example, judgments of loudness could reflect one's experience that softer sounds are further away than are louder ones (Warren, 1963). In a similar way, friendliness estimates on Barbara might have been low because she is not a good student or because she reads unscholarly fiction. You should note that these are also potential problems for the rating method. In any event, we should not forget that the magnitude estimation technique allows us to do something very important: we can get a pretty good measure of people's opinions.

Table 2-2			Fictitious Magnitude Estimates of Friendliness									
					Freshman							
Observer	Barbara	2	3	4	5	6	7	8	9	10	11	
1	2	265	35	400	270	260	22	255	400	100	375	
2	90	600	270	500	600	500	180	455	900	400	800	
3	3	250	90	320	300	200	60	190	375	160	350	
4	.05	50.5	25	25	40.5	50	5.5	50	100	45	90.5	
5	1	100	50	175	130	105	20	95	200	90	180	
6	1	530	150	560	550	525	80	500	1000	350	800	
7	100	5800	250	6200	6000	5500	200	5000	10000	700	7000	
8	25	175	75	250	175	160	55	150	275	150	250	
9	20	1200	300·	2000	1300	1110	200	1000	2000	900	1900	
10	.1	60	40	25	65	55	2	50	100	45	90	
Mean	24.2	903.1	128.5	980.1	956.1	846.5	82.4	763.5	1535	294	1183.6	

Note. In each row are the estimates given by a particular observer to each of the 11 freshmen. For example, observer 1 estimated Barbara's friendliness as a 2, and gave freshman 6 an estimate of 260. The column means are the average magnitude estimates for each freshman. The means are obtained by adding up the estimates for a particular freshman and dividing the sum by the number of estimates (10, one from each observer). In Barbara's case we add 2 + 90 + 3 + . . . + 20 + .1 and divide that sum by 10 to get a mean estimate of 24.2. Barbara received the lowest mean estimate, and freshman 9 received the highest mean estimate (1535).

We should tell you that when you use scaling techniques such as the ones we have just described, you are doing research in the oldest problem area in psychology; namely, the specification of psychological characteristics. This is usually called *psychometrics,* which simply means that you are trying to obtain a *metric* (i.e., a measurement) of *psycho-logical* characteristics. If we are measuring the judgment of stimuli along a known physical dimension, e.g., how bright lights of different intensities appear, we are engaging in *psychophysics.* Edwin G. Boring (1950), the eminent psychologist and historian of experimental psychology, claimed that the introduction of techniques to measure the relation between internal judgments (the "psycho" of psychophysics) and the external world (the "physics") marked the onset of scientific psychology. Psychophysics began in about 1850 and was then concerned with dimensions less complex than friendliness (e.g., brightness, heaviness, loudness). However, scaling techniques can be applied to almost any psychophysical or psychometric problem, so they continue to be very important. Science begins with analysis and analysis requires measurement. These scaling techniques and other data collection procedures discussed elsewhere in this text will help you to measure thought and behavior.

Reliability and Validity.   Because there was agreement among our fictitious observers on how to judge the freshmen, we can say that our measurement scales are *reliable.* A good measurement should be reliable —we want it to yield consistent, repeatable results (remember, science relies on self-correction and if our measures vary all over the place we cannot establish anything). Our measures must also be *valid,* which means they must measure what they are supposed to measure. We need some sort of *criterion* to determine the validity of our measurements. What this means is that we have some independent means of determining friendliness so that we can compare our measure of friendliness to the independent (criterion) measure. Our observers may not have judged friendliness on the basis of a profound knowledge of human personality. Rather, the judgments may have been based upon some other factor, such as social desirability. As noted above, it could be that Barbara has some other undesirable traits that brought forth low friendliness ratings and estimates. Likewise, it is possible that Student 9, who received the highest scores, is rich or exceptionally attractive, thus 9 received high scores for reasons other than exceptional friendliness. We will discuss the validity of an observation in some detail in Chapter 10. For now, you should note that validity is a crucial characteristic of all data—if we do not know what we are measuring, scientific progress is impossible. If we had actually done two scaling studies and found close agreement, then we could argue that there is indeed a friendliness dimension underlying the judgments in the two cases (Calfee, 1975). That is to say, the two scaling techniques have converged upon the same psychological metric. Such results from scaling studies would indicate that there is some validity to our observations. Alas, the results are fictional—perhaps you could obtain some real data on this topic.

Data Collection in Psychology

Collecting, interpreting, and reporting data about our fundamental question is what scientific psychology is all about. We have already indicated that it is difficult to lay down rules to help you become a curious, creative scientist. We can, however, help you with the more mundane aspects of science. So, in this section we introduce the advantages of the major data collection procedures used by scientific psychologists.

Naturalistic Observation

One of the most useful ways to go about exploring an unknown phenomenon, at least initially, is simply to watch it and describe it in as much detail as possible. This is called *naturalistic observation.* If you stumble across an aardvark one day and decide you want to know more about it, one of the best ways is simply to follow it day and night and record your observations. You will discover a great deal this way, but certainly not everything you want to know.

There are two primary characteristics typically associated with naturalistic observation. One is that it is concerned with naturally occurring phenomena. The second is that the observer usually stays out of the way and does not intervene. In fact, the observer in most cases does everything possible to be unobtrusive in naturalistic observation. When the researcher's presence is obvious (i.e., the presence is obtrusive), the observations are said to be *reactive.* That is, the observation of the natural phenomenon, say the behavior of the aardvark, is likely to be in part a reaction to the detected presence of the observer. This is especially true in research of certain aspects of human behavior, where people know how they are supposed to behave and, if they know they are observed, will simply behave as they should. So studies of shoplifting or speeding are likely to discover little of interest if the participants know they are observed. Since the researcher's interest is in naturally occurring behavior, efforts in naturalistic research must be taken to make the measures nonreactive or unobtrusive. An interesting book in its second edition by Webb, Campbell, Schwartz, and Sechrest (1981), describes many unobtrusive measures that may be taken in naturalistic research on human behavior.

Naturalistic research of interest to psychologists is perhaps most prevalent in the area of *ethology,* the study of animal behavior (often in the wild). A recent example, which has been popularly noted, is Jane van Lawick-Goodall's investigations of wild chimpanzees.

Simply observing the behavior of animals or humans allows one to gain a general impression of the characteristics and range of behavior, but one may soon desire more systematic observation. One way more systematic observations are made by ethologists is by listing different categories of experience for the organism under study and then recording the number of times the organism engages in each behavior. To illustrate, let us take a hypothetical human example. Suppose it were possible to follow about a college professor and unobtrusively record his or her daily behavior. Borrowing the checklist technique and scheme of activities developed by ethologists to study nonhuman behavior, we could record the frequency of his or her typical daily behaviors and their approximate durations, as in Table 2–3.

As you might imagine from this hypothetical example, it is difficult to apply the naturalistic observation method to the entire spectrum of human behavior, and often it can only be applied with difficulty to animals in their natural habitat because of the many practical problems involved. Application of the naturalistic method to humans in a number of settings has been attempted by Barker and his associates (for example, Barker and Wright, 1951; Barker, 1968), although a variety of behaviors, such as sex, have not been studied in great detail. Other

---

An illustration of the checklist technique developed by ethologists. The typical daily behaviors of a hypothetical college professor are recorded, as well as their approximate duration.

Table 2–3

Occurrences over time

Activity		1–15 min.	16–30 min.	31–45 min.	46–60 min.	Over 1 hr.	Total
Eating			XX	X			3
Sleeping						X	1
Drinking	Alcoholic		X				1
	Nonalcoholic	XXX	XX				5
Eliminating		XXXXX					5
Working	Lecturing				XX		2
	Preparing lectures					X	1
	Grading papers					X	1
	Talking with students					X	1
	Writing research report					X	1
Tennis						X	1

variants of the naturalistic observation approach have been used to study more sensitive aspects of human behavior. Some are briefly described here.

The Case Study. One of the most venerable forms of inquiry in psychology is the case study. Freud's psychoanalytic theory arose from his observations and reflections on individual cases. In general, a case study is the intensive investigation of a single case of some sort, whether of a neurotic patient, a spiritual medium, or a group awaiting the end of the world. An interesting case study of this last instance was provided by Festinger, Riecken, and Schachter (1956) who infiltrated a small group of persons who were indeed awaiting the end of the world. The members thought themselves in contact with beings from another planet who communicated to one member that the destruction of the earth was near. The group was expecting to be rescued by spacecraft before the catastrophe. Festinger and his colleagues were especially interested in the reactions of the group when (if?) the calamity did not occur. They observed that for many of the members of the group the belief in its delusional system actually increased rather than decreased after the predicted date of catastrophe had passed.

One advantage of the case study over standard naturalistic observation is that the case study is not necessarily limited to current thought and action. Rather, a good part of most case studies involves historical or retrospective analysis. When did our compulsive washer, Ruth L. from Chapter 1, first begin to bathe excessively? Did she feel these compulsions as a child? A case study is necessary to answer such questions, and an effective way to interpret important events in an individual's life is to use the technique of *deviant case analysis.* Here the researcher considers two cases that bear a number of similarities and yet differ in outcome. Suppose, for example, that Ruth L. had a twin sister (in fact she did not) who was not a compulsive washer. The researcher would attempt to pinpoint through careful comparison of the cases of Ruth and her sister the factors that were responsible for the difference in outcome.

Phenomenological Report. Another historically important naturalistic method in psychology is the subjective, or phenomenological, report of subjects. The method of *introspection* was of great importance early in the history of psychology. Introspection means to "look within"; that is, you report on your internal thoughts and sensations. In many other cases, subjects' reports have also been used as evidence. Much of the "evidence" for Freud's psychoanalytic theory is based on his interpretations of his patients' reports of dreams or free associations. Even today in some areas of psychology it is common to take reports by subjects as a type of evidence, especially in survey research.

Survey Research.   Case studies and phenomenological reports usually involve only a few subjects, and often these individuals are not at all representative of the population at large. Freud's theory, for example, is based mostly on the cases of neurotic Viennese housewives. It is often of interest to obtain information on a large random sample of people in a large geographic area (such as the United States), even though the amount of information obtained from any single person is necessarily quite limited. This technique is little used in most areas of psychology, though it is familiar to most of you through its use in predicting elections and the like. With the precise sampling techniques now available, relatively few people can be queried and the results will nonetheless generalize well to the population at large. It is difficult to imagine that this method will ever become popular with many psychologists because of the generally descriptive nature of the results obtained. Nonetheless, clever use of the method may allow contributions to some areas of psychology (for example, a developmental psychologist may sample Americans' beliefs about effective child rearing practices).

The survey technique can also be used to good advantage when it is necessary to examine a large number of people from a particular group. The high-school graduate research mentioned in Chapter 1 is an example of the survey technique in action. Here, the researchers obtained reports from over 17,000 graduates.

A combination of observation procedures is typical of the *participant-observer technique.* This form of observation is common in anthropological research, and, as the name implies, this technique requires the researcher to make observations while actually living with the subjects or engaging in similar activities. Much recent ethological research involves participant observation, and Bartell (1970) has extended this technique to the examination of married "swingers" in the United States. While Bartell apparently did not swing, he did spend much time in the homes of swingers, and he did attend their parties, in much the same way that a cultural anthropologist might live in a primitive village and engage in some, but not all, of the tribe's activities.

Miller (1977) has summarized some of the important roles that naturalistic observation can play in psychology. His comments were aimed specifically at comparative psychology, but they seem applicable to all kinds of descriptive research. The first role is at the heart of scientific psychology: "to study nature for its own sake." By being curious the observer is in a position to generate scientifically valuable questions, which lead to the second role: "naturalistic observations initially serve as a starting point for investigating certain behavioral phenomena and subsequently serve as a point of departure from which to develop a program of laboratory research." As noted earlier, the search for the causes of thought and action demands that we first know what there is to be studied (and in what quantity and how often it occurs; we need measurable data). According to Miller the third role can be viewed as the reverse of the second: "naturalistic observation can be used to validate or add substance to previously obtained laboratory findings." Creating mental images is an extremely effective way to improve memory in the laboratory (Bower, 1972), but do images help with "real-life" retention? It turns out that images and other mnemonic devices are extremely important for learning and retaining a second language (Atkinson, 1975). The fourth role is: "naturalistic observation can increase the efficiency of utilization of animals in the laboratory by providing useful information regarding species variables, or so-called biological constraints." This is relevant to all animals, including humans. Unless we have a "natural history" of bathing in Western society, it would be impossible to say Ruth L.'s washing rituals were abnormal. The fifth role noted by Miller is: "the use of the field as a natural 'laboratory' to test some hypotheses or theoretical concept via observational techniques and/or experimental manipulation." Squire and Slater (1975) used a questionnaire to see if the forgetting of natural events was similar to that obtained in laboratory situations.

The Correlational Approach

Scientists are not long contented with the type of descriptive data that is derived from observational studies. Of much greater interest is how two or more *variables* are related. (A variable is an aspect of research that can be measured or manipulated. More on this in the next section.) The use of correlational techniques permits us to specify and assess the degree of relation between or among the variables, so that we can then predict and select on the basis of the observed relationship. The assessment is usually made ex post facto, or from after the fact. All this means is that the data are collected and then one computes a *correlation coefficient,* which indicates the degree of relation. What is the correlation between high school performance and college performance? How does early TV preference correlate with teenage aggression? These questions, you will remember, are the kinds examined with the correlational technique.

In Chapter 6 you will learn how to calculate one kind of correlation coefficient. For now, it should be noted that almost all correlation coefficients have the property that they can vary from −1.00 through 0.00 to +1.00. Commonly they will not be one of these figures but something in between, such as +.72 or −.22. The magnitude of the correlation coefficient indicates the degree of relation (larger numbers reflecting greater relationships). The sign indicates the *direction* of the relationship, positive or negative, not the importance, which is indicated by the magnitude only. It is important to put the appropriate sign in front of the correlation coefficient, since otherwise one cannot know which way the two variables are related, directly or inversely. It is common practice, though, to omit the + sign before positive correlations. A correlation of .68 would be interpreted as positive. It is a better practice always to include the sign. An example of a *positive* correlation is the relation between lung cancer and smoking. As one variable increases, so does the other (though not perfectly, because the correlation coefficient is less than +1.00). There is also a documented *negative* correlation between smoking and another variable, namely grades in college. People who smoke a lot have tended to have lower grades than those who smoke less (Huff, 1954, p. 87).

In their examination of the relationship between TV preferences and aggression, Eron et al. (1972) found a correlation of +.31 between preference for violent TV in the third grade and the amount of aggression in the late teens. In contrast to this moderately large positive correlation coefficient, Eron et al. found a negligible correlation of –.05 between preference for violent TV in the late teens and teenage aggression. So, the correlational technique is a valuable way to extend descriptive data that result from naturalistic observation. Not only do third graders watch a lot of TV, and not only do some third graders prefer violent TV programs, but we can also make the prediction that there is a direct relation between the amount of violent TV observed and later aggressive behavior. The practical implications of this result seem straightforward, and there has been some effort on the part of the television industry to reduce the amount of violence available during time periods when young children are likely to be staring at the TV. In this instance, then, the correlation coefficient has been used to predict some aspects of behavior and also to make some programming decisions (i.e., select certain programs to be shown at certain times). The correlational technique is invaluable for prediction and selection.

We will briefly caution you here and then extend our caution later about making causal statements on the basis of correlation coefficients. Under usual circumstances a substantial correlation between two variables indicates that the variables are related and nothing more. We can predict and select on the basis of that coefficient, but we must be wary of asserting that one variable causes the other. Should we consider the negative correlation between college grades and cigarette smoking to mean that smoking causes low grades? We could just as easily say that low grades cause people to smoke more. On the basis of this single correlation we cannot rule out the possibility that some third factor is influencing or mediating the relation between grades and smoking. Students with poor grades may be more anxious and thus smoke more. Or more sociable students may smoke more and study less, and so on. These possible interpretations point to the potential for *confounding* that is inherent in correlational research. When two or more factors are varied at the same time or are assessed at the same time so that we cannot know whether one factor, the other factor, or both operating together produce some effect, we say that the factors are confounded. In Chapters 6 and 7 we will amplify on this difficulty, and we will also discuss some modifications of the correlational technique that permit one to make reasonable causal statements about the variables under investigation.

Experimentation

Imagine you are a student in a class in enviromental psychology and have received the following assignment: Go to the library and "defend" a table by preventing anyone else from sitting down for as long as you can. You must use only nonverbal means to accomplish this. To carry out this task you might wait in the crowded library until a table was vacant, quickly sit down and proceed to strew your books, clothing, and other belongings all over the table in hopes that this disarray might keep others away. After some time, say fifteen minutes or so, someone finally does sit down at your table, ending your assignment. Have you performed an experiment?

Before answering this question, let us sketch out the major criterion for an experiment as was briefly discussed in the preceding chapter. An experiment occurs when the environment is systematically manipulated in order to observe the effect of this manipulation upon some behavior. Aspects of the environment that are not of interest, and hence not manipulated, are held constant so as not to influence the outcome of the experiment. To answer the question above, we must introduce two special terms—*independent* and *dependent variables*—to describe how the environment is manipulated and how behavior is observed.

Many students are surprised to discover that the actions described above are not an experiment. All experiments require at least two special features called independent and dependent variables. The dependent variable is the behavior recorded by the experimenter, in this case the time until someone else sat down at your table. The independent variable is a manipulation of the environment controlled by the experimenter, in this case strewing articles on the table. *But in order to have an experiment there must be at least two ways, or levels, of manipulating the environment.* Sometimes these two levels might just be the presence or absence of manipulation. The library example above fails to meet this criterion, since there was only one level of the independent variable. How might we change the procedure to obtain an experiment? The simplest answer would be to have the experimenter repeat the actions by sitting down again, this time without strewing anything about. Then our independent variable would have the necessary two levels: items strewn about and no items strewn about the table. Now we have something to compare with the first condition. The possible outcomes of this experiment are three: (1) strewing articles on the table results in a longer time before the table is invaded by another person; (2) the time until invasion is the same whether or not articles are strewn about; (3) strewing articles results in a shorter time until invasion. Without the second level of the independent variable (no articles strewn about) these three outcomes cannot be evaluated. Indeed it is impossible to say anything about how effective articles are in defending library tables until there are two levels of the independent variable. When this library experiment is performed, the first possible outcome is obtained. A table can be better protected by a person plus assorted articles than by only a person.

To review, experiments must have at least independent and dependent variables. While the research techniques discussed previously did not allow or require manipulation of the environment, independent variables with at least two levels are necessary before an experiment can be established.

Advantages of Experiments

The main advantage of experiments over the other techniques is better control of extraneous variation. In the ideal experiment, all factors (variables) except the one being studied are not permitted to influence the outcome—in the jargon of experimental psychology we say that these other factors are *controlled.* In the ideal experiment, all factors but one (that under investigation) are held constant. Since these other factors are under the experimenter's control, we can logically conclude that any differences in outcome must be due to manipulation of that one independent variable. As the levels of the independent variable are changed, the resulting differences in the dependent variable can only occur because the independent variable changed. Putting this another way, changes in the independent variable *caused* the observed changes in the dependent variable. While nonexperimental research techniques are limited to statements about correlation—that is, variable A and variable B are related—experiments permit statements about causation—that is, independent variable A causes dependent variable B to change.

This does not mean that scientists never misinterpret experimental results. Scott and Wertheimer (1962) relate the story of a researcher working with fleas. The flea was trained to jump when the experimenter said "Jump." Then the researcher removed two of the flea's legs and said "Jump." The flea jumped. Finally the researcher removed all of the flea's legs and said "Jump." The flea sat unmoving. The investigator, so they say, concluded that removing all of a flea's legs causes it to become deaf.

Thus, in principle, experiments lead to statements about causation. In practice, these statements are not always true. No experiment is 100 percent successful in eliminating or holding constant all other sources of variation but the one being studied. However, experiments eliminate more extraneous variation than other research techniques. In later chapters we will discuss specific ways in which experiments limit extraneous variation.

Another advantage of experiments is economy. Using the technique of naturalistic observation requires the scientist to wait patiently until the conditions of interest occur. If you lived in Trondheim, Norway (near the arctic circle) and wanted to study the effects of heat upon aggression, relying on the sun to produce high temperatures would require great patience and time. The experimenter must be able to control the situation by creating the conditions of interest, thus obtaining data quickly and efficiently.

A good example of control leading to efficiency comes from a study by Middlemist, Knowles, and Matter (1976), who were interested in studying the effects of crowding in a men's restroom on the delay of onset and duration of urination. Since men prefer to stand apart at urinals whenever possible, a naturalistic study would be time consuming. The observers would have to wait until two men simultaneously used the urinals and then hope that the pairs of men would stand apart or adjacently often enough to yield reliable data for determining the effects of crowding. The experimenters controlled spacing of males at a row of three urinals by placing a bucket of water and a "Don't Use" in one of them. A conferederate of the experimenter was stationed at one of the end urinals. The distance was varied between the subject and the confederate by putting the bucket and sign either adjacent to the confederate or one urinal away. They found that the closer the confederate was to the subject the longer was the delay in beginning urination and the shorter was the duration of urination.

Ex Post Facto Studies

For one reason or another, there are many variables that cannot be manipulated directly. One deterrent to manipulation of variables in experiments are the ethical considerations all scientists must make (see Chapter 4 for a discussion of ethics in research). It is ethical to survey or otherwise observe the thoughts and actions of swingers with their permission. By no stretch of the imagination, however, would it be ethical to create a group of swingers and compare their activities to a nonswinging group that we created. A second barrier to manipulation is mother nature. Some attributes, such as the sex of our subjects, cannot be varied by the experimenter (except in very rare and controversial circumstances), and there are other variables, such as natural disasters (e.g., tornados) or unnatural disasters (e.g., wars and airplane crashes), that are both physically and morally difficult to implement. Can we do experiments that concern these phenomena? After all, the variables listed above and others like them are fascinating and may play an important part in human experience.

The answer to the question is (assuming you are an ethical scientist) you can and you cannot. We are not being silly here; rather we are emphasizing the fact that you cannot do real experiments on phenomena such as the ones listed above. You can conduct *quasi-experiments,* or what are often called *ex post facto studies*. The technique here is similar to the ex post facto examination in correlational research, except that two or more levels of the variable of interest are examined rather than correlated. So, we wait for mother nature to do her work, and then we compare the effects of that "independent variable" with the effects that occur when that variable is not present or differs in some way. If we compare the reading ability of men to that of women or children's reading versus that of adults , we have conducted an ex post facto experiment.

The advantages of ex post facto studies are obvious: they use naturally occurring independent variables, most of which have a high degree of intrinsic interest and important practical implications. In a quasi-experiment, we take advantage of observational and correlational procedures and combine them with the power of experimentation. If we want to find out about almost any inherent subject characteristic (age, sex, race, ethnic group), socially caused subject attribute (social class, region of residence, etc.), almost all disease and illness subject attributes (limb loss, mental illness, dietary phenomena, effects of disasters), we are going to have to conduct ex post facto research, unless it is possible to do the experiment directly on subhuman organisms. While ex post facto research is interesting and can be very important research, we should caution you here that the advantages to ex post facto research are gained at the expense of control. When the researcher has to take what is given, what is given may include several important confounding variables. We will discuss these problems more fully in later chapters.

Summary

Scientific psychology begins with measurement. A nominal measurement scale simply names or categorizes objects, and an ordinal scale tells you whether one thing is greater than (or less than) another. An interval scale can indicate how great the difference is between two objects, but it does not have a true zero point. A ratio scale does have a real zero point, which means that you can talk about ratios at this level of measurement (e.g., Tom is twice as heavy as Sally). Two typical measurement procedures are the rating technique and the method of magnitude estimation. These procedures require observers to assign numbers to attributes according to how they perceive them. In the rating technique, people assign attributes of objects to particular, experimenter-defined categories, while they assign numbers according to perceived ratios among attributes in the method of magnitude estimation. Data collection procedures include several observation techniques (descriptive research), the correlational method (predictive research), and experimentation (explanatory research). Observation techniques are flexible and easily used for "real-life" problems. The correlational method is indispensible for prediction and selection. Control is the major feature of experimentation, which means that causal statements about experimental results are possible.

Study and Review

Exercises

1. Identify the type of measurement scale for each of the following attributes: socio-economic level, a person's height, class rank, basketball jersey numbers, calendars.

2. Devise at least two ways to measure each of the following: attitudes toward premarital intercourse, the severity of crimes, sex appeal (in both men and women), the goodness of your psychology course.

3. Research Problem. (At the end of most chapters, some exercises will ask you to critique a research project in some way. You will be provided enough information in the question to answer it. If some procedural detail is omitted—e.g., the time of day the research was conducted, you may assume that the information is irrelevant. Base your discussion on the information provided.) In 1980 a researcher studied the attitudes toward war among various age groups. One group contained 7-year-olds, a second group contained 35-year-olds, and the last group was comprised of 60-year-olds. Marked differences in the attitudes toward war were observed. There is an important confounding variable in this study. What is it? Speculate on the effects of this confounding with regard to the attitudes of each age group. (Hint: You might think about this question in terms of the "generation gap.")

Key Concepts

analysis 25
measurement 26
data 26
ratio scale 27
ordinal scale 27
interval scale 27

nominal scale 28
rating technique 29
indirect measurement versus
    direct measurement 30
method of magnitude
    estimation 31

Suggested Readings

Probably the best place to obtain additional information about measurement in psychology is in: Gescheider, G. A. *Psychophysics: method and theory.* Hillsdale, New Jersey: Lawrence Erlbaum, 1976. A good source of additional information about all types of psychological research and measurement is: Kerlinger, F. *Foundations of behavioral research.* New York: Harper & Row, 1973.

WHAT TO LOOK FOR IN THE . . .

Abstract: What was done to whom and what was found

Introduction: What the author proposes; the hypotheses tested

Method: Dependent, independent, subject, and control variables; does the method test the hypothesis

Results: Do the results support or reject the hypothesis

Discussion: What conclusions are stated

References: Other reports you might read; are citations complete

WHAT TO INCLUDE IN THE . . .

Abstract: What you did to whom and what you found

Introduction: Why you are doing this research; the hypotheses you are testing

Method: A description of all variables; enough detail so that someone else can repeat your project

Results: Tables and/or figures that summarize your results; point the reader to the most pertinent data

Discussion: State how your results relate to the hypotheses tested; include relevant inferences and conclusions

References: All references cited in your paper belong here

How to Read and Write
a Research Report

3

Unless you read articles in journals of psychology, you may have difficulty understanding psychological research. The data base associated with a particular problem area resides in journals. Thus in order to understand those data, you will need to be able to comprehend the research reports. The first section of this chapter explains the format and style of articles and gives you some hints to help you become a critical reader. Because you will probably have to report the results of your own research, the second part of this chapter deals with writing a research report.

Overview

Trying to comprehend a psychology journal article can be difficult for the novice. In this section we prepare you for your first encounter with a journal article by explaining the format and style of journal reports. In addition, you will given some clues about how to be a critical reader of research reports.

How to Read a Journal Article

The Parts of an Article

The typical psychology article consists of seven parts: title and author(s), abstract, introduction, method, results, discussion, and references. The format of journal articles in psychology is governed by the *Publication Manual of the American Psychological Association,* which was revised in 1974. This manual is well worth reading, especially when you start to write your own research reports.

Title, Author(s), and Abstract.   From these sections you can decide whether or not you want to read the entire article. From the title and abstract you should know what variables were manipulated or selected, and you should be able to determine what was measured. The abstract should tell you something about the results that were obtained. If the title is mysterious or not particularly informative, the abstract should clear up any ambiguities. The name of the researcher is important for two reasons: you can make sure you have found the article you are looking for (referencing is done by author's surname); and if you are familiar with an author's research, you may be able to anticipate some of the contents of the article.

Introduction.   The introduction specifies the problem to be studied and tells why it is important. A good introduction also specifies the hypotheses to be tested and gives the rationale behind any predictions. You will find short references to other research reports, such as: *Brown (1979) found* ... or *It has been argued that (Brown, 1979)....* These statements refer to the author of another research report and the date when the report was published. The complete reference to the research is found in the reference section at the end of the report. Statements are referenced to indicate the source of hypotheses or research findings. You may find it necessary to read some of these other reports in order to fully understand the one you are currently reading.

Method.   The method section describes in detail the operations performed by the experimenter. It is usually printed in smaller type to conserve space, but this should not mislead you into believing it is an unimportant part of the article to be quickly skimmed over. The method section should contain enough information for another experimenter to replicate the study.

   It is customary to divide the method section into subsections that cover subjects, apparatus, and procedure. The *subjects* subsection tells how many subjects there were, how they were selected, and who they were (college students or rats). The *apparatus* subsection indicates any special equipment that was used. If the equipment is commercially available, then the brand name and model number are usually specified. If custom-built equipment was used, then construction details and measurements are presented. The *procedure* subsection explains what happened to the subjects, including instructions (for humans), special handling (for animals), statistical design features, and so forth. If uncommon materials such as special nonsense syllables, an original survey, or a new personality test were used, there may be a *materials* subsection. The materials subsection will provide details about the test or other novel materials and may contain a sample of the materials or even a listing of all materials used. Often you will find a *design* subsection that includes a description of the experimental plan and additional features of the statistical techniques.

Results.   This section tells what data were obtained. Descriptive statistics summarize the results (it is unusual to find raw data or individual scores reported). Inferential statistics are presented so that the reader can decide whether or not to believe the data. If you are unfamiliar with psychological statistics, further details are presented in Chapters 6 and 9. However, since you may be reading articles soon, you need to know that a statement like "$F(4, 60) = 2.93, p < .05$" means that the odds of obtaining an F-statistic at least as large as 2.93 by chance if the experiment were repeated would be less than 5 percent.

Either tables or graphs may be used to summarize data. Tables present a summary of the dependent variable similar to the tables that summarized the scaling of Barbara's friendliness (see Chapter 2). Graphs are called *figures,* and the way they are drawn can be misleading. If an article contains several figures, check to see if the scales are comparable so that the effects can be easily compared across different figures. In most figures the dependent variable (what is measured) is plotted on the *ordinate*—the vertical axis. The independent variable (what is manipulated in an experiment) or a subject variable (such as personality type or age in a quasi-experimental study) is usually graphed on the *abscissa* —the horizontal axis. The results of several conditions can be shown in the same figure by using different types of lines and symbols for each condition (see the article later in this chapter).

Discussion.   The discussion section is the most creative part of an article. Here the author presents conclusions about the results and often offers a theoretical analysis of them. In the words of the *Publication Manual:* "In the discussion section, you are free to examine, interpret, and qualify your results, as well as draw inferences from them." Authors are given enough rope to hang themselves in the discussion. Hence, while any part of an article should be approached with caution, an extra degree of skepticism is required for discussion sections. Freedom for the authors to interpret and draw inferences requires cautious, critical reading.

References.   These are found at the end of the article. For the student the references are primarily valuable as a guide to related information. The references cited will indicate the research that the author thinks is most relevant. When you have become familiar with a research area, you may know of additional, pertinent work that the author overlooked (or at least failed to cite). In this instance you might be able to make an important criticism of the work and develop some ideas for additional research.

Exceptions to the Format

Some exceptions to the standard format are common. The exception you are most likely to encounter involves a combination of the results and discussion sections. Fortunately such combinations are labeled "Results and Discussion." These combined sections often occur in short articles (such as those found in the *Bulletin of the Psychonomic Society*). Combined results and discussion sections are also found in articles that report more than one experiment—each study has its own results and discussion section. When more than one study is reported in an article, there is usually a final section devoted to interpretation of all the results. This last section is usually called "General Discussion" or "Conclusions."

Order of Reading Sections

Most readers start at the front of an article and dutifully plod their way to the references, except perhaps for those who enjoy mystery novels and so reverse this process. As you become more and more familiar with a research area, it becomes less necessary to follow the order printed in journals. For example, if you are truly an expert in an area, merely reading the results section may be enough for you to infer the rest of the article. After you have read a few articles, don't be afraid to depart from the usual order.

Checklist for the Critical Reader

In this section we offer some hints that should help you become a better consumer of the information presented in psychological journals. The major suggestion is for you to avoid rushing through the article. Instead, you should deliberately stop after each section and write down the answers to the questions we shall list below. This will be difficult at first, thinking is harder than reading, but with practice the process becomes automatic and requires little extra time. We suggest that you write down the answers for several articles. Once you get into the habit of being an active, critical reader, you may omit written answers to all the questions. However, as we suggest later, you should keep a written summary of the articles you read (on index cards or in a notebook). The purpose of these notes is to give you ready access to the data base relevant to a particular problem. The questions listed below indicate some of the information that should be in your summaries.

Introduction

1. What is the author proposing?

    Skeptics regard the introduction as a sales pitch for the article. While an experienced reader can figure out why the author is arguing for some point of view, beginners should be satisfied with a straightforward answer to the question.

2. What hypotheses will be tested?

    The answer to this question should be obvious and stated directly.

3. How would I test this hypothesis?

This is the key question for the introduction. You should answer this question *before* you go on to the method section. If the author has any skill as a wordsmith, once you have finished the next section you are likely to agree with the method advocated in the article. In fact, a really clever author will plant the seeds to this answer in the introduction itself, and this makes it harder for the reader to answer this question without being biased by the author's persuasiveness. Write down the major ideas for your method of testing the hypothesis.

Method

Compare your answer to question 3 with the author's. They probably will differ, if you have not peeked. Now answer question 4a.

4a. Is my proposed method better than the author's?

Regardless of who had the better method, you or the author, this forced comparison will make you think about the method section critically, instead of passively accepting it.

4b. Does the method actually test the hypothesis?

The hypothesis is sometimes the first casuality, disappearing between the introduction and method sections. Always check that the method used is adequate and relevant to the hypothesis at hand.

4c. What are the independent, dependent, subject, and control variables?

This is an obvious question and can be answered quickly. Listing the variables helps you avoid passive reading of the method section. After you have resolved differences between your proposed method and the author's, answer the next question.

5. Using the subjects, apparatus, and procedures described by the author, what results would I predict for this experiment?

Again it is essential that you answer this before reading the results section. You may well find it impossible to predict a single outcome. This is not really a problem, since the author probably had more than one prediction also, and then went back and "polished" the introduction once results were in. Draw a rough sketch illustrating the most likely outcomes you would expect.

Results

Compare the obtained results to your predictions. If they are the same go on to question 7. If not, answer question 6.

6. Did the author get unexpected results?

> After some thought you will reach one of two conclusions. Either your prediction was wrong or the results are hard to believe. Perhaps the method was inappropriate or perhaps these results would not be obtained again if the experiment were repeated. If you feel strongly enough, you might even try your own experiment.

7. How would I interpret these results?

> As before, you should answer this without first reading the discussion.

Discussion

Compare your interpretation with the author's. Answer question 8a or 8b, whichever is appropriate.

8a. Why didn't I think of that? (author wins)

8b. Why didn't the author think of that? (you win)

> The discussion section is the most difficult to evaluate. Often only future research can decide if it is correct. Some authors often have already done some of this future research but have not gotten around to reporting it yet. In such cases the discussion often sets up this "new" research.

Checklist Summary

If you have read your first article carefully, writing down the answers to all eight questions, by now you should be pleasantly exhausted. To help you recover, the next part of the chapter takes a typical psychology article and analyzes it according to the checklist summarized in Table 3–1.

Table 3-1   Questions for Critical Readers

Introduction
1. What is the author proposing?
2. What hypotheses will be tested?
3. How would I test this hypothesis?

Method
4a. Is my proposed method better than the author's?
4b. Does the method actually test the hypothesis?
4c. What are the independent, dependent, subject, and important control variables?
5. Using this method, what results would I predict?

Results
6. Did the author get unexpected results?
7. How would I interpret these results?

Discussion
8. Is my interpretation better than the author's?

Below we have reprinted a short article from the *Bulletin of the Psychonomic Society.* The answers to the checklist questions were distilled from answers given in one of the author's classes. Most of those students were college sophomores who had taken two courses in psychology. The article is about experiments that have been interpreted as showing that a particular type of brain wave (alpha waves) can be conditioned in human subjects.

In order to understand the following article, you will need some additional information. Most articles are written for experts in a particular area, so the authors of a report assume that their readers have some knowledge of the topic under investigation. In addition, most journals set page limitations on articles, which means that some information may be missing or presented very tersely. The assumptions made by the authors and the brevity of many articles pose a problem for the novice reader. The novice may have to read other articles or textbooks in order to understand a particular report. To help you understand the following report, we present some background information.

The article by Lindholm and Lowry is about learning to control a particular brain wave—the alpha wave. Alpha waves are prominent during meditation and relaxed wakefulness, and these waves are often associated with a pleasant emotional state that is called the alpha experience.

In a typical study about learning to control brain waves, the subject is connected to an electroencephalograph (EEG), a device that measures brain waves. The EEG is constructed so that it can provide a feedback signal to the subject when a particular brain wave, such as the alpha wave, is present. The feedback, usually a tone, is supposed to work as a reinforcer does in operant conditioning. That is, the feedback tells the subject when alpha is occurring. So, when the feedback is contingent upon the appearance of alpha waves (i.e., feedback occurs only when alpha occurs), the alpha waves should occur more often than when feedback is noncontingent (i.e., the occurrence of feedback is unrelated to the occurrence of alpha). The logic here is precisely the same as reinforcing a hungry rat with food when a particular response is made. If food is contingent upon a particular response, then that response will increase in likelihood. If food is presented noncontingently with respect to that response, then it will not increase in likelihood.

Some earlier alpha wave studies seemed to show that alpha would increase even when the feedback was noncontingent. Thus, Lindholm and Lowry wanted to examine the effects of false (i.e., noncontingent) feedback on alpha wave production. If alpha waves increase when feedback is noncontingent, then it can be concluded that something other than operant conditioning increases the frequency of alpha production.

Lindholm and Lowry also studied the effects of relaxation on the production of alpha. They do not detail the method of inducing relaxation for you, but we will. The procedure used was Jacobson's (1978) method of progressive relaxation. This technique involves training people to alternately tense and relax small groups of muscles until the entire body is in a state of relaxation. This progressive relaxation usually starts with the toes, works up through the legs, then the torso, arms, neck, and finally the face.

The following report is brief. One question you might want to try to answer is: "Could I replicate this study on the basis of the information presented?"

Alpha production in humans under conditions of false feedback

Ernest Lindholm and Steven Lowry
Arizona State University, Tempe, Arizona 85281

Subjects were pretrained in either Jacobson's relaxation or a control relaxation technique, then served in four daily sessions of biofeedback training. On some days, the feedback was veridical with respect to alpha production, while on other days, the feedback falsely indicated either success or failure at the control task. The results showed that alpha increased over trials, but this increase was independent of feedback contingency. Subjective reports of mood were not influenced by feedback falsely indicating success or failure at the control task, and there were no reliable relationships between mood and amount of alpha actually produced. Prior training on Jacobson's relaxation did not enhance alpha production. It is concluded that alpha production and positive mood states are not systematically related and that neither of these variables is operantly conditioned through biofeedback.

Brown (1970, 1971, 1974), Kamiya (1968, 1969) and others have reported that humans can learn to control their alpha production and that successful learning is accompanied by a variety of positive mood states (e.g., euphoria, well-being) collectively referred to as the "alpha experience." Others (e.g., Lynch, Paskewitz, & Orne, 1974) have argued that alpha production is not learned, that rather, subjects habituate to the strangeness of the experimental environment and over time, engage in fewer activities that tend to block alpha, such as visual fixation on objects in the room. Regarding mood states, Plotkin, Mazer, and Lowey (1976) found no relationship between mood and the amount of alpha produced, although they suggested the possibility that the subjects' perceived success or failure might influence subjective reports of mood; that is, subjects who thought they were successful might report more positive mood states than subjects who thought they were not successful at the control task.

The Lynch et al. (1974) position that alpha enhancement is not learned is questioned by the results of Brolund and Schallow (1976), who showed that combining feedback and reward led to greater alpha enhancement than feedback alone, suggesting that experimental contingencies were controlling the behavior (alpha production) to some reliable degree. Further, Lynch et al. (1974) employed a noncontingent feedback control in which the noncontingent feedback of one subject is a replay of the contingent feedback received by another. This may well be inappropriate for alpha learning experiments, since subjects do (by whatever means) increase alpha over trials, thus the replay of increasing density of feedback over trials might serve to fortuitously reinforce almost anything the control subject does which works in the direction of increasing alpha. This could introduce a bias in the direction of reducing group differences between contingent and noncontingent groups and obscure real differences between groups.

The other type of control group used in alpha experiments is the no-feedback control, which simply requires subjects to sit in a comfortable chair in a quiet room for the duration of the experiment (Browland & Schallow, 1976). The problem here is that these subjects receive less stimulation than subjects receiving feedback (contingent or otherwise) and thus might display enhanced alpha due to a movement toward a sleep or semisleep state. It appears, therefore, that while some argue that alpha enhancement is not a learned phenomenon, the lack of appropriate control groups detracts from the force of these arguments.

There appear to be four important questions that require evaluation before the worth of alpha conditioning experiments can be adequately evaluated: (1) Are alpha increases learned as a result of experimental contingencies? (2) Is the "alpha experience" closely related to the amount of alpha actually produced? (3) Is the intensity of the "alpha experience" influenced by the subject's perceived' success or failure? (4) Is the amount of alpha produced and the intensity of the "alpha experience" influenced by the subject's ability to relax? There is an implicit assumption that alpha density and relaxation are closely related, yet this assumption has never been directly tested by manipulating relaxation as an independent variable.

Question 1. What is the author proposing? The authors propose that the results of research concerned with learning to control alpha brain waves are equivocal. They seem to favor the idea that you cannot learn to control alpha.

Question 2. What hypotheses will be tested? The hypotheses are listed as "questions" to be answered before one can accept alpha conditioning: (1) does alpha increase because of the feedback provided? (2) what is the relation between the amount of alpha produced and the alpha experience? (3) what is the relation between the alpha experience and the subject's perceived failure or success? (4) what is the relation between the subject's ability to relax and the production of alpha (and the alpha experience)?

Question 3. How would I test these hypotheses? With respect to the first one, you could try to fool the subject in some way so that the feedback provided on the production of alpha is not correct. You could, for example, randomly present feedback to the subject—sometimes when alpha is being produced, and sometimes when it is not being produced. If alpha increases under random feedback, then it is not learned. With regard to the second hypothesis, you could correlate some measure of the subject's mood (the alpha experience) and the amount of alpha that is produced. For the third hypothesis you could tell some subjects that they are doing well and compare their alpha production to that of subjects who are told that they are not doing well. One way to examine the final hypothesis would be to provide a relaxing atmosphere for some subjects and compare their alpha to the alpha of subjects who are trained in a more tense environment.

Method

Subjects. Ten male and 10 female subjects were solicited by advertisement to participate in an experiment in which they could learn self-relaxation techniques and control of brainwaves. All were members of psychology classes regularly offered at Arizona State University.

Apparatus

Brain activity was recorded from occipital-occipital placements referenced to left mastoid using Grass silver disk electrodes and Grass electrode paste. Signals were amplified by a Beckman Type 411 dynograph, the high-level output of which was fed to the input of a DEC-LAB-8 computer that was programmed to detect alpha activity according to the following criteria: (1) There must be 1 1/2 cycles of activity falling within the 8- to 12-Hz frequency band, and (2) the amplitude of the activity must exceed the Schmitt trigger threshold set for each subject during the baseline sessions. When both criteria were met, the computer software turned on the biofeedback display which consisted of a 61 X 61 cm sheet of milk-white Plexiglas located 61 cm from the subject's face and back-lighted by a 15-W ac bulb. The Plexiglas formed the face of a plywood box, thus providing a diffuse low-intensity glow that covered a large portion of the visual field and minimized focusing.

Procedure

Relaxation training. The 20 subjects were divided into two groups of 5 males and 5 females each. The subjects in the Jacobson's group received 3 h of relaxation training, as did the subjects in the control relaxation group; the latter were told only to listen to white noise played at a low intensity and to relax as best they could.

Biofeedback training. Four 54-min sessions of biofeedback training were employed. Subjects were told that each session investigated a different brainwave, and that recent research indicated that relaxation enhanced control of all brainwaves, thus they should use their prior relaxation training to keep the feedback light on as much as possible. This was deception. In fact, the four sessions operated as follows: Contingent Day 1 (CD1) was the first day of feedback for all subjects. Feedback was contingent on alpha production, and this was true also for the fourth day (Contingent Day 4, abbreviated CD4). Days 2 and 3 were either false increasing (FI) or false decreasing (FD) feedback, counterbalanced across subjects. Under FI, the feedback density started at a low level and increased over trials, while the reverse was true for the FD condition. To make the illusion of "real" feedback convincing, the amounts delivered on Days 2 and 3 were based on individual subject's Day 1 performance, and were programmed for delivery according to an unpredictable computerized schedule, the only constraint being that feedback increased or decreased over trials for the FI and FD groups, respectively. Thus, the amount of feedback presented to each individual subject was both a familiar and credible amount, referenced to his or her Day 1 performance. The rationale for this particular design was as follows: The first day must be contingent to establish baseline performance, and the last day should also be contingent to assess time-dependent changes in alpha production. The middle 2 days were FI and FD to assess perceived success on mood and also to determine whether feedback contingency was systematically related to alpha production.

Question 4a. Is my method better than the authors'? Their methods are at least as good as ours, if not better.

Question 4b. Does the method actually test the hypotheses? Yes, the methods should test the four hypotheses. One problem that does exist is the fact that all subjects receive contingent feedback on the first day.

Although that procedure seems necessary to provide a baseline of alpha production, it is possible that its effects could carry over throughout the next three days and mask the other manipulations. However, the effects of false feedback on the second two days probably will not carry over because the order of presenting the two conditions was *counterbalanced* across subjects. Counterbalancing means that some subjects received false increasing feedback about their brain waves on the second day and decreasing feedback on the third day. The rest of the subjects received those conditions in the reverse order (counterbalancing is discussed in Chapter 5).

Question 4c.   What are the variables (independent, dependent, subject, control)? Independent variables: type of feedback, type of relaxation training, trials, and days. Dependent variables: amount of alpha, mood. It is not clear how or when mood will be assessed. Subject variables: sex. Control variables: amount of feedback on the false feedback days determined by the subject's alpha level on the first day, session length was controlled, as were the number of training days.

Question 5.   What do I predict? Since previous researchers have reported reliable alpha conditioning, we predict that increases in alpha will be observed only on the first and last days (i.e., only when the feedback is contingent on alpha production). Furthermore, we expect that alpha will increase with increases in the alpha experience and with perceived success. We expect that the ability to relax will enhance alpha.

Results and Discussion

The .95 confidence level was adopted throughout as indicating the presence of a reliable difference.

The percent alpha produced during all phases of the experiment are displayed in Figure 1. All functions superficially resemble "learning curves," since performance during Trial 4 was generally superior to performance during Trial 1. An ANOVA revealed main effects for trials and rest vs. feedback. The main effect for sessions approached the .05 level and was therefore further analyzed by comparing CD1 alone with CD2, as a test for extreme differences. This analysis also failed to detect reliable sessions differences. No other main effect or interaction approached significance in either ANOVA.

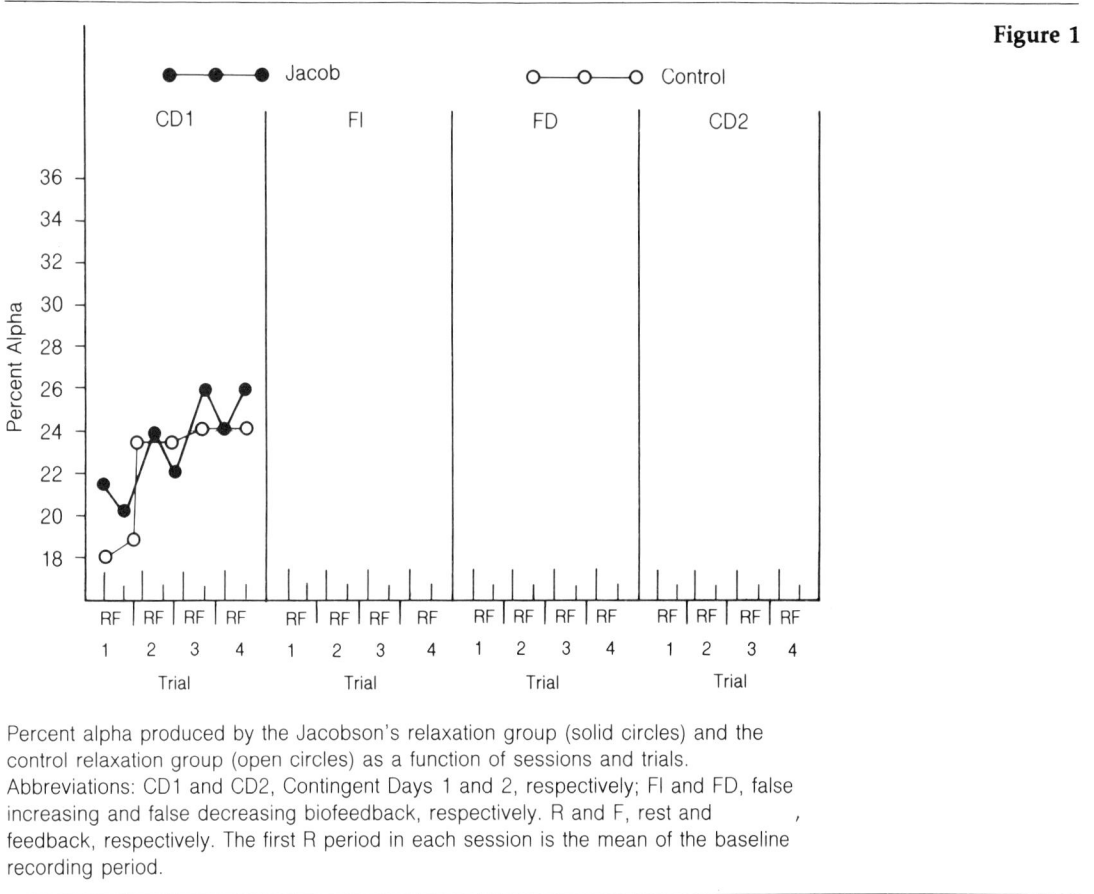

Percent alpha produced by the Jacobson's relaxation group (solid circles) and the control relaxation group (open circles) as a function of sessions and trials. Abbreviations: CD1 and CD2, Contingent Days 1 and 2, respectively; FI and FD, false increasing and false decreasing biofeedback, respectively. R and F, rest and feedback, respectively. The first R period in each session is the mean of the baseline recording period.

The interpretation of these results is straightforward: The Jacobson's relaxation and control relaxation groups behaved similarly throughout the experiment. Both displayed more alpha as a function of trials and both displayed more alpha during feedback than during rest periods. However, the amount of alpha produced was not affected by whether the feedback was veridical or false, demonstrating that alpha production was not under the control of the experimental contingencies. We also analyzed the data from the viewpoint of net alpha change, for example, alpha produced during each feedback period minus alpha produced during the preceding rest period. This "change score" produced functions (not shown) that varied in a nonsystematic manner and remained close to 0% change. An ANOVA in this case produced no main effects or interactions that approached reliability.

The mood scores (responses on the Mood Adjective Check List, MACL, Nowlis, 1965) were analyzed by ANOVA, Mann-Whitney U, and parametric and nonparametric correlational methods. None of these analyses even hinted at a reliable relationship among the variables of amount of alpha actually produced, subjective report of mood, prior exposure to relaxation training, or perceived success or failure on the control task. Differences attributable to sex of subject were sought in all of the above analyses, but none were found.

We purposely used visual feedback since the early positive reports of alpha conditioning used visual feedback while more recent, negative findings employed nonvisual feedback designs. Also, we designed control groups that we feel eliminated or circumvented the problems inherent in the control groups used by others. Additionally, we used a computerized system for detecting alpha activity that circumvented the "roll off" problems inherent in the "active filter" systems used by others. Finally, we gathered data on our subjects over a 4-day period (plus relaxation pretraining) which is longer than other published experiments. Nonetheless, there was no evidence that changes in alpha production were learned through operant conditioning, since the response (alpha production) was not under the control of reinforcement contingencies (biofeedback being veridical or false). We did replicate Brown's (1971) finding that alpha production is greater during feedback than during rest periods. While Brown interpreted this finding as evidence for alpha learning, we point out that feedback need not be contingent to produce this effect, and if alpha is considered to be change scores, no evidence for learning is apparent. Finally, the "alpha experience" appears to be nothing more than suggestibility; empirically, mood was not related to the amount of alpha produced nor to perceived success or failure.

References

Brolund, J. W., & Schallow, J. R. The effects of reward on occipital alpha facilitation by biofeedback. *Psychophysiology,* 1976, **13,** 236–241.

Brown, B. B. Recognition of aspects of consciousness through association with EEG activity represented by a light signal. *Psychophysiology,* 1970, **6,** 442–452.

Brown, B. B. Awareness of EEG subjective activity relationships within a closed feedback system. *Psychophysiology,* 1971, **7,** 451–464.

Brown, B. B. *New mind, new body.* New York: Harper & Row, 1974.

Kamiya, J. Conscious control of brainwaves. *Psychology Today,* 1968, **1,** 57–60.

Kamiya, J. Operant control of the EEG alpha rhythm and some of its reported effects on consciousness. In C. Tart (Ed.), *Altered states of consciousness: A book of readings.* New York: Wiley, 1969.

Lynch, J. J., Paskewitz, D. A., & Orne, M. T. Some factors in the feedback control of human alpha rhythm. *Psychosomatic Medicine*, 1974, **36,** 399–410.
Nowlis, V. Research with the mood adjective check list. In S. S. Tomkins & C. E. Izard (Eds.), *Affect, cognition, and personality.* New York: Springer, 1965.
Plotkin, W. B., Mazer, C., & Lowey, D. Alpha enhancement and the likelihood of an alpha experience. *Psychophysiology,* 1976, **13,** 466–471.

(Received for publication November 9, 1977.)

Question 6. Did the author get unexpected results? The only prediction of ours that was correct concerned the positive effect of false increasing feedback on the amount of alpha. However, that is a small "victory" since alpha also increased under false decreasing feedback. It looks as if the subjects who received real relaxation training did better on the last day or two than did the control subjects. However, the authors report that there were no interactions between relaxation and sessions. This means that the effects of relaxation training did not differ reliably across sessions. "ANOVA" refers to "analysis of variance," a type of statistical test discussed later in this text.

Question 7. How would I interpret the results? Subjects might have increased alpha because they wanted to. That is, the important variable in an alpha "conditioning" study is not the relation between feedback and alpha production. Rather, alpha waves may be perceived as desirable by the subjects so that it would be important for them to try to have an alpha experience. Since most college students have heard about meditation and brain waves, it is possible that these subjects actually tried to relax and increase alpha. Furthermore, since these subjects were introductory psychology students, it is likely that they knew quite a bit about alpha waves and the alpha experience.

Question 8. Is my interpretation better than the authors'? The authors simply point out that the results are not due to conditioning (alternative explanations are mentioned in the introduction). They do argue that the alpha experience is due to suggestibility, which is somewhat similar to our interpretation of the conditioning results.

If you are interested in alpha experiences and alpha conditioning, you will find a recent review by Plotkin (1979) to be thought provoking. Plotkin suggests that there are no unequivocal demonstrations of alpha conditioning, and he offers eight hypotheses for the development of the alpha experience during laboratory studies of alpha.

Table 11–1 in Chapter 11 lists many important journals that contain psychological research. You might examine these and start being a critical consumer of psychological research. Practice might not make you a perfect reader of journal reports, but it will help, especially if you follow the checklist for critical readers.

Writing a Research Report

You have gotten an idea, reviewed the pertinent literature, designed a procedure, collected your data, and analyzed the results. Now you may have to report your results. Your course may require a written record of your research. Even if it does not demand a report, you are obligated to publicize the results of a carefully done project. In order to maintain the self-correcting nature of science, we believe that it is important to publish good data. However, this does not mean that journals should be cluttered with information derived from every undergraduate project. If your research is promising, you will receive encouragement from your instructor. In this section we will review the format of a typical report and discuss some of the stylistic considerations that comprise a comprehensible paper.

If you follow our suggestions for reading articles, then you will have a pretty good idea about the format of a research report, and you will probably have a good feel for technical writing style. Some aspects of technical writing are not too obvious, so we will discuss them here. What we present are general guidelines. If you need additional information, you should examine R. J. Sternberg's book, *Writing the Psychology Paper.* The 1974 revision of the *Publication Manual of the American Psychological Association* will also help, because it is the official arbiter of style for almost all of the journals listed in Table 11–1 (Chapter 11), as well as for many other journals in psychology and education.

Format

Since you already know about the major content sections of a journal article from your active reading of research reports, the outline of a typical report in Figure 3–1 emphasizes the sequence of pages you will have to put together in your APA-style report. A run through that sequence will give you an idea of what you are supposed to include. Your cover page has the title of your project, your name, and your affiliation (your institution or place of business). If you were submitting your article for publication, you would also include a short title (running head) that would be used at the top of the pages of your published article. Usually the title page is not numbered. The next page, page 1, contains the heading *Abstract* and the abstract itself. On this page and on all subsequent ones except the figures, you should have an abbreviated title and the page number in the top right-hand corner of the page. Page 2 repeats the whole title and includes your introductory

Figure 3–1

Title Name(s) Affiliation(s) Running head (short title)	Running head 1 Abstract	Running head 2 Title (Introduction— no heading)	Running head 3 Method Subjects Apparatus Procedure
Running head 4 Results Insert Fig. 1 here	Running head 5 Discussion	Running head 6 Reference Notes	Running head 7 References
Running head 8 Footnotes (General acknowledge- ments are not numbered.)	Running head 9 Table 1 (Title) (Successive ta- bles are on sep- arate pages.)	Running head 10 Figure captions Figure 1 Figure 2	(Figures are on final pages with one per page. Put run- ning head on the *back* of each.)

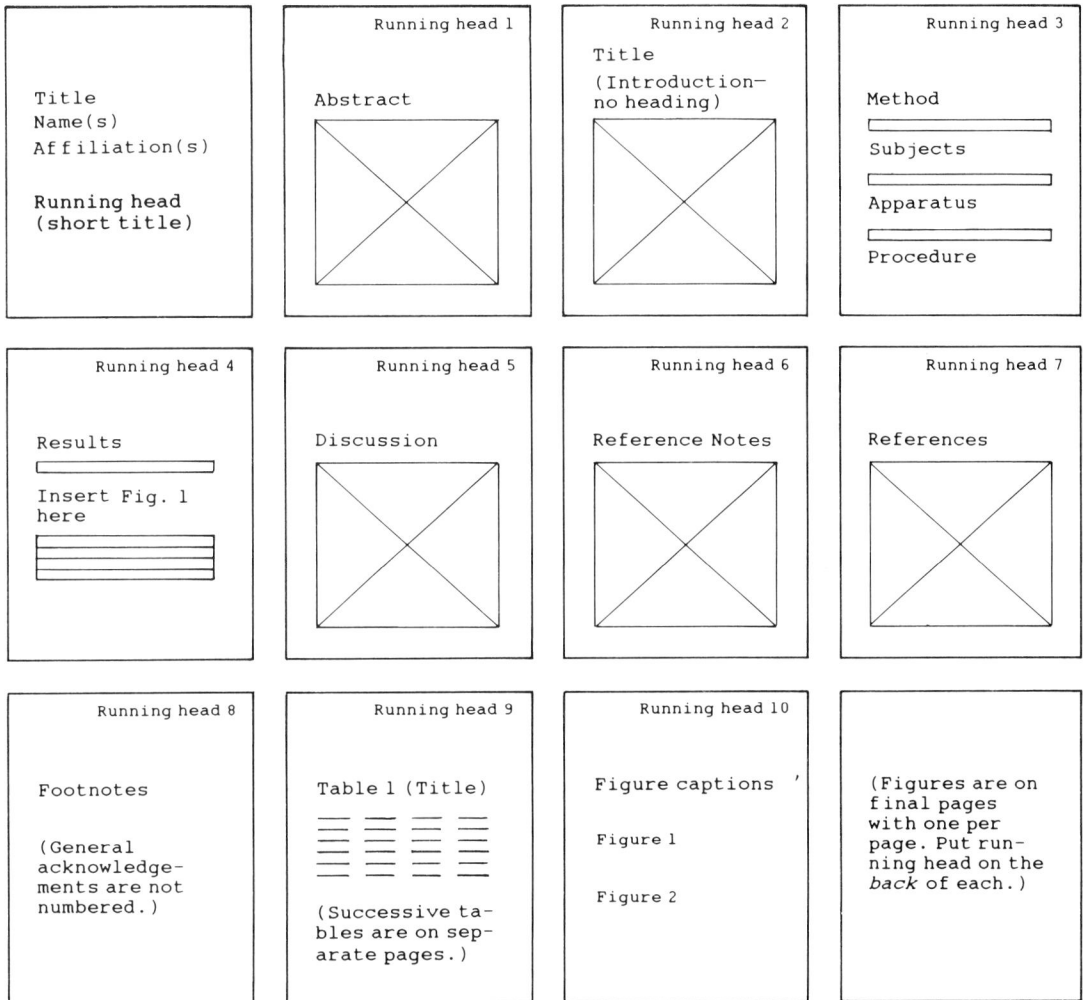

Page sequence for a report in APA format

material. Ordinarily, you do not have a heading for the introduction. After your introduction is finished, the method section begins. Note the format shown for the headings on page 3 in Figure 3–1. The side headings, like *Subjects* and *Apparatus,* help point the reader to pertinent information. The results section immediately follows the method. You do not include your figures and tables in the body of this section (they come at the end of the report). Instead, you indicate their approximate location as shown in page 4 of Figure 3–1. Next comes the discussion, which ends the major textual portion of your report.

Reference notes appear on a separate page after the discussion. Reference notes refer to unpublished works, papers presented at conferences, and personal communications from other researchers. They occur in the reference note list in the order in which they are mentioned in the text (Note 1, Note 2, etc.). If your report is a follow-up of one of your previous projects that has not been published, then you would cite your previous work as a reference note. The regular references begin on a separate page. The format for presenting references is complex, and you should use care in preparing them. The article reprinted in this chapter has most of the different styles of references that you will have to document. Look them over carefully, and, if you have any questions, ask your instructor. (The authors also want to warn you that the references at the end of this text are *not* in APA format, so don't get confused by them.) You might also study the APA manual and recent journal articles. Any footnotes are on a separate page after the references and are listed in numerical order. For most college laboratory reports, footnotes are not necessary. When you prepare something for publication, you may acknowledge financial and intellectual support that would appear on the footnote page. General acknowledgments are not numbered. Other, perhaps peripheral, information would appear as numbered footnotes, but such footnotes are generally discouraged.

Following the footnotes are your data tables mentioned in the results section. Each table should be on a separate page and numbered consecutively, according to its appearance in the results section. Make the titles of your tables short but communicative. Captions for your figures are numbered consecutively and appear on a separate page following the data tables. Finally, you have your figures, each on a separate piece of paper. Put your name (or the short title) and the number of the figure on the back.

Style

Now that you have some idea of the format, let us consider style. After you have suffered through some obscurely written article, we are sure you recognize the advantage of clear, unambiguous writing. The APA format helps standardize the order and general content. However, making sure that the reader understands what you are saying is up to you. We have read many research reports prepared for our classes—some good, some awful, most of them in between—and we have found that the biggest problem is transition, or flow, from one section to the next. Deliberately or not, many students write as if they were composing a surprise-ending short story when their report should be as straightforward as possible.

Your abstract should include your variables (independent, dependent, and important control variables), number and type of subjects, major results, and important conclusions. The body of your report should then expand upon the abstract. (This is why most abstracts are written last, by the way, even though the report might be clearer if it were written first as an outline for the main part of the report.) You should remember the following: in your introduction you state why you are interested in particular variables and what other investigators have found; in your method you state how you examined those variables; in the results you state what happened when you examined the variables; and in your discussion you state what the effects of the variables mean. Thus the body of your report should represent a tight "package," not a disjointed essay containing sections that seem independent of each other. You have to tell your readers what you were trying to do, and tell them, and tell them, and . . .

Perhaps the best way to think about your report is as follows: do not be afraid to be somewhat redundant by having each section build on the previous one. If you repeat the purpose of your research often enough as you go through each section of the report, even the dullest reader will have gotten something from your report by the time he or she gets to the reference list.

Shown in Table 3–2 is a summary of the information that should be included in each section of your report.

The APA publication manual outlines style problems as follows: use the precise word, avoid ambiguity, order presentation of ideas, and consider the reader. These warrant some discussion.

Scientific writing demands clarity, so each word has to be chosen carefully. Consider these sentences that regularly appear in undergraduate research reports: "I ran the subjects individually." "The white, albino rat was introduced to the Skinner box." Actually, none of the subjects in the study from which the first sentence was pulled did any running during the course of the project. What the author meant to say was, "I tested the subjects individually," or "The subjects were tested individually." From reading about rats introduced to Skinner boxes, you might conclude that the researcher had very clever rats. The rat did not shake hands with a box; all that happened was that the rat was put into the operant conditioning chamber. Furthermore, "white, albino" is redundant. All albino rats are white. The lesson here is that in scientific writing you must be careful to choose the correct word or phrase and avoid ambiguity. You should also remember to be careful with pronouns like *which, this, that, these,* and *those.* Many students find it irresistible to begin a paragraph with one of these pronouns, and more often than not the referent for the pronoun is not very easy to deter-

Table 3-2	A Summary of the Information in Each Section of a Research Report

Section	Content
Title	Experiments: state independent and dependent variables— "The effects of X on Y." Other studies: state the relationships examined— "The relation between X and Y."
Abstract	In less than 150 words, state what was done to whom and summarize the most important results.
Introduction	State what you plan to do and why (you may have to review results from related research). Predicted results may be appropriate.
Method	Present enough information to allow someone else to repeat your study exactly the way you did it. For clarity use subheadings (*Subjects, Apparatus,* etc.), and make sure that dependent, independent, subject, and control variables are specified.
Results	Summarize important results in tables or figures. Direct the reader to data that seem most relevant to the purpose of the research.
Discussion	State how the results relate to the hypotheses or predictions stated in the introduction. Inferences and theoretical statements are appropriate.
References	In APA format list only those references that were cited in your report.

mine. You can usually avoid any ambiguity by including the referent of the pronoun each time it is used.

After you have decided upon your words and phrases, you have to put them together carefully. A common problem is to shift tenses of verbs abruptly. In general, you should use the past tense in the review of other studies in your introduction (Smith *found* . . .) and in your method (The subjects *were* . . .). When you are describing and discussing your data, the present tense is usually appropriate (The data *show* that . . ., which *means* that . . .).

Make sure that collective and plural nouns agree with their verbs and pronouns. Plural words that end in *a* are troublesome, such as *data, criteria,* and *phenomena.* Each of those nouns is plural, so they each require plural verbs and pronouns. "These data are" is correct, but "this phenomena is" is not correct. The singular forms for those nouns are: *datum, criterion,* and *phenomenon* ("This phenomenon is").

Many scientific writers overuse the passive voice in their reports. Consider this statement: "It is thought that forgetting is caused by interference." While that statement is fairly concise and it is precise, it is also stuffy and less direct than, "We think that interference causes forgetting," which is really what was meant in the first statement. In general, you should be careful about using either the active or passive voice too much. If you overuse the passive voice, you become stuffy. If you overuse the active voice you may take interest away from what you did and place too much emphasis on yourself (I think . . ., I did . . ., etc.). If you want to emphasize what was done and not who did it and why, use the passive construction. On the other hand, if you think that the agent of the activity is also important, or if the reason for the action is important, then you should use the active voice.

Publishing an Article

Assume that your article has been written, proofread, corrected, and the last page has just emerged from a steaming typewriter. Now what? Although it is unlikely that your first student effort will produce an article of professional quality, you may nevertheless find it interesting to discover what happens when an article is submitted to a journal by a professional psychologist.

The first step is to send copies of the manuscript (the technical term for an unpublished work) to a small number of trusted associates who can check it over to make sure it has no obvious or elementary flaws and that it is written clearly. Once the comments come back, the indicated corrections are made and, with some trepidation, the author commits the manuscript to the mails addressed to the editor of the most appropriate journal. After this it is necessary to forget about it entirely for the next few months or otherwise exhibit great patience. The reviewing process is slow. The editor who receives the manuscript is a harried, overworked, tired individual who often regrets accepting the editorship. Editors of journals, like elected politicians, serve a fixed term of office, usually 4–6 years. About two or three weeks after submitting the potential article, the author will receive a form letter of thanks for interest in the journal and acknowledging receipt of the manuscript. The manuscript gets a number (like 81–867) and if an associate editor has been assigned to handle it the author is instructed to direct all future correspondence to that editor.

The editor then sends copies of the manuscript to one or two reviewers. It is unlikely that both of them will be good friends of the author. Blind reviewing, where an author conceals his or her identity, can be used with some journals for those who do not believe in the impartiality of reviewers. The reviewer, who may also review for several other journals, puts the manuscript in the pile on his or her desk with a muttered curse. A conscientious reviewer may take up to a day or two to carefully read and evaluate a manuscript. When each reviewer gets around to it, a summary statement is sent to the editor. When the reviewers are in agreement, the editor's decision is easy. Should the reviewers disagree, the editor must carefully read the manuscript and sometimes may request a third opinion. Finally, an editorial decision is reached and the author receives a letter stating either (a) why the manuscript cannot be published, (b) what kind of revisions are needed to make the manuscript acceptable, or (c) that the journal is happy to publish the article. Since rejection rates are quite high in most journals (above 80%), editors spend a great deal of time devising tactful letters of rejection.

Whether or not the article was accepted, the comments of the reviewers are most valuable. The best psychologists in the area have provided, free of charge, their careful opinions about the research. Of course, reviewers can also make mistakes. Anyone who disagrees with a review has the privilege, even the responsibility, of writing a reply to the editor. This usually will not get the article accepted, but it is important that rejected authors have the right to appeal or protest. Anyway, there are always other journals.

If the article was perchance accepted for publication, the author is not yet finished. Some revision may be required. The copyright for the article is signed over to the publisher. Some months later the author receives galley or page proofs from the publisher. These must be carefully checked to ensure that the words and tables set in type by the printer match the original manuscript. After making corrections, and authors are charged for excessive corrections that do not result from printer's errors, the article is returned. Some additional months after this the article finally appears in print in the journal. The entire process, from submitting the manuscript until final publication, takes a year or more. Authors do not get paid for articles in journals, but on the other hand neither do they get charged for the privilege of appearing in print.

As you might expect, it is a great thrill to see your name in print, especially for the first time. An even greater thrill, however, is the knowledge that you may have added some small amount to our understanding of why people think and act as they do.

Summary

When you read a research report, it is important that you read actively and critically, so you can derive maximum benefit from other people's research. The checklist for critical readers is designed to get you into the habit of actively asking questions about the reports you read: What hypotheses are being tested, how are they being tested? Does the method test the hypotheses? Do the results speak to the hypotheses? How does the author relate the results to the purposes of the research? What interpretations and inferences are made by the author? You should also consider these questions when you write your own report. The APA format provides a framework for your report, but it is up to you to write clearly. Writing and (possibly) publishing the results of a project may be a tedious process. However, remember that the purpose of psychological research is to find out why people think and act as they do. In order for psychological science to be self-correcting, reports must be published and knowledgeable consumers must read them.

**Study and
Review**

Exercises

1. Go to the library and practice being a critical reader of psychology articles. In Chapter 11 there is a list of some of the relevant psychology journals. Be sure to use the checklist.

2. Frequently you will have to write a research report that includes more than one study. Examine several journal articles that contain two or more studies and note how the articles are broken up into sections. There are no set rules here, but you should be aware of the general techniques that are used.

Key Concepts

Title 47
Author 47
Abstract 47
Introduction 47
Method 48
Results 48
tables 49
figures 49
ordinates 49

abscissa 49
Discussion 49
References 49
Checklist for Critical Readers
    50–52
APA format 63
Subjects 64
Appratus 64
report contents 66

Suggested Readings

The following two publications will give you more detail about writing journal articles: American Psychological Association. *Publication manual of the American Psychological Association* (2d ed.). Washington, D.C.: Author, 1974; and Sternberg, R. J. *Writing the psychology paper.* New York: Barron's, 1978.

QUESTIONS THAT SHOULD BE ANSWERED
BEFORE THE RESEARCH IS CONDUCTED

How will the participants in my project react?

Is my naturalistic observation unobtrusive? Can I assess normal and motivated forgetting in my case study by corroborating evidence? Is my test able to counteract the problem of response styles? Does my experimental plan contain ''blinding'' or other procedures to insure that the subjects react appropriately to the independent variable?

How will I, the researcher, influence the results of my project?

Will my personal characteristics influence the behavior of the subjects? Have I defined a research plan that permits me to treat all participants the same (except for deliberate variation)? Do I have to be blind to certain aspects of the research in order to be unbiased? Am I aware of my own biases and preconceptions? Am I an objective researcher?

Do other scientists understand what I am investigating?

Are my terms operationally defined?

Does my project represent a valid attempt to determine why people think and act as they do?

Are my subjects representative? Have I selected meaningful variables to examine and vary? Is the setting I plan to use ecologically valid?

Is my project designed in accordance with contemporary ethical standards?

Will I treat my subhuman subjects in a humane fashion? Do I understand the ethical principles behind drug research? Will my human subjects be treated in a dignified fashion without violating their personal freedom and damaging their physical and emotional health? Have I read and understood the ethical principles espoused by the American Psychological Association?

Pitfalls in Conducting Research

4

Conducting a good research project is difficult because there are numerous pitfalls waiting to sabotage your work. The purpose of this chapter is to forewarn you about many of these problems. Most of the difficulties have to be confronted before all the details of your research plan have been determined. Thus, we should consider these pitfalls before discussing how to conduct research. There are other pitfalls that can influence how you interpret the *results* of research that will be examined in a later chapter. The problems discussed in this chapter are: (1) how the researcher and subject react to being involved in research; (2) ways to ensure accurate communication among scientists; (3) how to try to determine the validity of your research procedure; and (4) whether or not your project violates ethical standards.

Overview

Good research requires careful planning and careful interpretation. There are several pitfalls that can hurt both the conduct of research and its interpretation. In this chapter we are concerned with the pitfalls that can arise while you are conducting your research. We will warn you about several problems that can be avoided by carefully planning ahead —forewarned is forearmed. In a later chapter we will examine problems associated with interpreting the results of research.

In many areas of psychological research, we can view the reactions of the participants not only in terms of the project itself, but also in terms of "normal" social interaction. Suppose you are responding to a survey that asked you to estimate the number of times a day you think about sex. Go ahead and make a guess. Now, suppose you were asked the same question in a personal interview. Would your answer in the interview be the same as the one given in the survey? You might be reluctant to say "I think about sex at least 15 times a day." On the other hand, writing "15" in response to the question on the anonymous survey might not bother you at all. In general, ordinary social interaction may put demands on a research participant that changes the way he or she responds. *Demand characteristics,* a phrase coined by Orne (1962,

Pitfalls Due to the Reactions of the Participants

1969), highlights the pressures put on people participating in research. If people respond in ways they think the research demands, rather than naturally, an accurate interpretation of the data may be difficult or impossible. The effects of unnatural responding show up in all types of psychological research. We will consider some specific examples of demand characteristics and some possible solutions.

Demand Characteristics of Descriptive Research

Naturalistic Observation.   As noted in Chapter 2, *unobtrusive measures* are often used in naturalistic research. In most instances the reasons seem obvious and the solutions straightforward. Have you ever climbed a tree and peeked at the baby birds in a nest? Your presence usually results in loud fussing by the nestlings (apparently they think you are Mom or Dad bringing home the bugs), and this fussing usually attracts one or both of the parents. If you have disturbed the nest of an aggressive bird, such as a wren or an eagle, you are likely to be dive-bombed by an angry parent. The lesson here is that almost all animals (including humans) do not like strangers invading their territories. Thus, long-range camera lenses, binoculars, and blinds are basic equipment in naturalistic observation.

Sometimes, however, either the subjects themselves, the terrain, or some other aspect of the project demand close contact. It is in these situations that *participant observation* (see Chapter 2) often provides a solution. For example, Fossey (1972) has spent a great amount of time observing the mountain gorilla. The mountain gorilla lives in central Africa, and its habitat is threatened by human beings who are moving into that area. Since the mountain gorilla's normal habitat is in the mountainous rain forest, long-range, unobtrusive spying is out of the question. Fossey was particularly concerned with the free-ranging behavior of the gorillas, so she decided to become a participant observer. This was difficult, because the gorillas are not tame. She had to make a fool of herself in front of the gorillas so that they would become accustomed to her presence. She mimicked aspects of the animal's behavior, such as eating, grooming, and making weird gorilla-like vocalizations. As she said, "one feels like a fool thumping one's chest rhythmically or sitting about pretending to munch on a stalk of wild celery as though it were the most delectable morsel in the world. But the gorillas have responded favorably" (p. 211). It took several months for Fossey to gain the confidence of the gorillas, and it will probably take one or two decades for her to complete her project. How would you like to act like a gorilla for 10 or 15 years?

Case Studies.   Case studies are individual histories, which means that much of the evidence in the studies is *retrospective* in nature (i.e., it comes from looking back into the past). Looking backward often causes problems. One difficulty is that the evidence may be inaccurate due to ordinary forgetting. We may not remember what our thoughts and actions were in nursery school because what has happened since that time interferes with our memory of early events. A second problem has to do with a demand characteristic—*motivated forgetting* may occur. This refers to the active way in which humans reconstruct their past experiences. People often distort unpleasant events, which results in "remembering" the wrong things. The bad things are forgotten (e.g., the shoplifting episodes as a nine-year old), and the good things are remembered and sometimes made even better (the stellar piano recital or the 47 merit badges in scouts). Research has shown that mothers often misremember events about their own children's very early years (Garmezy, 1971). This distorted remembering usually has to do with emotionally related phenomena, such as the child's reactions to toilet training and weaning. One way around this problem is to get corroborating evidence from other individuals. This may be difficult to do, and the corroboration is also subject to both kinds of forgetting.

Surveys, Interviews, and Tests.   Demands that lead to motivated forgetting are also present in other forms of descriptive research. Since many of the responses on tests and surveys are not retrospective, we talk about the possible contamination as *response style* or response *sets.* Different people may have habitual ways of answering questions. These habits may be due to how they view themselves, or they may be due to the expectations of the researcher and society (more on this latter point later). In general, there seem to be three kinds of response styles: "yea saying" or *response acquiescence,* "nay saying" or *response deviation,* and *social desirability.* College-bound high school graduates respond "no" to the question, "Do you use marijuana daily?" Does this answer reflect the true behavior of these people, or does the answer reflect the habitual tendency to say "no" (response deviation)? Alternatively, the answer could be a socially desirable one because marijuana is a controlled substance and many authorities frown upon its use. The high school graduates not heading for college tended to answer "yes" to this question twice as often as the college bound (see Bachman and Johnston, 1979). Is this answer a "true" one, or does the "yes" simply indicate that these people are likely to acquiesce and say "yes" no matter what the question is? Based on the answer to this one question, we cannot determine if the answer is a true one or if it is one resulting from a particular response style.

Edwards (1953, 1957) has developed an interesting solution to the response-style problem. The respondent is presented with a question that demands a *forced choice* between equally desirable or undesirable alternatives. On Edwards' test, the Personal Preference Schedule, the respondent has to select one of two activities or indicate which of two thoughts or feelings reflect the characteristics of the respondent. For example, the respondent might have to choose between painting a picture or writing a play. This forced-choice technique is designed to minimize contamination due to response styles.

Associated with the problem of response styles is a problem more difficult to cope with. Volunteer subjects differ in a number of ways from potential participants who do not volunteer (e.g., Rosnow and Rosenthal, 1970). Volunteers tend to be more intelligent, better educated, more cooperative, better adjusted, and higher in need for social approval than nonvolunteers. All of these differences could have a strong effect on the reactions of a subject to a particular project. These characteristics of volunteers are somewhat like a super response style: everything about the subject plays a role in determining the sorts of responses that are given. Furthermore, the volunteer problem might also limit the generality of your results.

What the volunteer problem means for your own research is that you have to be careful in sampling from the population of participants available to you. If your test or survey is boring and requires the respondent to go to extreme lengths to be cooperative (trudging through a blizzard at 11:00 P.M. to the psychology building), then your answers may be based upon a biased sample of opinion. The problem is also serious, as Rosnow and Rosenthal point out, in opinion surveys that rely on volunteer mailings or phone-ins. What are we to make of the results of a magazine survey that relies on voluntary compliance of the readers? Or, how about the radio survey that solicits calls from its listeners? In both cases we do not know anything about the people who did not respond, nor do we know anything about the people who do not read that magazine or listen to that station. We can find out about the nonrespondents by expending a great deal of time and effort. Usually, this effort is not made.

There are two solutions to the nonrespondent problem. In the first place, you can get a random sample of the entire population that is available to you. This means that every potential respondent has an equal chance of being questioned. In the second place, you could give the nonrespondents some kind of extra incentive to participate in your project. They could be offered money, or they might be given detailed information about the research project. The extra inducements might bias the results, however, by treating some subjects differently from others prior to participation in the project.

Correlational Research.   Since test results and survey data often provide the basis for correlations, the problems mentioned above are applicable here. Demands on participants might be magnified in correlational research that involves two measures of the people closely in time. Participants do not usually react passively to the inquiries of the researcher. Instead, they often try to figure out what is going on and respond according to their perceptions of the project (Orne, 1962, 1969). For example, suppose you surveyed a college population about their sexual and religious attitudes. Simultaneously (or a little while later) you also asked them about their use of drugs. It would have to be a very slow college student who could not figure out at least some purposes of the project.

Experimentation. Walk up to a stranger and say, "please do me a favor by doing ten push-ups." Repeat your request to several others. Then, repeat the procedure, but this time say, "I'm doing a psychology experiment, please do me a favor by doing ten push-ups." The odds are that you will get very little compliance in the first group of people and very few refusals in the second group. People will do things in the name of science and experimentation that they will not ordinarily do (Orne, 1962). Put another way, experiments may not only examine behavior, they may produce it! Demand characteristics are an important source of contamination of experimental data.

Orne (1962, 1969) has noted that subjects entering an experiment have some general notions of what to expect and are usually trying to figure out the specific purpose of the experiment. They are likely to believe that reasonable care will be taken for their well-being and that whatever the experimenter asks them to do will serve a useful purpose. They will also want to know this purpose and seek clues in the experimental situation. Because many psychological experiments would provide uninteresting results if the true purpose of the study were known, elaborate deceptions are often used to mask the true purposes of the experiment. But, as Orne points out, these might sometimes be rather transparent. At any rate, the general problem exists as to how the subject's expectations affect or determine her or his behavior in an experiment. As Orne notes:

Insofar as the subject cares about the outcome, his perception of his role and of the hypothesis being tested will become a significant determinant of his behavior. The cues which govern his behavior—which communicate what is expected of him and what the experimenter hopes to find—can therefore be crucial variables. Some time ago I proposed that these cues be called "demand characteristics of an experiment." . . . They include the scuttlebutt about the experiment, its setting, implicit and explicit instructions, the person of the experimenter, subtle cues provided by him, and, of particular importance, the experimental procedure (Orne, 1969, p. 146).

Demand characteristics of the experimental situation may be a potent problem in generalizing the results of an experiment because, if the results were produced by demand characteristics of the experimental situation, they will not generalize to other situations. It is well known that when people know they are being observed as part of an experiment their behavior will be greatly affected. One famous case of this is the *Hawthorne effect,* named after the Western Electric Company plant at which an experiment was conducted on factors affecting worker productivity (see Homans, 1965). Six average women workers were chosen for a longitudinal study of factors affecting the rate at which they assembled telephone relays. After an initial period measuring the baseline rate of producing relays, the women were placed in a special test room, and, after a period of adjustment to their new circumstances, experienced a number of changes in their daily routine that were supposed to affect productivity. During one period of the study, rest pauses were inserted into their schedule, and later the frequency of pauses was increased. During another period, their method of payment was changed, and during yet another, a light lunch was provided, and so on. The experiment lasted for more than a year and the results were quite surprising. With a few exceptions, no matter what changes were made —whether there were many or few rest periods, whether the work day was made longer or shorter, etc.—the women tended to produce more and more telephone relays. Although it is hard to pinpoint the reason for this change, since a number of variables were confounded, it seems quite likely that it was largely due to the fact that the women knew they were in an experiment, felt the special attention, and wanted to cooperate. They knew that the experimenters expected the changes in the working conditions to affect them, so they did. They kept working harder and harder. (For a different interpretation see Parsons, 1974.)

Since the changes in behavior apparently resulted from the fact that the woman were in an experiment and not because of the independent variables that were manipulated, we can say that the Hawthorne effect represents one kind of demand characteristic. Orne argues that to some extent experiments with humans always have this feature built in. The person is an active participant interested in what is happening and usually eager to "help." Orne and his associates have done a great deal of research on demand characteristics in experimentation. Some of the most interesting studies dealt with demand characteristics in hypnosis research.

Investigators interested in the effects of hypnosis have asked subjects in this altered state of consciousness to do all sorts of things, often with notable success. One apparently well-established finding is that subjects under deep hypnosis can be led to perform various antisocial and destructive acts such as throwing nitric acid in the face of a research assistant and handling venomous snakes (Rowland, 1939; Young, 1952). Orne and Evans (1965) suspected that this might have been due more to the demand characteristics of the situation than the effects of hypno-

Figure 4–1

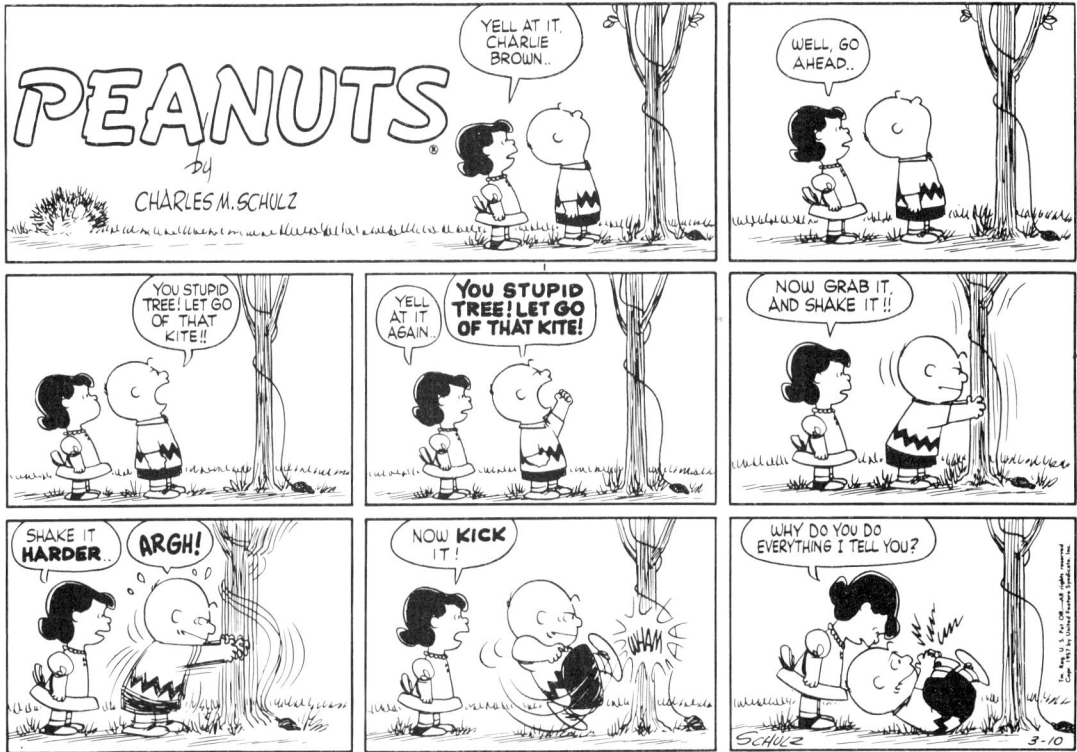

Drawing by Charles Schulz: © 1957 United Features Syndicate, Inc.

Most people will resist the suggestions of another person more than our gullible friend Charlie Brown, but when placed in an experiment most of us become like him. Orne might well have asked his subjects the same question Lucy asked in the cartoon.

sis. They asked subjects to perform a series of dangerous acts such as grasping a venomous snake, taking a coin from fuming acid, and throwing the acid in the experimenter's face under several treatment conditions: (a) subjects under deep hypnosis, (b) a group of subjects told to simulate or pretend that they were under hypnosis, (c) a group of awake control subjects who were not asked to simulate hypnosis, but who were pressed by the experimenter to comply with the requests, (d) other awake control subjects who were not pressed to comply, and (e) people asked to perform the task without being made part of an experiment. The results are summarized in Table 4–1 as the percentage of people carrying out the tasks in each condition. Not surprisingly, people not in the experimental setting refused to carry out the antisocial tasks, but as others had reported, a high percentage of hypnotized subjects did carry

Table 4-1

Percentage of subjects who performed dangerous tasks in response to requests by the experimenter (adapted from Orne & Evans, 1965).

Subject group	Grasp venomous snake	Take coin from acid	Throw acid at experimenter
Real hypnosis	83	83	83
Simulating hypnosis	100	100	100
Waking control— press to comply	50	83	83
Waking control— without press to comply	50	17	17
Nonexperimental	0	0	0

out the tasks as instructed. However, *all* simulating control subjects also performed the tasks and even the nonsimulating controls performed them to a large extent if they were pressed to comply, demonstrating the power of the experimental situation. The conclusion to be drawn is that hypnosis is not necessarily responsible for performing the antisocial acts. Rather, demand characteristics of the experimental situation, including the setting, the instructions, and the way subjects think they are supposed to behave while under hypnosis, are sufficient to produce the antisocial acts. The inference should not be drawn that antisocial acts cannot be elicited from people under deep hypnosis, only that the studies currently available do not offer good evidence to support this idea. It should be mentioned, in passing, that the experimenter in this study was blind to (i.e., did not know) the conditions of the subjects, so as not to affect their behavior.

Countering the effects of demand characteristics in experimentation is often very difficult. Unobtrusive measures may not work in a laboratory setting, because most people know that they are in an experiment. Consequently, many psychologists do their experiments in a natural setting. These *field experiments* are similar to naturalistic observation with the addition of a real or ex post facto independent variable. Going into the field, where people may be unaware that they are being experimented upon, poses two additional problems: (1) loss of control that is characteristic of laboratory experiments; and (2) unobtrusive measures may violate some of the ethical standards of research.

One way to insert unobtrusive measures into a laboratory experiment is to use *deception*. Deception can push the demand characteristics in a particular direction, so that the subject will respond naturally to the true independent variable. In a famous example of deception by Milgram (1963), the participants were led to believe that they were giving shocks to a "learner" in order to improve the rate of learning. In fact, the shock apparatus was fake and the learner just pretended to receive strong shocks. Many people regard this sort of deception as unsatisfactory because of the ethical problems it raises. However, deception by omission sometimes may be acceptable. Typical behavior may be elicited without *necessarily* violating ethical standards when certain facts about the study are not mentioned. For example, half the subjects in a memory experiment may receive special instructions on how to learn and remember. A second group, the control group, does not receive these special instructions. The control group serves as a baseline for "natural" memorizing. Whenever deception by omission is used, you must be careful to maintain the dignity of the person being studied (see the later section on ethics).

When we withold some pertinent information from the participant, we say that the experiment is being run *blind.* A good example of a blind study is one by Carver, Coleman, and Glass (1976), who were concerned with the suppression of fatigue by Type A and Type B people. Type As are aggressive people who really strive to win in competitive situations. People with the Type A behavior pattern are prone to coronary heart disease. Type Bs are less aggressive and competitive, and they are less likely to have heart problems. Type As and Type Bs were put on an exercise treadmill to see how long they would exercise relative to their maximum capacity. Carver et al. also got subjective estimates of fatigue from the subjects. During the course of the experiment, every attempt was made to remove any hint of competition—both against the clock or against other people's performance on the treadmill. In fact, the people were told that they would be removed from the treadmill after a predetermined time. The time on the treadmill was actually determined by the participant who indicated when he had had enough. Confronting the Type As with evidence of competition might have enhanced their competitive drive. The experimenters wanted the As to become fatigued in the absence of any apparent competition. So, making the subject blind to the nature of the experiment seemed important. In this instance the deception does not appear unethical. The results found by Carver et al. indicated that the Type As worked longer on the treadmill than did Bs. Despite the extra effort, the As reported less fatigue than did the Bs.

A final way to control for demand characteristics in experiments is the approach used by Orne and Evans (1965) in their hypnosis study. They had people *simulate* (or pretend) to be hypnotized in addition to subjects who were hypnotized. The logic here is straightforward. The demand characteristics of the situation are assumed to be the same for subjects in both the experimental condition and the simulating control condition. If the experimental manipulation (say, hypnosis) is truly effective, then the behavior of the experimental group should differ reliably from that of the simulating group.

The technique of using simulating participants is sometimes called a *thought experiment* (e.g., Richman, Mitchell, and Reznick, 1979). In general, the approach is to test an independent variable on the experimental group. Then, you tell your simulating subjects about the independent variable, and you ask them to indicate what they would do in that situation. If the results of the thought experiment are highly similar to the results due to the independent variable, we can conclude that there are important demand characteristics contaminating the effects of the independent variable.

A summary of demand characteristics is presented in Table 4–2.

Table 4-2	Summary of Demand Characteristic Pitfalls and Their Solutions		
	Research Procedure	Type of Pitfall	Possible Solution
	Observation	Reactivity	Unobtrusive measures
	Case Study	Motivated forgetting	Corroborating evidence
	Surveys, Tests, and Correlation	Response styles	Forced-choice responding
		Volunteer problem	Random sample, extra incentives
	Experimentation	Reactivity (Hawthorne effect)	Deception ("blind")
			Simulated experiments

Researcher Effects

While you are carefully watching your subjects to make sure that there are no disruptive demand characteristics in your project, there is someone else you should be spying on—yourself. Barber (1976), who makes a distinction between the *investigator,* the person responsible for designing, analyzing, and interpreting research, and the *experimenter,* the person actually conducting the study, has presented an extensive and valuable discussion of ten investigator and experimenter effects. Since you are likely to be both investigator and experimenter in your own research, we combine our discussion of these problems under one heading—researcher effects.

The researcher, just like the subject, is a fallible individual. So, we should recognize where and when the researcher can have detrimental effects on the outcome. Pitfalls associated with the researcher can occur either deliberately or inadvertently. We hope that there are few deliberate effects, but they can be very costly, so we discuss them first.

Deliberate Researcher Effects. When one engages in research, a great deal of time and effort are expended. Therefore, it is not surprising that there have been instances of deliberate fabrication. A researcher who is enamored with a particular theory may fudge the data enough to support the theory. A researcher with strongly held political or social beliefs may report some results and suppress others. In the same way these biased researchers may design their projects in such a way that negative or ideologically "bad" results will be unlikely to occur. Surely there is no place in scientific psychology for such insidious practices.

How do we guard against deliberate bias? We have to assume that scientific training emphasizes objectivity and the acquisition of knowledge. The goal of scientific psychology is to find out why people think and act as they do—it is not to support particular theories or political credos. Scientists must be as objective as possible, especially when data conflict with personal interest.

How do we detect deliberate bias? Science is self-correcting and truth will out. Unfortunately it may take a long time for fakery to be discovered. A sure way to speed up detection is to increase the number of direct replications (Barber, 1976). Direct replications involve an exact repetition of an experiment (see Chapter 10). If important pieces of research are not directly repeatable, then the scientifically valid data will make their appearance in the literature by replacing the bogus findings.

Inadvertent Researcher Effects. Inadvertent effects are probably more widespread and harder to detect than deliberate researcher bias. Just how often they occur is difficult to determine, because there are many parts of the research process that may be inadvertently contaminated. A scientist's political beliefs, for example, could result in an incomplete survey that assesses some attitudes and not others. This does not necessarily indicate deliberate bias, but may merely represent the fallibility of the individual scientist. The scientist can only think about a limited number of things at a time, so the research designs will partially reflect the scientist's personal preferences. This sort of problem can have very subtle manifestations. For example, animal learning is not a politically sensitive research area. However, the research design, apparatus, and species of animal can be determined by the researcher's preconceptions of animal learning (Barber, 1976). There are two solutions to this problem: (1) researchers should be aware of their own underlying preconceptions (these preexisting notions are what philosophers of science call "paradigms"; Kuhn, 1962); and (2) a variety of attacks on a problem should be undertaken by many scientists.

Another source of researcher bias derives from treating participants in a project differently over and above any *planned* differences in treatment. A great deal of evidence indicates that how the researcher treats the subjects can have a profound effect on the results (Barber, 1976). An example will illustrate the possible effect and a way to prevent the researcher from inadvertently influencing the outcome. Suppose you were the researcher in the study by Carver et al. (1976) about fatigue suppression in Type As and Type Bs. You would know ahead of time that half of your subjects (the As) were particularly prone to coronary heart disease. You have to record the exercise time on the treadmill as the subjects are working at or beyond their maximum oxygen consumption. Would you treat Type As and Type Bs differently? Would subtle body movements or the tone of your voice clue the Type As to take it easy so they do not have a heart attack? (This was unlikely, since the Type As were young—they had the *potential* for coronary problems later in life).

There are two ways to minimize bias that can lead to differential treatment. In the first place, the researcher must be expected to conduct the project as uniformly as possible for all participants. The only differences in treatment should be those that are deliberately introduced—independent variables, different questions in a survey, different observing times, etc. Type As must be treated exactly like Type Bs. This was done by Carver et al. (1976), who even went so far as to eliminate the data of one subject who was personally acquainted with one of the data collectors.

A second way to minimize inadvertent differential treatment is to make the researcher *blind* with respect to potentially important attributes of the participants or the task. The experimenters in the study by Carver et al. did not know if an individual was a Type A or a Type B. This diminished the chances of treating the Type As differently on the treadmill. This tactic of making the researcher blind is the other side of the coin of making the subjects blind to aspects of the task. If both the subject and the researcher are blind, we have what is called a *double blind* design.

Double blind designs are common in medical experiments that test the effectiveness of drugs. The experimental group is given the drug, and the control group is given a placebo substance. A *placebo* (the word is derived from a Middle English word meaning to be pleased) is a pharmacologically inert substance (a "sugar pill") given to control subjects to fake them out. They, along with the experimental group, assume that they are receiving a real drug, so the expectancies will be the same for the two groups. Not only are the placebo subjects blind, so is the researcher. The researcher does not know who is receiving the placebo and who is getting the real drug. In the typical drug experiment, the substances are given code numbers that cannot be deciphered by the person who actually administers the substances. However, someone else will know who received the placebo and who received the drug. All of these precautions decrease the possibility that the control subjects will be treated differently from the experimental subjects, with one exception—the independent variable.

The personal attributes of a researcher may bias the actions of the participants. The age, sex, race, and authority of the researcher may determine how the subjects react. In a personal interview it has been shown that subjects are more likely to report sexual thoughts when the interviewer and the respondent are of the same sex than when they are of the opposite sex (Walters, Shurley, and Parsons, 1962). The easiest way to solve this problem is to use more than one researcher and to make sure that each one follows the research protocol exactly. In your own research it may not be possible to enlist assistance from others. Therefore, you should try to treat each person identically.

We have emphasized strict adherence to procedure as one way to minimize inadvertent researcher effects. This is especially important for minimizing the possibility of incorrectly recording data. In every condition for every subject, data must be recorded in the same way. This means that before the project begins you will have to define exactly what an acceptable datum is (see below). Furthermore, in animal work you will have to guard against the pitfall of *anthropomorphism.* This refers to the tendency to attribute human characteristics to nonhumans, especially internal thoughts and feelings. Anthropomorphism is sometimes obvious as in, "The dog loved and respected its master" and sometimes not so obvious, "The rat was hungry so it ate a lot." A similar pitfall occurs in the description of the thoughts and feelings of primitive tribes. An observer might attribute standard western thought to primitives as in, "Their love of individual liberty conflicted with the socialist ideology of the tribal council." All of these examples are actually theoretical statements that may not be warranted on the basis of the data. How do we define "love" in a dog? Does it mean that the dog wagged its tail or came when it was called? What is hunger for a rat? These sorts of issues are examined in the next section.

Reliability of Communication

No serious discussion, scientific or otherwise, can progress very far unless the participants agree to define the terms they are using. Imagine that you and your date are having a friendly argument about who is the best athlete of the year. How do you define athlete? You both would agree about such common sports as tennis, swimming, and gymnastics. But what about more esoteric sports like frisbee throwing, hang-gliding, and hopping cross-country on a pogo stick? Should practitioners of these activities be considered for your athlete-of-the-year award? Until this question of definition is answered, your discussion may just go around in circles.

Similar problems can arise in scientific discussions. Let's imagine that scientists in psychophysical laboratories in West Lafayette, Indiana, and Clayton Corners, Arkansas, are studying tail-flicking responses to flashes of light in the horseshoe crab. One laboratory finds that its crabs give tremendous tail-flicks while crabs in the other lab hardly move their tails at all. The scientists are very concerned and exchange terse letters and autographed pictures of their respective crabs. Eventually the reason for the discrepancy is discovered. They were each defining the flash of light differently, since their flashes were of different durations, even though the brightness of the two flashes was similar. When they adjusted their flashes to be the same, both labs obtained the same results. This example is a little farfetched since, as we all know, crabs can't autograph their pictures. Furthermore, all good psychologists know the importance of defining the stimulus exactly, so that this confusion would probably not have occurred in the first place. But this example does show what *could* happen if scientists were not very careful about defining their terms.

While social conversation and scientific discourse both require definitions, the requirements for scientific definition are more stringent. Terms that are perfectly adequate for ordinary conversation are most often too vague for scientific purposes. When you state that someone has a pleasant personality, other people have a good enough idea of what you mean so that a need for better definition does not arise. But when a psychologist uses the term "personality" in a technical sense, a great deal of precision is necessary. This important distinction between *technical* usage and *common* usage occurs frequently in psychology. It is all too easy to slip and use technical language imprecisely. Words like *information, anxiety, threshold,* etc., have broad everyday meanings that must be precisely limited when they are used in a technical sense. The most common way of providing such technical meaning is by way of an *operational definition.*

An operational definition is a formula for building a construct in a way that other scientists can duplicate. "Take the eye of a newt, the leg of a frog, three oyster shells and shake twice" is an operational definition, although it is not entirely clear what is being defined. However, this recipe can be duplicated and so meets the major criterion for an operational definition. You can tell from this example that an operational definition does not have to make any sense, as long as it is clear and can be copied. For instance, we might operationally define a construct called "centigrams" as the product of your height in centimeters and your weight in grams. Since any scientist can easily determine the "centigram" score, this is an operational definition. Of course, it probably could not be used for any important scientific purpose, but the potential utility of an operational definition is a separate issue from its clarity.

The major virtue of operational definitions is that they help prevent us from confusing technical concepts with their equivalents in common language. We can illustrate this by referring to an experiment where participants were faced with two rows of ten lights and one row of ten buttons (Morin and Grant, 1954), as shown in Figure 4–2. A stimulus lamp went on and a correct button press would extinguish it and present

Figure 4–2

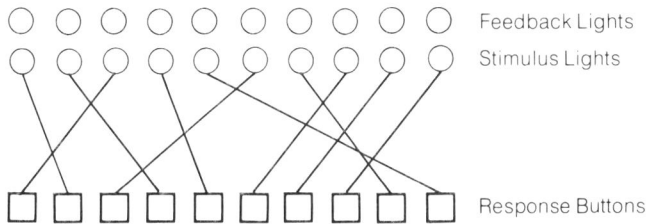

Stimulus lights and response buttons are not connected in any obvious relationship. For example, pressing the leftmost response button does not control the leftmost light, but instead turns off the third light from the left (after Morin and Grant, 1954).

the next stimulus lamp and so forth. This would be a simple task if each light were connected to the button directly underneath it. However, lights and buttons were haphazardly joined. This was why the top row of feedback lights was used. Pressing any button lit up a feedback light showing which stimulus light (that is, the one directly below the feedback light) was controlled by that button. After several days of practice, participants were tested to see if they had learned the light-button relationships. All participants could correctly draw a diagram linking lights and buttons, so the experimenters disconnected the feedback lights. The time taken to press the buttons went up dramatically. A similar effect occurs when you learn to operate a typewriter. It does not take long to be able to diagram the relationship between keys and letters. But even though you know where each letter can be found on the keyboard, it takes a fair amount of practice until you can type equally well with eyes open or closed. This seems like a contradiction. On the one hand, being able to draw the diagram correctly is evidence that the light-button relationships had been learned. On the other hand, the increase in time is evidence that the relationships were not learned.

This apparent contradiction stems from using the term "learning" in its common language sense. But technically, learning can never be observed directly. Instead it is inferred from a change in behavior—that is, we need at least two measures of behavior before we can state that learning occurred. In the light-button experiment, one measure of learning was the decrease in time needed to press the buttons with succeeding days of practice. However, these data occurred with the row of feedback lights connected, so that a reversal (an increase in time required) when conditions are changed by removing feedback lights is not really astonishing. The other measure of learning—drawing a diagram —assumes that no one could do this before the start of the experiment, since participants would have had no experience with the arbitrary connections between lights and buttons. So there was no need to obtain two drawings, before and after, and only one, after, was requested. This showed learning. Note that the two operational definitions of learning are quite different. The first uses time as a measure, while the second uses ability to draw a diagram. Since these definitions differ, it should not be odd that the results of two different measures of learning also differ. Our confusion arises from the common language habit of calling both of these measures indices of learning. Since they have separate operational definitions, it would be better to call them by different names, for example Learning (time) and Learning (drawing). Thus, measurement of any process that cannot be directly observed, but must instead be inferred, should be tied to operational definitions.

The way in which terms are operationally defined is illustrated in Table 4–3. In this example the concept, learning, is defined by the operation used to produce it (practice on the button-pressing task) and the operations used to measure it (drawing a diagram vs. time to perform the task). Since "learning" was examined in an experimental situation, we can specify both the causes of learning (changes in the independent variable) and the results of those causes (changes in the dependent variables). If we simply measured or assessed learning by means of observation or test (or survey), then we could only define our concept in terms of dependent variables. The additional operational specification that results from experimental manipulation indicates another advantage of experimentation over other forms of research. When independent variables are varied, both "sides" of a concept can be tied to the operations that are performed. When there are no independent variables, it may not be possible to point to the operations that produced the concept under investigation.

The difficulty with having a few dozen varieties of learning, each with its own operational definition, is that so many definitions can make it difficult to get any kind of theoretical integration. There is considerable economy or parsimony in only having to discuss just one kind of

---

Table 4-3	Operational Definitions of Learning in the Morin and Grant Experiment

Operation Producing Learning	*Concept Defined*	*Measurements*
Button-pressing practice ⟶	Learning ⟶	Time to perform
Button-pressing practice ⟶	Learning ⟶	Drawing accuracy

Note. Practice, the antecedent condition, produces learning, which is reflected in the behaviors that were measured (the dependent variables). Since antecedent conditions are rarely manipulated directly in nonexperimental research (e.g., tests, surveys, and naturalistic observation), we usually have to guess at or infer the conditions that produced what we are studying.

learning. Psychology, like any science, strives for general concepts that unify data. From this viewpoint, undue preoccupation with operational definitions might seem to be pushing us in the wrong direction. The solution is to seek operational definitions that come together upon common theoretical constructs. This notion of converging operations is so important that it is covered as a topic in its own right (see Chapter 10). Since giving up operational definition entirely, as some philosophers of science have suggested, is too risky—it would lead to difficulties as in the earlier example of the light flashes and horseshoe crabs— we must aim for a theoretical framework that pulls our operational definitions together.

When we link our operational terms, we make them *valid.* That is, our concepts become useful, reasonable explanations, not just clear, reliable ones. In a very real sense, then, the goal of scientific psychology is to provide valid explanations (concepts) for why we think and act as we do.

Validity of the Research Procedure

Does our research have anything to do with why people think and act as they do? Have we selected an object of study that is representative of people? Is our research setting one that will yield a valid answer to our fundamental question?

Students of psychology typically demand a higher level of relevance in their psychology courses than they expect from other sciences. Students who are not at all dismayed that their course in introductory physics did not enable them to repair their automobile are often disturbed that their course in introductory psychology did not give them a better insight into their own motivations, did not cure their neuroses, and failed to show them how to gain eternal happiness. If you did not find such information in introductory psychology, we doubt that you will find it in this text either.

The data that psychologists gather may at first seem unimportant, since you may not find an immediate relationship between basic psychological research and pressing social or personal problems. It is natural for you to then doubt the importance of this research and to wonder why the federal government, through agencies like the National Institute of Mental Health, is funding researchers to watch rats press bars or run through mazes.

The difficulty, however, is not with the research but with your expectations as to how "useful" research should be conducted. As has been noted by Sidman (1960), you expect progress to occur when researchers establish laboratory situations that are analogous to real life situations: "In order to study psychosis in animals we must learn how to make animals psychotic." This is off the mark. The psychologist tries to understand the underlying *processes* rather than the physical situations that produce these processes. The physical situations in the real world and the laboratory need not be at all similar provided that the same processes are occurring. Let's say we would like to know why airplane accidents occur. A basic researcher might approach this problem by having college sophomores sit in front of several lights that turn on in rapid succession. The sophomore has to press a key as each light is illuminated. This probably seems somewhat removed from midair collisions of aircraft. Yet although the physical situations are quite different, the processes are similar. Pressing a key can be an index of attention, because psychologists can overload the human operator by presenting lights faster than he or she can respond. Thus, this simple physical situation in a laboratory allows the psychologist to study failure of attention in a carefully controlled environment. In addition to the obvious safety benefits of studying attention without having to crash airplanes, there are many scientific advantages to the laboratory environment. Since failures of attention are responsible for many kinds of industrial accidents (DeGreene, 1970), studying attention with lights and buttons can lead to improvements outside the laboratory.

By the same token, establishing similar physical situations does not guarantee similarity of processes. We can easily train a rat to pick up coins in its mouth and bury them in its cage. But this does not necessarily mean that the "miserly" rat and the miserly human who keeps coins under a mattress both do so because the same psychological processes are controlling their behaviors.

Despite these assertions about the validity of basic research, you must confront some pitfalls concerning validity before you begin your own project. These problems were loosely summarized above, but more specific names for them are subject representativeness, variable representativeness, and setting representativeness.

Subject Representativeness

Basic research in psychology relies heavily on two subject populations: white rats and college students. Are these organisms representative? Are data from these organisms pertinent to general statements about psychological processes?

One way to answer these questions is to say that rats and college students *have* to be representative. For ethical reasons some research cannot be done on humans, so animals are used. Rats and college students are readily available to most researchers, so they are examined. The justifications for using rats and college students (some might claim that they are being overused) are convenience and ethics. Thus, some psychological problems have to be analyzed with rats and college students as subjects.

This rationale does not mean that limiting your observations to these populations is problem free. Let us consider some difficulties with using animals in psychological research. A major problem is that of *reversability* (Uttal, 1978). In mathematics, reversability refers to an attempt to determine the problem or equation from a solution. As an example, consider the answer *7*. Can you figure out what led to *7?* Not without a great deal of additional information. The answer *7* could have come from *4 + 3 = ?, 377 − 370 = ?, $\sqrt{49}$ = ?, How many days are in a week?,* and an infinite number of other possibilities. If we damaged a rat brain in order to understand how the human brain works, we would have to assume that the brain of a rat works the same way (i.e., it has the same equation) as the human nervous system. Physiological psychologists make the assumption that the solution (the rat's behavior) is unique to a particular equation (the nervous system). In other words, it is assumed that by reversing the solution one arrives at the problem.

"So what?" some of you might say. "I'm not going to be a physiological psychologist." However, Uttal's point is also relevant to behavioral research that ignores physiological interpretations. Looking for "learning" in rats or other subhumans presupposes a mechanism for the process in the same way that damaging a rat brain assumes a unique mechanism. Harry F. Harlow, an eminent psychologist who has done famous work on learning and love in monkeys, has summarized the dilemma this way: "Basically the problems of generalization of behavior between species are simple—one cannot generalize, but one must. If the competent do not wish to generalize, the incompetent will fill the field." (Harlow, Gluck, and Suomi, 1972, p. 716.)

If we view the results of subhuman research as a model or functional analogical theory (see Chapter 1), then we recognize that our cross-species generalizations are always tentative. Many tests on many species may have to be done before strong conclusions can be made.

The difficulties we have just examined also pertain to research using college students. How representative are the results obtained from college students? The answer to this question is vague—it depends. The answer depends on the purposes of the research and the boldness of the investigator. If we are concerned with processes that are likely to be shared by all humans, such as basic sensory processes or simple forms of learning and retention, then we can be fairly sure that our data will represent humans other than college students.

A difficulty arises, however, when we are interested in complex psychological processes. Language, problem solving, and sophisticated memorizing strategies require that the subject possess characteristics that may not be common to everyone. We cannot limit our psychology to normal human adults. Young children, Ibo tribesmen in Africa, and deaf mutes are likely to possess abilities that are different from the typical college student. Imagery may enhance memory in college students (Atkinson, 1975; Bower, 1972), but there are some limits to its success for young children (Tversky and Teiffer, 1976), and there are cross-cultural differences in the use of imagery as well (Cole, Gay, Glick, and Sharp, 1971).

The moral here is that you should be careful in generalizing on the basis of a single sample of subjects from a subset of the population at large. If you are too bold ("Imagery always aids retention, no matter who uses it"), you run the risk of being wrong. Again, if we view the college student as a model for psychological processes in the same way that we view the white rat as a model, then we will recognize that some of our conclusions must be tentative. This is particularly the case when basic research findings are going to be used for applied purposes. The generalization should be tried out on the target population before a particular policy or practice is implemented. Based just on Bower's (1972) work with college students, time and effort would be wasted if imagery training were instituted in a nursery school for the blind.

Variable Representativeness

Because science is analytic, the scientist usually designs a project that is manageable and direct in its purpose. What this means in practice is that the research project nearly always departs from real life. This is true even in naturalistic observation, where the observer selects only a subset of the behaviors to record. Scientists also simplify their projects because they do not possess unlimited memory and attention spans. How do we select variables that are reasonable and worthwhile?

The answer to this question is seemingly simple, and part of the answer is obvious. In the first place, we can select variables simply because we are interested in them. Curiosity is not the only basis of science; it is also true that scientific nosiness is a perfectly respectable attribute. If you are interested in the mating rituals of blue-footed boobies, you go out and observe blue-footed boobies. The role of curiosity in part begs the question, however, because curiosity alone does not provide any clues as to what aspects of the boobies' mating behavior should be observed.

This is where the less clear answer to our problem enters. As we discuss in detail in Chapter 11, a good researcher must be familiar with the data base of a research problem. You should know what has been done in the past so you do not waste time studying something that has been established as relevant or completely irrelevant. For example, an analysis of the boobies' feeding activity may be completely unrelated to their mating behavior. Here, too, theoretical predictions may be of crucial importance. Remember, one of the important criteria of a good theory is testability. A theory should tell you what to look for in a particular problem area. From your standpoint, a theory is good as long as it is reasonably explicit in making predictions. Unfortunately, very few psychological theories make straightforward predictions. This ambiguity means that a lot of hypothesis testing depends upon the wit and wisdom of the researcher, a state of affairs that makes it difficult to list a set of rules for hypothesis testing.

Assuming you have selected variables to observe or manipulate, eventually you will have to consider their representativeness. This can be determined in the same way that subject representativeness was dealt with. After you examine the data base and relevant theories, then repeat your research with minor variations in the variables to begin establishing their representativeness.

Setting Representativeness

Perhaps the major issue associated with representativeness has to do with the setting—often called *ecological validity.* This is a serious problem in experimentation, where, by definition, the experimental setting is an artificial one. The most straightforward way to find out if your laboratory experiment is representative is to conduct the same experiment in the field, that is, in a natural setting. *Field experiments* lack the control available in laboratory work and may involve using unobtrusive measures. Thus, using a natural setting may not be the best way to determine the ecological validity of a laboratory experiment.

Recently Bem and Lord (1979) introduced a promising way of determining the ecological validity of laboratory research. Their procedure is called *template matching,* and it focuses on whether or not people respond in the laboratory as they do in real life. Instead of trying to determine if the laboratory setting is analogous to a natural one, Bem and Lord try to see if similar behaviors occur naturally and in the laboratory. First, the behavior in a laboratory task is defined by a *template.* A template in this case is a description of how the person is supposed to behave in that situation. Second, they assess the natural behavior of a person by means of tests and ratings by friends. Finally, ecological validity is determined by *matching* the natural behavior (determined by friends and tests) with the idealized template (how they should respond in the laboratory). Ecological validity is assumed if natural behavior and laboratory behavior match. If they do not match, the assumption is that the experiment is not representative. Let us consider an example. A template for a bargaining task indicates that the ideal cooperative subject will bargain so as to be helpful to other bargainers. Suppose a real subject has been described as being cooperative in everyday affairs. If our real subject fails to be cooperative in the laboratory task, then we can question the ecological validity of the task.

Although template matching may be useful, there are some drawbacks. In the first place, it may be difficult to develop realistic templates.

Knowing how to describe ideal behavior on a task assumes that a great deal is already known about that laboratory setting. In the second place, getting personality assessments of the real subjects may be time consuming. Finally, we have to be sure that the personality assessments are valid. If the tests or the subject's friends are in error, then the template matching will be in error. Our experiment might be valid and our personality assessments invalid (we really had an uncooperative subject in the above example). Nevertheless, the template matching technique is a useful alternative to field research for problems that require ecological validity of the laboratory task.

Ethical Considerations in Research

You have an obligation to conduct your research in accordance with contemporary ethical standards (American Psychological Association, 1973). Some of these ethical standards are obvious (e.g., you will not excise the brains of college sophomores), but there are some that are not so obvious, and these can pose serious problems. In this section we will examine a number of ethical considerations that must be made by all people engaged in research.

Ethics in Animal Research

Subhumans are studied because they are interesting. They are also used in psychological research when we cannot study humans, as is the case in many physiological experiments. Animals are used because they develop faster than humans, and there is a great deal of control over the heredity and environment of animals. Using animals does not mean that they can be treated cruelly. You are obligated to treat your goldfish, worms, guinea pigs, rats, etc. according to certain humane criteria. These guidelines are reprinted in Tables 4–4 and 4–5.

Table 4–4 contains the rules specified by the National Institutes of Health for people who have a government grant or research contract. The information in Table 4–5 was devised by the American Psychological Association for you, the student researcher. Both guidelines emphasize decent care and treatment. Both also mention additional regulations. Before using animal subjects, you should understand the contents of these two tables, and you should also become familiar with relevant state and local humane regulations.

Listed in Table 4–6 are guidelines for the use of drugs in research involving both humans and subhumans. The primary purpose for reprinting these guidelines is to discourage most undergraduate research on drugs, especially projects using humans. Special government permits are required for research with controlled substances (including marijuana), and most student projects neglect to include appropriate "after

---

Guidelines for Use of Experimental Animals
National Institutes of Health

Table 4-4

The personnel

1. Experiments involving live warm-blooded animals and the procurement of living animal tissues for research must be performed by, or under the immediate supervision of, a qualified biological or medical scientist.

2. The housing, care, and feeding of all experimental animals must be supervised by a properly qualified veterinarian or other biological scientist competent in such matters.

The research

3. The research should be such as to yield fruitful results for the good of society, not feasible by other methods or means of study, and not random and unnecessary in nature.

4. The experiment should be so designed and based on knowledge of the disease or problem under study that the anticipated results will justify its performance.

5. The experiment should be so conducted as to avoid all unnecessary suffering and injury to the subject animals.

6. The scientist in charge of the experiment must be prepared to terminate it whenever he believes that its continuation may result in unnecessary injury to the subject animals.

7. If the experiment is likely to cause greater discomfort than the attending anesthetization, the subject animals must first be rendered incapable of perceiving the pain and be maintained in that condition until the experiment is ended. The only exception to this guideline should be in those cases where anesthetization would defeat the purpose of the experiment, and then the procedures must be carefully supervised by the principal investigator.

8. If it is necessary to sacrifice an experimental animal, the subject animal must be killed in a humane manner in such a way as to insure immediate death in accordance with procedures approved by an institutional committee. *No animal shall be discarded until death is certain.*

9. Post-experiment care of subject animals must be such as to minimize discomfort, in accordance with acceptable practices in veterinary medicine.

The facilities

10. Standards for the construction and use of housing, service, and surgical facilities should meet those described in the publication, "Guide for Laboratory Animal Facilities and Care," Public Health Service Publication No. 1024, or as otherwise required by the U.S. Department of Agriculture regulations established under the terms of the Laboratory Animal Welfare Act (PL 89-544) as amended December 24, 1970.

Source: National Institutes of Health (4206), No. 7, June 14, 1971.

---

care" for their human participants. You are responsible for accidents, antisocial behavior, and worse yet, addiction that could result from an experimentally induced high. If you are compelled to engage in drug research, use animals as your subjects and legal substances. If you do, be sure you understand the rules in Table 4–6 as well as the other legal documents that are mentioned therein.

Table 4-5	APA Guidelines for the Use of Animals in School Science Behavior Projects

1. In the selection of science behavior projects students should be strongly urged to select small animals that are easy to maintain or invertebrates as subjects for evaluation.

2. All experiments *must* be preplanned and conducted in such a manner that respect for basic animal life and all humane considerations are fully understood and carried out by the student.

3. Each student undertaking a science project using animals *must have a qualified supervisor*. Such a supervisor shall be a person who has had training and experience in the proper care of small and laboratory-type animals. The supervisor *must* assume the primary responsibility for all conditions of the experiment. The following requirements must be fulfilled:
   a. The student shall research and study the appropriate literature concerning previous work done in the student's chosen area.
   b. A written preliminary outline of the student's plan of action and anticipated outcome for the science project shall be submitted and be available for evaluation. Such an outline should include the specific purpose of the research and a justification of the methodology.

4. Legislation and guidelines for specific care and handling of all animals do exist. Students, teachers, and supervisors *must* be cognizant of such legislation and guidelines. Copies of appropriate humane laws are available by contacting the local humane organization and the American Humane Association, P.O. Box 1266, Denver, Colorado 80201. Each state also has specific animal health regulations which must be considered. Copies of animal health regulations are obtainable from the state veterinarian or state public health office.

5. No student shall undertake an experiment which includes the use of drugs, surgical procedures, noxious or painful stimuli such as electric shock, extreme temperature, starvation, malnutrition, ionizing radiation, etc., except under extremely close and rigorous supervision of a researcher qualified in the specific area of study.

6. Students using animals *must* insure for the proper housing, food, water, exercise, cleanliness, and gentle handling of such animals at all times. Special arrangements *must* be made for care during weekend, holiday, and vacation periods. The comfort of each animal, by meeting its basic daily needs, shall be of prime concern. Caution must be taken to avoid the animals being teased or harmed by other students.

7. When the research project has been completed and the student does not wish to maintain the animal(s) as a pet, arrangements shall be made for proper disposition by the supervisor. *Under no circumstances should the student be allowed to provide "experimental" euthanasia.*

8. Specifications for the detailed treatment of animals are available from the American Psychological Association, Office of Scientific Affairs, 1200 Seventeenth Street, N.W., Washington, D.C. 20036.

9. A copy of these Guidelines shall be posted conspicuously wherever animals are kept and projects carried out.

Note. The guidelines were devised for sub-college projects, but seem relevant to the undergraduate laboratory as well.

Source: American Psychological Association, Committee on Precautions and Standards in Animal Experimentation.

General Principle: A psychologist or psychology student who performs research involving the use of drugs shall have adequate knowledge and experience of each drug's action or shall work in collaboration with or under the supervision of a qualified researcher. Any psychologist or psychology student doing research with drugs must comply with the procedural guidelines below. Any supervisor or collaborator has the responsibility to see that the individual he supervises or collaborates with complies with the procedural guidelines.

Definition of a Qualified Researcher

1. A qualified researcher possesses a PhD degree based in part upon a dissertation that is experimental in nature and in part upon training in psychology, pharmacology, physiology, and related areas, and that is conferred by a graduate school of recognized standing (listed by the United States Office of Education as having been accredited by a recognized regional or national accrediting organization).

2. A qualified researcher has demonstrated competence as defined by research involving the use of drugs which has been published in scientific journals; or continuing education; or equivalent experience ensuring that the researcher has adequate knowledge of the drugs, their actions, and of experimental design.

Definition of a Drug

In these Guidelines, the term drug includes (a) all substances as defined by the term drug in the "Federal Food, Drug, and Cosmetic Act" (21 USC 321) and (b) all substances, Schedules I-V, as listed in the "Comprehensive Drug Abuse Prevention and Control Act of 1970" (21 USC 812; PL 91-513, Sec. 202) in its present form or as amended (Federal Food, Drug and Cosmetic Act, 21 USC, Sec. 201 (g), Appendix A). Copies of these acts are available from the Superintendent of Documents, United States Government Printing Office, Washington, D.C. 20402.

Procedural Guidelines

1. All drugs must be legally obtained and used under conditions specified by state and federal laws. Information concerning these laws should be obtained from federal or state authorities.

2. Proper precautions must be taken so that drugs and drug paraphernalia that are potentially harmful are available only to authorized personnel. All such drugs used in experiments should be kept in locked cabinets and under any additional security prescribed by law.

3. All individuals using or supervising the use of drugs in research must be familiar with PL 91-513, the "Comprehensive Drug Abuse Prevention and Control Act of 1970," and its implementing regulations as well as all amendments to the act and other drug laws relevant to their research.

4. The use of drugs must be justified scientifically.

5. All individuals using or supervising the use of drugs in research must familiarize themselves with available information concerning the mode of action, toxicity, and methods of administration of the drugs they are using.

6. In any experiment involving animals, the welfare of the animal should be considered as specified in APA's "Precautions and Standards for the Care and Use of Animals."

7. Research involving human subjects is governed by additional guidelines as set forth in APA's "Ethical Standards for Psychological Research."

8. The present Guidelines should be brought to the attention of all individuals conducting research with drugs.

9. The present Guidelines should be posted conspicuously in every laboratory in which psychologists use drugs.

Source: American Psychological Association Ad Hoc Committee on Guidelines for the Use of Drugs and Other Chemical Agents in Research.

Ethics in Human Research

Psychologists are extremely concerned with the ethics of research with human participants. While some of this concern is pragmatic, due to fear of restriction of research funds and loss of access to subject populations, most psychologists are ethical persons who have no desire to inflict harm on anyone. The mad researcher, who will do anything to obtain data, is largely a fiction.

Since it is difficult for an experimenter to be completely impartial and objective in judging the ethical issue concerning his or her own research, most universities and research institutions have peer committees that judge the ethicality of proposed research. Indeed, all federally funded research must be approved by such a committee before any funding is granted. These committees are guided by several principles advocated by the American Psychological Association (1973).

The general purpose of these principles, which are summarized in Table 4–7, is to uphold the dignity of research participants and prevent them from being physically and psychologically abused. Interpretation of these principles is not easy, and many research areas seem particularly susceptible to difficult ethical issues.

Consider the experiment by Middlemist, Knowles, and Matter (1976) that was discussed earlier. Subjects were forced via a sign and a mop bucket to select a urinal immediately adjacent to a toilet stall in a public lavatory. One of the experimenters was seated in that stall, and a periscope was fixed so that the onset and duration of urination could be measured secretly. The subject could not be identified by the person peering through the periscope. This surreptitious observation violates several of the principles in Table 4–7 (3, 4, 5, 6, and 8), involving informed consent and an honest and open agreement between the investigator and participant. So, it is not surprising that this research has received public condemnation (Koocher, 1977). In a reply to Koocher's critique, Middlemist et al. (1977) argued that Principles 7, 9, and 10, involving confidentiality and minimal harm to the participant were upheld by violating principles 3, 4, 5, 6, and 8. Middlemist et al. noted that none of their subjects suspected that they were being observed, and they stated "If someone were going to be upset by the experiment, debriefing would precipitate rather than ameliorate this upset, since the observations had already been made" (p. 123). Clearly, there is disagreement over the ethicality of this research.

Ethical decisions are usually not decided upon empirically. Rather, the decisions are based upon a pragmatic criterion. This criterion focuses on the potential value of the research. The potential worth of the research is balanced against the potential harm to the participants. Is the knowledge obtained by Middlemist et al. worth the sorts of indignities denounced by Koocher? Imagine you are on an ethics committee and

1. In planning a study the investigator has the personal responsibility to make a careful evaluation of its ethical acceptability, taking into account these principles for research with human beings. To the extent that this appraisal, weighing scientific and humane values, suggests a deviation from any principle, the investigator incurs an increasingly serious obligation to seek ethical advice and to observe more stringent safeguards to protect the rights of the human research participant.

2. Responsibility for the establishment and maintenance of acceptable ethical practice in research always remains with the individual investigator. The investigator is also responsible for the ethical treatment of research participants by collaborators, assistants, students, and employees, all of whom, however, incur parallel obligations.

3. Ethical practice requires the investigator to inform the participant of all features of the research that reasonably might be expected to influence willingness to participate and to explain all other aspects of the research about which the participant inquires. Failure to make full disclosure gives added emphasis to the investigator's responsibility to protect the welfare and dignity of the research participant.

4. Openness and honesty are essential characteristics of the relationship between investigator and research participant. When the methodological requirements of a study necessitate concealment or deception, the investigator is required to ensure the participant's understanding of the reasons for this action and to restore the quality of the relationship with the investigator.

5. Ethical research practice requires the investigator to respect the individual's freedom to decline to participate in research or to discontinue participation at any time. The obligation to protect this freedom requires special vigilance when the investigator is in a position of power over the participant. The decision to limit this freedom increases the investigator's responsibility to protect the participant's dignity and welfare.

6. Ethically acceptable research begins with the establishment of a clear and fair agreement between the investigator and the research participant that clarifies the responsibilities of each. The investigator has the obligation to honor all promises and commitments included in that agreement.

7. The ethical investigator protects participants from physical and mental discomfort, harm, and danger. If the risk of such consequences exists, the investigator is required to inform the participant of that fact, secure consent before proceeding, and take all possible measures to minimize distress. A research procedure may not be used if it is likely to cause serious and lasting harm to participants.

8. After the data are collected, ethical practice requires the investigator to provide the participant with a full clarification of the nature of the study and to remove any misconceptions that may have arisen. Where scientific or humane values justify delaying or withholding information, the investigator acquires a special responsibility to assure that there are no damaging consequences for the participant.

9. Where research procedures may result in undesirable consequences for the participant, the investigator has the responsibility to detect and remove or correct these consequences, including, where relevant, long-term aftereffects.

10. Information obtained about the research participants during the course of an investigation is confidential. When the possibility exists that others may obtain access to such information, ethical research practice requires that this possibility, together with the plans for protecting confidentiality, be explained to the participants as a part of the procedure for obtaining informed consent.

Source: American Psychological Association.

97

decide whether or not you would allow the following examples of proposed research:

1. An environmental psychologist sits in a crowded library and keeps detailed records of seating patterns.

2. An environmental psychologist takes videotapes of seating patterns in a library. These tapes are maintained indefinitely and library patrons do not know they have been filmed.

3. An experimental psychologist tells students that he is interested in their reading comprehension when in reality he is recording the speed of their responses rather than their comprehension.

4. A social psychologist is studying bystander intervention in a liquor store. Permission has been obtained from the store manager. In clear view of a patron, an experimenter "steals" a bottle of liquor. A second experimenter approaches the patron and asks, "Did you see him steal that bottle?"

5. A social psychologist connects surface electrodes to male participants, with their prior approval. These participants are told that the electrodes are connected to a meter in front of them that measures sexual arousal. In reality, the meter is controlled by the experimenter. Participants are then shown slides of nude males and females. The meter gives high readings for pictures of males, leading the participants to believe they have latent homosexual tendencies.

Since it is difficult to gain agreement on ethical issues, we cannot make definitive judgments about the above examples. However, informal discussions with our colleagues reveal that only the first example was unequivocally considered ethical. Since the psychologist is merely observing and does not know the people, informed consent was not deemed necessary. Any individual, psychologist or not, could easily observe these same people in the library. The potential harm to participants is small.

You may be surprised that objections were raised to every other example. Number 2 was thought to invade personal privacy since the tapes were not erased after the data had been abstracted. Number 3 would be acceptable only if the experimenter carefully debriefed participants by explaining the nature and reasons for this minor deception. Subjects may get upset over what they think is poor performance even in a harmless laboratory test of reading speed. Potential psychological harm may result from any task, harmless or not. We have had subjects cry, cheat, and swear in standard laboratory tests of learning and memory. Number 4 was actually performed; a patron denied seeing the theft and then called the police as soon as she left the store. The investigator had to go down to the police station to bail out the experimenters.

Number 5 was also performed, and it too was considered unethical, even with debriefing. It is not clear if the potential psychological harm of leading the participant to think he had hidden homosexual tendencies could be removed by even immediate extensive debriefing. This would especially be the case if the person did indeed have latent homosexual tendencies.

These examples should show that there is no clear answer as to what is ethical. The responsibility rests upon the researcher, review committees, and also upon journal editors who review research for publication. While deception and concealment may be justified in limited instances, great caution is demanded in such research. One of the first things you should do when you design a project is to consider the ethics of your procedure. You should get advice from your friends and from your instructor. Deceit and danger are not prerequisites to good research; they should be avoided as much as possible.

Summary

Before you actually conduct a research project, you will want to make sure that the design minimizes contamination from several sources. One problem has to do with demand characteristics, which you can control by making your subjects blind to relevant aspects of the procedure. Frequently, it will be necessary to blind yourself so that your reactions do not inadvertently influence responding. In any project the procedure should be followed as exactly as possible for all subjects. Another problem is sloppy communication. Our concepts should be operationally defined so that other investigators will understand us. Operational definitions will also ensure that we adhere to the procedure. It is often difficult to make sure that our research is representative. Using just white rats or college students as participants may limit the generality of our results. Also, we have to try to select representative variables to investigate. Our setting, especially if it is an experiment, may not be ecologically valid. We can resort to field experiments, or we can select experimental tasks that elicit behaviors similar to those found in natural situations. Finally, our procedures must be ethically acceptable. Degrading and dangerous research should be avoided regardless of whether you use human or subhuman participants.

Study and Review

Exercises

1. *Design problem.* Two men, about to be promoted to the position of assembly-line foreman, were sent by their company to the American School for Supervisors (ASS) in order to learn how to be good supervisors. Because the classes at ASS were oversubscribed, one of the men received a course in Behavioral Administration Development (BAD), and the other took a course

in Workers Organizational Reeducation Studies and Training (WORST). Upon returning to their home office the men were put in charge of two different shifts of the same assembly line, and after two months the productivity of each shift was determined, and the job satisfaction of the male and females workers was assessed. Productivity under the BAD foreman was about the same as that under the WORST foreman. Furthermore, job satisfaction was only slightly better on the WORST shift than on the BAD shift. The company president decided that the similarity of the performance of BAD and WORST indicated that the ASS programs were a waste of time, and that in the future no new foreman would be sent there. Why might the conclusion of the president be wrong? What pitfalls can you detect in this training program?

2. Which of the following terms or phrases does not belong with the others? *Hunger, anxiety, learning, response, motivation.* Why?

3. You want to do a laboratory experiment on the effects of various mnemonic devices on the learning and retention of textbook material. How would you determine the ecological validity of your task?

4. In a laboratory experiment concerned with the effects of motivation on learning, some college sophomores were told that their performance on the task was indicative of their IQ, while other similar subjects received no such instructions. What are some ethical pitfalls in this study? How can they be avoided?

Key Concepts

demand characteristics 71
unobtrusive measures 72
participant observation 72
retrospective 72
motivated forgetting 73
response styles 73
response deviation 73
response acquiescence 73
social desirability 73
forced choice tests 73
random sample 74
volunteer subjects 74
Hawthorne effect 76
field experiments 78
deception 78
blind 79

simulated experiment 79
thought experiment 79
researcher bias 80
double blind 82
placebo 82
anthropomorphism 83
operational definition 84
subject representativeness 88
problem of reversability 89
variable representativeness 90
setting representativeness 91
ecological validity 91
template matching 91
ethics in animal research 92
drug research 95
ethics in human research 96

Suggested Readings

You should read the entire monograph, *Ethical principles in the conduct of research with human participants,* American Psychological Association, 1973. Each of the principles is discussed in detail, and several cases illustrating each principle are included.

Robert Rosenthal has written extensively on subject and experimenter reactivity in research. While some of his work concerning inadvertent experimenter effects may be overstated (see Barber, 1976), you will find any of his works valuable.

You will find T. X. Barber's little book, *Pitfalls in human research: ten pivotal points.* New York: Pergamon, 1976, to be an excellent resource for information about investigator and experimenter bias. Barber also details many solutions to these pitfalls.

Parsons has suggested that most of the Hawthorne effect can be attributed to operant conditioning (i.e., the rewards and feedback provided the assembly-line workers). You might find the article interesting: Parsons, H. M. What happened at Hawthorne? *Science,* 1974, *183:* 922–931.

EXPERIMENT: **A Particular Comparison is Produced
While Other Variables are Held Constant**

Independent variables: At least two levels of a variable are manipulated to provide a standard of comparison. Interactions may occur when there are two or more independent variables.

Dependent variables: A specific behavior is measured in an experiment.

Control variables: In the ideal experiment, all other variables are held constant.

Experimental design—minimizing confounding

Between-subjects design: In the simplest case, the experimental group receives the independent variable and the control group does not. To minimize the confounding of subject characteristics with group membership, randomly assign participants to conditions or match their characteristics between groups.

Within-subjects design: Each participant receives all levels of the independent variable. To minimize confounding due to carry-over effects, the order of testing each level of the independent variable must be counterbalanced or randomized.

Small-*n* design: A small number of subjects receives repeated observation under a *within-subjects* design. Counterbalancing of the order of testing by means of ABA or ABAB designs insures that causal explanations are appropriate.

Basic Experimentation

5

A tightly designed, well-conducted experiment is the goal of psychologists who attempt to answer the question why we think and act as we do. In this chapter we will consider some of the characteristics of a good experiment. The essential ingredient of an experiment is control over the variables that are manipulated so that causal conclusions can be made. Therefore the procedures in basic experimentation must ensure that the dependent variable is influenced by the independent variable and not by some other variable(s).

Overview

Experiments are tests designed to arrive at a causal explanation (e.g., Cook and Campbell, 1979). How do we know when a test permits a causal inference? The conditions necessary for arriving at explanations were set forth in the nineteenth century by the philosopher John Stuart Mill (1843). The conditions he outlined provide a good definition of an experiment.

Mill argued that three interrelated methods permit one to distinguish causality from observation. The first of these methods is called the *Method of Agreement,* which in application cannot by itself determine causality. The Method of Agreement asserts that if event A is always followed by a particular result (let's call the result X), then it is *likely* that A causes X. A causal interpretation based on agreement (A leads to X) may not be valid unless the observer has direct control over the occurrence of A. For example, Mill noted that simple agreement between the occurrences of A and X could lead to conclusions such as day causes night or vice versa and he knew as well as we do today that this is a simplistic assumption. So without control over the appearance of A, the Method of Agreement results in a correlation which by itself cannot lead to inferences about causation.

Valid causal statements require a second method, the *Method of Differences.* According to the Method of Differences, if X always follows A, but X does not occur when A does not occur, then A surely causes X. The important point here is that the Method of Differences suggests a basis for comparison (i.e., a true test): control the occurrence or nonoccurrence of A and then assess the two levels (or values) of A. In other

What Is an Experiment?

103

words, we have an independent variable that can be changed in such a way that we can compare the effects of one level to the effects of another level (we can compare the effects of A on X to the effects of some other variable on X). This is essentially how we defined an experiment in Chapter 2.

Mill's third method, the *Method of Concomitant Variations,* summarizes what we have just said about the joint effects of the other two methods. Concomitant variation means that there are a series of tests that allow one to make comparisons of differences. For example, there might be several different values of A, and their effects on X are compared two at a time.

Boring (1954) has noted that the concept of *control* in experimentation derives from Mill's methods. One way we can view control is in terms of direct manipulation (A occurs or does not occur), which, according to the Method of Differences, leads to a basis for comparison (hence, the term *control group,* as explained later). Control also suggests that we can eliminate alternative explanations of our results. Usually control in experimentation is thought of in three ways: (1) there is a control condition for purposes of *comparison;* (2) the levels or values of the independent variable can be *produced;* and (3) the experimental setting can be controlled by holding certain aspects *constant* (e.g., type of apparatus or method of measurement). These three types of control —comparison, production, and constancy—are crucial to the conduct of an experiment that will yield an explanation of why people think and act as they do.

In an Experiment a Particular *Comparison* is *Produced* While Other Aspects of the Situation are Held *Constant.*

Advantages of Experimentation

One characteristic of modern life is that many of us are subjected to changes in atmospheric pressure during air travel. Furthermore, a substantial portion of the world's population lives at elevations of between 2000 and 10,000 feet. What this means is that many people are subjected to mild decompressions in barometric pressure. Are these decompressions hazardous like so many other things in the world today (e.g., pollution, pesticides, or food additives, etc.)? This question was the impetus for experiments conducted by Graessle, Ahbel, and Porges (1978). Early research indicated that greatly reduced barometric pressure (like that of altitudes greater than 10,000 feet) can retard both fetal and newborn development. Graessle et al. wanted to see if lesser decompressions, more like those experienced during air travel, also affected the development of infants.

To study this problem Graessle et al. experimented with pregnant rats. The general procedure was to subject the rats to a series of mild decompressions similar to those experienced during air travel (around 6000 feet), and then compare the growth and behavior of rats born to the mothers that experienced decompression to the growth and behavior of rats born to mothers kept at ground level (728 feet in this instance).

Now for some particulars of their research. Pregnant rats were randomly divided into two groups: one group received seven daily decompressions for 20 days during pregnancy, and the second group of mothers was kept at ground level. Changes in pressure for the one group (up to a pressure equaling an altitude of 6000 feet) lasted about 20 minutes. The changes in pressure were gradual, simulating the sorts of changes that occur during air travel. Following birth, all infant rats were weighed daily and received periodic testing of their ability to grasp a thin wire, turn over (the righting reflex), move on an inclined plane, and climb (pull themselves up a thin wall when suspended by their forepaws).

To summarize, the *independent variable* (what was varied) was atmospheric pressure, and the *dependent variables* (the things observed and measured) included the weight of the babies and the various behaviors mentioned above. At this point we need to mention a third class of variables, the *control variables,* (the variables that the experimenter holds constant). In this experiment, control variables included: similar housing and feeding conditions for all animals at all times, identical testing procedures, and the fact that the treated and untreated mothers were of the same strain of rats.

Ordinarily we call the group of subjects that receives the independent variable the *experimental group;* the designation for the untreated subjects is the *control group.* (Note, a control group is not the same as a control variable. The meaning of a control group will become clear momentarily.) So, the decompressed mothers and their pups comprise the experimental group. The mothers and their pups who were kept at ground level as a comparison or baseline group are called the control group. Note that the experimental/control label makes some sense; that is, the control group receives a different (in this case no) treatment, and an examination of its behavior serves to indicate changes that would occur in the absence of the independent variable. Thus, the control group *controls* for changes that may occur whether or not any particular variable is introduced into the situation. The experimental group, of course, defines the experiment for us. The experimental group is the one that receives the treatment of interest—decompression—in the present instance. (Note, we are using Mill's Method of Differences to arrive at an explanation.) Graessle et al. found that rats who were given decompressions before birth began to climb at a later age than did the control animals and that the prenatally decompressed rats gained weight more slowly than did the controls.

The results of this experiment are intriguing and may have important practical implications. If you were interested in this topic, you might have considered the possibility of doing this experiment with pregnant humans. The ethics of that tactic would be questionable without knowing the effects of mild decompressions in advance. That is why we do many types of experiments, especially preliminary ones, on subhumans. An alternative approach to the problem might be to do the research ex post facto. We would find infants whose mothers had flown during pregnancy. Then we would compare their development to infants whose mothers had remained at ground level during pregnancy. Other than the tedious job of identifying the subjects in the first place, the major drawback to the ex post facto procedure is a loss of control. As we will detail in Chapter 7, it is very difficult to hold potentially relevant variables constant after the fact. In particular, we would be hard put to find two groups of subjects whose only difference was that some had flown prenatally and some had not.

We can conclude, therefore, that this animal study about the effects of mild decompression is more ethical, more economical, and better controlled than are alternative research procedures. This is not to say that this experiment is problem free. You might find it worthwhile to reconsider some of the pitfalls associated with experimentation within the context of the experiment just described. One obvious problem concerns generalizing from rat development to human development.

Variables in Experimentation

Variables are the gears and cogs that make experiments run. Effective selection and manipulation of variables makes the difference between a good experiment and a poor one. This section covers the three kinds of variables that must be carefully considered before starting an experiment: *independent, dependent,* and *control* variables. We conclude by discussing experiments that have more than one independent or dependent variable.

Independent Variables

Independent variables are those *manipulated* by the experimenter. The brightness of a lamp, the loudness of a tone, the number of decompressions given to a rat are all independent variables, since the experimenter determines their amount. Independent variables are selected because an experimenter thinks they will cause changes in behavior. Increasing the intensity of a tone should increase the speed with which people respond to the tone. Increasing the number of decompressions given to a mother may change the rate of development of her pups. When a change in the level (amount) of an independent variable causes a change in behavior, we say that the behavior is under control of the independent variable. Failure of an independent variable to control behavior, often called *null results,* can have more than one interpretation. First, the experimenter may have incorrectly guessed that the independent variable was important and the null results may be correct. Most scientists will accept this interpretation only reluctantly and so the following alternate explanations of null results are common. The experimenter may not have created a valid manipulation of the independent variable. Let's say you are conducting an experiment on second grade children and your independent variable is the number of small treats (chocolates, peanuts, etc.) they get after each correct response in some task. Some children get only one while others get two. You find no difference in behavior between the two groups. Perhaps if your independent variable had involved a greater range–that is, if it went from one piece of candy to ten pieces of candy—you would have obtained a difference. Your manipulation was not sufficient to reveal any effect of the independent variable. Or perhaps, unknown to you, the class had a birthday party just before the experiment started and your subjects' little tummies were filled with ice cream and birthday cake. In this case maybe even ten pieces of candy would not show any effect. This is why, in studies of animal learning with food as a reward, the animals are deprived of food before the experiment starts. Thus, experimenters are careful to produce a strong manipulation of the independent variable. Failure to do so is a common cause of null results. Other common causes of null results are related to dependent and control variables, to which we now turn.

Dependent Variables

The dependent variable is that *observed* and *recorded* by the experimenter. It *depends* upon the behavior of the subject. The time to press a switch, the speed of a worm crawling through a maze, the age when a rat climbs all are dependent variables, since they are observed and recorded by the experimenter.

One criterion for a good dependent variable is reliability. When an experiment is repeated exactly—same subject, same levels of independent variable, etc.—the dependent variable should yield about the same score as it did previously. Unreliability can occur due to some deficit in the way we measure the dependent variable. Assume we wish to measure the weight in grams of an object, say, a candle before and after being lit for fifteen minutes. We use a scale that works by having a spring move a pointer. The spring contracts when it is cold and expands when it is hot. So long as our weight measurements are taken at constant temperatures they will be reliable. But if temperature varies while objects are being weighed, the same object will yield different readings. Our dependent variable is then unreliable.

Null results can often be caused by deficits in the dependent variable even if it is reliable. The most common cause is a restricted or limited range of the dependent variable so that it gets "stuck" at the top or bottom of its scale. Imagine you are teaching a rather uncoordinated friend how to bowl for the first time. Since you know from introductory psychology that reward improves performance, you offer to buy your friend a beer every time he or she gets a strike. Your friend gets all gutter balls so you drink the beer yourself. Thus you can no longer offer a reward, which means that the unrewarded performance should decrease. But since it is impossible to do any worse than all gutter balls, you cannot observe any decrement. Your friend is already at the bottom of the scale. This is called a *floor effect*. The opposite problem, getting 100 percent correct, is called a *ceiling effect*. Ceiling and floor effects (see Chapter 10) prevent the influence of an independent variable from being accurately reflected in a dependent variable.

Control Variables

A control variable is a potential independent variable that is held constant during an experiment. It does not vary because it is *controlled* by the experimenter. For any one experiment, the list of desirable control variables is quite long, far longer than can ever be accomplished in practice. In even a relatively simple experiment, for example requiring people to memorize three-letter syllables, many variables should be controlled. Time of day (diurnal cycle) changes your efficiency, and ideally this should be controlled. Temperature could be important since you might fall asleep if the testing room were too warm. Time since your last meal might also affect memory performance. Intelligence is also related. The list could be extended. In practice an experimenter tries to control as many salient variables as possible, hoping that the effect of uncontrolled factors will be small relative to the effect of the independent variable. The smaller the size of the effect produced by the independent variable, the more important it is to carefully control other extraneous factors. Holding a variable constant is not the only way to remove extraneous variation. Design techniques that we shall discuss later in the chapter also control extraneous variables. However, holding a variable constant is the most direct experimental technique for controlling extraneous factors, and so we shall limit our definition of control variables to only this technique. Null results often occur in an experiment because there is insufficient control of these other factors—that is, they have been left to vary unsystematically. This is especially true in studies outside of laboratories where the ability to hold control variables constant is greatly decreased. Remember, we call these unintended effects *confoundings,* since their influence confounds (or confuses) the proper interpretation of the results.

Independent variable is *Manipulated*
Dependent variable is *Observed*
Control variable is held *Constant*

Name the Variables

Because understanding *independent, dependent,* and *control* variables is so important, we have included some examples here for you to check your own understanding. For each situation name the three kinds of variables. Answers are provided at the end of this section.

1. An automobile manufacturer wants to know how bright brake lights should be, in order to minimize the time required for the driver of a following car to realize that the car in front is stopping. An experiment is conducted to answer this. Name the variables.

2. A pigeon is trained to peck a key if a green light is illuminated, but not if a red light is on. Correct pecks get rewarded by access to grain. Name the variables.

3. A therapist tries to improve a patient's image of himself. Every time the patient says something positive about himself the therapist rewards this by nodding, smiling, and being extra attentive. Name the variables.

4. A social psychologist does an experiment to discover if men or women give lower ratings of discomfort when six people are crowded into a telephone booth. Name the variables.

Answers

1. Independent (manipulated) variable:	Intensity (brightness) of brake light
Dependent (observed) variable:	Time from onset of brake light until depression of brake pedal by following driver
Control (constant) variables:	Color of brake light, shape of brake pedal, force needed to depress brake pedal, external illumination, etc.

2. Independent variable: Color of light (red or green)

   Dependent variable: Number of key pecks

   Control variables: Hours of food deprivation, size of key, intensity of red and green lights, etc.

3. Independent variable: Fakeout—this is not an experiment because there is only one level of the independent variable. To make this an experiment we need another level, say rewarding positive statements about the patient's mother-in-law. Then the independent variable would be kind of statement rewarded.

   Dependent variable: Number (or frequency) of positive statements about self.

   Control variables: None. This is a poor experiment.

4. Independent variable: Sex of the participant. Note: this is not a true independent variable, because the experimenter did not manipulate it. This is an ex post facto experiment.

   Dependent variable: Rating of discomfort

   Control variables: Size of telephone booth, number of persons (6) crowded into the booth, etc.

More Than One Independent Variable

It is unusual to find an experiment reported in a psychological journal in which only one independent (manipulated) variable was used. The typical experiment manipulates from two to four independent variables simultaneously. There are several advantages to this procedure. First, it is often more efficient to conduct one experiment with, say, three independent variables than to conduct three separate experiments. Second, experimental control is often better since with a single experiment some control variables—e.g., time of day, temperature, and humidity—are more likely to be held constant than with three separate experiments. Third, and most important, results generalized across several independent variables—that is, shown to be valid in several situations—are more valuable than data that has yet to be generalized. Fourth, just as it is important to establish generality of results across different types of experimental subjects and settings, we also need to discover if some result is valid across levels of independent variables. For example, let's say we wish to find out which of two kinds of rewards facilitate learning geometry by high school students. The first reward is an outright cash payment for problems correctly solved and the second reward is early dismissal from class—that is, each correct solution entitles the student to leave class five minutes early. Assume that the results of this hypothetical experiment showed early dismissal to be better. Before we make early dismissal a universal rule in high school, we should first establish its generality by comparing the two kinds of reward in other classes such as history and biology. Here subject matter of the class would be a second independent variable. It would be better to put these two variables into a single experiment than to conduct two successive experiments. This would avoid problems of control like one class being tested the week of the big football game (when no reward would improve learning), while the other class was tested the week after the game was won (when students felt better about learning).

When the effects produced by one independent variable are not the same across the levels of a second independent variable we have an *interaction.* The search for interactions is a major reason for using more than one independent variable per experiment. This can be best demonstrated by example.

Kantowitz and Bartell (1977) were interested in the effects of personal space invasion upon a person's willingness to loan money to a stranger. The degree of spatial invasion (the first independent variable) was manipulated by selecting either small (two-person) or large (four-person) tables in a university cafeteria. As you will recall from Chapter 2, this manipulation of spatial invasion is ex post facto since the experimenters had no control over the kind of person who sat at a small table versus one who picked a large table. Thus the potential for confounding type of person and table size exists in this experiment, unless it is assumed that subjects randomly select tables based upon the first vacancy rather than upon table size. The experimenter waited until he could find a student seated alone at either a large or small table. After asking permission to be seated, the experimenter proceeded to eat lunch. The second independent variable concerned what the experimenter did after eating half a peanut butter and jelly sandwich. In a condition designed to increase helping behavior, the experimenter left the table to get a drink, implying that the seated person should watch the lunch. A confederate dressed as a cafeteria clean-up attendant then approached the table and asked the person if the remaining half sandwich belonged to him. Before the person could explain that the owner of the sandwich would be right back, the attendant grabbed the lunch and dumped it into a trash can. Then the experimenter returned, asked what happened to his lunch, and tried to borrow money for a new lunch. The dependent variable was how much money the subject was willing to loan. In a second condition the experimenter dropped his lunch on the floor and then tried to borrow money. So the second independent variable has to do with whether the lunch was dropped or thrown out by the attendant.

The outcomes of this experiment are shown in Figure 5–1, with each variable alone. People were more willing to loan greater amounts if the table was small[1] and if the lunch had been thrown out by the attendant rather than dropped by the experimenter. However, as Figure 5–2 shows, the results were really more complicated than this because an *interaction* occurred. People loaned more money for the thrown-out lunch only at the small table. People sitting at large tables loaned about the same small amount of money regardless of whether the lunch was dropped or thrown out by the attendant.

Figure 5–1

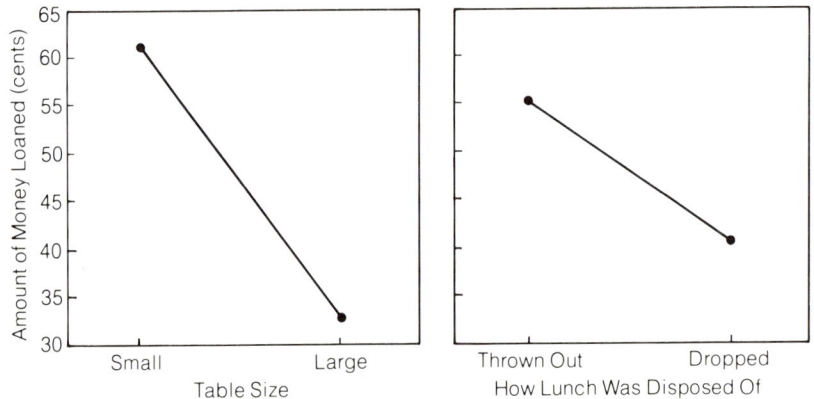

Effects of two independent variables (table size and how lunch was disposed of) upon the amount of money loaned in a cafeteria. Each variable is plotted separately (data from Kantowitz and Bartell, 1977)

[1]The ex post facto nature of this field experiment might suggest the proper conclusion is that rich students prefer to sit at small tables and poorer students at large tables. A post experimental questionnaire was administered and no difference in amount of money was found between occupants of small and large tables. But even though subjects were matched on amount of pocket money, as with any ex post facto design the possibility of some confounding always remains.

Figure 5–2

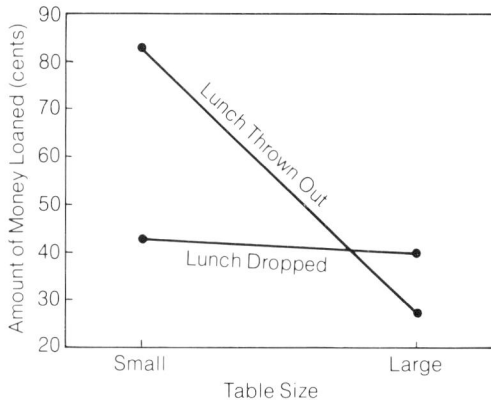

Effects of two independent variables on amount of money loaned. The variables are plotted together to show an interaction (data from Kantowitz and Bartell, 1977).

In summary, an interaction occurs when the effects of one independent variable are determined by the levels of other independent variables. When interactions are present, do not discuss the effects of each independent variable separately. Because the effects of one variable also depend upon the levels of the other variables, we are forced to discuss interacting variables together.

More Than One Dependent Variable

The dependent (observed) variable is used as an index of behavior. The experimenter must decide which aspects of behavior are relevant to the experiment at hand. While some variables are traditional, this does not mean that they are the only, or even the best, index of behavior. Take, for example, the behavior of a rat pressing a bar or a pigeon pecking a key. The most common dependent variable is the number of presses or pecks observed. But the force with which a key is pecked can also lead to interesting findings (see Notterman and Mintz, 1965), as can the latency or time to respond. Researchers can usually come up with several dependent variables that may be appropriate. Let's say we wish to study the legibility of the type that you are now reading. We can't observe "legibility," of course. What dependent variables might we observe? Here are some that have been used in the past: retention of meaningful information after reading text, time needed to read a fixed number of words, number of errors in recognizing single letters, speed in transcribing or retyping text, heart rate during reading, and muscular tension during reading. And this list is far from exhaustive.

Reasons of economy argue for obtaining as many dependent measures at the same time as is feasible. Despite this, the typical experiment uses only one or at most two dependent variables simultaneously. This is unfortunate since, just as the generality of an experiment is expanded by having more than one independent variable, it is also expanded with several dependent variables. One reason for not using several measures is that the results may be hard to interpret. Sometimes it may not be possible to determine whether the dependent variables are measuring the same or different things. Another reason more dependent variables aren't used is that it is statistically difficult to analyze several dependent variables at once. Although modern computer techniques make the calculations quite feasible, many experimental psychologists have not been well trained in these multivariate statistical procedures and thus hesitate to use them. While separate analyses could be conducted for each dependent variable, this loses information in much the same way that separate analysis of independent variables ignores interactions. Because multivariate analysis is complex, we will not treat it here. Nevertheless you should be aware that it is often advantageous to use more than one dependent variable in an experiment. (See Table 5-1.)

Table 5-1	The Important Variables in an Experiment		
	Type of Variable	*Operation Performed*	*Examples*
	Independent	At least two levels of a variable are *MANIPULATED*	Atmospheric pressure; Types of memorizing instructions
	Dependent	Certain behavior is *MEASURED*	Infant growth and movement; number of words remembered
	Control	Other variables are *HELD CONSTANT*	strain of rats; mode of decompression; type of words memorized and number of trials to learn

Note. The examples come from the experiment by Graessle et al. (1978) who were interested in the effects of different amounts of atmospheric pressure on the development of rats and from the work by Bower (1972) that was concerned with effects of different types of memorizing instructions on the retention of unrelated words.

Experimental Design

The purpose of experimental design is to minimize extraneous or uncontrolled variation, thereby increasing the likelihood that an experiment will produce reliable results. Entire books have been written about experimental design. Here we will cover only a sample of some common techniques used to improve the design of experiments. While this treatment is necessarily less complete than that of an entire text devoted to the subject, it should give you an understanding of the aims of the psychologist designing an experiment, even though it will not give you all the techniques that could be used.

Within- and Between-subjects Designs

One of the first design decisions an experimenter must make is how to assign subjects to the various levels, i.e., the different values, of independent variables. The two main possibilities are to (a) only assign some subjects to each level, or (b) to assign each subject to every level. The first possibility is called a *between-subjects* design and the second a *within-subjects* design. This can be shown with a simple example. Thirty students in introductory psychology have signed up for your experiment that tests ability to remember nonsense words. Your independent variable is the number of times you will say each item, one or five times. You expect that an item that is presented five times should be learned better than an item presented only once. The between-subjects design calls for you to divide your subjects in half—that is, into two groups of fifteen students each—with one group receiving five repetitions and the other one repetition. (How to select which subjects to put in each group will be discussed shortly.) The within-subjects design has all thirty subjects learning with both levels of the independent variable—that is, each is tested with one repetition and again with five repetitions. (How to determine the order in which each subject gets these two treatments will also be discussed later.) Which design should you use?

The between-subjects (two groups) design is conservative (safe) because there is no chance of one treatment contaminating the other, since the same person never receives both treatments. Nevertheless, most experimental psychologists would prefer the within-subjects (one group) design. It is more efficient since each subject is compared to himself or herself, which means that we do not have to have separate groups. Any differences resulting from one versus five repetitions cannot be due to differences between the people in the two groups, as would be the case for the between-subjects design, since the same people get all treatments. However, the between-subjects design must deal with differences among people and this decreases its efficiency—that is, its ability to detect real differences between one and five repetitions of the memory items. But there is a risk in the more efficient within-subjects design. Imagine that all thirty subjects first learned items with five repetitions and then learned items with one repetition. As a result of their earlier experience with five repetitions they might decide to repeat the item that was only presented once to themselves four more times. This would destroy any differences between the two levels of the independent variable. The danger is that an early part of the experiment might change behavior in a later part of the experiment, because the effects of one treatment would carry over to the other treatment. This, of course, ruins the experiment. We can minimize this danger by *counterbalancing* (discussed below), but we cannot eliminate it entirely. So if an experimenter suspects that the effects of one treatment may linger on to alter a later treatment, the between-subjects design should be used. Because it is less efficient it will require that a much greater number of subjects be tested, but this is preferable to a within-subjects design in which effects have been carried over from an early part of the experiment to a later part.

Randomization and Matching. In any between-subjects design the experimenter must somehow guarantee that there are as few differences as possible among the subjects in the two or more treatment groups. Clearly, if we took the five best memorizers and deliberately placed them in the one repetition group, and put the five worst in the five repetition group, we might wind up after our experiment with no difference in results or even, perhaps, with the one repetition group doing better than the other group. To prevent this outcome, the experimenter tries to have groups that are equivalent at the start of the experiment. One way to do this is to administer a memory test to all thirty subjects before the regular experiment starts. Then pairs of subjects could be formed from those subjects who had equal or very similar scores. One member of each pair would be randomly assigned to one group and the other member to the second group. This technique is called *matching.* One difficulty with matching is that an experimenter cannot match for everything. Thus, there is always the possibility that the groups, even though matched on some characteristic(s), differ on some other characteristic that may be relevant. So, matching is done on the basis of the most likely confounding variables. Even so, matching on one variable may cause a mismatch on another variable.

A more common technique to ensure that equivalent groups are formed is *randomization.* In our repetition experiment, one way to form two groups by randomization would be to draw names out of a hat. Or we could ask each person to step forward, and then throw a die. Even throws would be assigned to one group and odd throws to the other. Or if you didn't have any dice, a table of random numbers could be used to generate even and odd digits. This method of assigning subjects to experimental conditions has no bias since it ignores all characteristics of the subjects; so we expect that groups so created would be equivalent on any and all relevant dimensions. However, randomization does not guarantee that the groups will always be equal. By chance more of the better memorizers might have been assigned to one of the groups. The odds of this rare occurrence can be calculated by the methods of statistics. This is why experimental design and statistics are often treated as the same topic. However, design is concerned with the logic of arranging experiments, while statistics deals with calculating odds, probabilities, and other mathematical quantities. So if we are sure that all relevant dimensions have been dealt with, matching is preferable to randomization. Since we seldom are sure, randomization is used more often.

Counterbalancing. While the within-subjects (one group) design avoids problems of forming equivalent groups since there only is one group, it has the analogous difficulty of determining the order in which treatments should be given to subjects. One solution is again to use randomization by drawing treatments out of a hat, or random number table, or computer. The logic behind this is the same as that just discussed. However, while randomization produces equivalent orders in the long run, it is less likely to be suitable when there is only a small number of treatments. In most experiments the number of subjects exceeds the number of treatments, so randomization is a good technique for assigning subjects to treatments.

Complete counterbalancing makes sure that all possible treatment orders are used. In the repetition experiment, this is easy since there are only two orders: one and five repetition, five and one repetition. So half the subjects would receive one repetition followed by five repetitions while the other half would get the opposite order. As the number of treatments increases, the number of orders gets large indeed. Three treatments have six different orders, four treatments have twenty-four different orders, five treatments have one hundred and twenty different orders, etc. As the levels of an independent variable increase, complete counterbalancing soon becomes impractical. Instead experimenters must settle for incomplete counterbalancing where each treatment occurs equally often in each position—that is, treatment A occurs first, second and third equally often, and ditto for treatments B and C. This arrangement is called a *Latin square* design. Some Latin squares are shown in Figure 5–3.

Counterbalancing does not eliminate the effects of order, rather it balances them across subjects. In each time period of the experiment, each treatment occurs, which means that each treatment has the same chance of being influenced by confounding variables. Hence we have the term counterbalancing—it names a situation in which we counter the effects of potential confounding variables by balancing them over the periods when the treatments are administered.

Counterbalancing allows experimenters to evaluate possible order effects. If such effects are present, and especially if they result in interactions with more important independent variables, steps need to be taken

Figure 5–3

Subject Number	Order 1st	2nd	3rd	4th	Order 1st	2nd	3rd	4th	Order 1st	2nd	3rd	4th
1	A	B	C	D	A	B	C	D	A	B	C	D
2	B	D	A	C	B	D	A	C	B	D	A	C
3	C	A	D	B	C	A	D	B	C	A	D	B
4	D	C	B	A	D	C	B	A	D	C	B	A

Three Latin squares for counterbalancing the order of four treatments. Letters represent treatments. Thus, the first subject receives treatment A first, B second, and then C followed by D. Note that each treatment occurs only once in each row and each column. In the second and third squares, the *order* of treatments is balanced— each treatment precedes and follows every other treatment equally often.

to correct the design. For example, the experimenter might decide to repeat the experiment using a between-subjects design to avoid order effects.

The order of treatments within a Latin square could be determined randomly, in which case we would have a *randomized blocks procedure.* Usually, however, when the number of treatments is greater than two, but not much greater than seven or eight, the *balanced Latin square* design is the most appropriate. In Figure 5–3, the middle and right-hand squares are balanced, which means that when each condition is tested it will, across subjects, be preceded and followed in equal frequency by every other condition. This last feature is very useful in minimizing carry-over effects among conditions and makes the balanced Latin square preferable to other counterbalancing schemes.

Constructing a balanced Latin square is easy, especially if there are an even number of treatments. Let us label the four conditions in an experiment from A to D. A balanced Latin square can be thought of as a two-dimensional matrix where the columns (extending vertically) represent conditions tested and the rows (extending horizontally) represent subjects. In the right-most square of Figure 5–3, subjects are labeled 1–4, and the order in which they receive treatments is determined by reading across the row. Thus, in this example, Subject *1* receives the conditions in the order A, B, D, C. The general formula for constructing the first row of a balanced Latin square is A, B, X, C, $X-1$, D, $X-2$, and so forth, where X stands for the final or total numbers of conditions (in this case D is the last treatment). After the first row is in place, then just go down the columns with the successively designated treatments, starting over when you get to X. (Note how this procedure was followed in the third square in Figure 5–3.) When using a balanced Latin square design, subjects must be run in multiples of the number of treatments (in this case four), in order to appropriately counterbalance conditions against carry-over effects.

When an experiment contains an odd number of conditions, it becomes a bit more complicated to use a balanced Latin square. In fact two squares must be used, the second of which is the reverse of the first, as can be seen in Figure 5–4, where once again numbers indicate subjects and letters stand for conditions in the experiment. When a balanced Latin square is used with an odd number of treatments, each subject must be tested in each condition twice. The case shown in Figure 5–4 is for five conditions. In general the first square is constructed in exactly the same manner as when there are an even number of conditions, and then the second square is an exact reversal of the first.

To repeat, the balanced Latin square is an optimal counterbalancing system for many purposes, since each condition occurs, on the average, at the same stage of practice and each condition precedes and follows every other equally often.

Counterbalancing is useful not only for the assignment of treatment orders, but also to determine the order of testing when there is more than one dependent variable. The primary concern is to balance any potential carry-over effects for any given subject. To illustrate, let us reconsider the decompression study mentioned earlier. Suppose there is reason to believe that how the infant rats did on one test, e.g., climbing, could influence behavior on another test, e.g., grasping. So, even though the different measures are not independent variables in the

Figure 5–4

Order of Testing

Subjects	Square 1					Square 2				
1	A	B	E	C	D	D	C	E	B	A
2	B	C	A	D	E	E	D	A	C	B
3	C	D	B	E	A	A	E	B	D	C
4	D	E	C	A	B	B	A	C	E	D
5	E	A	D	B	C	C	B	D	A	E

Balanced Latin square for five experimental conditions (A–E) to be presented to each subject. Rows indicate the order in which subjects 1–5 are to receive the experimental conditions. When there is an odd number of treatments, each one must be given to each subject twice for a balanced Latin square.

usual sense, the order in which they are administered may affect what is measured. One test might make the infant rats tired or could, conceivably, enhance muscle tone. If we have two measures, *A* and *B*, we could completely counterbalance the order of assessment across subjects so that the average effect would be balanced.

What do we do for an *individual subject?* One solution to this problem, and the one most psychologists would pick, would be to use an *ABBA* design. This would unconfound each assessment with time of assessment, since each measure would occur at the same time on the average ($1 + 4 = 5$ for *A* and $2 + 3 = 5$ for *B*, where the numbers refer to the order of test). But perhaps the specific order of testing might also matter. If *A* is the grasping test and *B* the climbing test, it is possible that climbing is so fatiguing that the results of the grasping test are biased.

Two solutions to differential order effects are possible. One would be to simply increase the number of subjects and just get one test from each subject. Of course this would defeat the purpose of multiple testing and using the subject as its own control. Another solution would be to use more than one within-subject counterbalancing scheme. For example, half the subjects might get the reverse of the scheme that the other half receives. So half the subjects would be tested in the *ABBA* order and the other half would be tested in the order *BAAB*. Across subjects, as well as within subjects, therefore, we would balance the testing of the subjects.

You should note that the above counterbalancing procedures are useful in a variety of different ways. They can be used to assign subjects to treatments, to determine the order of testing, to determine when certain materials are given to particular subjects, and, in general, to minimize the effects of one aspect of an experiment on another.

Mixed designs. Experiments need not be exclusively within-subjects design or between-subjects design. It is often convenient and prudent to have some independent variables treated as between-subjects and others as within-subjects in the same experiment (assuming the experiment has more than one independent variable, of course). If one variable seems likely to cause transfer or carry-over effects, for example, administering a drug, it can be made a between-subjects variable while the rest of the variables are within-subjects. This compromise design is not as efficient as a pure within-subjects design, but it often is safer.

Control Conditions

Most experiments contain some control group (between-subjects design) or control condition (within-subjects design). In its simplest form the control group is the group that does not receive the levels of interest of the independent variable. (Sometimes this is phrased as the group that does not receive the independent variable, but this shorthand is misleading, since all independent variables by definition must have at least two levels, one of which may be the control level.) For example, an experimenter might be analyzing the effect of noise upon studying. Using a between-subjects design, one group of subjects would be exposed to loud noise for half an hour while they were studying; this is the level of interest of the independent variable. A control group would study the same material for half an hour but in a quiet setting. Then both groups would be tested on the material. Any obtained difference on the test between the two groups would be attributed to the effect of noise.

The control group does not always receive no treatment as in the example above where no noise was introduced. In the study on decompression, the control condition was ground-level pressure at 728 feet. Another control condition could have been sea level (zero altitude). In another part of the country, 1000 feet might have been the appropriate control altitude. The important characteristic of a control condition is that it provides a *baseline* against which some variable of the experiment can be compared. Sometimes the best baseline is no particular treatment, as noted above, but many times the best baseline requires some activity. A frequent example occurs in memory research where a group of subjects is required to learn two different lists of words; the experimenter is interested in how learning one list interferes with learning the other. The experimental group (receiving the level of interest of the independent variable) first learns list A, then learns list B, and then is tested again on list A. The experimenter would like to show that learning list B interferes with list A. But before any conclusion of this sort can be reached, a comparison control condition is required. Merely, comparing the final test of list A with the first test is insufficient since subjects might do more poorly on the last list A test simply because they were tired or do better because of extra practice. A control condition with no treatment would have a group learn list A, then sit around for the time it took the experimental group to learn list B, and then be tested again on list A. But this would be a poor control condition because subjects might practice or rehearse list A while they were sitting around. Practicing would improve their final performance on the last list A test and incorrectly make the experimental group look as if list B interfered more than it really did with list A. As shown in Figure 5–5, a proper baseline condition would occupy the control group during the time the experimental groups was learning list B—perhaps by having them do arithmetic or some other "busy work" that would prevent rehearsal.

Sometimes the control condition is contained implicitly within the experiment. Recall the memory experiment discussed earlier where the independent variable was the number of repetitions of an item, one or

Figure 5–5   Examples of experimental and control groups for list learning.

	First Period	Second Period	Third Period
Experimental Group	Learn List A	Learn List B	Test List A
Control Group	Learn List A	Do arithmetic	Test List A

five. No experimenter would bother to include a control group or condition with zero repetitions, since no learning could occur under this odd circumstance. The control condition is implicit, in that five repetitions can be compared to one and vice versa. Since the experimenter might well be as interested in effects of a single repetition as in five repetitions, we probably would not explicitly call the one-repetition level a control condition. But it does provide a baseline for comparison—and so for that matter does the five-repetition condition, since the one-repetition results can be compared with it.

Choosing an Experimental Design

We have noted that the between-subjects design precludes carry-over effects from one treatment to another, while the within-subjects design does not confound subjects with conditions. Furthermore, we have suggested that the within-subject design is usually more efficient than the between-subject design, so obtaining repeated observations from the same subjects may be preferable to using independent groups. In this section, we will consider some rules of thumb for selecting an experimental design, regardless of the particular research topic. At the end of this section, there are several experimental problems for which you are to choose a design.

Carry-Over Effects

If your independent variable is likely to have a permanent effect on the subject that would prevent subsequent unconfounded testing, then a between-subjects design should be used. What sorts of independent variables would operate in this way? One would be prenatal decompression or any other independent variable that permanently alters the development of the subject. Some other variables that might be similar in their effects to decompression include: prenatal nutrition, nearly all kinds of physiological damage (brain lesions, some drugs, toxic chemicals, etc.), most time-dependent variables (the effect of persuasion on later consumer behavior or the effects of a particular reading technique on second-grade achievement), and any other variable whose effects are likely to be irreversible. Most subject variables (sex, age, ethnic group, etc.) require a between-subjects design, but these variables are not true independent variables. The special problems associated with research involving subject variables will be examined in Chapter 7.

If you are interested in changes in behavior over time, such as improvements in learning or retention, changes in strategy in a particular task, or optimal performance on a task, then you will want to use some variant of a within-subjects design. Either you will need repeated measures from the subjects (the rats are placed in the maze twice each day for a month) or you will want to have each subject receive several treatments over time. In effect, you are looking for a carry-over effect, which is really what a great deal of learning research is all about.

Individual Differences

You might think it trivial for us to say that people differ from each other. However, individual differences among subjects are not a trivial problem when it comes to designing a good experiment. If your subject pool contains individuals who are markedly different from each other or if you expect that large individual differences in thought or behavior are likely to show up in your experiment, you may be better off using a within-subjects design rather than a between-subjects design. The within-subjects design automatically takes care of differences among your subjects. As long as you counterbalance appropriately and carry-over effects are not a problem, then you can control for these individual differences in a within-subject design.

A case in point is testing the effectiveness of drugs. Drug manufacturers know that people (and animals too) differ in their sensitivity to drugs. Once the drug is marketed, many different types of people will be taking the drugs. Therefore it is imperative that many different types of people be tested, and that several drugs are tested on the same person. Within-subjects administration of several levels of a drug compared to a placebo will also control for individual differences that may appear on the behavioral or attitudinal task used to assess drug effects. For example, if the effects of a drug on pain tolerance are being tested, it is important to do this study within-subjects, because we know ahead of time that there are tremendous individual differences in reaction to pain in the absence of any externally administered substance.

Obviously, if a drug is likely to have long-term effects, a between-subjects design must be used. An additional reason that many clinical tests of drug effectiveness use between-subjects designs is that subjects are selected with certain diseases. They are given the drug, and a control group with the same disease is given a placebo or another drug for comparison. For humanitarian reasons, if one of the drugs is effective, then all patients receive it after the experimental comparison is completed.

Many research problems pose a particular dilemma to you: you must balance off carry-over effects with the possible contaminating effects of large individual differences. There is no easy solution to this problem. Sometimes the easiest way out is to do the study one way (e.g., within-subjects) and then do it the other way (e.g., between-subjects). While such a tactic may seem inefficient, in the long run multiple experimentation will add to the generalizability of the results.

Design Problems

For each of the following problems, decide upon a within- or between-subjects design. If you think the situation warrants it, set up your experiment with both types of design. For practice you should indicate the independent, dependent, and control variables. If you choose a within-subjects design, specify the counterbalancing procedures, and if you use a between-subjects design, indicate how subjects will be assigned to conditions. Regardless of your design, indicate your reasons for selecting either the within- or between-subjects configuration.

1. A researcher wants to see which is easier to learn: hard to pronounce syllables (e.g., WMH, JBT, SJK) or easy to pronounce syllables (e.g., LEJ, NAM, HEK). Lists containing either 20 pronounceable syllables or 20 hard to pronounce syllables will be prepared. Each element in a list will be shown for 2 seconds. At the end of the series the subjects will try to write down the syllables from memory.

2. A cleanser manufacturer is interested in the effects of package color on the sales of Scrubbo super-duper cleanser. Identical cartons of Scrubbo will be prepared that differ only in the background color of the label (maroon, pink, or aqua). Sales are to be monitored for the next four months.

3. A child psychologist wants to determine the effects of cloth versus paper diapers on toilet training. Day-old infants will be used in the project. The age at which diapers are no longer needed (to the nearest week) will be determined.

4. The importance of training regimen on the learning of a complex maze by rats is under investigation. A comparison will be made of massing practice trials (one trial every ten seconds) to distributing practice trials (one every ten minutes) on the number of trials it takes the rats to travel the maze without error.

5. The Burpo beer company is test marketing flavored "light" beers. They want to see if consumers prefer strawberry-, licorice-, or avocado-flavored Burpo. Several bottles will be made of each flavor. Consumers will fill out a questionnaire on how much they like the flavor, body, and aroma.

In many areas of psychological research and in many areas of applied psychology, it is not possible to use a large number of subjects in a control-group (between-subjects) or control-condition (within-subjects) design as we have just considered. Rather, a large number of observations are made upon a small number of subjects (usually designated small-n, referring to the number and not the size of the subjects). As the observations are being made, independent variables are introduced into the situation, and changes in behavior are measured. Since small numbers of subjects are used, economy and control are exerted through the use of variants of the within-subjects procedures mentioned above. Some of these small-n experiments require special control procedures that we shall now consider.

Small-n Experiments

Psychophysical Experiments

Psychophysics, you will remember from Chapter 2, refers to the branch of psychology that attempts to relate psychological judgment to the characteristics of physical stimuli. In the typical psychophysical experiment, a small number of subjects may make a number of judgments about a large number of stimuli. Very often a subject will be required to rate or otherwise judge the same event several times. The reason that a small number of subjects usually participate in psychophysical studies has to do with economy. If we want to determine the subject's sensitivity to dim flashes of light, we might present test flashes of varying intensities as many as 7000 times. Obviously doing this with 20–30 subjects would be extremely time consuming. The general tactic is to get reliable measures from a few subjects, and, if we are examining rather simple psychophysical judgments, we do not have to worry too much about individual differences. Where individual differences may play a more important role, say in judging the degree of abstractness of common English nouns, then a larger number of subjects may be tested. Spreen and Schulz (1966), for example, had 58 college students rate 329 nouns for their concreteness, specificity, and pronounceability.

What sorts of control procedures should be instituted in a psychophysical study? Regardless of whether a small or large number of subjects are tested, carry-over effects from one judgment to the next must be balanced across subjects. In the Spreen and Schulz study, carry-over effects were handled by presenting the 329 words in a different random order to each subject.

One particular problem that occurs in psychophysical scaling tasks involves changes in adaptation level (Helson, 1964). The *adaptation level* refers to the context or reference level for making a particular psychophysical judgment. Suppose you are given the task of rating these acts for seriousness: treason, running a red light, failing to signal a turn, and keeping excess change at the grocery. You might have some difficulty deciding which of the last three crimes is bad relative to each other and the awful crime of treason. Compare your rating of that series with the following: child abuse, rape/murder, treason, arson, and keeping excess change at the grocery. In this instance, keeping excess change is relatively "good," and you may have some difficulty in rating the other crimes.

A considerable amount of research has been concerned with adaptation level and its effects on psychophysical judgment (e.g., Parducci, 1968). The moral for you is that you should be alert for adaptational effects and present your stimuli in such a way as to minimize them. In addition to random presentation of the stimuli (Spreen and Schulz, 1966), other forms of counterbalancing may help to minimize carry-over effects from one judgment to the next.

Operant Conditioning Experiments

The work of Skinner (e.g., 1938) and his associates (Sidman, 1960) is classified as small-n because most of their experiments involve the conditioning of a small number of subjects under a number of tightly controlled conditions. The general approach has been dubbed the *experimental analysis of behavior,* and a journal, *Journal of the Experimental Analysis of Behavior,* is devoted to such small-n experimentation. Unlike psychophysical research, the argument for using few subjects in operant conditioning experiments does not reside in economy. Proponents of this approach argue that by very carefully controlling the experimental setting and by taking numerous and continuous measures of the dependent variable powerful control can be obtained and valid conclusions can be reached. In contrast to standard experimental procedures where conclusions are based on average performance of large numbers of subjects randomly assigned to conditions, this small-n approach relies on a detailed examination of the behavior of a small number of organisms.

Nearly all operant conditioning research, relying as it does on a small-n, is done within-subjects. We will consider just two of the within-subjects control procedures used in the experimental analysis of behavior.

The Reversal Design. The logic behind the reversal design is straight-forward: first obtain a baseline measure of the subject's behavior, then see how that behavior changes when an independent variable is introduced, and finally reverse the conditions back to the original and measure the behavior again under this second baseline. In its basic form this design is labeled the *ABA* design, where *A* and *B* refer to the different phases of the experiment. Just using an *AB* design would not allow an experimenter to make definite statements about the effects of the variable introduced during the *B* phase. If there is a change in the dependent variable when the treatment is administered in the *B* phase, the experimenter cannot conclusively establish that it was due to the independent variable because of a lack of control comparisons. The change in the dependent variable might have occurred anyway, without the treatment variable being applied, due to confounding from some uncontrolled variable the experimenter might not have observed. Note that in the *AB* design there is always a time confounding with the introduction of *B* following *A*. The third phase in the *ABA* design, the reintroduction of a baseline, serves to rule out the effects of confounding by returning the conditions of the experiment to their original, baseline level with the independent variable no longer applied. If behavior in the second *A* phase returns to its baseline level, an experimenter can conclude that it was the independent variable that effected the change during the *B* phase. The only time this generalization would not apply is when a secondary variable, not detected by the experimenter, happened to be perfectly correlated with the independent variable. Such situations are unlikely.

The results of an applied reversal design are shown in Figure 5–6. In this interesting experiment, Hart, Allen, Buell, Harris, and Wolf (1964) wanted to decrease the excessive crying of Bill, a nursery school student. During the *A* phases, the nursery school teacher simply counted the number of Bill's crying episodes and tried to comfort him. During the *B* phases the teacher attempted to decrease crying by extinguishing it. That is, the teacher ignored his crying episodes and rewarded Bill with attention every time he responded to minor calamities (such as falls or pushes) in a more mature way. Usually the teacher paid attention to Bill's crying in the *A* phases. Since it would be counter to the purpose of the experiment to leave Bill in an *A* phase (crying excessively), a second *B* phase was instituted to reduce crying. As shown in Figure 5–6, the number of crying episodes decreased markedly in the first *B* phase, which completes the *AB* phase of the design. But we cannot be certain that the combination of extinction and reward of appropriate behaviors were responsible for Bill's improved behavior. Perhaps he was getting along better with his classmates, his parents were treating him better at home, or some other factor could have improved his disposition. So, the *A* phase was reintroduced; that is, Bill was again reinforced via attention for crying. As shown in the third panel of Figure 5–6, it took only four days to reestablish the baseline level of crying, leading to the conclusion that reward by attention to appropriate behavior and ignoring of crying were responsible for the termination of crying in the first *B* phase. Since the second *B* phase also resulted in the extinction of crying, the reward hypothesis is supported, not to mention the fact that Bill is now a more enjoyable student for his teacher.

Although the reversal design is commonly used in applied settings as in the case of Bill, it is also frequently seen in basic experiments. Boe and Winokur (1978) used a reversal design to study what controls a person's choice of words in conversations. The subject's task was to orally answer three questions in each of three sessions that occurred at weekly intervals. The questions contained target words that Boe and Winokur thought the subjects would echo in the course of answering each question. The first and last sessions (the *A* phases) had the following target words: changes, feel, society, employment, wages, and training. The target words in the questions of the *B* phase were synonyms of those used in the *A* phases: effects, believe, culture, hiring, salaries, preparation. All of the questions were about the women's liberation movement, and Boe and Winokur expected that answers concerned with job payment would include *wages* in the *A* phases and *salaries* in

Figure 5–6

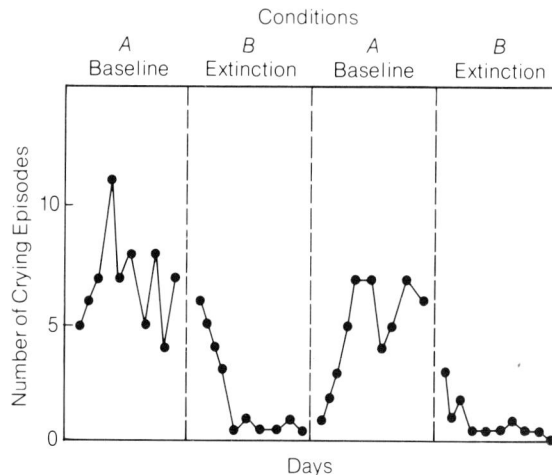

The number of crying episodes exhibited by Bill, a nursery school student, during the four phases of an *ABAB* design initiated to control his problem crying (after Hart et al., 1964).

the *B* phase if the subjects were echoing the wording of the questions. The results followed expectation: more *B* words were emitted during the *B* phase than during the *A* phases and vice versa for the *A* words. Use of the *ABA* design allows us to conclude that the specific content of the question exerted some control over the content of the answers. Use of the *AB* design would not have permitted that conclusion.

Extensions of the Reversal Design.   Just as is the case in the standard within-subjects experiment, small-*n* experiments often include carry-over effects that prohibit using the reversal design. If the treatment introduced in the *B* phase has long-term effects on the dependent variable, then reversal is impractical. Furthermore, the experimenter may want to obtain several samples of the subjects' behavior under either the same independent variable or under several independent variables. There are several ways around these problems, but a complete enumeration is beyond the scope of this book. We will consider one extension of the reversal procedure and direct your attention to the book by Craighead, Kazdin, and Mahoney (1976) for additional small-*n* designs.

Rose (1978) used what could be called an *ACABCBCB* design, where *A* refers to baseline conditions, and *B* and *C* are phases that include different independent variables. Rose was interested in the effects of artificial food coloring and hyperactivity in children. Two hyperactive eight-year-old girls were subjects. They had been on a strict diet, the K-P diet (Feingold, 1975), that eliminates foods containing artificial flavors and colors and foods containing natural salicylates (e.g., many fruits and meats). On the basis of uncontrolled case studies (*AB* designs), Feingold reported that the K-P diet reduced hyperactivity.

Rose's *A* phase was the behavior of the two girls under the ordinary K-P diet. The *B* phase was another type of baseline. It involved the introduction of an oatmeal cookie that contained no artificial coloring. The *C* phase included the independent variable of interest: oatmeal cookies containing an artificial yellow dye. This artificial color was chosen because it is commonly used in the manufacture of foods, and it had the additional benefit that it did not change the taste or appearance of the cookies. (When asked to sort the cookies on the basis of color, judges were unable to do so systematically with regard to the presence of the dye.) The subjects, their parents, and the trained observers who watched the children were blind to when the child had eaten the dye-laced cookie. Several aspects of the childrens' behavior were recorded during school by several different observers.

All measures are in agreement for both girls, so we show in Figure 5–7 the percentage of time one of the girls was out of her seat (i.e., when

Figure 5–7

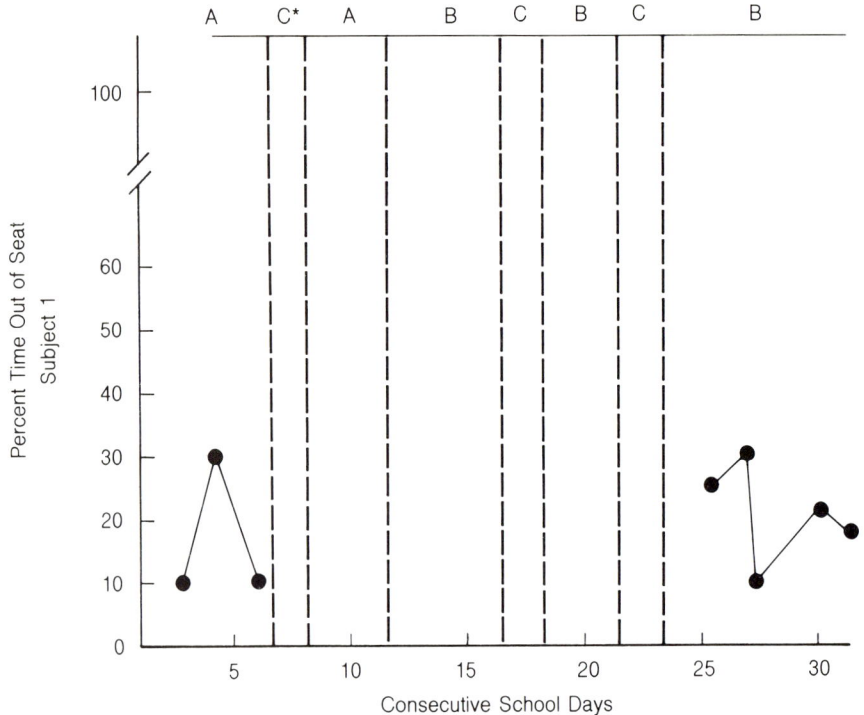

Percentage of time out of seat during baseline (*A*), placebo cookie (*B*), and artificially colored cookie (*C*) phases. *Indicates a *C* phase resulting from a violation of the diet, but one that was inadvertent and not experimentally introduced. (After Rose, 1978.)

she was overactive). Notice that hyperactivity occurred only in the *C* phase, when the child had ingested a cookie with artificial coloring in it. There was no placebo effect (*B* phase), since the behavior during the *A* and *B* phases is essentially the same. Thus, Rose concluded that artificial colors can lead to hyperactivity in some children.

Summary

A well-designed experiment insures that changes in the dependent variable result from the independent variable. This control over the situation also insures that causal statements are reasonable. In a between-subjects experiment, independent groups of subjects are assigned to the different levels of the independent variable. In the simplest case, the control group does not receive the independent variable, while the experimental group does receive it. Otherwise the two groups are as alike as possible. Random assignment to the two conditions is the best way to insure the comparability of the subjects in the two conditions. Another way to insure comparability is to match the subjects in the two conditions on the basis of some potentially relevant attribute, such as intelligence for a learning experiment. Matching on the relevant variables is often difficult, because, in the extreme case, if you knew all the relevant attributes, you would not have to do the experiment. In a within-subjects experiment, the same subject receives all levels of the independent variable. This procedure guarantees that the subjects in control and experimental conditions are identical, except when there is carry-over from one treatment to the next. Various counterbalancing procedures are used to minimize these carry-over effects by balancing them over time or across subjects. Small-*n* experiments pose specific within-subject problems, so a reversal design is often used. In the typical reversal design an independent variable is introduced after a period of baseline measurement, which is then repeated to determine if the independent variable rather than some confounding variable changed behavior in the second, independent variable phase. Shown in Table 5–2 is a summary of the control procedures used in experiments.

Summary of Control Techniques for Between- and Within-Subjects Designs			**Table 5-2**
To Control for:	*Between-Subjects Design*	*Within-Subjects Design*	*Small-n*

Individual differences (sex, age, I.Q.)	1. Randomized assignment— unbiased assignment of subjects to groups
	2. Matched assignment
	  a. hold variable constant across groups (run just females)
	  b. equate variables across groups (use equal numbers of smart and dull subjects)
		Individual differences automatically controlled	Individual differences automatically controlled

Situational differences (time of day the data are collected, room temperature, etc.	1. Randomize the effects of these variables 2. Hold constant or equate these variables	Same as between subjects	Same as between subjects

Carry-over effects (order of testing, assignment of materials)	Usually carry-over effects do not occur. If they do, same techniques as in within subjects.	1. Intrasubject counterbalancing (ABBA)
		2. Intragroup counterbalancing
		  a. randomized order
		  b. complete counterbalancing
		  c. incomplete counterbalancing (Latin-square designs)
			1. Same as within subjects, and
			2. Reversal designs
			  a. *ABA*
			  b. *ABAB*
			  c. variants of the above

Study and Review

Exercises

1. An experimenter examined the effects of LSD on complex learning of rats. One group of rats was given a very small dose of LSD, so small a dose that it was unlikely to have any behavioral effects. A second group was given a large dose. Then, both groups ran through a complex maze several times. The dependent variable was the number of errors the rats made before obtaining the food reward at the end of the maze. The large dose group made 4.5 times as many errors as the small dose group, and the experimenter concluded that LSD can mess up complex learning. Comment on the design of this experiment: what would improve the design? Comment on the conclusion by the experimenter.

2. What is wrong with the following experimental design? In order to study the effects of imagery on memory, an experimenter used a within-subjects design that involved the following: a long list of unrelated words was presented to the subjects, with each word being presented one at a time. Half the words were printed in red ink and the other half in black ink. The subjects were told to create a vivid mental image of the red words and to simply say the black words over and over to themselves until the next word was shown. After all the words were presented, the subjects had to write down as many of the words that they could, in any order they wished.

Key Concepts

experiment 103
Method of Agreement 103
Method of Differences 103
Method of Concomitant
Variations 104
    control 104
independent variable 105
dependent variable 105
control variable 105
experimental group 105
control group 105
ex post facto 106
floor effect 108
ceiling effect 108
confounding 109
interaction 111

between-subjects design 115
within-subjects design 115
matching 116
randomization 116
counterbalancing 117
Latin square 117
balanced Latin square 118
randomized blocks 118
ABBA conterbalancing 120
mixed design 120
baseline 121
carry-over effects 122
individual differences 123
small-*n* experiments 125
adaptation level 126
reversal *(ABA)* design 127

Suggested Readings

A complete discussion of the advantages and disadvantages of between- and within-subjects designs can be found in: Kerlinger, F. *Foundations of behavioral research.* New York: Harper & Row, 1973.

The following book contains an excellent discussion of small-n research as applied to behavior modification: Craighead, W. E., Kazdin, A. E., and Mahoney, M. J. *Behavior modification: principles, issues, and applications.* Boston: Houghton Mifflin, 1976.

USEFUL COMPUTATIONAL FORMULAE

Measures of Central Tendency

Mode	the most frequent score
Median	the middle score
Mean	$\bar{X} = \Sigma X/n$

Measures of Dispersion

Variance	$s^2 = \dfrac{\Sigma X^2}{n} - \bar{X}^2$
Standard Deviation	$s = \sqrt{\dfrac{\Sigma X^2}{n} - \bar{X}^2}$

Correlation

Pearson r	$r = \dfrac{n\Sigma XY - (\Sigma X)(\Sigma Y)}{\sqrt{[n\Sigma X^2 - (\Sigma X)^2][n\Sigma Y^2 - (\Sigma Y)^2]}}$

FACTS ABOUT THE NORMAL DISTRIBUTION

1 Of all scores 68 percent are within $\pm$ 1 standard deviation of the mean

2 Of all scores nearly 96 percent are within $\pm$ 2 standard deviations of the mean

3 Of all scores 99.74 percent are within $\pm$ 3 standard deviations of the mean

4 Standard scores (z-scores) are differences between individual scores and the mean expressed in units of standard deviations

X and **Y** are individual scores (data)	**n** is the number of observations or subjects	Σ refers to the act of adding (or summing)
X^2 is each score squared, so	Σ**X**^{2} refers to adding up the scores after each has been squared	$(\Sigma$**X**$)^2$ means to square the sum of the raw scores

Descriptive Statistics

6

So you have conducted a research project? What do you do now? Before you can hope to understand the data you have collected, you need some way to summarize or describe those data. The purpose of this chapter is to give you some idea as to why an understanding of statistics is crucial to the description of psychological data. In Chapter 9 you will encounter more advanced principles of statistical reasoning. For now we want to emphasize ways to summarize data.

Overview

You have conducted research in order to collect data about a psychological topic. Measures are taken and numbers are produced. What are you going to do with them? As a first step you should want to systematize and organize them. We know that it is difficult, if not impossible, to think about and understand more than a few things at a time. Instead of looking at a whole array of numbers produced by 200 people on a 50-item attitude questionnaire, you would find it more useful to briefly describe the numbers. Descriptive statistics provide the summarizing and systematizing function. The two main types of descriptive statistics are *measures of central tendency* and *measures of dispersion* (variability).

Let us take a hypothetical experimental situation. A drug company has sponsored a test of the effects of LSD on the behavior of rats, so we decide for starters to see how it affects their running speed. Forty food-deprived rats have been trained to run a straight alley maze for a food reward. We randomly assign them to two groups. To one group we administer LSD by injection and observe the effect on the speed with which they run the alley for food 30 minutes after the injection. The other group is tested in a similar manner 30 minutes after receiving an injection of an inert substance. The following are the running times for the 20 control subjects in seconds: 13, 11, 14, 18, 12, 14, 10, 13, 13, 16, 15, 9, 12, 20, 11, 13, 12, 17, 15, and 14. The running times for the subjects receiving the LSD injections are 17, 15, 16, 20, 14, 19, 14, 13, 18, 18, 26, 17, 19, 13, 16, 22, 18, 16, 18, and 9. Now that we have the running times,

Descriptive Statistics: Telling It Like It Is

Figure 6–1

Drawing by C. Schulz. Copyright © 1967 United Features Syndicate. Inc. Used by permission.

Many psychology students seem to freeze up—much like Sally—when faced with simple mathematical calculations involved in elementary statistics. Don't worry: Anyone knowing arithmetic and just a little algebra can follow this chapter.

what do we do with them? One thing we might want is some sort of graphical representation of the numbers. One type of graph is the *histogram* shown in the two panels of Figure 6–2, where the running speeds in seconds appear along the abscissa (X axis) and the frequency with which each occurred in the two conditions is displayed along the ordinate (Y axis). Running times for the control subjects are in the top histogram, while those for the experimental subjects are represented in the bottom one. Another way to represent the same information is a *frequency polygon*. Its construction is equivalent to that of the histogram; you can think of it as constructed by connecting the midpoints of the bars in the histogram. Examples of frequency polygons can be seen later in Figure 6–3. Notice that in both conditions in Figure 6–2 the greatest number of scores occurs in the middle and they tend to tail off in frequency as scores (time) become smaller or larger. Both the histogram and frequency polygon are types of *frequency distributions*. They help systematize the data, but there are more efficient summary descriptions.

Central Tendency

The most common summary description of data is a measure of central tendency which, as the name implies, indicates the center of the distribution of scores. By far the most common measure of central tendency in psychological research is the *arithmetic mean*. The mean $(\overline{X})$ is simply the sum of all the scores (ΣX) divided by the number of scores (n), or $\overline{X} = \Sigma X / n$. It is what most people think of as the average of a set of numbers, although the term average technically applies to any measure of central tendency. The sums of the running times for the experimental and control conditions of the hypothetical experiment discussed above were 338 and 272 seconds, respectively. Since there were 20 observations in each condition, the means are 16.9 seconds for the experimental condition and 13.6 for the control.

The mean is by far the most useful measure of central tendency and almost all inferential statistics, which we come to later, are based on it. Therefore it is always the statistic used where possible. However, two other measures of central tendency are sometimes used. Next most common to the mean is the *median*; it is the score above which half of the distribution lies and below which the other half lies. The median, then, is the midpoint of the distribution. When there is an odd number of scores in the distribution, such as 27, the median is the 14th score from the bottom or top since that score divides the distribution into two groups of 13 scores. When the number of scores *(n)* is an even number, the median is the arithmetic mean of the two middle scores, if the scores are not tied. So the median of the scores 66, 70, 72, 76, 80, and 96 is (72 + 76)/2, or 74. When the two middle scores are tied, as in the distribution of scores from the hypothetical LSD experiment, the convention is to designate the median as the appropriate proportion of the distance between the *limits* of the particular score, where the limits are a half score above and below the tied score. This will be clearer with an

Figure 6–2

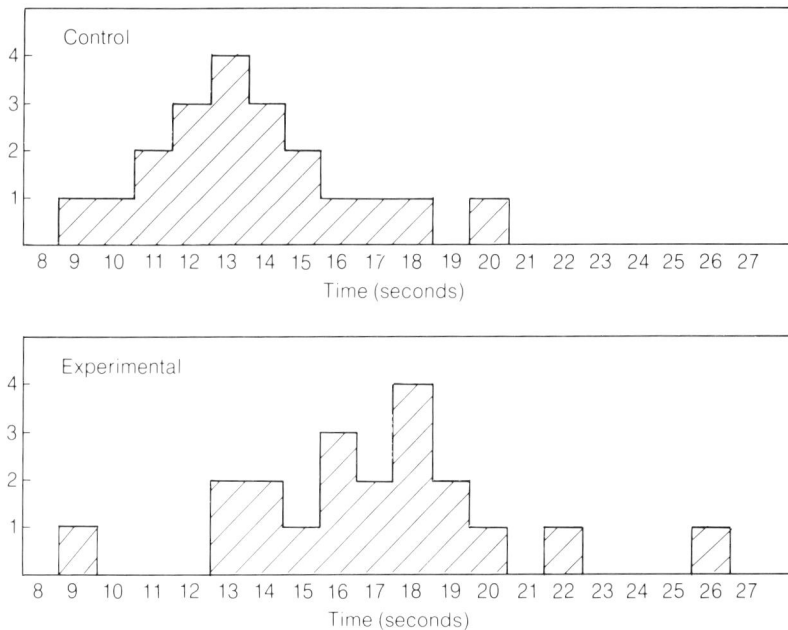

Histograms representing scores for 20 subjects in the control and experimental conditions of the hypothetical LSD experiment.

example. Consider the distributions of scores from our experiment. If you arrange the 20 control running times from lowest to highest you will discover that the 8th, 9th, 10th, and 11th scores are all 13. Under such conditions the 10th score is considered the median and it is considered to lie three quarters of the distance between the limits of 12.5 and 13.5. So the median would be 12.5 + .75, or 13.25, for the control subjects. By the same reasoning, and you should try it yourself, the median for the experimental subjects is 17.

Why is the median used? The primary reason is that it has the (desirable) property of being insensitive to extreme scores. In the distribution of scores of 66, 70, 72, 76, 80, and 96, the median of the distribution would remain exactly the same if the lowest score were 1 rather than 66 or the highest score were 1223 rather than 96. The mean, on the other hand, would differ widely with these other scores. Often this benefit can be extremely useful in summarizing data. In our LSD experiment, suppose that one of the rats given LSD had stopped halfway down the alley to grok on a particularly interesting feature of the runway before continuing on its way to the goal box. Thus its time to complete the runway was 45 minutes or 2700 seconds. If this score replaced the 26 second score in the original distribution, the mean would go from 16.9 seconds to 150.6, or from 3.30 seconds greater than the control mean to 137.0 seconds greater. This is only because of one very deviant score. In such cases researchers frequently use the median score rather than the mean to represent the central tendency. Using the mean seems to give an unrepresentative estimate of central tendency because of the great influence of the one score. However, using the median often limits severely any statistical tests that can be applied to the data.

The final measure of central tendency, almost never reported in psychological research, is the *mode* or the most frequent score in the distribution. In the distribution of control scores above, it is 13, while in the distribution of experimental scores, it is 18.

Measures of Dispersion: Variability in Data

Measures of central tendency indicate the center of the scores, while measures of dispersion indicate how the scores are spread out about the center. The simplest measure of dispersion is the *range,* which is the difference between the highest and lowest scores in the distribution plus one. For the control rats in the LSD experiment the range is 12 (20 − 9 + 1), while for the experimental rats it is 18 (26 − 9 + 1). Since the range only indicates the extreme scores, it is rarely used.

The most useful measures of dispersion are the *standard deviation* and the *variance* of a distribution. The standard deviation is most useful as a descriptive statistic, while the variance of a distribution is used in inferential statistics. As we shall see, the two are closely related.

In deciding on a measure of dispersion, we want to provide a number that reflects the amount of spread that the scores exhibit around some central tendency measure, usually the mean. One such measure that would be appropriate is the *mean deviation*. This is calculated by taking the difference between the mean and every score in a distribution, summing these differences, and then dividing by the number of scores. However, it is actually necessary to take the mean absolute difference (that is, to ignore the sign of the difference or whether the score was greater or less than the mean). The reason for this is that the sum of the deviations of scores about the mean is always zero, a defining characteristic of the mean (see Table 6–1). Thus the mean deviation must be the *absolute* mean deviation. The mean deviations for our hypothetical experimental conditions in the LSD experiment are calculated in Table 6–1. The symbol $||$ indicates the absolute value of a number, so $|-6| = 6$.

The absolute mean deviation of a set of scores is an adequate measure of dispersion and is based on the same logic as finding the mean

Calculation of the mean deviation and absolute mean deviations from two sets of scores. Notice that the sum of the deviations (differences) in calculating the mean deviation is zero, which is why it is necessary to use the absolute mean deviation.

Table 6–1

	Control group			Experimental group	
X	$(X - \bar{X})$	$|X - \bar{X}|$	X	$(X - \bar{X})$	$|X - \bar{X}|$
9	−4.60	4.60	9	−7.90	7.90
10	−3.60	3.60	13	−3.90	3.90
11	−2.60	2.60	13	−3.90	3.90
11	−2.60	2.60	14	−2.90	2.90
12	−1.60	1.60	14	−2.90	2.90
12	−1.60	1.60	15	−1.90	1.90
12	−1.60	1.60	16	− .90	.90
13	− .60	.60	16	− .90	.90
13	− .60	.60	16	− .90	.90
13	− .60	.60	17	+ .10	.10
13	− .60	.60	17	+ .10	.10
14	+ .40	.40	18	+1.10	.10
14	+ .40	.40	18	+1.10	1.10
14	+ .40	.40	18	+1.10	1.10
15	+1.40	1.40	18	+1.10	1.10
15	+1.40	1.40	19	+2.10	2.10
16	+2.40	2.40	19	+2.10	2.10
17	+3.40	3.40	20	+3.10	3.10
18	+4.40	4.40	22	+5.10	5.10
20	+6.40	6.40	26	+9.10	9.10

$\Sigma X = 272$ Total = 0.00 Total = 41.20 $\Sigma X = 338$ Total = 0.00 Total = 52.20
$\bar{X} = 13.60$ $\bar{X} = 16.90$

Absolute mean deviation $= \dfrac{41.20}{20} = 2.06$ Absolute mean deviation $= \dfrac{52.20}{20} = 2.61$

of a distribution. However, the standard deviation and variance are preferred to the mean deviation because they have mathematical properties that make them much more useful in more advanced statistical computations. The logic behind their calculation is quite similar to that of the mean deviation, which is why we have considered the mean deviation here. In calculating the mean deviation it was necessary to take the absolute value of the difference of each score from the mean so that these differences would not sum to zero. Instead of taking the absolute difference, we could have gotten rid of the troublesome negative numbers by squaring the differences. This is exactly what is done in calculating the variance and standard deviation of a distribution.

The *variance* of a distribution is defined as *the sum of the squared deviations from the mean divided by the number of scores*. Or, in other words, each score is taken, subtracted from the mean, and squared; then all these values are summed and divided by the number of scores. The formula for the variance is

$$s^2 = \frac{\Sigma(X - \bar{X})^2}{n} \tag{6-1}$$

where s^2 represents the variance, X the individual scores, $\bar{X}$ the mean, and n the number of scores or observations. The *standard deviation* is simply *the square root of the variance,* and is therefore represented by s. So

$$s = \sqrt{\frac{\Sigma(X - \bar{X})^2}{n}}. \tag{6-2}$$

Calculation of the standard deviations for the control and experimental conditions from the LSD experiment by the mean deviation method is illustrated in Table 6–2.

The formulas for the variance and standard deviation of a distribution given in Equations 6–1 and 6–2 are rather cumbersome, and in practice the equivalent computational formulas given below are used. The standard deviation formula is

$$s = \sqrt{\frac{\Sigma X^2}{n} - \bar{X}^2} \tag{6-3}$$

where ΣX^2 is the sum of the squares of all the scores, X is the mean of the distribution, and n is the number of scores. Similarly, the formula for variance is

$$s^2 = \frac{\Sigma X^2}{n} - \bar{X}^2. \qquad \textbf{(6-4)}$$

The standard deviations for the experimental and control scores are calculated with the computational formula in Table 6–3. Notice that the value in each case is the same as when the definitional formula is used.

In describing an array of data, psychologists typically present two descriptive statistics, the mean and the standard deviation. Although there are other measures of central tendency and dispersion, these are most useful for descriptive purposes. Variance is used extensively, as we shall see, in inferential statistics.

Calculation of the standard deviation, s, for the control and experimental conditions by the mean deviation method.

Table 6–2

	Control group			Experimental group	
X	$(X - \bar{X})$	$(X - \bar{X})^2$	X	$(X - \bar{X})$	$(X - \bar{X})^2$
9	−4.60	21.16	9	−7.90	62.41
10	−3.60	12.96	13	−3.90	15.21
11	−2.60	6.76	13	−3.90	15.21
11	−2.60	6.76	14	−2.90	8.41
12	−1.60	2.56	14	−2.90	8.41
12	−1.60	2.56	15	−1.90	3.61
12	−1.60	2.56	16	− .90	.81
13	− .60	.36	16	− .90	.81
13	− .60	.36	16	− .90	.81
13	− .60	.36	17	+ .10	.01
13	− .60	.36	17	+ .10	.01
14	+ .40	.16	18	+1.10	1.21
14	+ .40	.16	18	+1.10	1.21
14	+ .40	.16	18	+1.10	1.21
15	+1.40	1.96	18	+1.10	1.21
15	+1.40	1.96	19	+2.10	4.41
16	+2.40	5.76	19	+2.10	4.41
17	+3.40	11.56	20	+3.10	9.61
18	+4.40	19.36	22	+5.10	26.01
20	+6.40	40.96	26	+9.10	82.81

$\Sigma X = 272$ Total = 0.00 $\Sigma(X - \bar{X})^2 = 138.80$ $\Sigma X = 338$ Total = 0.00 $\Sigma(X - \bar{X})^2 = 247.80$

$\bar{X} = 13.60$ $\bar{X} = 16.90$

$s = \sqrt{\dfrac{\Sigma(X - \bar{X})^2}{n}}$ $s = \sqrt{\dfrac{\Sigma(X - \bar{X})^2}{n}}$

$s = \sqrt{\dfrac{138.80}{20}}$ $s = \sqrt{\dfrac{247.80}{20}}$

$s = 2.63$ $s = 3.52$

Table 6–3

Calculation of the standard deviation, *s*, for the control and experimental conditions by using the computational formula (also called the raw score method). Notice that the same values are obtained as when the definitional formula is used (see Table 6–2), but that the calculations are much easier to perform.

X	X^2	X	X^2
9	81	9	81
10	100	13	169
11	121	13	169
11	121	14	196
12	144	14	196
12	144	15	225
12	144	16	256
13	169	16	256
13	169	16	256
13	169	17	289
13	169	17	289
14	196	18	324
14	196	18	324
14	196	18	324
15	225	18	324
15	225	19	361
16	256	19	361
17	289	20	400
18	324	22	484
20	400	26	676

$$\Sigma X = 272 \qquad \Sigma X^2 = 3838 \qquad \Sigma X = 338 \qquad \Sigma X^2 = 5960$$

$$\bar{X} = 13.60 \qquad\qquad\qquad\qquad \bar{X} = 16.90$$

$$\bar{X}^2 = 184.96 \qquad\qquad\qquad\qquad \bar{X}^2 = 285.61$$

$$s = \sqrt{\frac{\Sigma X^2}{n} - \bar{X}^2} \qquad\qquad s = \sqrt{\frac{\Sigma X^2}{n} - \bar{X}^2}$$

$$s = \sqrt{\frac{3838}{20} - 184.96} \qquad\qquad s = \sqrt{\frac{5960}{20} - 285.61}$$

$$s = 2.63 \qquad\qquad\qquad\qquad s = 3.52$$

The Normal Distribution

In the histograms in Figure 6–2 (on page 137) representing the running times of the rats in the two conditions of our hypothetical experiment, most of the scores pile up in the center and they tail off towards the ends (or tails) of the distribution, especially for control subjects. Most psychological data tend to look like this when represented graphically. When they are graphed, psychological data often approximate the *normal curve* or *standard normal distribution,* where scores are most numerous in the middle, decline in frequency with distance from the middle, and do so in a symmetrical way. A score 10 points above the middle is about as common as a score 10 points below it. Several examples of normal curves are pictured in Figure 6–3, where some characteristics of all normal curves may be noted. First note that in all three distributions the

Figure 6–3

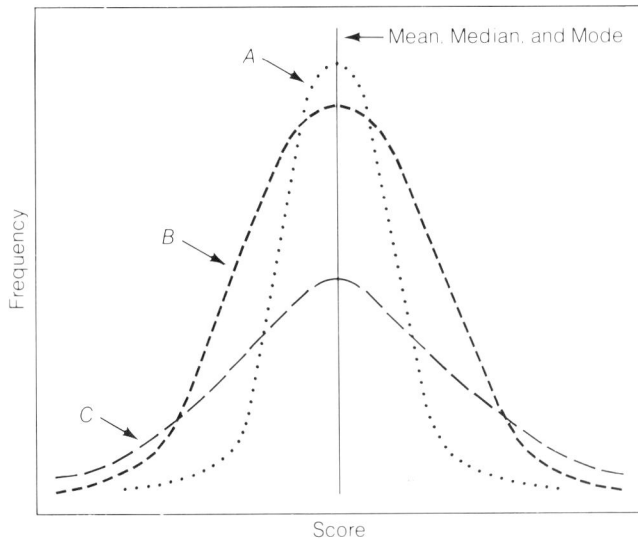

Three examples of the normal curve that differ in variability. (C) has the greatest variability and (A) the least. The normal curve is a symmetrical distribution in which the mean, median, and mode all have the same value.

mean, median, and mode fall on top of one another. The main difference in the distributions is in their variability. The tall, thin curve in A has a smaller variance (and, of course, standard deviation) than the other two, while the flat, broad curve C has a larger variance than the others. All three curves, though, are normal curves.

Notice that on each side of the normal curve there is a point where the curve slightly reverses its direction; it starts bending outward more. This is called the *inflection point* and is labeled in the normal curve in Figure 6–4. The inflection point in the curve is always one standard deviation from the mean. In fact, the normal curve has the useful property that specific proportions of the distribution of scores it represents are contained within specific areas of the curve itself. About 68 percent of all scores are contained within one standard deviation of the mean (34 percent on each side). Similarly, almost 96 percent of the scores are contained within two standard deviations of the mean, and 99.74 percent of the scores are within three standard deviations. The percentage in each area is shown in Figure 6–4. This is true of all normal curves, no matter how sharp or flat they are.

This property of normal curves is extremely useful because if we know an individual's score and the mean and standard deviation in the distribution of scores, we also know the person's relative rank. For example, most I.Q. tests are devised so that the population mean is 100 and the standard deviation is 15. If a person has an I.Q. of 115, we know that he or she scored higher than 84 percent of all people on the test (50 percent of the people below the mean and 34 percent above). Similarly, a person with an I.Q. of 130 scored higher than almost 98 percent of all people, while an I.Q. of 145 is greater than those of 99.87 percent of the population. See if you can arrive at these percentages by adding up the appropriate areas in Figure 6–4.

Figure 6–4

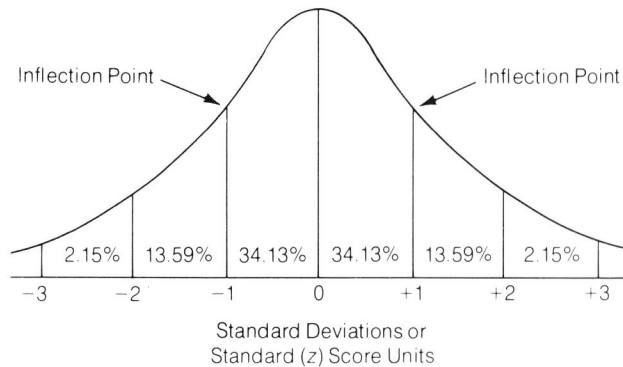

Proportions of scores in specific areas under the normal curve. The inflection points are one standard deviation from the mean.

Most distributions of scores in psychological data are, or at least are assumed to be, normal. (Often with small samples, as in our hypothetical data in Figure 6–2, it is difficult to tell whether or not the distribution is normal.) It is commonplace to compare scores across normal distributions with different means and variances in terms of *standard scores* or *z scores*. This is simply the difference between an individual score and the mean expressed in units of standard deviations. So an I.Q. of 115 translates to a z score of 1.00, that is, [115 – 100]/15, while an I.Q. of 78 translates to a z score of – 1.47, that is, [78 – 100]/15. Standard scores are useful since they allow comparison of the relative ranks of scores for a person across distributions in which the means and standard deviations vary greatly. Grades in courses should be calculated in terms of z scores if the means and standard deviations of the scores vary widely from one test to the next. Thus a person's eventual rank in the class is calculated more faithfully by finding the mean of the z scores than the mean of the raw scores of the tests.

When it is said that data in some experiment or other are *normally distributed* it means that, if they were graphed, they would form a normal distribution as in Figure 6–4. Thus normal, as it is used in psychological research, usually refers to a type of distribution and not a value judgment as to the goodness or badness of the scores. (There are various sorts of other distributions besides normal ones, but we cannot tarry here to consider some of the other more prevalent types.)

The Correlation Coefficient

As we saw in Chapter 2, psychologists are particularly interested in how two variables are related to one another. The use of correlational techniques, you will remember, permits us to see how two variables co-vary, or correlate. Now we will consider some statistical procedures that will allow us to specify the degree to which two things vary.

There are actually several different types of correlation coefficient, and which is used depends on the characteristics of the variables being correlated. However, as an example of calculation of a correlation coefficient, we shall consider one commonly used by psychologists, *Pearson's product-moment correlation coefficient,* or Pearson r. You should remember that this is only one of several and if you actually need to compute a correlation on some data, you should consult a statistics text to determine which is appropriate for your particular case.

Let us imagine that we are one of the bevy of psychologists who devote their careers to the study of human memory. One of these psychologists hits upon a simple, intuitive idea concerning head size and memory, which goes like this. Information from the outside world enters the head through the senses and is stored there. An analogy can be made between the head (where information is stored) and other physical vessels, such as boxes, where all kinds of things can be stored. On the basis of such analogical reasoning, which is common in science, one can make the following prediction about the properties of physical containers: as head size of a person increases, so should the person's memory. More things can be stored in bigger boxes than smaller, and similarly more information should be stored in larger heads than smaller ones.

This "theory" proposes a simple relationship, that as head size increases so should memory. A positive correlation between these two variables is predicted. A random sample of the population could be taken and the persons chosen could be measured on two dimensions, head size and how many words they can recall from a list of 30 presented to them once at the rate of one word every three seconds. Three hypothetical sets of results from ten subjects are presented in Table 6–4. Notice that for each individual there are two measures, one of head size and the other of number of words recalled. Also notice that the two types of measures need not be similar in any way to be correlated. They do not have to be on the same scale. Just as one can correlate head size with number of words recalled, one could also correlate I.Q. with street address number, or any two sets of numbers at all. Box 6–1 provides an example of how Pearson r is actually computed. (You need not work through this example to understand the rest of the discussion of correlation.)

Box 6–1

Computing Pearson r

Let us call one set of numbers in Table 6–5 X scores and the other set Y scores. For example, head sizes might be X scores and words recalled Y scores. The formula for computing Pearson r from the raw scores in panels (a), (b), or (c) is as follows:

$$r = \frac{n \, \Sigma XY - (\Sigma X)(\Sigma Y)}{\sqrt{[n \, \Sigma X^2 - (\Sigma X)^2][n \, \Sigma Y^2 - (\Sigma Y)^2]}} \qquad (6\text{–}5)$$

Then n refers to the number of subjects on which observations are taken (ten here); the terms ΣX and ΣY are the totals of the X and Y scores, respectively; ΣX^2 and ΣY^2 are the sum of all the X (or Y) values after each is squared; and the $(\Sigma X)^2$ and $(\Sigma Y)^2$ are the total of all the X or Y values with the entire total or sum squared. This

---

Table 6–4

Three hypothetical examples of data taken on head size and recall representing (a) a positive correlation, (b) a low (near zero) correlation, and (c) a negative correlation.

	(a)			(b)			(c)	
Subject	Head size (cm.)	Recall (words)	Subject	Head size (cm.)	Recall (words)	Subject	Head size (cm.)	Recall (words)
1	50.8	17	1	50.8	23	1	50.8	12
2	63.5	21	2	63.5	12	2	63.5	9
3	45.7	16	3	45.7	13	3	45.7	13
4	25.4	11	4	25.4	21	4	25.4	23
5	29.2	9	5	29.2	9	5	29.2	21
6	49.5	15	6	49.5	14	6	49.5	16
7	38.1	13	7	38.1	16	7	38.1	14
8	30.5	12	8	30.5	15	8	30.5	17
9	35.6	14	9	35.6	11	9	35.6	15
10	58.4	23	10	58.4	16	10	58.4	11

$r = +.93 \qquad\qquad\qquad r = -.07 \qquad\qquad\qquad r = -.89$

Calculation of Pearson r for the data in the first (a) column of Table 6–4 by the raw score formula (Equation 6–5)

Table 6–5

Subject number	X Head size (cm.)	X^2	Y Words re-called	Y^2	$X \cdot Y$
1	50.8	2580.64	17	289	863.60
2	63.5	4032.25	21	441	1330.50
3	45.7	2088.49	16	256	731.20
4	25.4	645.16	11	121	279.40
5	29.2	852.64	9	81	262.80
6	49.5	2450.25	15	225	742.50
7	38.1	1451.61	13	169	495.30
8	30.5	930.25	12	144	366.00
9	35.6	1267.36	14	196	498.40
10	58.4	3410.56	23	529	1343.20

$n = 10 \quad \sum X = 426.70 \quad \sum X^2 = 19{,}709.21 \quad \sum Y = 151 \quad \sum Y^2 = 2451 \quad \sum XY = 6915.90$

$$r = \frac{n \sum XY - (\sum X)(\sum Y)}{\sqrt{[n \sum X^2 - (\sum X)^2][n \sum Y^2 - (\sum Y)^2]}}$$

$$r = \frac{10(6915.90) - (426.70)(151)}{\sqrt{[(10)(19{,}709.21) - (426.70)^2][(10)(2451) - (151)^2]}}$$

$$r = \frac{69{,}159.00 - 64{,}431.70}{\sqrt{[197{,}092.10 - 182{,}072.89][24{,}510 - 22{,}801]}}$$

$$r = \frac{4727.30}{\sqrt{[15{,}019.21][1709]}} = \frac{4727.30}{\sqrt{25{,}667{,}829.89}}$$

$$r = \frac{4727.30}{5066.34}$$

$$r = +.93$$

leaves the value ΣXY, or the sum of the cross products. This is obtained very simply by multiplying each X-value by its corresponding Y and then summing these products. You may see other formulas for calculation of Pearson r besides the raw score formula in equation 6–5, but these will be equivalent (in general) to the one presented here. An illustration of how Pearson r is calculated using this raw score formula is presented in Table 6–5 using the data from the (a) column of Table 6–4. You should try to work out the values for Pearson r for the (b) and (c) panels yourself to make certain you understand how to calculate the values and to gain an intuitive feel for the concept of correlation. The values of r are given below the appropriate columns in Table 6–4.

Scatter Diagrams

In order to give you a better idea of the graphical representation of correlations, the data in the three panels of Table 6–4 are presented in the three panels of Figure 6–5, where head size is plotted along the horizontal X-axis (the abscissa) and number of words recalled is plotted along the vertical Y-axis (the ordinate). Such graphs are usually called *scatter diagrams* because they show how two sets of scores scatter when plotted against each other. Notice that the high positive correlation between head size and number of words recalled in the (a) panel in Table 6–4 is translated into a visual representation that tilts upward to the right, while the negative correlation in panel (c) is depicted as sloping downward to the right. Thus you can see how knowing a person's score on one variable helps predict (though not perfectly in these cases) the level of performance on the other. So knowing a person's head size in the hypothetical data in the (a) and (c) panels helps predict recall, and vice versa. This is the primary reason correlations are useful: they specify the amount of relationship and allow predictions to be made. Notice that this last statement cannot be made about the data in panel (b) where there is essentially a zero correlation. The points are just scattered about and there is no consistent relationship, which is just what a low Pearson r reflects. Even in the cases where the size of the correlation is rather large, it should be noted that it will not be possible to predict perfectly an individual's score on one variable given his or her

Figure 6–5

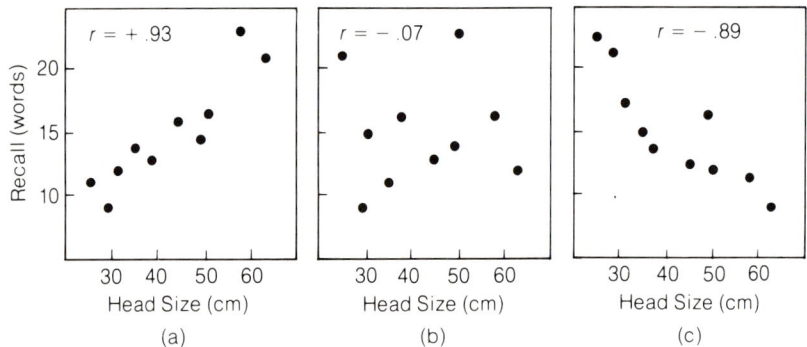

Graphical representation of the data in Table 6–4 showing the characteristic pattern of (a) a high positive correlation, (b) an essentially zero correlation, and (c) a strong negative correlation.

position on the other. Even with $r = +.75$ between head size and number of words recalled, it is still quite possible for a person with a large head size to recall few words and vice versa. Unless the correlation is perfect ($+1.00$ or -1.00), prediction of one score when given the other will not be perfect, either.

What do you think the real correlation would be between head size and recall of a random sample of the population at large? Although we have not actually done such a study, we think it quite likely that it would be rather large and positive (perhaps $+.60$ to $+.70$), in support of our theory of memory storage based on head size. (You will see why we think this below.) What can we conclude from this? How can correlation coefficients be interpreted? We turn to this issue next.

Interpreting Correlation Coefficients

An important warning is always given in any discussion of correlation: The existence of even a sizable correlation implies nothing about the existence of a causal relationship between the two variables under consideration. On the basis of just a correlation, one cannot say whether Factor X causes Factor Y, Factor Y causes Factor X, some underlying third factor causes both, or the two are completely unrelated. Let us consider some examples. Suppose we have found a correlation of $+.70$ between head size and recall of words. This is in general agreement with our theory that larger heads hold more information, but certainly there are other interpretations of this relationship. In particular it could be argued that the high positive correlation between head size and recall is *mediated* or produced by some third factor underlying both, such as age. We know that people's heads grow as they age and that recall also improves with age. Therefore age (or one of its correlates) might actually be responsible for the large positive correlation we have found between head size and number of words recalled.

In correlational studies we cannot conclude that any one factor produced or caused another since there are likely to have been a number of factors which varied simultaneously with those of interest. In an experiment one attempts to avoid this problem by directly manipulating one factor while holding all the others constant. Then the influence of the manipulated factor on whatever it is we are measuring can be directly attributed to the factor of interest. When two factors (or more) are varied at the same time so that we cannot know whether one factor, the other factor, or both operating together produce some effect, we say that the factors are confounded. *Confounding* is inherent in correlational research and leads to the interpretational difficulties with such research. In the example of the correlation between head size and recall we cannot say that variations in head size produced or caused differences in recall since head size was confounded with at least one other factor, age. We have relied just on the Method of Agreement (Chapter 5), and we have not produced a comparison by the Method of Differences.

In other cases the relationship between two factors may seem to allow a causal interpretation, but again this is not strictly permitted. Some studies have shown a positive correlation between the number of handguns in a geographic area and the number of murders in that area. Proponents of gun control might use this evidence to support the contention that an increased number of guns leads to (causes, produces) more murders, but again this is not the only plausible interpretation. It may be that people in high crime neighborhoods buy handguns to protect themselves. Or that some third factor, such as socioeconomic class, actually mediates both. So no conclusion is justified simply on the basis of a moderate or even high correlation.

Since correlations can be calculated between any two sets of scores, it is apparent that often even very high correlations are accidental and not linked to one another at all. Since 1950 there may be a very high correlation between the number of preachers and the number of pornographic movies produced each year, with both being on the increase. But it would take an unusual theory to relate these two in a causal manner.

A high degree of correlation is given greater weight in cases where obvious competing explanations (from confounding factors) seem less plausible. We have already mentioned that most of the early evidence linking cigarette smoking to lung cancer was correlational, yet the conclusion was drawn (over the protests of the cigarette manufacturers) by the 1964 Surgeon General's report that cigarettes were likely to lead to or cause cancer. This eventually led to warnings on cigarette packages and a ban of advertising for cigarettes on television, among other things. So the correlation was taken as indicative of a causative relationship, probably because competing hypotheses seemed implausible. It seems unlikely, for example, that having lung cancer causes one to smoke more cigarettes (to soothe the lungs?). More plausible, perhaps, is that some underlying third factor (such as anxiety) produces the relationship or that it is accidental. We should mention, by the way, that the link between cigarette smoking and lung cancer has now been established by experimental studies with nonhuman animals, typically beagles.

As a final example of the pitfalls of the correlational approach, consider the negative relationship mentioned previously between cigarette smoking and grades (Chapter 2). More smoking has been related to poorer grades. But does smoking cause poorer grades? It seems unlikely, and certainly there are ready alternative interpretations. Students with poor grades may be more anxious and thus smoke more. Or more sociable students may smoke more and study less, and so on. Once again, no firm conclusions on the causal direction of a relationship between two variables can be established simply because the variables are correlated, even if the correlation is perfect. Like the observational method, the correlational method is very useful for suggesting possible relationships and directing further inquiry, but it is not useful for establishing direct causal relationships. The correlational method is superior to the observational method because the degree of relation between two variables can be precisely stated and thus predictions can be made about the (approximate) value of one variable if the value of the other is known. Once again, the greater the correlation (nearer +1.00 or −1.00), the better is the prediction.

Low Correlations: A Caution

If high correlations cannot be interpreted as evidence for some sort of causal relationship, one might think it should at least be possible to rule out a causative relationship between two variables if their correlation is very low, approaching zero. If the correlation between head size and recall had been −.02, would this have ruled out our theory that greater head size leads to better recall? Or if the correlation between smoking and lung cancer had been +.08, should we have abandoned the idea that they are causally related? The answer: sometimes, under certain conditions. But other factors can cause low or zero correlations and may mask an actual relationship.

One common problem is that of *truncated range.* In order to calculate a meaningful correlation coefficient, there must be rather great differences among the scores in each of the variables of interest; there must be a certain amount of spread or variability in the numbers. If all the head sizes were the same in the panels of Table 6–4 while the recall scores varied, the correlation between the two would be zero. Work it out yourself. If we only looked at the correlation between head size and recall in college students, it might be quite low because the differences in head size and recall among college students may not be very great compared with the population at large. This could happen even though there might be a positive (or negative) correlation between the two variables if head size were sampled over a wider range. So the problem of restricted range can produce a low correlation even when there is an actual correlation present between two variables.

You might think that everyone would recognize this problem and avoid it, but it is often more subtle. Consider the problem of trying to predict success in college from Scholastic Aptitude Test scores at a school with very high admission standards. The scores on the verbal and quantitative subtests can range from 200 to 800, with average (mean) performance of just below 500. Imagine that mean scores at our hypothetical college are 700 on each subtest. The admissions officer at this college computes a correlation between combined SAT scores and freshman grades and finds it to be +.10, very small indeed. Her conclusion: SAT scores cannot be used to predict grades in college. The problem, however, is that the only scores considered were ones from a very restricted range, specifically very high ones. People with low scores were not admitted to the college. So the truncated range problem is very likely to be a factor here. If the college had randomly admitted people and then after the fact the correlation had been determined between SAT scores and grades it might have been much higher. Since psychologists often use homogeneous populations such as college students, the restricted range problem must be carefully considered in interpreting correlations.

A final problem in interpreting low correlations is that one must be certain that the assumptions underlying the use of a particular correlation coefficient have been met. Otherwise its use may well be inappropriate and lead to spuriously low estimates of relationship. These have not been discussed here, but we have said to check on these assumptions in a statistics book before employing Pearson r or any other correlation coefficient. For example, one assumption underlying Pearson r is that

Figure 6–6

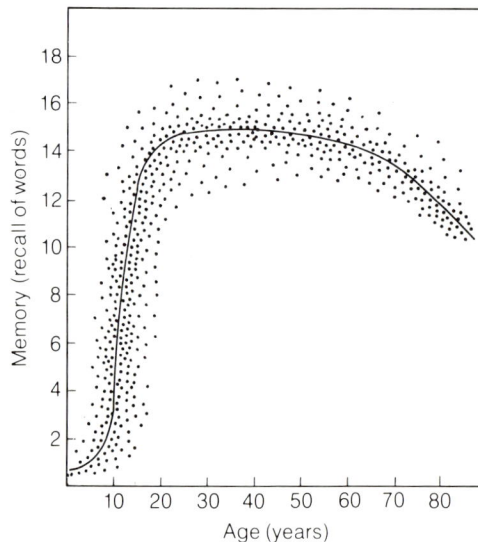

A hypothetical figure depicting a curvilinear relationship between memory and age. Although memory is related to age in a systematic fashion and one could predict recall by knowing age, Pearson r would be quite low since the relationship is not linear.

the relationship between the two variables is linear (can be described by a straight line) rather than curvilinear as in the hypothetical (but plausible) relationship in Figure 6–6 between age and long-term memory. At very young ages the line is flat, then it increases between ages 3 and 16, where it again levels off until late middle age, where it drops slightly, until very old age, where it decreases at a greater rate (Craik, 1977). Thus one can predict recall of words from age fairly well, but Pearson r will be rather low since the relationship is not linear between the two variables. This could of course, always be checked by plotting a scatter diagram as in Figure 6–5 or Figure 6–6. Low correlations, then, may not reflect an absence of relationship, but only that the assumptions of the particular coefficient employed were not met.

Exercises

1. One good way to summarize this chapter is to have you calculate some important descriptive statistics. Calculate the median, mean, and standard deviation for the following individual reaction times (in seconds) from a study in which subjects were asked to generate images in their minds to common English nouns: 1.10, 1.38, 1.44, 1.06, 0.93, 1.80, 1.10, 0.97, 1.56, 1.33, 1.51, 1.03.

2. In the table below are some fictitious data from a college's admissions office. For ten students we have the scores from the verbal portion of their Scholastic Aptitude Test (SAT) as well as their freshman grade point average (GPA). The GPA is on a four-point scale where $F = O$, $D = 1$, $C = 2$, $B = 3$, and $A = 4$. Calculate the correlation coefficient between these two sets of scores. What might you conclude?

Study and Review

Student	Verbal SAT	Freshman GPA
1	471	2.00
2	403	1.50
3	510	2.25
4	485	2.00
5	575	2.25
6	445	1.75
7	400	2.50
8	590	3.25
9	560	2.50
10	555	2.75

Key Concepts

central tendency 135	variance 138
dispersion 136	normal curve 142
histogram 136	inflection point 143
frequency polygon 136	standard scores (z scores) 144
frequency distributions 136	product-moment correlation
mean 136	coefficient 145
median 137	Pearson r 145
mode 138	scatter diagrams 148
range 138	confounding 149
standard deviation 138	truncated range 151

Suggested Reading

An excellent statistics text that includes details of descriptive statistics and correlation is: Thompson, J. B. and Buchanan, W. *Analyzing psychological data.* New York: Charles Scribner's Sons, 1979.

INCREASING INTERNAL VALIDITY IN THE ABSENCE OF DIRECT CONTROL

How does one try to make valid causal statements in . . .

Correlational Research

Use *cross-lagged panel correlation procedure:* examine patterns of correlations over time to aid in determining the direction of causality

---

Quasi-experimental Research

Case Studies:

Use *deviant case analysis* (a nonequivalent control "group"); examine several dependent variables

---

Interrupted Time Series:

Use *nonequivalent control group;* study several dependent variables; search for additional natural treatments

---

Subject Variables:

Use matching on potentially relevant characteristics; beware of regression artifacts

---

Developmental Research (Age):

Use *cross-sequential design* to minimize generation and time-of-test confoundings; include *true independent variable* and look for interactions

Correlational and
Quasi-Experimental Research

7

In this chapter we consider situations in which the researcher plays a less active role than in the typical laboratory experiment. Most correlational research and field experimentation, especially those field studies that use subject variables, are ex post facto in nature. This means that the researcher does not control all the relevant variables, rather the "manipulations" occur naturally or before the researcher has a chance to investigate the problem. Ex post facto research often poses difficult control and interpretive problems, many of which are examined in this chapter.

Overview

**Control
in Scientific
Research**

Discovering why people think and act as they do usually requires an analytic breakdown of that question into manageable units. In a properly conducted experiment, the situation is controlled so that changes in dependent variables result solely from changes in the independent variables. Another way of describing the value of an experiment is that, in the ideal case, it is *internally valid* (for example, Cook and Campbell, 1979). A study that is internally valid allows straightforward causal statements to be made about the outcome. Thus, by means of control (the Method of Differences) the researcher rules out inadvertent confounding, and the results reflect the effects of the intended variables. As discussed in Chapter 5, Graessle et al. (1978) were able to assert that mild decompressions caused decrements in the growth and behavior of rats. They designed the experiment to maximize the effect of their independent variable, prenatal decompressions, and minimize the effects of extraneous variables. This means that their research was internally valid.

A single laboratory experiment may not be *externally valid*. Externally valid research has generality, so it should be representative of the real world and not distort the question under investigation. By their very nature, laboratory experiments are artificial, which means that the setting, subjects, and variables may be unrepresentative. We may have to conduct several interrelated experiments to converge on a generalizable explanation. Graessle et al. studied rats in a compression chamber;

157

they did not study pregnant humans in airplanes. On the basis of their research, we cannot state that they arrived at an externally valid conclusion with regard to the effects of air travel on human development.

In contrast to laboratory experiments, most ex post facto research is likely to be externally valid but may not be internally valid. Correlating TV preferences with later aggression focuses upon reasonable aspects of human behavior—"real" behaviors in "real" situations are studied. However, without special techniques we may not be able to conclude that TV preferences cause later aggression. This means that we cannot make any conclusions about the effects of TV even if it is an interesting variable. We will examine some of the threats to internal validity in ex post facto research and some ways to minimize those threats.

Internal Validity in Correlational Research

Does watching violent TV programs cause aggressive behavior? Eron et al. (1972) measured children's preference for violent programs and how aggressive the children were as rated by their peers. For these third graders, Eron et al. found a moderate positive correlation, $r = +.21$, indicating that more aggressive children tended to watch more violent TV (and less aggressive children tended to watch less violent programs). How are we to interpret this positive correlation? Can we say that watching violent programs causes aggressiveness? The answer is "no," and to see why this is the case, all we have to do is turn our causal statement around and assert that being aggressive causes a preference for violent TV. Based on this one correlation coefficient, we have no reasonable way to decide upon the direction of causality. In other words, we are hard put to have an internally valid causal statement that is based on a single correlation.

When we do not know the direction of causality (violent TV causes aggression versus aggressive traits cause a preference for violent programs), there is the strong possibility that some *third*, confounded variable is the cause of the obtained relation. Since the researchers did not control either the programs watched or the initial aggressiveness, they cannot rule out other variables, such as genetic differences in aggressiveness or differences in home life. It is difficult if not impossible to make internally valid causal statements on the basis of a single correlation coefficient.

The internal validity of correlational research can be enhanced by examining patterns of correlations over time. This technique is called the *cross-lagged panel correlation procedure*, and it was used with effectiveness by Eron et al. They conducted a ten-year follow-up study of the same children in the "thirteenth" grade and the results are summarized in Figure 7–1. The correlation between a preference for violent TV and aggression was essentially zero ($r = -.05$) in the thirteenth grade. Similarly, the relation between preference for violent TV in the third and thirteenth grade was negligible ($r = +.05$), but there was a moderate relation between aggressiveness in the two grades ($r = +.38$), indicating that it is a somewhat stable trait. Of more interest are the cross-lagged correlations (the ones along the diagonals of the figure) in assessing the direction of the relation. Do aggressive people watch violent TV, or does watching violent TV produce aggressiveness? We can determine which of these two possibilities holds true by examining the diagonal correlations. There is essentially no relationship between aggressiveness in the third grade and watching violent TV in the thirteenth ($r = +.01$). However, there is a fairly substantial correlation between a preference for watching violent TV in the third grade and aggressiveness in the thirteenth ($r = +.31$). In fact, the relationship is even greater than between these two variables in the third grade. Thus the direction of relationship seems to be that watching violent TV programs in the third grade may produce aggressiveness later. The underlying assumption is that if one variable causes the other, measurement of the first variable (watching violent TV programs) at one point in time should be more strongly related to the second variable (aggressiveness) at a later point in time than when the second (effect) variable is measured at the same time as the first (cause). That is, causes should take some time to produce their effects. (See Figure 7–1.)

Figure 7–1

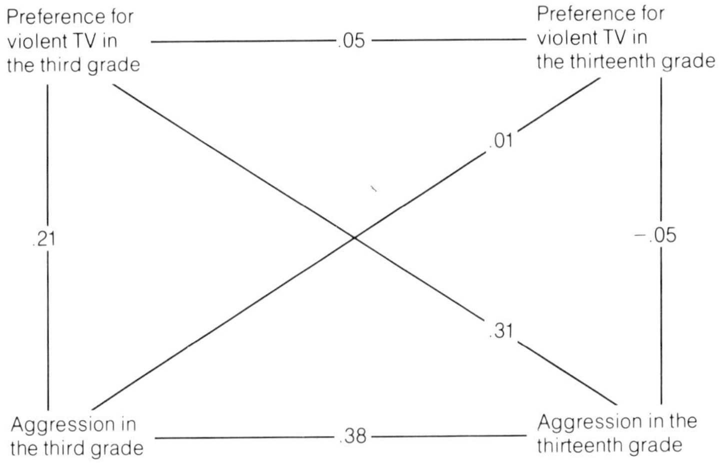

Correlations between a preference for violent television programs and aggression as rated by peers for 211 males over a 10-year period. The important cross-lagged correlations are on the diagonals (after Eron, Huesman, Lefkowitz, and Walder, 1972).

Using these cross-lagged panel correlations and other complex analyses, Eron et al. concluded that watching violent TV programs early in life probably causes, in part, aggressive behavior later in life. Of course, there are many other factors contributing to aggressiveness, but this is an excellent example of how cross-lagged panel correlations can contribute to determining cause and effect relations. You should note that our causal statements cannot be as strong as those from experiments because the Method of Differences was not used.

The general strategy of the cross-lagged procedure, then, is to obtain several correlations over time, and then, on the basis of the size and direction of the *r*s, determine what leads to what. The cross-lagged technique is fairly new to psychological research and has the obvious drawback that the research project may be very time-consuming. Nevertheless, this method for enhancing the internal validity of correlational research has been used effectively in several problem areas, such as showing that a large vocabulary enhances spelling more than vice versa and that air pollution is an important cause of the death rate in large cities rather than mortality causing pollution (Cook and Campbell, 1979, Chapter 7).

In addition to cross-lagged panel correlations, there are several other statistical procedures used to gain a better understanding of causation in correlational research. Some of these include *partial correlation*, *multiple regression analysis*, and *path analysis*. As is true of the cross-lagged procedure, these other techniques involve an examination of several relationships and not just a single correlation. These are described in numerous statistical texts (see especially Cook and Campbell, 1979) and, since this is not a book concerned primarily with statistical techniques, we shall only note their existence here as an aid to interpreting correlational research. As a general rule you should remember that internal validity is always suspect in correlational research because of possible third variable confounding. Causal statements should not be made on the basis of a single correlation, but on a pattern of correlations that permits one greater confidence in ruling out alternative causes of the observed relations.

Internal Validity in Quasi-experiments

The phrase *quasi-experiment* refers to those experimental situations in which the experimenter does not directly manipulate variables as in a typical laboratory experiment. In a quasi-experiment some or all of the variables are ex post facto, which means that they are not under direct control of the experimenter. Either the effects of natural "treatments" (such as disasters) are observed or particular subject variables (such as age, sex, weight) may be of interest. In either case, we must be wary of internal validity, because the experimenter does not manipulate the variables. That is, the Method of Differences is not under direct control. In Chapter 2 we noted that quasi-experiments have the advantage of being intrinsically interesting, and they also allow the examination of variables that would be unethical to manipulate directly. Here we consider the pitfalls of quasi-experiments and how to minimize those problems.

Natural Treatments

Ex post facto analyses of the effects of some naturally occurring event, such as a disaster or a change in school curricula, are usually interesting and important, but are often difficult to interpret in a causal fashion. Most quasi-experiments involving naturally occurring treatments have a structure that is similar to the small-n experiments (ABA) discussed in Chapter 5. We might, for example, have records of third-grade achievement before and after (the A phases) the introduction of a new method for teaching reading (the B phase). Note carefully: this example does not comprise a true reversal design, because there is not a removal of the treatment to allow a return to the original baseline. In fact, most quasi-experiments of the general form *observation*, *treatment*, *observation* cannot be true reversal designs for two reasons: (1) the treatment is not, of course, under the experimenter's control; and (2) most natural treatments, such as curriculum revision, are likely to have long-term carry-over effects. Not only must we be concerned with carry-over effects, but we must also worry about the changes in the subjects themselves. If we examine the effects of a new reading program on third-grade achievement, one thing that is confounded with the introduction of our treatment is a change in the age of our subjects. While age itself does not cause anything (see below), many important changes correlate with age: more experience in school, better test taking, improved linguistic skills, better social adjustment, biological maturation, and the like.

Thus, two particular threats to internal validity with naturally occurring treatments are the history of the subject and any changes in the subject that occur over time. Either or both of these factors could vary directly, inversely, or not at all with the intended treatment. Ways to minimize these difficulties (for example matching) generally involve more active participation on the part of the experimenter. One thing we could do in our ex post facto analysis of the effects of reading techniques is to find a control third-grade class that did not have this new technique imposed upon them. So, we might end up with a quasi-experimental design similar to the one shown in Table 7–1. This looks like an ordinary experimental design, but remember—we have no direct control over the situation, and, as we shall see below, by adding a matched control group we have incurred additional threats to internal validity. This type of design is sometimes called a *nonequivalent control group* design because

Table 7-1	A Hypothetical Quasi-Experimental Design for Examining Curricula Changes on Third-Grade Achievement Scores

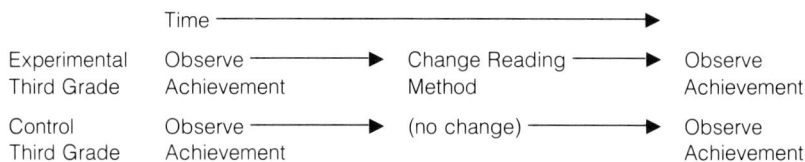

Time ──────────────────────────────────────▶

Experimental Third Grade	Observe ────────▶ Achievement	Change Reading ────────▶ Method	Observe Achievement
Control Third Grade	Observe ────────▶ Achievement	(no change) ────────────▶	Observe Achievement

Note. The two third-grade classes are assumed to be highly similar, differing only on the imposed curriculum change. There was not random assignment to the two groups, and usually the control group is determined ex post facto. Thus, this design includes a *nonequivalent control group*.

random assignment to conditions is not used, and matching is attempted after the fact.

We will now consider two quasi-experimental designs that appear in the psychological literature on some topics: the one-shot case study and the interrupted time series design.

One-Shot Case Studies

We can view the one-shot case study in the following way: we have a long-term treatment on an individual and after the fact we obtain some measurements of that individual's thought and action. If we use the same notation that we used for the reversal design, we can call this an AB design (where A is the history and B stands for current behavior). "Treatments" occur and then we observe their effects. Note, the "treatments" don't allow baseline observations. Viewing the one-shot case study as an AB design immediately points to the threat on internal validity—there is no baseline or control condition. As noted in Chapter 2, the *deviant case analysis* is one way to obtain a "control" group in case study research. We take an individual as similar as possible to our case except for a crucial missing treatment (a drunkard for a father, a disabling illness, and so forth) and determine how the individuals deviate from each other. The similar individual is a nonequivalent control, not a true control.

In a sense, therefore, interpretation of a case history is similar to detective work. The typical case study involves a large number of dependent variables. Thus, the researcher who wishes to make causal statements on the basis of a case study has to look for important clues and then interpret the meaning of those clues in the context of all the other observations. In the case of Ruth L., who had the severe washing compulsion, it is possible that her early experience with extremely fussy governesses and a desire to please her mother by being very neat and clean combined to make her anxious in the presence of dirt as an adult.

You should be careful in how you interpret the above discussion. As a laboratory research design, the one-shot case study with only one or two dependent variables would be sloppy and internally invalid. However, in the typical case study, where a great deal of information is available, causal "detective" work is often more reasonable and more likely to lead to internally valid conclusions. The researcher gains control by increasing the number and complexity of the observations. If you remember that case studies involve retrospective reports, which means that the life history "facts" may be forgotten or distorted, then a cautious investigator might tentatively accept the reports as internally valid.

Interrupted Time Series Design

The *interrupted time series design* is often encountered in quasi-experimental research, and it represents the logical extension of the general *observation*, *treatment*, *observation* design (see Table 7–1). In the simplest time series design, we have a single experimental group for which we have multiple observations before and after a naturally occurring treatment. Instead of examining just one or two third-grade classes, we could observe third-grade classes in a school system over several years. Or we could follow the achievement of the pupils across their entire school career. What we need to know is when the time series is interrupted by some treatment. Then we compare observations before and after the treatment to see if it had any effect. Suppose we had records of public school achievement for a city that added fluoride to its water one year. In this instance we would plot achievement against time and look for changes in achievement subsequent to fluoridation.

Such a hypothetical time series analysis is shown in Figure 7–2. What we look for in a time series analysis are changes following interruption by the treatment. In the hypothetical example you will note that there is a rather dramatic increase in achievement following the introduction of fluoride. Can we assert that fluoride causes better achievement? No, and the answer is no for the same reason that we have difficulty in interpreting a single correlation coefficient. It is possible that fluoride had an indirect effect, which means that some confounding factor is the principal cause. Perhaps fluoride reduced absenteeism for the purposes of dental work, and it was the reduced absences that permitted higher achievement. The possibility of such indirect effects makes it difficult to arrive at internally valid conclusions.

In the present example we could examine the absence rate before and after the introduction of fluoride. This could be done by plotting absence rate over time as well as achievement. Alternatively we could try to find a control group that was similar to our experimental group but was untreated with fluoride. Finding a satisfactory control group

Figure 7–2

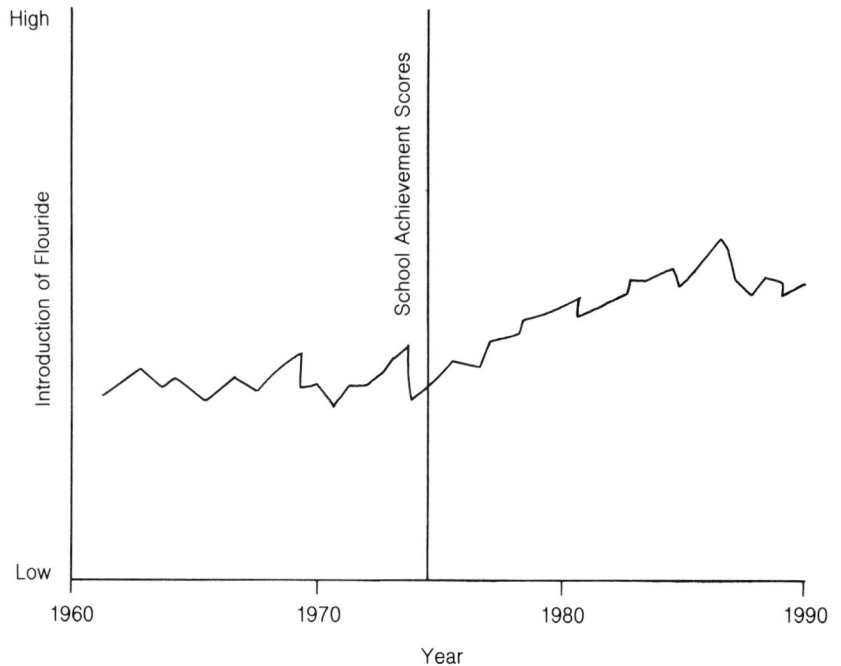

An hypothetical example of a time series analysis of the effects of flouride on school achievement scores.

might be difficult (imagine trying to find a town that differed from yours on only one dimension). Furthermore, using such a control group would leave us open to the problems of matching (see below). Of course, any control group we did use would have to have an absence rate similar to that of the experimental group, but it would still be nonequivalent because random assignment was not used.

While a no-treatment control group is often desirable, there are other things to look for in a time series analysis that may be helpful (back to the detective's clues). Not only can we use multiple dependent variables, such as absenteeism and the number of extracurricular activities, we can also examine other treatments in much the same way that a case study is combed for additional hints. Since time series often involve a long time period, the researcher has to rely on the availability of complete and accurate records. In our example we would need to have detailed records of every student, the administration, and the faculty in order to make internally valid statements. Without these records we could not rule out plausible alternative explanations.

Even with the records, there may be difficulties. The innumerable other changes that can take place mean that confounding is always a threat to internal validity. Over a 30-year period performance in school could change for several reasons, and these natural treatments could operate independently or they could interact. Teachers and administrators change, the curriculum changes, pupils graduate or move away, there may be economic changes, and so on.

The above difficulties of the interrupted time series design are magnified when the effect of the treatment is delayed or masked by other variables (Cook and Campbell, 1979). The effects of fluoride are unlikely to be immediate. Cavities take time to develop, and fluoride does not eliminate cavities once they have taken hold. Thus, the effects of fluoride might be delayed, and we would not be in a position to interpret what caused the changes in achievement. Furthermore, the effects of fluoride could be masked by the intrusion of some variable that counteracts its effects, such as a bubble gum factory moving to town.

These cautions notwithstanding, the interrupted time series design is very useful, especially in applied research. A good example of a recent time series analysis is a study by McSweeny (1978) who showed that the introduction of a small charge for directory assistance (the "information" operator) dramatically reduced the number of directory assistance calls. Since most such calls were for numbers and addresses that were widely published, the telephone company wanted to eliminate these nonessential calls in order to keep the lines open for essential assistance. The number of daily calls in Cincinnati dropped by about 70,000 following the introduction of the 20-cent fee, showing that the strategy was an effective one.

Designs Employing Subject Variables

Much research in psychology is concerned with differences among classes of people in the way they behave. A *subject variable* is some characteristic of people that can be measured. Examples are numerous and include intelligence (I.Q.), weight, anxiety, sex, age, need for achievement, attractiveness, race, ability to recall dreams, as well as many types of pathological conditions (schizophrenia, alcoholism, and so on). Subject variables are often used in psychological research, but their use demands special consideration since their investigation is after the fact. Thus designs employing subject variables are one more type of ex post facto design.

In experiments an investigator has control over manipulation of the independent variable, so that it can be manipulated while all else is held constant. So if we are interested in the effect of pornographic movies upon physiological arousal and later sexual excitement, we can take two statistically equivalent groups of people (or the same people at different times), show them a movie with pornographic scenes included or omitted (holding other variables constant), and measure their responses. One can then have confidence (but never certainty) that the difference between the movies produced any observed differential effect in arousal. The case is very different with subject variables, though. An experimenter cannot manipulate a subject variable while holding other factors constant; he or she can only select subjects who already have the characteristic in some varying degree and then compare them on the behavior of interest. If the subjects in the different groups (say, high, medium, and low I.Q.) differ on the behavior, we cannot conclude that the subject variable difference produced or is responsible for the difference in behavior. The reason is that other factors may vary with the subject variable and thus be confounded with it. So if high I.Q. subjects perform some task better than low I.Q. Subjects, we cannot say that I.Q. produced or caused the difference, because the different groups of subjects are likely to vary on other relevant dimensions such as motivation, education, and the like. When subject variables are investigated we cannot safely attribute differences in behavior to them, as we can with true experimental variables. Such designs, then, essentially produce correlations between variables. We can say that the variables are related, but we cannot say that one variable produced or caused the effect in the other variable.

This is a very important point, so let us consider an example. Suppose an investigator is interested in the intellectual functioning (or lack thereof) of people suffering from schizophrenia. People diagnosed as belonging to this group are given numerous tests meant to measure various mental abilities. As a control the researcher also gives these tests to another group of people, so-called normals. He or she discovers that schizophrenics do especially poorly relative to normals in tests involving semantic aspects of language, such as those that involve understanding the meaning of words or comprehending prose passages. The investigator concludes that the schizophrenics perform these tests more poorly *because* they are schizophrenics and that their inability to use language well in communication is a likely contributing cause of schizophrenia.

Studies like this are common in some areas of psychology. Despite the fact that conclusions similar to the one in the example above are often drawn from such studies, they are completely unwarranted. Both conclusions are based on correlations, and other factors could well be the critical ones. Schizophrenics may do more poorly than normals for any number of reasons. They may not be as intelligent, as motivated, as educated, or as wise at taking tests. It may simply be that they have been institutionalized for a long time with resulting poverty of social and intellectual intercourse. So we cannot conclude that the reason that the two groups differ on verbal tests is schizophrenia or its absence in the two groups. Even if we could, it would certainly not imply the other conclusion, that language problems are involved in causing schizophrenia. Again, all we would have is a correlation between these two variables, with no idea of whether or how the two are causally related.

Use of subject variables is very common in all of psychological research, but it is absolutely crucial in areas such as clinical and developmental psychology, so the problems with making inferences from such research should be carefully considered. A primary variable in developmental psychology is age, a subject variable, which means that much research in this field is correlational in nature. In general, the problem of individual differences among subjects in psychology is one that is often ignored, though there are often appeals to consider this problem as crucial (for example, Underwood, 1975). Let us consider some ways of attempting more sound inferences from experiments employing subject variables.

Matching

The basic problem in the investigation of subject variables, and in other ex post facto research, is that whatever differences are observed in behavior may be due to other confounded variables. One way to try to avoid this problem is by *matching* subjects on the other relevant variables. In the comparison of schizophrenics and normals we noted that the two groups were also likely to differ on the other characteristics, such as I.Q., education, motivation, institutionalization, and perhaps even age. Rather than simply comparing the schizophrenics to normals, we might try to compare them to another group more closely matched on these other dimensions so that, hopefully, the main difference between the groups is in the presence or absence of schizophrenia. For example, we might use a group of neurotics who, on the average, are similar to the schizophrenics in terms of age, I.Q., length of time institutionalized, sex, and some measure of motivation. When the two groups have been matched on all these characteristics, then we can more confidently attribute any difference in performance between them to the factor of interest, namely, schizophrenia. By matching, investigators attempt to introduce the crucial characteristic of experimentation—being able to hold constant extraneous factors to avoid confoundings—into what is essentially a correlational observation. The desire is to allow one to infer that the variable of interest (schizophrenia) produced the observed effect.

There are several rather severe problems associated with matching. For one thing it often requires a great deal of effort because some of the relevant variables may be quite difficult to measure. Even when one goes to the trouble to take the needed additional measures, it may still be impossible to match the groups, especially if few subjects are involved before matching is attempted. Even when matching is successful, it often greatly reduces the size of the sample on which the observations are made. Thus we then have less confidence in the reliability of our observations (that is, that they are stable and repeatable).

Another problem with matching involves the introduction of the dreaded *regression artifact*. This is discussed in Chapter 10, but we will explain it briefly here. Under certain conditions in many types of measurements a statistical phenomenon occurs known as *regression to the mean*. The mean of a group of scores is what most people think of as the average, the total of all observations divided by the number of observations. For example, mean height in a sample of 60 people is the sum of all their heights divided by 60 (see Chapter 6). Typically, if people who received extreme scores (that is, very high or very low) on some characteristic are retested, their second scores will be closer to the mean of the entire group than were their original scores. Consider an example. We give 200 people a standard test of mathematical reasoning for which there are two equivalent forms, or two versions of the test that we know to be equivalent. The average (mean) score on the test is 60 of 100 possible points. We take the 15 people who score highest and the 15 who score lowest. The means of these groups are, say, 95 and 30, respectively. Then we test them again on the alternate form of the test. Now we might find that the means of the two groups are 87 and 35. On the second test the scores of the two extreme groups regressed toward the mean; the very good group scored more poorly while the very poor group had somewhat better scores. Basically it happens for the high scoring group because some people whose "true scores" are somewhat lower than actually tested lucked out and scored higher than they should have on the test. When retested, people with extreme high scores tend to score lower, nearer their true score. The situation is reversed for the low scoring group.

This regression toward the mean is always observed under conditions when there is a less than perfect correlation between the two measures, and the more extreme the selection of scores, the greater the regression toward the mean. It also occurs in all types of measurement situations. If abnormally tall or short parents have a child, it will likely be closer to the population mean than the height of the parents. As with most statistical phenomena, regression to the mean is true of groups of observations and is probabilistic (that is, it may not occur every time). For example, a few individual subjects may regress away from the mean in the second test of mathematical reasoning, but the group tendency will be toward the mean.

How does regression toward the mean affect ex post facto research where subjects have been matched on some variable? Again, consider an example. This one, like much ex post facto research done on applied societal problems, has important implications. Let us assume we have an educational program that we believe will be especially advantageous for increasing the reading scores of black children. This is especially important because black children's scores are typically lower than those of whites, presumably due to different cultural environments. We take two groups of children, one black and one white, and match them on several criteria including age, sex, and most importantly, initial reading ability. We give both groups of children the reading improvement program and then test their reading ability after the program. We find, much to our surprise, that the black children actually perform *worse* after the reading program than before it, while the white children improve. We conclude, of course, that the program helped white children but actually hurt black children, despite the fact that it was especially designed for the latter.

This conclusion, even though it may seem reasonable to you, is almost surely erroneous in this case because of regression artifacts. Consider what happened when the black and white children were matched on initial reading scores. Since the populations differed initially with blacks lower than whites, in order to match two samples it was necessary to select black students with higher scores than the mean for their group and white students with lower scores than their group mean. Having picked these extreme groups, we could predict because of regression to the mean that when retested, the black children would have poorer scores and the white children would have better ones, on the average, even if the reading improvement program had no effect at all! The exceptionally high-scoring black children would tend to regress toward the mean of their group, while the low-scoring whites would regress toward the mean for their group. The same thing would have happened even if there were no program and the children were simply retested.

The same outcome would likely have been obtained if children were matched on IQ's instead of reading scores, since the two are probably positively correlated. So simply finding another matching variable may be no solution. One solution would be to match very large samples of black and white children and then split each group, giving the reading program to one subgroup but not the other. All would be retested at the end of the one subgroup's participation in the program. (Assignment of subjects to the subgoups of black and white children should, of course, be random). Regression to the mean would be expected in both subgroups, but the effect of the reading program could be evaluated against the group that had no program. Perhaps black children with the reading program would show much less drop (regression to the mean) than those without, indicating that the program really did have a positive effect.

Ex post facto research with subject variables is conducted quite often to evaluate educational programs, so its practitioners need to be aware of the many thorny problems associated with its use. Without matching one may not be able to say much with regard to the results or draw important conclusions because of confoundings. Matching helps alleviate this problem in some cases where its use is possible, but then one introduces the possibility of regression artifacts. And many researchers seem unaware of this problem. One famous blooper in such evaluational research, very similar to the hypothetical study outlined here, is discussed in Chapter 10.

When matching is a practical possibility, and when regression artifacts are evaluated, we can feel somewhat more confident of conclusions from our results. But we should still remember that what we have is still only a correlation, albeit a very carefully controlled one. Matching is useful, but it's not a cure-all. In our earlier example comparing schizophrenics to others on mental test performance, if the schizophrenics still perform worse than the new matched control group of neurotics, can we then conclude that schizophrenia *produces* inferiority in language usage? No, we cannot. It could still be something else, some other difference between the two groups. We can never be sure we matched on the relevant variables. Perhaps neurotics are superior in their use of language!

Age as a Variable

One subject variable, age, deserves its own discussion for two reasons. In the first place, developmental psychology is a popular and important part of scientific psychology. In the second place, age as a variable poses very difficult confoundings that have generated some interesting and powerful research designs.

Let us suppose that you are interested in determining the effects of age on the ability to use two types of learning strategies. One type of strategy should improve recall (Tversky and Teiffer, 1976) because when your subjects use this strategy correctly they will be able to associate one thing with another. In the case of remembering the names of simple objects (for example, *knife*, *tree*, and *cat*) the recall of one object will help you recall another object (for example, recalling *cat* reminds you of *tree* because cats climb trees and trees make you think of *knife* because you carve your initials in a tree with a knife). We will call this the recall strategy. A second strategy might help you recognize things (as in a multiple-choice test), because in this recognize strategy you look for minute differences among objects so that later on you can specify which of several similar objects was actually shown to you.

You have decided to see how children of different ages utilize these two strategies. How are you going to design your project? The most straightforward (and also the most likely) method is the *cross-sectional method*. In this method, we would select children of different ages (for example, 5, 8, and 12) and then randomly assign half of each age group to one of the strategy conditions. An alternative way of doing this study would be the more time-consuming *longitudinal method*. In a longitudinal study, we would test a subject when he or she was five, then at eight, and then again at age twelve. In the cross-sectional method we are figuratively cutting through the age dimension, and in the longitudinal method we follow a particular individual along the age dimension. These two developmental methods are highly used in studies where age is a variable, yet they both contain serious confoundings that could make the internal validity of the studies highly suspect.

What are some of these serious confoundings? Before we can discuss them we need to discuss age itself. Since age is a subject variable, it cannot be considered a true independent variable. Age is a dimension; in particular, it is a time dimension along which we can study behavior. Some developmental psychologists have suggested that we should consider age as a dependent variable since it is a variable that varies with other subject characteristics from birth to death (Wohwill, 1970).

In any event, we cannot directly vary age so we must be wary of any concomitant variables associated with it. Different research designs have different confoundings. In the cross-sectional method, age is confounded with the generation of birth. Not only is one of the authors of this textbook 22 years older than his son, he and his son also differ in terms of generation of birth, and generation itself is a complex variable. In this sense the generation gap is real—someone born in 1942 is not just 22 years older than someone born in 1964. The older person was born into a different world populated by different people who had different attitudes and educations than the counterparts (what the developmental psychologists call *cohorts*) of the younger person.

Since there are problems with the cross-sectional method, let us consider the longitudinal method. In this method we follow a particular individual who will maintain the same cohorts. In the longitudinal method, therefore, we do not have to worry about the generation/age confound. However, the longitudinal method confounds age with time of treatment or testing. If you test the memory of a child at age five and then at age twelve, not only is the person seven years older on the second test, but the world has changed in the interim. Using the longitudinal method, we might find that college students' attitudes about energy conservation in 1982 have changed since they were five years old in 1968. Is the change in attitude due to a change in age or to a change in the world?

Shown in Figure 7–3 are some research designs that can be used when age is a variable. Note that the *time lag* design (the design indicated along the diagonal) aims at determining the effects of time of

Figure 7–3

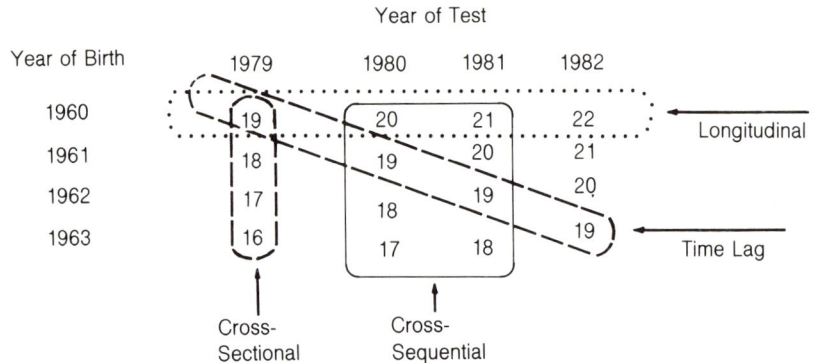

Some quasi-experimental designs when age is a variable at the time of testing.

testing while holding age constant (only 19-year olds are tested in this example). As is true of the cross-sectional design, the time lag design confounds cohorts of the subjects with the target variable.

Schaie (1977) has outlined many sophisticated designs to overcome the confoundings we have just described. One of these designs is illustrated in Figure 7–3. The *cross-sequential design*, indicated by the vertical dashes, involves testing two or more age groups at two or more time periods. A complex cross-sequential study might involve all 16 of the groups indicated in the table. You should note that the cross-sequential design includes features of the other three designs we have mentioned. Different ages are tested at the same time as in the cross-sectional method, an individual is tested successively as in the longitudinal method, and the time lag design is represented by testing different subjects of the same age at different times (19- and 20-year olds in this case). In the cross-sequential design, therefore, the researcher can determine the effects of most of the potential confoundings. The effects of age are tested both longitudinally and sectionally (a 20-year old can be compared to other ages in 1980, and that 20-year old is tested again in 1981). If the effects of age are the same in both of these comparisons, then we can rule out cohorts and time of testing as important confoundings.

An obvious drawback to the cross-sequential design is that it is cumbersome. Many subjects would have to be tested over a period of time, which may make a research project impractical. Because of this, the cross-sequential design is not used as often as it probably should be. Instead, most developmental researchers stick to the more manageable cross-sectional design.

A typical cross-sectional experiment has age as a quasi-independent variable as well as another true independent variable. In the

Tversky and Teiffer (1976) study outlined earlier, three age groups were tested following instructions about either the recall strategy or the recognize strategy. The recall strategy improved retention at all ages (5, 8, and 12), but only the oldest children benefited from the recognize strategy. Such results are an example of an *interaction* (see Chapters 5 and 8), which means that the effects of one variable are dependent upon the level of the other variable—the effects of type of strategy depended upon the age of the subjects.

The tactic of using age and a true independent variable in developmental research means that one outcome the researcher expects is an interaction. Whatever variables are confounded with age (in the Tversky and Teiffer study, age was confounded with grade in school in addition to the usual confoundings associated with a cross-sectional design) might be differentially affected by a true independent variable. The clever psychologist tries to pinpoint what components of age determine thought and behavior, and the search for particular interactions may help. In the next chapter we will discuss interactions in laboratory experiments. For the moment you should note that the purpose of both the cross-sequential design and the search for interactions is to enhance the internal validity of developmental research. Age is a complex variable, and we must simplify it in order to have a valid analysis.

Summary

In research that is internally valid, it is possible to make straightforward statements about cause and effect. In ex post facto research, where there is no direct control over the variables—they are examined after the fact —causal statements may not be possible because of confoundings. The internal validity of correlational studies may be enhanced by using the cross-lagged panel correlation technique, which involves obtaining correlations over time in order to determine the direction of causality. Quasi-experiments have one or more ex post facto components: either naturally occurring variables or subject variables (or both). One-shot case studies and the interrupted time series design are two quasi-experimental procedures with low internal validity. The researcher must be a good detective to determine the causal agents in these two procedures. Likewise, the researcher needs to be a good detective when he or she tries to handle subject variables by matching subjects on the basis of particular characteristics. Just what characteristics are to be matched often poses a difficult problem, and those characteristics may regress toward the mean in many instances. Age as a subject variable provides many real threats to internal validity because it is confounded with numerous other factors. Using the cross-sequential design and looking for interactions of age with true independent variables are two ways to enhance the internal validity of developmental research. Threats to internal validity and possible ways to overcome these threats are summarized in Table 7–2.

Table 7–2	Threats to Internal Validity in Correlational and Quasi-experimental Research with Some Solutions		
	Research Procedure	*Threat to Internal Validity*	*Ways to Enhance Internal Validity*
	Correlational	Direction of causation; "third variable" problem	Cross-lagged panel correlations
	Case Studies	Source of causation; baseline "condition"	Deviant case analysis (a non-equivalent control); detective work
	Interrupted Time Series	Changes in subjects and environment; delayed effects	Nonequivalent control group; detective work
	Subject variables	Dimensions on which to match regression artifacts	Matching; include true independent variable and seek interactions
	Age as a Variable	Confoundings with: time of testing, generation of birth	Cross-sequential design; include a true independent variable and seek interactions

Study and Review

Exercises

1. A considerable amount of evidence indicates that there is a positive correlation between birth order and intelligence (Zajonc and Marcus, 1975). Birth order refers to the order in which children enter the family unit (first born, second born, and so on). Intelligence tends to be lower for later born children than for the earlier ones. List as many factors as you can that might be confounded with birth order. How might you determine which of these factors is important in influencing intelligence? That is, how do we enhance internal validity when birth order is the variable?

2. The *Journal of Applied Psychology* often reports studies that used an interrupted time series design. Examine several recent issues and note, in particular, any control conditions that are included.

3. Age as a variable in geriatric research (the study of old age) is often more difficult to analyze than in child development studies. Why?

Key Concepts

internal validity 157
external validity 157
cross-lagged panel correlation
    158
quasi-experiment 160
observation-treatment
  observation 161
nonequivalent control group 161
one-shot case study 162
deviant case analysis 162
interrupted time series 163

subject variable 165
matching 167

regression artifact 168
regression to the mean 168
age 170
cross-sectional method 171
longitudinal method 171
time lag design 171
cross sequential design 172
interaction 173

Suggested Readings

Donald T. Campbell has written a great deal about quasi-experimental research. The best place to begin is with the first book listed below. More detail is presented in the second one. Campbell, D. T. and Stanley, J. C. *Experimental and quasi-experimental designs for research*. Chicago: Rand McNally, 1963. Cook, T. D. and Campbell, D. T. *Quasi experimentation: design and analysis issues for field settings*. Chicago: Rand McNally, 1979.

COMPLEX EXPERIMENTS HAVE MORE THAN ONE INDEPENDENT VARIABLE— LOOK FOR INTERACTIONS

Complex Between-subjects Experiments

2 X 2 Factorial Design

2 independent variables, each with 2 levels yielding 4 independent groups

look for 2 main effects and an interaction of the 2 variables

control for confounding of subjects with groups

2 X 2 X 2 Factorial Design

3 independent variables, each with 2 levels yielding 8 independent groups

3 main effects and there may be 4 interactions; carry-over usually not a problem

see above and the complex interaction may be uninterpretable

Complex- Within-subjects Experiments

2 X 2 Within Factorial Design (treatments X treatments X subjects)

each subject receives each level of each independent variable—4 treatments in a 2 X 2

more efficient than between designs; each subject is own control; main effects and interactions can be determined

confounding via carry-over effects must be minimized— counterbalance or randomize; use several observations in each condition to increase reliability

Mixed Designs

A combination of independent variables manipulated both between- and within-subjects

each subject receives each level of the within-subjects variable, and separate groups are determined by the levels (and types) of between-subjects variables

has virtues of the above; very good for looking at interaction of practice (trials) with another independent variable

all controls above must be considered, but carr-over is usually a variable, so its effects are measured

Complex Experimentation

8

The purpose of this chapter is to discuss the design and interpretation of experiments with more than one independent variable. Such multifactor experiments emphasize the interaction between independent variables. As noted at the end of the previous chapter, researchers are often particularly concerned with how the effects of one variable are influenced by the level of the other. Multifactor experiments can be viewed as extensions of one-variable experiments. Some designs vary the independent variables between subjects and some within subjects. It is also possible to have a mixture of a between-subjects and within-subjects manipulation of the independent variables. We will consider all three of these possibilities here.

A 2 × 2 Experiment

Between-Subjects Factorial Designs

Why complex experiments?   If science progresses by analysis, it might have occurred to you to question the logic of including more than one independent variable in an experiment. We have already noted that increased control in quasi-experiments comes about by including both subject variables and true (externally manipulated) independent variables in the study. Increased control is not the primary reason for conducting laboratory experiments with more than one independent variable. Rather, the major reason has to do with the complexity of thought and behavior. Limiting experimental analysis to a one-at-a-time variable manipulation cannot mirror the numerous, intertwined forces that influence people outside of the laboratory. Therefore, multifactor experiments are likely to have better ecological validity (i.e., they are more representative) than single-factor experiments. We can increase the generality of our results by doing experiments that attempt to match the complexity of forces that combine to influence our thought and behavior. In addition, *complex* causal statements can be made, which should increase internal validity.

Does the above mean that what we have said before about analysis is invalid? No. In any research problem, the basic factors need to be determined before we can make more complex observations. In much the same way that naturalistic observation and correlational studies often precede basic experimentation, simple experiments often provide the groundwork for more complex ones. Scientific maturity occurs gradually. The data base is slowly built, and the theories are gradually developed. We begin with description and prediction, and we end with explanation. Explanation itself goes through a developmental process— from simple experiments to complex ones.

Factorial Design in Memory Research. Bower (1972) has reported that creating mental images can triple the number of unrelated words you can remember from a long list. In a typical one-factor (that is, one independent variable), between-subjects experiment on imagery, one group of subjects (the experimental group) received instructions on how to create mental images, and another separate group of subjects was given no special instructions. The latter group was the control group and it provided a baseline of ordinary memorization against which the effects of mental images were compared. This design assumed that the controls were not using imagery. Some probably were, which would work against the hypothesis and against the observed effects.

This simple design seems fine as far as it goes, but you may have asked yourself, "Are the effects of mental imagery the same for all types of words?" When a question like this is posed, the investigator is asking if the effects of mental imagery interact with the characteristics of the words. It is fairly easy to imagine a *kitchen* or an *elephant*, but most people find mental images are poorer for words such as *fate* or *criterion* (for example, Elmes and Thompson, 1976). You might expect that mental images would assist retention only when good mental images can be created. If you cannot create a good image for the word *criterion*, then using the mental imagery strategy should not aid memory. This expectation leads to the following prediction: in an experiment on memorizing words, mental images will benefit the retention of high imagery words more than the retention of low imagery words.

The prediction includes an interaction: the effects of creating mental images should depend upon the characteristics of the words. This prediction can be tested by what is called a *2 X 2 factorial experiment*. In a 2 X 2 factorial design, there are two factors (independent variables) of interest, and there are two *levels,* or values, of each factor. This study is more complicated than a single factor one that just examines the effects of mental imagery. In the 2 x 2 factorial design, we can determine the *main effects* of each independent variable separately (that is, we can see if memorization strategy influenced retention, and we can also see what the effects of imagery value were on memory). We can also see how the variables affect the influence of each other—the *interaction effect* or simply the interaction. A 2 X 2 factorial experiment done by one of the authors examined the effects of both memorization strategy and word characteristics on memory. The design of this experiment is outlined in Table 8–1.

We call the two independent variables in this experiment *rehearsal instructions*, to refer to how the subjects were told to memorize the words, and *imagery value*, to refer to the characteristics of the words. In one type of rehearsal instruction the subjects were told to create mental images and elaborate associations to the words. The other type of rehearsal instruction was rote, in which the subjects were instructed to repeat the words over and over. The two levels of imagery value were determined by the results of a previous magnitude estimation experiment (see Chapter 2). High imagery words (for example, elephant) received high imagery estimates, and low imagery words (for example, criterion) received low estimates (Elmes and Thompson, 1976).

Table 8–1 shows that there are four independent groups with ten subjects in each group. The subjects were college students who were randomly assigned to one of the four groups. In a between-subjects factorial design, the number of groups is equal to the product of the number of independent variables times the number of levels of the independent variables, which simply means that all possible combinations of levels and variables are tested. In the present instance we have the following four groups (2 X 2): subjects memorizing high imagery words under rote instructions; subjects memorizing high imagery words

Design of a 2 x 2 Factorial Experiment (Between-Subjects) **Table 8-1**

High Imagery Words		Low Imagery Words	
Rote Rehearsal	Elaborative Rehearsal	Rote Rehearsal	Elaborative Rehearsal
Subject 1	S 11	S 21	S 31
S 2	S 12	S 22	S 32
S 3	S 13	S 23	S 33
S 4	S 14	S 24	S 34
S 5	S 15	S 25	S 35
S 6	S 16	S 26	S 36
S 7	S 17	S 27	S 37
S 8	S 18	S 28	S 38
S 9	S 19	S 29	S 39
S 10	S 20	S 30	S 40

Note. The individual subjects are numbered 1–40 for illustrative purposes, they were not tested in order from 1 to 40. Rather they were randomly assigned to one of the four conditions when they came to the laboratory, so the order of arrival at the laboratory was not confounded with the particular group. The mean number of words recalled in each group appear in Figure 8-1, and the raw scores are shown in Box 9-7 in the following chapter.

using elaborative instructions; subjects memorizing low imagery words under rote rehearsal; and subjects memorizing low imagery words using elaborative instructions.

Before considering the results of this experiment, some additional details of the procedure will be mentioned. Subjects in all conditions were shown ten words, one at a time for three seconds each. Before and after each word was presented, the subjects had to do some mental arithmetic—a long string of digits was shown to them and they had to figure out the sums of adjacent digits. They called out the sums as fast as they could, doing the mental arithmetic for 20 seconds before and after each word was shown. After the final session of mental arithmetic, the list was repeated again in exactly the same way, and then the subjects had to write down as many of the words as they could in any order they wished. The intervening mental arithmetic was included to minimize inter-associations among the words and to make the recall task somewhat difficult. If every subject recalled every word, we would have a ceiling effect that would not allow us to discriminate among the conditions. Remember, half the subjects were told to repeat each word over and over when it was presented (rote rehearsal), and half were told to generate a mental image for each word (elaborative rehearsal). Half of each rehearsal group was shown high imagery words, and half was shown low imagery words.

The results of the experiment are shown in Figure 8–1. The mean numbers of words recalled are plotted against the imagery value of the words. The parameters (that is, the connected data points) are the two rehearsal conditions. Shown in parentheses are the mean values for each point. The first thing you should do when considering the results of a multifactor experiment is draw a figure if the results are given in tabular form. Then you should examine the general characteristics of the figure: in Figure 8–1 you should note that the two lines are not parallel. The elaborative rehearsal line is higher than the rote rehearsal line, and the two points for high imagery words are higher than the points for the low imagery words.

We can summarize these data as follows: elaborative rehearsal results in better recall than does rote rehearsal; more high imagery words are recalled than low imagery words; and recall is highest when high imagery words have been memorized under elaborative rehearsal instructions. These assertions are supported by a statistical analysis reported in Chapter 9. In the terminology introduced earlier: there are main effects of type of rehearsal instructions and imagery values, and there is an interaction between these two factors.

When an independent variable has the same effect regardless of the level of the other independent variable, we say that the effects are additive (that is, the effects of one simply add on to the effects of the other). An interaction will appear whenever the effects of the independent variables are not additive. This would mean that the combination of variables has a multiplicative effect. The multiplicative combination

Figure 8–1

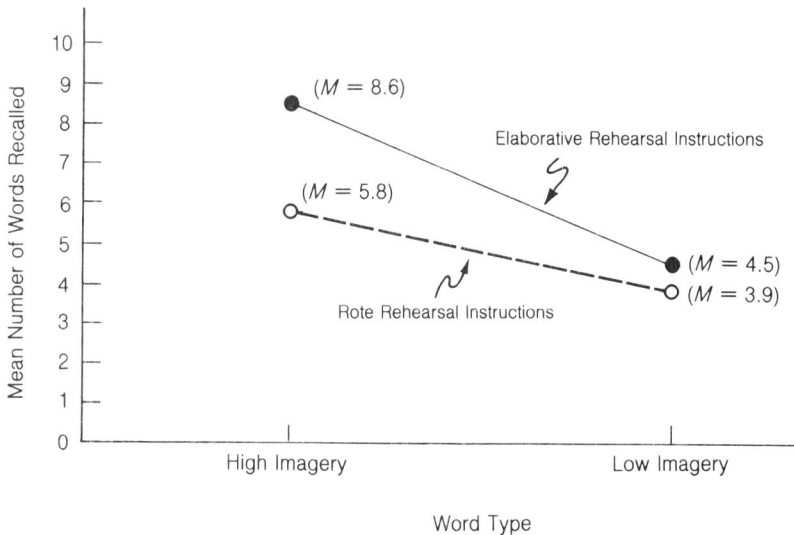

Mean number of words recalled under rote and elaborative rehearsal as a function of the imagery value of the words. A 2 X 2 factorial design (between-subjects). Mean recall of high imagery words = (8.6 + 5.8)/2 = 7.2. Mean recall of low imagery words = (4.5 + 3.9)/2 = 4.2. Mean recall under the rote rehearsal = (3.9 + 5.8)/2 = 4.9. Mean recall under elaborative rehearsal = (8.6 + 4.5)/2 = 6.6. The fact that the two lines are not parallel indicates an interaction between word imagery and rehearsal instructions. The effects of type of rehearsal depend upon word imagery: elaborative rehearsal leads to much better recall of high imagery words than does rote rehearsal, but the effectiveness of elaborative rehearsal is smaller when low imagery words are memorized.

will show up in a figure as functions (lines connecting data points) that are not parallel, which is why it is a good idea to graph results to illustrate any possible interaction. You can calculate the main effects shown in the caption of Figure 8–1 by averaging the appropriate pairs of data points. After you have "eye-balled" your data, you may then want to verify the significance of your results via statistical tests. Such tests are described in the next chapter.

We can conclude from this experiment that the effects of type of rehearsal are dependent upon what is being memorized—the effects of rehearsal instructions and word imagery interact. Using elaborative rehearsal that involves creating mental images of the words aids retention, especially when high imagery words are to be remembered.

Interactions are very important in psychological research, so in Figure 8–2 we have illustrated several possible additional outcomes to our memory experiment to help you practice interpreting data from multifactor experiments. In a multifactor experiment, there are many possible results. In a 2 X 2 design, there can be two, one, or no main effects, and each of those results may or may not be accompanied by an interaction. Some of these possibilities are shown in Figure 8–2.

Figure 8–2

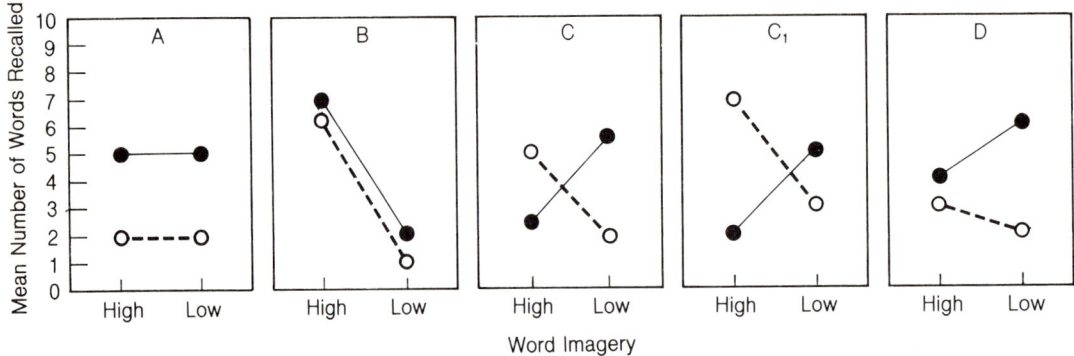

Hypothetical results for the memory experiment outlined in Table 8–1. Elaborative rehearsal is represented by the filled circles; rote rehearsal is designated by the open circles. Panel *A*: main effect of rehearsal; Panel *B*: main effect of imagery; Panel *C*: cross-over interaction, no main effects and C_1: cross-over interaction, main effect of rehearsal; Panel *D*: interaction, main effect of rehearsal.

Panel *A* depicts one main effect (rehearsal instructions) and no interaction with type of word since the lines are approximately parallel. There is no main effect of word imagery. Panel *B* indicates one main effect, in this case just imagery influences recall, and there is no interaction between rehearsal instructions and word imagery.

There is a very obvious interaction in Panel *C*. The effects of rehearsal instructions are exactly opposite, depending upon the imagery value of the words. This type of interaction is called a *cross-over interaction* because the lines connecting the points cross. In this example of a cross-over interaction, there are no main effects. That is, neither rehearsal instructions nor word imagery influenced recall by themselves (to demonstrate this to yourself, get the average score for each rehearsal instruction and for each level of imagery). Shown in Panel C_1 is a cross-over interaction and a main effect of rehearsal instructions. There is no main effect of word imagery in the example shown in this panel.

Panel *D* illustrates an interaction and one main effect (rehearsal instructions). You can determine that there is one main effect because, when averaged over the type of rehearsal instruction, about the same number of words are recalled regardless of the level of imagery.

If we had done the memory experiment with three values of word imagery (for example. high, medium, and low), we would have done a 3 X 2 factorial experiment that involved six (three levels of imagery times two levels of rehearsal) independent groups. There is no limit to the number of levels of the independent variables that can be used, although in between-subjects designs you will rarely find more than four levels of a given independent variable.

A 2 X 2 X 2 Experiment

Another way of adding complexity to an experimental design besides increasing the levels of the independent variables is to increase the *number* of independent variables themselves. So, we could have an *n* X *n* X *n* factorial design, where each *n* refers to the number of levels of three different independent variables. In between-subjects factorial designs, you will rarely find an experiment that has more than three factors, and usually there are just two or three levels of each factor. The reasons for these limitations are partially practical in nature. If you have between 10 and 20 subjects in each group, you would have to test an extraordinary number of subjects if you had a 4 X 3 X 2 X 2 X 2 design. This design would give you 96 conditions, and with just 10 subjects in a group you would need 960 subjects. In addition, multivariable interactions (more than three) are difficult to interpret.

We will illustrate the design and results of a 2 X 2 X 2 factorial experiment to give you an idea of what to expect from such a complex design. In this design there are eight independent groups (2 X 2 X 2 = 8). Such an experiment is shown in Table 8–2, and if it looks familiar to you, it should, because it is the complete design of the experiment outlined in Table 8–1. Earlier we presented a portion of the design for ease of explanation; now we give you the entire experiment as it was actually conducted. The additional independent variable was the number of presentations of each word: two for half the subjects and one for

---

Design of a 2 X 2 X 2 factorial memory experiment from which Table 8-1 was taken.

Table 8-2

2 Presentations

High Imagery Words		Low Imagery Words	
Rote Rehearsal	Elaborative Rehearsal	Rote Rehearsal	Elaborative Rehearsal
S 1 through S 10	S 11 through S 20	S 21 through S 30	S 31 through S 40

1 Presentation

High Imagery Words		Low Imagery Words	
Rote Rehearsal	Elaborative Rehearsal	Rote Rehearsal	Elaborative Rehearsal
S 41 through S 50	S 51 through S 60	S 61 through S 70	S 71 through S 80

Note. The scores for each subject in this experiment are presented in Box 9-8 in the following chapter. The means scores for each group are shown in Figure 8-3.

the other half. The results of the 2 X 2 part of this experiment shown in Figure 8–1 are for the subjects who had the words presented twice.

There are several ways to present the data for the eight groups in this experiment. The important thing to remember when you graph your own data is to try to make it as meaningful as possible. Design your figures so that any interactions and main effects will be obvious. Initially you will want to try to put all your data points in a single figure. If that is too cluttered, you may then want to make two or more graphs. In the present case, we could have had two graphs: one graph showing the effects with two presentations (as in Figure 8–1) and a second one showing the results when there was one presentation. Instead, we have combined all data points in a single figure, Figure 8–3, because it seems to illustrate the important features of the results. A clear figure is important because in a 2 X 2 X 2 design there are a total of four interactions to worry about: imagery and rehearsal, imagery and number of presentations, rehearsal and number of presentations, and the three-way interaction of all three variables. The last interaction is called a *higher order interaction*, because it involves more than two variables. It is worth repeating that higher order interactions are often very difficult to interpret, which is another reason why you will not see many factorial designs with more than three factors. An interaction involving five or six factors would be very confusing. The investigator would probably be kept wondering, along with the rest of the world, what, if anything, it means.

Figure 8–3

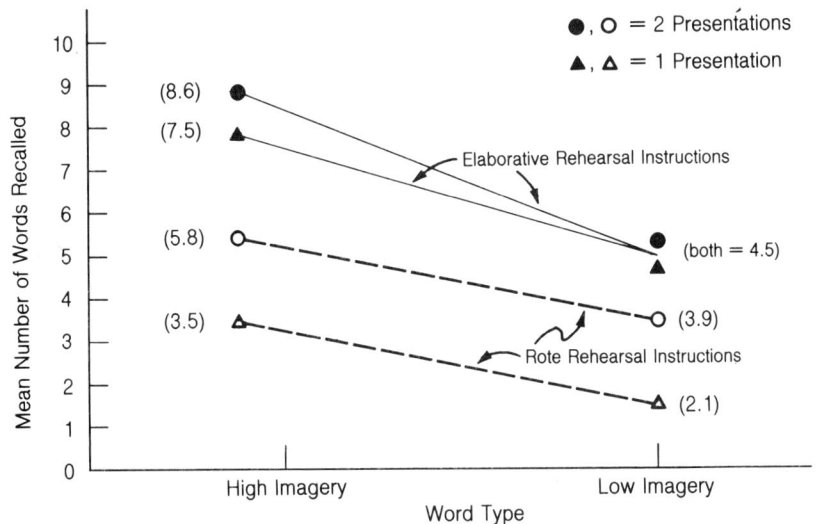

Mean number of words recalled as a function of the imagery values of the words. Number of presentations and type of rehearsal are the parameters. A 2 X 2 X 2 factorial design. The numbers in parentheses are the mean scores.

Let us examine Figure 8–3 in some detail. In addition to the effects noted in Figure 8–1, there is a main effect of the number of presentations such that recall is higher after two presentations than after one. This effect of number of presentations holds true for both levels of imagery, which means that these two variables do not interact. However, there is an interaction between rehearsal and the number of presentations. Under rote rehearsal, recall was much higher after two presentations than after just one, but there was only a small effect of the number of presentations when the subjects used elaborative rehearsal. From this figure, or almost any for that matter, it is difficult to determine exactly if there is a higher order interaction. You can make a good guess that there isn't by noting that the overall tendency of the data points is in the same direction—moving from the upper left to lower right in this instance. If there had been a marked cross-over of one or more points, a higher order interaction may have resulted. The statistical analysis of these data presented in Chapter 9 confirms that there is not a reliable higher order interaction.

Control in Factorial Designs

In a between-subjects design, we want to make sure that the characteristics of the subjects are not confounded with group membership. In the ideal case we would randomly select our subjects and then randomly assign them to our conditions. Ordinarily, we are never able to have total random selection of our subjects because we do not have the procedures available to select from *all* rats or *all* college students in an unbiased fashion. It is essential, therefore, that we assign our subjects in our sample to conditions in such a way that minimizes the possibility of confounding their traits with our manipulations. With many groups in a factorial design, unbiased assignment is crucial, and it can be effected according to the procedures outlined in Chapter 5.

An additional way to assign subjects to groups that is not random, but nevertheless is unbiased, is to use a balanced Latin square to determine group membership. Chapter 5 details the procedures for constructing balanced Latin squares. The way to use this counterbalancing technique for subject assignment in a 2 X 2 design is as follows: the four groups are labeled (for example A, B, C, and D) and then a balanced square is made for those symbols. We would then use the order of conditions in the rows of the resulting Latin square to determine assignment. The first subject to appear in the laboratory would be assigned to condition A, the second to B, the third to D, and the fourth to C. Then the next row would be used to assign the next four subjects, and so on until all subjects are tested. We may have to construct many squares or repeatedly use the same square if there are more subjects than cells in our square. Note that the purpose of this procedure is the same as random assignment to conditions: to make sure that there is little relation between the subject's characteristics and assignment to a particular group. One advantage of the Latin square technique is that in a large experiment that takes a long time to conduct, the order in which the treatments are conducted is known well in advance and also balanced across time. So, any historical factors that might be confounded here are balanced across groups.

Other control aspects that are particularly important in any type of experiment include balancing of materials in a way that minimizes confounding their characteristics with other features of the experimental design. For example, in our memory experiment we had to be concerned about the particular order of the words within the presentation sequence. Some words are easier to remember than others, even at a given level of imagery. Moreover, words at the beginning and end of a list are remembered better than words presented in the middle. Since it is possible that these factors could interact with our independent variables, we devised ten different orders of both high and low imagery words, and we gave different subsets of subjects in each condition one of the ten orders. The ten orders assured that each word was presented at each presentation position by the time all subjects had been tested. This means that the characteristics of the words were counterbalanced across list position.

In general, randomization, counterbalancing, and other control techniques minimize potential confounding variables from interacting with the independent variables. Your design should try to reduce the possibility of such unwanted interactions. You might have noticed that we sometimes used randomization, sometimes a Latin square, and once used another form of incomplete counterbalancing (the ten list orders). There are no hard and fast rules for choice of control technique. The ones we used were chosen pragmatically. We did not generate a 10 X 10 balanced Latin square to determine the order of words in a list, because that would have resulted in 100 orders and we only tested 80 subjects. Also, it is unlikely that there are any important (or interpretable) confoundings that may have resulted from having item order determined by rotating them through the list rather than using the balanced Latin square. The particular control procedure you use is up to you: make sure that confoundings are minimized and your controls are easy to implement.

Our discussion of between-subjects designs has been limited to what is often called a *random groups design*, a reference to the fact that assignment of subjects to conditions is random. An alternative method of assignment is *matching* (see Chapters 5 and 7). In a *matched groups design* the experimenter tries to reduce the variability of observations between groups due to subject differences by matching the subjects in the groups on other variables. Thus, in the memory experiments we just described, subjects could have been matched on the basis of IQ before they were randomly assigned to conditions. (Each subgroup of matched subjects is randomly assigned to the groups.) In our earlier discussions we pointed out the difficulty of matching on relevant variables. Some subject variables, such as sex and age, can be matched across groups, or they could serve as a quasi-independent variable. If matching is going to be difficult, then you might want to use a complex within-subjects design, which we discuss next.

The within-subjects design is usually superior to a between-subjects design, because within-subjects manipulation is more economical (requires fewer subjects) and automatically controls for individual differences. Of course, if permanent carry-over effects are likely, a within-in-subjects design may be inappropriate.

Complex Within-Subjects Designs

The economical aspect of within-subjects designs is especially obvious when there is more than one independent variable. In the between-subjects factorial design illustrated in Table 8–2, 80 subjects were tested. In a highly similar experiment in Elmes and Bjork (1975, Experiment 3), just 12 subjects were used in a within-subjects design that had three independent variables: rehearsal instructions, number of presentations, and length of time involved in extraneous mental arithmetic.

Using a within-subjects design can, therefore, result in a substantial reduction in the number of subjects needed for testing. However, the reduced number of subjects may require you to increase the number of observations per subject in each condition to ensure that your data are reliable. We should obtain numerous samples of a subject's behavior, just as is done in a small-n experiment. By doing so we reduce the likelihood that some extraneous factor has influenced the results. For instance, in many learning, memory, perception, and reaction time experiments, events occur rapidly, placing great demands on the subject. If the subject coughs or blinks at an inappropriate time, we may incorrectly underestimate performance on that trial.

Thus instead of testing a large number of subjects as in the between-subjects design, we obtain several observations on a small number of subjects in a within-subjects design. Even with numerous observations per subject, the within-subjects design is usually more efficient than the between-subjects one.

A Complex Within-Subjects Experiment

Figure 8–4 is based upon one of the experiments reported by Elmes and Bjork (1975). We have simplified the presentation here to explain some of the features of within–subjects designs. A typical memory trial is shown in Figure 8–4. The two boxes with the word *or* in them illustrate the implementation of the two independent variables. The symbols

Figure 8–4

(warning signal)	READY	(1 sec)
(rehearsal cue)	XXXXX or OOOOO	(2 sec)
(words to remember)	SPOT ZEST VINE NEWS DOOR	(4 sec)
(time for rehearsal)		(6 sec)
(retention interval)	52 212 417 869 633 - - -	(2 or 12 sec)
(time to recall)	RECALL	(8 sec)
(rest period)		(6 sec)

(next trial)	READY	(1 sec)
	XXXXX or OOOOO	(2 sec)
	FROG MINE BOOM TREE SWAN	(4 sec)
		(6 sec)
	27 897 245 678 328 - - -	(2 or 12 sec)
	RECALL	(8 sec)
		(6 sec)

Outline of two trials in which each frame represents what was seen in the window of a high-speed memory drum. The time intervals are indicated in the parentheses. The function of each frame is noted on the left. Adapted from Elmes and Bjork (1975).

were a rehearsal instruction: for some subjects *XXXXX* signaled rote rehearsal for the upcoming words, and *OOOOO* indicated that the next group of words should receive elaborative rehearsal. For the remaining subjects, the symbol/instruction relationship was reversed (*XXXXX* meant elaborative rehearsal and *OOOOO* meant rote rehearsal). This means that the symbol/instruction relationship was completely counterbalanced across subjects.

The second independent variable was the length of the retention interval for the words. The length of this interval was either 2 or 12 seconds. During the interval, the subjects had to mentally figure the sums of groups of digits, say the sums aloud, and then tell whether the sum was an odd or even number. The subjects practiced this task before the experiment began, and they were told to do it as quickly and as accurately as they could. At the end of the adding interval, the subjects tried to recall as many of the five words as they could in any order that they wished. So, the mental arithmetic served as a distraction for either 2 or 12 seconds between the presentation and rehearsal of the words and the time at which they were recalled. Brown, 1958; Brown and Peterson, 1959).

During the six-second rehearsal period following the words, the subjects either repeated the words over and over (rote rehearsal) or tried to generate mental images or associations that connected the five words in a group (elaborative rehearsal). The type of rehearsal on a given trial was determined by the cue presented at the beginning of the trial. Each subject received 16 trials like the ones shown in Figure 8–4. On each of the trials, five different words were presented. The 16 trials represented four replications of each combination of rehearsal instruction (rote and elaborative) and retention interval (2 and 12 seconds).

This study can be considered a 2 X 2 within-subjects factorial design: the two types of rehearsal and the two retention intervals yield the four conditions. When treatments are administered within subjects, the design is usually not called a factorial. Rather, it is called a *treatments X treatments X subjects design*, a designation derived from the type of statistical analysis employed for such a design (see Chapter 9). Since all combinations of factors are tested, within-subjects factorial is a good shorthand designation.

The results of the experiment are shown in Figure 8–5. You should look for two main effects (one for type of rehearsal and one for length of the retention interval) and the interaction of the two variables. Note that there is an overall decline in recall as the length of the retention interval increases. Overall, recall is higher under elaborative rehearsal than under rote rehearsal. Finally, you should note that the lines are not

Figure 8–5

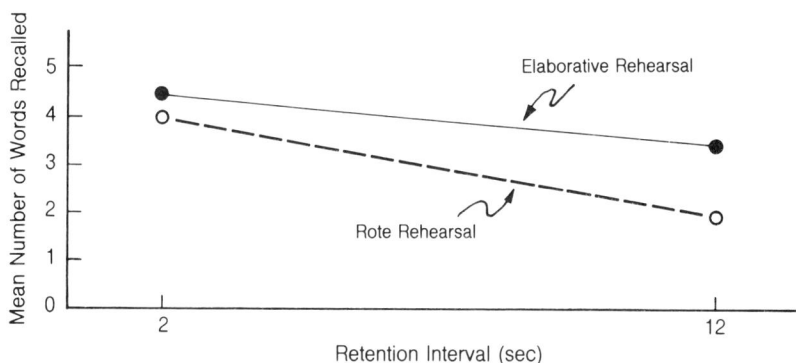

Mean number of words recalled on each trial under rote and elaborative rehearsal as a function of the length of the retention interval. Adapted from Elmes and Bjork (1975).

parallel, which means that the effects of the two variables interact. Elaborative rehearsal results in markedly better recall only at the longest retention interval. Thus, we examine a complex within-subjects experiment in the same way that we examine the results of a complex between-subjects design, by looking for main effects and interaction(s).

Control in Complex Within-subjects Designs

Adequate counterbalancing in complex within-subjects designs is essential. We have to be concerned about the carry-over effects that are inherent in any within-subjects experiment, and we have to guard against many of the kinds of confoundings that can occur in any multifactor experiment.

We mentioned that Elmes and Bjork completely counterbalanced the symbol/instruction relationship across subjects. Let us examine some other control features of their experiment. They had to worry about two carry-over effects: (1) the type of rehearsal on one trial could change performance on the next trial; and (2) the length of the retention interval on one trial could influence performance on the next. They also had to be concerned about the possibility of confounding groups of words and digits with the effects of the independent variables.

Randomization or counterbalancing could handle these problems. Elmes and Bjork chose to use counterbalancing to minimize carry-over effects and balance materials across conditions. Each of the four combinations of rehearsal instruction and the length of the retention interval was tested once before a given combination was tested again. This was done by setting up the test orders in blocks of four—each combination was tested once in each block. Since there were 16 trials, there were four of these test blocks.

This blocking procedure ensures that each treatment occurs in each fourth of the list. Elmes and Bjork went further and rearranged the order of treatment combinations within those blocks for subgroups of subjects. This rearrangement resulted in each treatment combination being tested at each of the 16 positions equally often by the time the final subject had been tested. Within a test block each treatment combination followed every other combination an equal number of times. So, the end result of this elaborate counterbalancing scheme was to minimize the possibility that one treatment combination could regularly influence the results of another.

In order to make sure that each group of five words (and each set of digits) appeared equally often in each condition, each subject saw the same sets of words and digits in the same order. Since the order of the treatment combinations was counterbalanced, holding word order constant means that each set occurred in each condition. However, word and digit groupings were confounded with practice. It is unlikely that this confounding had any differential effect on the results because the conditions of interest are balanced across practice. Randomizing the order of presenting word sets would have added some elegance to the design. However, this would have made counterbalancing the important variables more difficult, so elegance was sacrificed for practicality.

Mixed Designs

Since there are advantages and disadvantages to both pure within- and pure between-subjects designs, it is not surprising that many people have used *mixed designs*. In a mixed design there are one or more between-subjects independent variables and one or more within-subjects conditions. Mixed designs are very common in learning and physiological research, where the interest is in the effects of some variable over time or practice. Usually the variable of primary interest has strong carry-over effects (such as brain damage) so it is manipulated between subjects. Practice or time is necessarily a within-subjects variable in this case, because the same organism is repeatedly measured. (You will often see within-subjects designs, especially those involving large numbers of practice trials, called *repeated measures designs*). In such a mixed design, the experimenter is frequently interested in an interaction between the two variables. Does behavior under the different levels of my between-subjects factor differ across trials (or whatever the within-subjects factor may be)?

In order to illustrate a mixed design we will consider an experiment concerned with a classic problem in the psychology of learning: the *partial reinforcement effect*. We will examine only one aspect of this phenomenon; namely, behavior is usually more persistent following intermittent presentation of reinforcement than after continuous presentation. This means that when a reinforcer is withheld, responding persists longer after partial reinforcement than after continuous reinforcement. One way to study this phenomenon is to reinforce some animals in a maze on every trial and some less than 100 percent of the time. After the animals have learned, we withdraw all reinforcement and see how long the behavior of running the maze lasts, or, in the jargon of learning, how long it takes the behavior to extinguish.

The simplest sort of maze is the straight alley, which is composed of a start box where the animal is placed, an alley through which the animal runs when the start box door is opened, and the goal box where the animal is reinforced. The reinforcement is typically food, and usually the animal has been deprived of food prior to the experiment. The dependent variable is running speed or time to run the straight-alley maze. Often the animal's speed in each section of the runway is measured, so that one finds a speed for leaving the start box, traversing the alley, and approaching the goal. Learning is indicated by the fact that after a number of trials the rat's speed increases (the latency decreases). At first the rat dawdles along, but on later trials it really hustles.

Suppose we now wanted to ask a straightforward question about learning in this situation: How is learning affected by the amount of reinforcement? Intuitively you might expect that learning should increase as the amount of reinforcement increases. But if you read Chapter 4 carefully, you should realize that this depends on how the "amount of reinforcement" and "learning" are defined. We could vary the amount of reinforcement by varying the percentage of trials on which subjects receive reward, or by varying the magnitude of reward after each trial. We could also measure learning in at least two ways. One might be running speed, the other resistance to extinction. The latter measure is found by seeing how long after training an animal will continue running a maze when it no longer receives reinforcement. Let us confine our interest to the case where we vary the percentage of rewarded trials. The experiment we need to do to answer the question we are interested in has now become more manageable. We vary the percentage of trials on which the animals receive reward for running the maze (the independent variable), and we measure the time it takes the animals to run the maze and their resistance to extinction (or running speeds during extinction training).

If subjects are rewarded only on some percentage of trials and we want to see how this affects extinction of maze running, should we use a within-subjects or between-subjects design? If we use a within-subjects design we would need fewer subjects and the variability within conditions would be less. But in using a within-subjects design we would have to be concerned with the effects of one training schedule on the others used. Once an animal has learned a task under one reinforcement schedule, it will not approach the task as though it were new when it relearns the task under a new schedule of reinforcement, even if there has been extinction of the response after it was first learned. (Extinction does not eliminate the memory of the training, it simply stops the animals from responding.) Because of the danger of such carry-over effects from one condition to another in this situation, it would probably be better to use a between-subjects design. An experiment in which the percentage of trials on which subjects received reinforcement was varied between subjects was conducted by Weinstock (1958).

Weinstock tested female rats under six conditions of reinforcement in a simple maze. The rats were tested after 22 hours of water deprivation and access to water in the goal box was the reinforcer. Each rat was given only one trial a day. If more than one trial a day were given, then rats who received water on the early trials would be less motivated to run on later trials than rats that did not receive water on the early trials. Having rats run only one trial per day at a constant 22 hours of water deprivation eliminates this problem, but makes the experiment quite lengthy and onerous for the experimenter. It took Weinstock about half a year, testing rats eight hours a day, to complete this experiment.

For the first 12 trials all rats received continuous reinforcement (CRF), and were rewarded with water after each trial. On trials 13 to 108 the subjects were tested on one of six reinforcement schedules in a between-subjects design. It is easiest to think of these 96 trials as composed of eight blocks of 12 trials, with the partial reinforcement schedule as the number of reinforced and nonreinforced trials in each block of 12. One group of subjects received continuous reinforcement (12 reinforced and 0 nonreinforced, or 12–0), while five other groups received partial reinforcement. One group received 10 reinforced and 2 nonreinforced trials in each block of 12, other groups can be labeled 8–4, 6–6, 4–8, and 2–10, according to the number of reinforced and nonreinforced trials in a block of 12. It was randomly determined within a block of 12 trials which trials would be reinforced and which not for each condition. After 96 trials under one of these six schedules of reinforcement, all rats were given 60 further trials during which they received no reinforcement. Thus these are extinction trials. Weinstock's experiment is outlined in Table 8–3.

The extinction running speeds from Weinstock's experiment are shown in Figure 8–6. Running speeds during extinction declined with increases in the percentage of trials for which the subjects received reward during acquisition. The continuously reinforced subjects ran the slowest during extinction, while the groups that received the fewest rewarded trials ran the fastest. Thus partial reinforcement schedules produce learning that does not extinguish as rapidly as learning on continuous reinforcement schedules. This is the partial reinforcement extinction effect.

An outline of Weinstock's (1958) experiment on the effects of partial reinforcement on maze running speed.   **Table 8–3**

		Days		
1–7	*8–19*	*20–115*		*116–176*
	Trials 1–12	Trials 13–108	RF-NRF*	Trials 109–169
All rats were handled 6–8 minutes per day.	All rats received continuous reinforcement for 12 trials.	Rats received reinforcement according to six schedules of reinforcement for 96 trials in blocks of 12 trials.	12–0 10–2 8–4 6–6 4–8 2–10	All rats received nonreinforced (or extinction) trials.

* The number of trials in each block of 12 trials for which subjects received reinforcement (RF) or nonreinforcement (NRF).

The results in Figure 8–6 show an interaction. The effects of one variable depend upon the level of the other. Performance decreases in extinction (across nonreinforced trials), but it extinguishes more rapidly in some conditions (Group 12–0) than in others (Group 2–10). In general, when one of the variables in a mixed design involves repeated measures, one of the things to look for is an interaction indicating a differential effect of the between-subjects variable over trials.

In most mixed designs the sorts of control procedures we have already considered will be applicable. Obviously, when trials or practice is an independent variable, you will have carry-over effects. In that instance you want to observe or measure them rather than eliminate them, as would be the case when trials or practice simply co-vary with the independent variable under investigation.

Figure 8–6

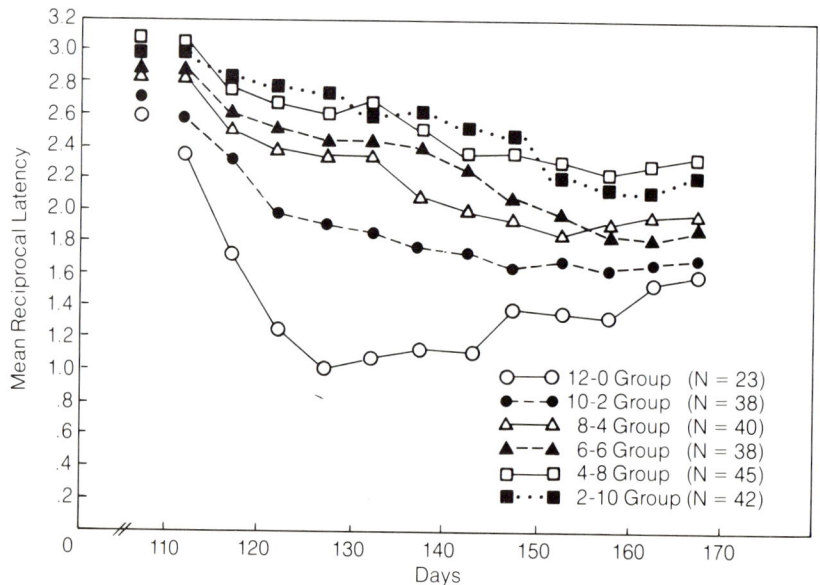

Mean reciprocal latency (speed) of maze running as a function of trials (in blocks of five) during extinction in Weinstocks experiment. The less reinforcement the rats received during acquisition (the fewer trials on which they were reinforced), the greater their speed during extinction, or the more slowly the behavior extinguishes. This is the partial reinforcement extinction effect (from Weinstock, 1958. Figure 2).

Summary

Multifactor experiments contain more than one independent variable, and these variables may have more than two levels. Multifactor designs may vary the independent variables between-subjects, within-subjects, or in a mixed design. The primary reason for conducting multifactor experiments is to increase the complexity of the experiment, and, thereby, increase the generality of the results. The results of a multifactor experiment can show both main effects of the independent variables and the interaction effect of the independent variables. Complex, higher order interactions that involve more than two independent variables are often very difficult to interpret. Control procedures associated with multifactor designs include randomization and counterbalancing techniques that are appropriate to single-factor experiments. Since multifactor studies are so complex, the application of standard control procedures requires good planning to control for the many potential confoundings. A summary of several complex designs, including their features and their control, appears at the beginning of this chapter.

Exercises

Study and Review

1. Go through several recent journals and try to find a complex experiment with more than three factors. Examine the results carefully and note any higher order interactions. What do those interactions mean?

2. In a straight-alley maze, a researcher varied the size of the food reinforcement that was given the rats; it was either large or small. Time to run down the alley was the dependent variable, and the mean time in seconds for each block of ten trials was:

	Block 1	*Block 2*	*Block 3*	*Block 4*
Large Reward	38	30	20	15
Small Reward	52	32	16	12

   The experimenter concluded that since the overall time was slower in the small reward group, large rewards lead to more rapid learning. What other conclusions can be drawn from the data in the above table? Draw a figure showing these results.

3. An experimenter is interested in studying the effects of practice on retention. If a within-subjects design is used and the independent variables are types of rehearsal (rote and elaborative) and number of presentations (1, 2, 3, and 4), indicate how the words to be remembered could be counterbalanced over the four different numbers of presentations. What are some additional confoundings that must be eliminated?

Key Concepts

main effects 178

2 X 2 factorial design 178

interaction effects(s) 179

cross-over interaction 182

2 X 2 X 2 factorial design 183

higher order interaction 184

random groups design 186

matched groups design 186

treatments X treatments X
    subjects design 189

repeated measures designs 191

mixed designs 191

Suggested Readings

Several complex experiments are reprinted in: Elmes, D. G., *Readings in experimental psychology*. Chicago: Rand McNally, 1978. See articles 14 and 25, in particular.

.

WHAT STATISTICAL TEST SHOULD I USE WHEN—

I have one independent variable that has two levels?

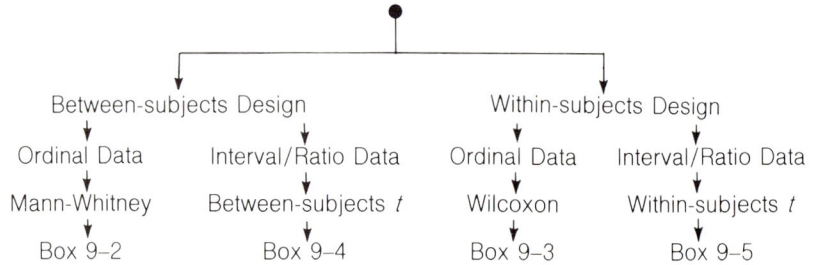

- Between-subjects Design
  - Ordinal Data
    - Mann-Whitney
    - Box 9–2
  - Interval/Ratio Data
    - Between-subjects *t*
    - Box 9–4
- Within-subjects Design
  - Ordinal Data
    - Wilcoxon
    - Box 9–3
  - Interval/Ratio Data
    - Within-subjects *t*
    - Box 9–5

I have one independent variable that has more than two levels?

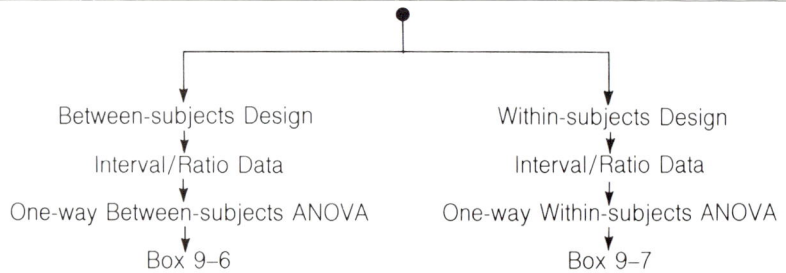

- Between-subjects Design
  - Interval/Ratio Data
    - One-way Between-subjects ANOVA
    - Box 9–6
- Within-subjects Design
  - Interval/Ratio Data
    - One-way Within-subjects ANOVA
    - Box 9–7

I have two independent variables, each with at least two levels?

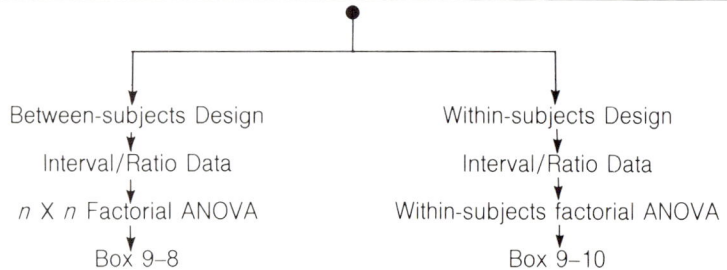

- Between-subjects Design
  - Interval/Ratio Data
    - *n* X *n* Factorial ANOVA
    - Box 9–8
- Within-subjects Design
  - Interval/Ratio Data
    - Within-subjects factorial ANOVA
    - Box 9–10

I have three independent variables, each with at least two levels?

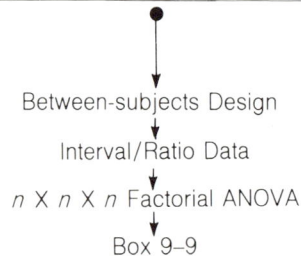

- Between-subjects Design
  - Interval/Ratio Data
    - *n* X *n* X *n* Factorial ANOVA
    - Box 9–9

Inferential Statistics

9

After we have collected and summarized our data, we need some way to help us determine whether our results are due to our manipulation or to chance factors. The purpose of this chapter is to give you some tools to help you make some decisions about your data. Inferential statistics allow you to make inferences about your data: where did the effect come from? Was it due to chance or was it due to my manipulation? In this chapter you will find many tests to help you make inferences, and you will also be treated to some information on the logic behind hypothesis testing.

Statistical Reasoning

Descriptive statistics, you will remember, are concerned with describing or summarizing data. Let us return for a moment to our hypothetical LSD experiment that was outlined in Chapter 6. The results of that study can be summarized by saying that the mean of the control group's running times was 13.60 seconds with a standard deviation of 2.63, while the experimental rats injected with LSD had a mean of 16.90 seconds and a standard deviation of 3.52 seconds. The experimental rats ran slower than the controls (the difference between the means was 3.30 seconds), but should we take this difference seriously? Perhaps it is due merely to chance factors such as measurement error or a few rats in the control group having a particularly good day and thus feeling like running a bit faster. How can we judge the likelihood that the difference between the two conditions is "real" or reliable, that it is not a fluke? How large must the difference be for us to conclude that it is unlikely to have occurred merely by chance alone? Inferential statistics are used to answer these questions.

In actual practice it is not too complicated to answer the questions. An appropriate statistical test is chosen for the experimental situation, a few straightforward computations are performed on a calculator (or computer), and then one consults a special table. The table informs us of the probability that the difference we found between our conditions is due to chance factors. If it is sufficiently unlikely to have occurred by chance, we conclude that the difference is statistically significant, or reliable. But while the actual computational procedures followed are often quite simple, the logic behind them needs to be understood so you will appreciate how statistical inferences are made.

Sampling

A *population* is a complete set of measurements (or individuals or objects) having some common observable characteristic. (See Box 9–1.) Examples of populations are all U.S. citizens of voting age, or all albino rats that have had injections of LSD, or all people asked to remember a list of 50 words. These are all populations we might be interested in for one reason or another, but of course it is impossible to study the entire population in any of these cases. If we could measure the entire population of rats for running speed after either an injection of LSD or an injection of a chemically inert substance, then we should better know what the effects of LSD were, since we would have measured the entire population. (Any difference could still, of course, be attributable to measurement error.) But since it is almost always impractical to measure an entire population, we must *sample* from it. A *sample* is a subset of a population, and it is what we are almost always examining when we compare experimental conditions. We make statistical inferences, then we draw a conclusion about an entire population that is based on only a sample of observations. We really want to know about the effects of LSD and the inert substance on rats in general, but we hope to draw this conclusion from a sample of, say, 20 rats in each condition.

Samples should always be as *representative* as possible of the population under study. One way of accomplishing this is *random sampling,* where members are picked from the population by some completely arbitrary means. Technically, one can only *generalize* about the population from which one has sampled, although if taken literally this would make experimental research hardly worth doing. If we received 50 rats from a supply house for our hypothetical experiment and selected a sample of 40 and randomly assigned them to the two conditions of the experiment, then would our conclusions only be true of the population of 50 rats? Well, perhaps technically, but no one would care about the result if this were so, and no one would have wasted the time doing the experiment. We would at least want to assume that the results are characteristic of that strain of rats, and, hopefully, that these results also generalize to other species, including humans. The problem is the same in experimental psychological research with humans. Suppose you are a researcher at the University of Toronto interested in studying some aspect of social behavior. You ready your experiment, which has three conditions, and plan to use students from introductory psychology courses as subjects, a common practice. You put up a sheet for them to sign up, randomly assign them to the three experimental conditions when they arrive at the experiment, and collect your data. To whom do your conclusions generalize? To introductory psychology students at the University of Toronto who volunteered for your experiment? If so, who cares what you found? In practice, psychologists assume that their results generalize more widely than the limited population from which they sampled for their experiment. We consider the problem of generality of results and the basis of this assumption more fully in Chapters 4 and 10.

Statistical Notation

Box 9–1

Characteristics of a population of scores are called *parameters*, while characteristics of a sample of scores drawn from a larger population are *statistics*. The mean of an entire population of scores is a parameter, while the mean of a sample is a statistic. To keep these distinctions straight, different symbols are used for population parameters and sample statistics. Below are some of the most frequent. Some of the concepts have already been explained and the others will be in the next few pages.

N	= Number of scores in a population
n	= Number of scores in a sample
μ	= Population mean (μ is pronounced mu)
$\bar{X}$	= Sample mean
σ^2	= Population variance (σ is pronounced sigma)
s^2	= Sample variance $\dfrac{\Sigma(X - \bar{X})^2}{n}$
$\hat{s}^2$	= Unbiased estimate of population variance $\dfrac{\Sigma(X - \bar{X})^2}{n - 1}$
σ	= Population standard deviation
s	= Sample standard deviation
$\hat{s}$	= Sample standard deviation based upon the unbiased variance estimate
$\sigma_{\bar{X}}$	= Standard error of the mean, $\dfrac{\sigma}{\sqrt{N}}$
$s_{\bar{X}}$	= Estimated standard error of the mean, $\dfrac{s}{\sqrt{n}}$ or $\dfrac{s}{\sqrt{n} - 1}$

The Distribution of Sample Means.   One way we could ask about the reliability of our LSD experiment with the rats would be to perform it repeatedly with new groups of rats. Of course we would be very unlikely to get exactly the same mean running times for the experimental and control conditions in these replications. The means in seconds for the experimental and control conditions in four replications might be 17.9 and 12.5, 16.0 and 13.4, 16.6 and 14.5, and 15.4 and 15.1. Since the experimental rats that receive the LSD always run slower than the control rats that do not, this would increase our confidence in the original finding, although the difference is rather small in the last replication. If we repeated the experiment like this and plotted the distribution of the sample means obtained in the two conditions, these distributions would tend to be normal. Thus they would have all the characteristics of the normal distribution, such as a certain proportion of the scores falling under a certain part of the curve. You could also find the difference between the two means in each experiment and plot the distribution of the differences between the sample means. These differences would also be normally distributed.

To give you a better idea of the *distribution of sample means* concept, let us borrow an example from a class demonstration by Horowitz (1974, pp. 179–182). Horowitz manufactured a population of 1000 normally distributed scores so that the mean and standard deviation of the entire population would be known. This is almost never the case in actual research situations, of course. His 1000 scores ranged from 0 to 100 and had a mean of 50 and a standard deviation of 15.8. The scores were listed on 1000 slips of paper and placed in a container. Horowitz had 96 students take samples of 10 slips from the container and calculate the mean. On each draw from the container, a slip was taken out, its number noted, and then replaced. The slips were mixed somewhat and another number was removed, and so on. After each student calculated the mean of the 10 scores in his or her sample, Horowitz collected all 96 and plotted the sampling distribution of means, which is represented in Table 9–1. In Table 9–1 the intervals between which means might fall are on the left and the number of means falling within each interval is on the right. Notice that the distribution is almost perfectly symmetrical, with almost as many scores in any interval a certain distance below the true mean of the population (50) as above it. Also, the mean of the 96 sample means (49.99) is quite close to the actual mean of the population (50). But the main thing you should notice in Table 9–1 is the great variability among the sample means. Although each sample of 10 was presumably random and not biased in any way, one sample had a mean of 37.8 while another had a mean of 62.3. Obviously these are very disparate means, even though they were sampled from the same population. If you were doing an experiment and found two very different sample means like this and were trying to decide whether they came from the same underlying distribution or two different distributions, you might think that such a large difference would indicate that they came from different distributions. In other words, you would think that the experimental treatment produced scores reliably different (from a different distribution) than the control scores. Usually this is a good rule —the larger the difference between means in the conditions, the more likely they are to be reliably different—but as we have seen even random sampling from a known distribution can produce sample means that differ greatly from each other and from the true population mean, which is known in this case. This lesson should be kept in mind while pondering small differences between means. Is the 3.30 second difference between experimental and control means in our mock LSD experiment really reliable?

The Standard Error of the Mean.   The standard error of the mean is the standard deviation of a distribution of sample means. In the data in Table 9-1 it is 5.01. The standard error of the mean gives you some idea as to the amount of variability in the distribution of sample means, or how likely the value of any particular sample mean is to be in error. Large standard errors indicate great variability, while small ones tell you that any particular sample mean is likely to be quite close to the actual population mean. Thus the standard error of the mean is a very useful number.

You might be wondering why we bother to tell you about the standard error of the mean if in order to calculate it you must repeat an

---

The distribution of sample means for the 96 samples taken by students in Horowitz' class. Each sample mean was based on ten observations (after Horowitz, 1974, Table 8.1).

Table 9–1

Interval	Frequency
62.0–63.9	1
60.0–61.9	1
58.0–59.9	3
56.0–57.9	7
54.0–55.9	9
52.0–53.9	12
50.0–51.9	15
48.0–49.9	15
46.0–47.9	13
44.0–45.9	9
42.0–43.9	6
40.0–41.9	3
38.0–39.9	1
36.0–37.9	1
	96 samples

Mean of sample means = 49.99
Standard deviation (s) of sample means = 5.01

experiment numerous times to get the sampling distribution of means and then calculate its standard deviation. Fortunately, you don't. The formula for finding the standard error of the mean (represented by $\sigma_{\bar{x}}$) is simply the standard deviation of the population (σ) divided by the square root of the number of observations ($\sqrt{n}$). Or

$$\sigma_{\bar{x}} = \frac{\sigma}{\sqrt{n}} \qquad (9\text{--}1)$$

Now, if you are still with us you might well be thinking, "Terrific. What good does this do me since the standard deviation of the population, the numerator in Equation 9–1, is never known?" That has occurred to statisticians, too, so they have devised a method for estimating the standard deviation of the population from the standard deviation of a sample. If you look back at Equation 6–2, where the formula for the standard deviation of a sample *(s)* appears, and simply replace the *n* in the denominator by $n - 1$, then you have the formula for getting an unbiased estimate of σ, the standard deviation of the population. The equation for finding the standard error of distribution of sample means (called the standard error of the mean or $s_{\bar{x}}$) is

$$\text{Estimated } \sigma_{\bar{x}} = s_{\bar{x}} = \frac{s}{\sqrt{n - 1}} \qquad (9\text{--}2)$$

Obviously we want the standard error of the mean to be as small as possible, since it represents the error we have in assuming that our sample mean represents the population mean. Equations 9–1 and 9–2 tell us how to do this: increase the size of the sample, *n,* which increases the denominator in the equations. The greater is *n,* the sample size, the smaller will be the standard error of the mean, $s_{\bar{x}}$. This should be no surprise. If the population involves 1000 scores, the sample mean should be closer to the population mean if there are 500 observations in the sample rather than only 10.

Horowitz drove this point home to the 96 students in his class by having them repeat the exercise of drawing slips from the population of 1000 scores and calculating the mean again, but this time he had them sample 50 slips rather than only 10. The resulting distribution of sample means is in Table 9–2. This time, with larger samples, there is much less variability in the sample means the students obtained. They are much closer to the actual population mean of 50. The standard deviation of the distribution of sample means, or the standard error of the mean, is 2.23, as opposed to 5.01 when the sample size was only 10. If $n = 100$ in a sample from the 1000 scores, the standard error of the mean would be 1.59; with a sample of 500 it would be .71, and with 1000 scores in a sample it would be only .50. (These were calculated from Equation 9–1 since the standard deviation (σ) is known for the entire population.) The reason you might not get the population mean even with a sample

The distribution of sample means for the 96 samples taken by students when sample size *(n)* = 50. The distribution is again normal, as in Table 9–1, but when each sample is based on a larger sample size, as it is here, the variability of the distribution (represented by the standard error of the mean) is much smaller (after Horowitz, 1974, Table 8.2).

Table 9–2

Interval	*Frequency*	
55.0–55.9	1	
54.0–54.9	3	
53.0–53.9	5	
52.0–52.9	9	
51.0–51.9	13	Mean of sample means = 49.95
50.0–50.9	17	Standard deviation *(s)* of sample means = 2.23
49.0–49.9	16	
48.0–48.9	14	
47.0–47.9	9	
46.0–46.9	6	
45.0–45.9	2	
44.0–44.9	1	
	96 samples	

of 1000 is that the sampling was done with *replacement;* that is, after a slip was drawn it was returned to the container and thus it might be drawn more than once while some slips are never drawn.

The lesson to be learned is that one should always try to maximize the number of observations—the sample size—in experimental conditions so that the statistics obtained will be as close as possible to the population parameters.

Testing Hypotheses

Scientists set up experiments to test hypotheses. The conventional statistical logic for testing hypotheses runs something like this. An experimenter arranges conditions, such as the experimental (LSD) and control (placebo) in our experiment with rats in Chapter 6, in order to test an *experimental hypothesis.* The experimental hypothesis in this case is that LSD will have some effect on running speed. This is tested by pitting it against the *null hypothesis,* which maintains that the two conditions do not differ in their effects on running speed. Stated another way, the experimental hypothesis is that the samples of running speeds come from two different underlying populations (that is, populations with different distributions), while the null hypothesis is that the two samples come from the same distribution. What statistical tests allow us to do is to find the likelihood with which the null hypothesis can be rejected. How unlikely must a null hypothesis be to be rejected? If an experimental result differs from that to be expected by the null hypothesis so much that a difference that great would be expected on the basis of "chance" (random factors) only 5 times in 100, we conclude that the null hypothesis can be rejected. This .05 *level of confidence* is just a convention; many psychologists prefer a more conservative .01 level for rejection, so that a null hypothesis is rejected only if the experimental result is likely to occur by chance in one case in 100. At any rate, the experimental hypothesis is tested, in a sense, indirectly. It is not affirmed, but the null hypothesis is rejected.

The logic of pitting an experimental hypothesis against the null hypothesis has come under attack in recent years for several reasons. Some argue that it gives a misleading idea as to how scientists operate. For one thing, not many researchers wander about the world losing any sleep or investing any thought into the null hypothesis. In general, experiments are set up to test theories and what is of primary concern is how their results can be interpreted or accounted for in light of our theories. Of special interest is the case where important experimental results seem irreconcilable with the major theories of a phenomenon. So experiments are important because of what they tell us about our theories and ideas—this is why we designed them in the first place—and not about whether or not the null hypothesis was rejected. But the null hypothesis testing logic is widely used as an introduction, however oversimplified, of the way scientific inference proceeds. Thus we present it here. Do not be misled, though, into thinking that psychologists spend their days dreaming up experimental hypotheses to pit against the null hypothesis. This is so in part, but the processes of scientific inference are fortunately much more varied and complicated than the logic of using the null hypothesis would lead one to believe.

The logic of testing hypotheses against the null hypothesis can be aptly illustrated in cases where the parameters of a population are known and we wish to determine if a particular sample comes from the population. Such cases are quite unusual in actual research, of course, since population parameters are rarely known.

Suppose you were interested in whether the members of your experimental psychology class were reliably above the national mean in intelligence as measured by I.Q. tests. (Or reliably below, as the case may be.) We know the population parameters in this case; the mean is 100 and the standard deviation is 15. You could test your class easily enough by giving them the short form of some intelligence test, such as the Otis, developed for group testing. Suppose you randomly sampled 25 people from your class of 100 and found the mean I.Q. of the sample to be 108 with a standard deviation of five.

How do we go about testing the experimental hypothesis that the class is reliably brighter than the population as a whole? First let us consider the hypotheses. The experimental hypothesis is that the students are brighter than people in the nation as a whole, or that the I.Q. scores of the students sampled come from a different population than randomly selected people. It's not exactly an exciting hypothesis, one in the vanguard of psychological research, but it will do for our purposes. The null hypothesis is, of course, that there is no reliable difference between our sample and the national mean, or that the students in the class are a sample from the same national population. If the null hypothesis were actually the case, the difference between the sample mean of 108 and the population parameter mean (μ) of 100 would be due to random factors. And certainly this is not implausible on the face of it because we have seen from our discussion of the sampling distribution of means how much a sample mean can differ from a population parameter, even when the sample was selected in an unbiased manner. Remember Horowitz' classroom demonstration, the results of which are portrayed in Tables 9–1 and 9–2.

Deciding how likely the null hypothesis is to be false is achieved by combining some concepts we have already met, including the normal curve, the sampling distribution of means, and z scores (standard scores). When unbiased samples are taken from a larger population, the means of these samples are normally distributed. With normal distributions we can specify what proportion of the distribution falls under each part of the curve, as seen in Figure 6-4. Finally, remember that z scores are the calculation of any score in a normal distribution in terms of standard deviation units from the mean.

All this is by way of review. Now how does this help us? What we do in testing the hypothesis that the sample is actually from a population with a mean IQ greater than the population at large is to treat the sample mean as an individual score (in terms of our earlier discussion) and calculate a z score on the basis of the deviation of the sample mean from the population mean. In our case we know the population mean is 100 and the class mean of the randomly selected students is 108. In order to calculate the z score we also need to know the standard error of the mean, the standard deviation of the sampling distribution of means. So the equation for the z score here is

$$z = \frac{\bar{x} - \mu}{\sigma_{\bar{x}}} \qquad \textbf{(9–3)}$$

The standard error of the mean ($\sigma_{\bar{x}}$) in this case is found by dividing the standard deviation of the population (σ) by $\sqrt{n}$ (see Equation 9–1), so $\sigma_{\bar{x}}$ is $15/\sqrt{25}$, or 3. So z is $(108 - 100)/3$, or 2.67.

Big deal, you say, what does a z of 2.67 buy us? A lot. It allows us to reject the null hypothesis with reasonable confidence and conclude in favor of the alternative hypothesis, that the class is actually superior to the population at large in terms of I.Q. We establish this by asking the question: How likely is a z score of 2.67 to occur when a sample mean is drawn from a larger population when the mean of the population is actually 100? The answer is that it will occur only .0038 of the time, or 38 times in 10,000. (We will come to how this was calculated in the next paragraph.) The custom in rejecting the null hypothesis is that if it could only occur one time in 20 by chance, we would reject it, so the difference in the class sample mean is *reliably different* or significantly different from the mean of the population.

To explain how this rather remarkable conclusion is reached we need to refer again to the special property of the normal curve of a certain proportion of cases falling under each part of the curve. Referring back to Figure 6–4 or to Figure 9–1 you can see that having a z score of ±2.00 is highly improbable. Greater scores in either direction occur only 2.15 percent of the time. Or in the other words, the probability of such an occurrence is .0215. This is also below the 5 percent or .05 *level of significance* or *level of confidence.* The .05 level of confidence is a convention adopted by psychologists, indicating that results occurring by chance 5 percent of the time (or less often) are reliable or *significant* results. So any mean score two or more standard deviations from the population mean is considered, using the logic we have outlined here, reliably (significantly) different from the population mean. In fact, the critical z value for rejecting the null hypothesis at the .05 level of confidence is ±1.96. In the Appendix in Statistical Table A-1 are presented (a) z scores from zero to four, with (b) the amount of area between the mean and z, and (c) most importantly, the amount of area beyond z. The amount of area beyond z is the probability of finding a score that distant from the mean on the basis of chance alone. Once again, when this probability falls below .05 as it does with z's of ±1.96 (or more), we reject the null hypothesis. Notice that with a z of 2.67, as in our I.Q. example, the probability of such a rare occurrence is only .0038. See Figure 9–1.

The statistical problem we have just considered—comparing a sample mean to a population parameter to see if the sample came from that population—is rather artificial, since population parameters are rarely known. But this example does exhibit characteristics of most common statistical tests. In all tests, some computations are performed on the data or raw scores gathered from an experiment, a value is found as in the z score just calculated, and then this value is compared to a distribution of values to see the likelihood that such a value could be obtained if the null hypothesis were in fact true. This distribution tells you, then, with what probability your result could be attributed to random variation. If this is less than five cases in 100 ($p < .05$), then by convention we say the null hypothesis can be rejected. This probability is sometimes called the *alpha (a) level* and, as already mentioned, some psychologists prefer values of .01 or even .001 (one in a hundred or thousand, respectively) to be more certain that the rejection of the null hypothesis is made correctly.

Figure 9–1

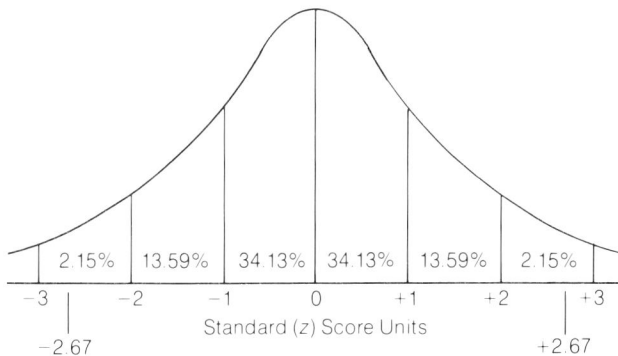

This is the standard normal distribution which was presented in Figure 6–4. There are two sides or tails to the distribution, positive and negative. If an experimenter simply asserts that there should be a difference between an experimental and control condition but does not specify the direction of the difference, this is called a nondirectional hypothesis. If a $z = 2.67$ is found, it is necessary to look up the probability that this will occur in both the positive and negative tails of the distribution and add the two, since the experimenter did not specify whether the difference should be positive or negative. When the experimenter has specified the direction of difference, one need only look up the probability in one tail. Since the distribution is symmetrical, the probability that the null hypothesis can be rejected is half as great with a one-tailed as with a two-tailed test. The less certain one is about the outcome of an experiment, the greater the difference between conditions must be for it to be decided that it is not due to chance.

Our z score test can also serve to introduce you very briefly to other important statistical concepts. First, let us consider two types of errors that can be made by applying statistical tests to experimental data according to the null hypothesis testing logic. Some dullard named them type I and type II errors so that students could henceforth confuse them whenever possible. A *type I error* is rejection of the null hypothesis when it is actually true, and the probability that this error is being made is indexed by the alpha level, which the experimenter selects. If the alpha level is $p = .05$, then we shall mistakenly reject the null hypothesis in 5 cases in 100. This points up the probabilistic nature of inferential statistics; we are not absolutely certain that a null hypothesis can be rejected, only reasonably certain. Thus the lower a level or p level we employ in determining statistical significance, the less chance we have of making a type I error. However, this increases the probability of a *type II error,* which occurs when we fail to reject the null hypothesis when it is actually false. Thus by setting a levels at different points we systematically decrease and increase the two types of errors. They trade off against one another.

Scientists are typically conservative in such matters, so the α level is typically kept fairly small, such as .05 or .01 (rather than, say, .10 or .15). Thus we minimize the error of rejecting the null hypothesis when it is true, or claiming a difference in our results when it is not there. As a consequence, though, we increase the type II error probability. A *conservative* statistical test minimizes type I errors, while more *liberal* statistical tests increase the probability of a type I error but decrease that of a type II error.

Unfortunately we can never know for sure in our experimental situations if we are committing type I or type II errors. We find this out primarily by experimental replications of our results. However, we can also find this out by calculating the power of a statistical test. The *power of a test* is the probability of rejecting the null hypothesis when it is actually false, so obviously we always want to maximize the power of our statistical tests. This is not the place to go into calculation of the power of tests, but we can note the two main factors that influence power. Look back to the z score formula in Equation 9–3. Whatever would make the z score larger would increase the power of the statistical test, or the likelihood of rejecting the null hypothesis. The value μ, the population mean, is fixed. Thus only two changes in the values of Equation 9–3 can affect z. One is the difference between the sample mean and the population mean ($\bar{x} - \mu$) and the other is n, the size of the sample. If the discrepancy between μ and $\bar{x}$ is increased (or in other cases if the difference between sample means in an experimental comparison is increased), so will the probability of rejecting the null hypothesis that there is no difference between the sample and the population means (or the means of the different samples).

But there is nothing we can do about the size of the difference between means; it is fixed. What we can do to increase the power of our statistical tests is to increase the sample size. As the sample size is increased, the power of the statistical test is increased. The reason for this, in brief, is that with larger samples we can be more confident that our sample means represent the mean of the populations from which they are drawn, and thus we can be more confident that any difference between a sample mean and a population mean (or between two sample means) is reliable. Sample size can have a great effect on the power of a test as can be seen in Table 9–3. Presented there are the z scores and p values for our difference between a sample mean of 108 I.Q. points and the population mean of 100 as the sample size varies. Obviously as the sample size varies, so will our conclusion as to whether or not the sample came from a national population or a more restricted, high I.Q., population. If we assume that the null hypothesis is actually false here, then by increasing sample size we decrease the probability of a type II error, or increase the power of the test we are using.

Table 9–3

How varying sample size *(n)* affects the power of a statistical test, or how likely one can reject the null hypothesis when employing the test. The example is from the *(z)* calculated in the text on a mean sample I.Q. of 108 where

$$z = \frac{\overline{X} - \mu}{\sigma_{\overline{X}}}$$

If the mean difference remains the same but *n* increases, *z* increases because

$$\sigma_{\overline{X}} = \frac{\sigma}{\sqrt{n}}$$

n	$\overline{X} - \mu$	$\sigma_{\overline{X}}$	*z*	*p*†
2	8	13.14	.61	.2709
5	8	6.70	1.19	.1170
7	8	5.67	1.41	.0793
10	8	4.74	1.69	.0455*
12	8	4.33	1.85	.0322*
15	8	3.88	2.06	.0197*
17	8	3.64	2.20	.0139*
20	8	3.35	2.38	.0087*
25	8	3.00	2.67	.0038*
50	8	2.12	3.77	.0001*
75	8	1.73	4.62	<.00003*
100	8	1.50	5.33	<.00003*

*All these values meet the conventional level of statistical significance. *p* < .05 (one-tailed). †*p* values are one-tailed (see below).

One final issue to be considered is specification of *directionality* of statistical tests. According to conventional logic involved in testing an alternative hypothesis against the null hypothesis, the alternative hypothesis may be *directional* or *nondirectional.* If one has an experimental and control group in an experiment, a nondirectional alternative hypothesis would simply be that the two groups would differ in performance on the dependent variable. But a directional hypothesis would state in addition the predicted direction of the difference; for example, the experimental group might be predicted to do better than the control.

This distinction is important, because if directionality of a hypothesis is stated, a *one-tailed* (or *one-sided*) *statistical test* is used, but if the alternative hypothesis is nondirectional a *two-tailed* (*two-sided*) test is used. One versus two "tails" refers to whether or not in looking up a *p* level associated with some determined value of the statistical test (say, *z* = 1.69), you consider one tail or both tails of the distribution.

This should be clearer with reference to our earlier example (see Figure 9–1). We took a sample (*n* = 25) of students, determined that the mean I.Q. of the sample was 108, and calculated a *z* = +2.67 in testing to see if this were different from the mean population I.Q. of 100. If we had no prior expectation of how the sample I.Q. should deviate from the normal population—if we thought it could be either greater or lower —this would have been a nondirectional hypothesis. In fact we did expect the sample I.Q. to be greater than 100, so we were testing a directional hypothesis and thus used a one-tailed test. This means we looked up the resulting z score in only one tail of the normal distribution, that greater than zero. A $z = +2.67$ leads to a one-tailed p value of .0038. If the hypothesis were nondirectional, then we have no *a priori* right to expect the resultant z score to be greater instead of less than zero. The z could fall in the positive or negative tail. Since the difference could have occurred in either direction, we use a two-tailed test. In practice, since the two tails of the distribution are symmetrical, we simply double the p level for the one-tailed test. In our example, if the hypothesis had been nondirectional, p would equal $2 \times .0038$, or .0076, still well below .05.

Two-tailed tests are more conservative and less powerful than one-tailed tests—it is harder to reject the null hypothesis. If you are uncertain about the outcome of an experiment, you need a greater value of the statistic to allow you to declare a difference. In practice, most investigators prefer to use the more conservative two-tailed test with sufficient power ensured by fairly large sample sizes.

Tests for Differences Between Two Groups

There is a bewildering variety of statistical tests for almost every purpose. At present we are interested in discussing tests that assess the reliability of a difference between two groups or conditions. How do we pick an appropriate test from all those available? There is no hard and fast rule. Tests vary in the assumptions they make, their power, and the types of situation for which they are appropriate. Perhaps the most popular test for the difference between two means in psychological research is the t test. Since the t test provides the same estimate of reliability as does the simple analysis of variance (discussed next) we will first concentrate on two other tests, the Mann-Whitney U test and the Wilcoxon signed-ranks test. These tests also are useful in introducing another type of statistical test besides that represented by the analysis of variance and the t test.

The Mann-Whitney and Wilcoxon tests are *nonparametric statistical tests* as opposed to *parametric tests.* Parametric statistical tests, such as analysis of variance and t, are those that make assumptions about the underlying population parameters of the samples on which the tests are performed. Common assumptions of parametric tests are that the variances of the underlying populations compared are equivalent, that the underlying distributions are normal, and that the level of measurement is at least an interval scale. If these assumptions are not met, then the test may be inappropriate. But how can we ever know whether or not the assumptions underlying the test are met since we do not know the population parameters? Typically we cannot, except by estimating population parameters from sample statistics. However, if we turn to nonparametric statistics the problem does not arise, because nonparametric statistical tests are those that make no assumptions about the underlying population parameters. This is why these tests are often called distribution-free statistics. Since these cannot be known anyway, this provides an important reason for using nonparametric tests. Another reason is that they are typically very easy to calculate and can often even be done by hand. On the other hand, though, nonparametric tests are typically less powerful than parametric tests employed in the same situation; that is, they are less likely to provide a rejection of the null hypothesis.

The *Mann-Whitney U test* is used to compare two samples and decide whether they come from the same or different underlying populations. It is used when the two samples are composed of different subjects, or in between-subjects designs. We cannot take space to provide the underlying rationale for the Mann-Whitney test, but can only tell you how to compute it in a rather cookbook fashion. In general, though, the logic is the same as in other statistical tests in which a value is computed from the test and compared to a distribution of values in order to determine whether or not the null hypothesis should be rejected. The way in which the Mann-Whitney test is applied to actual data is outlined in Box 9–2 where the reliability of the difference between the two samples in our hypothetical LSD experiment is tested.

The *Wilcoxon signed-ranks test* is also used for testing for the difference between two samples, but in this case the design must be a *related measures design.* In other words, either the same subjects must serve in both the experimental and control groups (a within-subjects design) or they must be matched in some way. Of course precautions must be taken in within-subjects designs to ensure that a variable such as practice or fatigue is not confounded with the variable of interest by using counterbalancing procedures (see Chapter 5). But assuming the experiment has been done well, the Wilcoxon signed-ranks test is an appropriate tool for analysis of the results.

Calculation of a Mann-Whitney U test on hypothetical experimental data previously discussed (see Table 6-2 on page 141.).   **Box 9–2**

Step 1. Rank all the numbers for *both* groups together beginning with the smallest number. Assign it the lowest rank.

Control (Placebo)		Experimental (LSD)	
Latency (sec.)	Rank	Latency (sec.)	Rank
9	1.5	9	1.5
10	3	13	11.5
11	4.5	13	11.5
11	4.5	14	17
12	7	14	17
12	7	15	21
12	7	16	24.5
13	11.5	16	24.5
13	11.5	16	24.5
13	11.5	17	28
13	11.5	17	28
14	17	18	32
14	17	18	32
14	17	18	32
15	21	18	32
15	21	19	35.5
16	24.5	19	35.5
17	28	20	37.5
18	32	22	39
20	37.5	26	40
	Σ rank$_1$ 295.5		Σ rank$_2$ 524.5

Note: When scores are tied, assign the mean value of the tied ranks to each. So for both 9 second times in this example, the rank 1.5 is assigned (the mean of 1 and 2).

Step 2. The equations for finding U and U' are below, where n_1 is the size of the smaller sample, n_2 is the size of the larger sample, ΣR_1 is the sum of the ranks of the smaller sample, and ΣR_2 is the sum of the ranks of the larger sample. Obviously the subscripts are only important if the sample sizes are unequal, which is not the case here.

$$U = n_1 n_2 + \frac{n_1(n_1 + 1)}{2} - \Sigma R_1 \qquad \textbf{(9–4)}$$

$$U = (20)(20) + \frac{(20)(21)}{2} - 295.5$$

$$U = 400 + 210 - 295.5$$
$$U = 314.5$$

$$U' = n_1 n_2 + \frac{n_2(n_2 + 1)}{2} - \Sigma R_2$$

$$U' = (20)(20) + \frac{(20)(21)}{2} - 524.5 \qquad \textbf{(9–5)}$$

$$U' = 85.5$$

Actually it is only necessary to compute U or U', because the other can be found according to the equations.

$$U = n_1 n_2 - U'$$
$$\text{or}$$
$$U' = n_1 n_2 - U$$

Step 3. Take U or U', whichever value is *smaller*, and look in Statistical Table A–2 to see if the difference between the two groups is reliable. The values in Statistical Table A–2 are recorded by different sample sizes. In this case both samples are of size 20, so the critical value from the table is 88. In order for the difference between the two groups to be judged reliable, the U or U' from the experiment must be *less than* the appropriate value in Table A–2. Since 85.5 is less than 88, we can conclude that the difference between the two groups is reliable at the .001 level of confidence.

Note: Statistical Table A–2 is only appropriate for situations when the sizes of the two samples are between 8 and 21. For other cases, you should consult an advanced text.

Before considering the signed-ranks test it is appropriate for us first to examine its simpler cousin, *the sign test,* which is also appropriate in the same situations. The sign test is the essence of simplicity. Suppose you have 26 subjects serving in both conditions of an experiment in which you are predicting that when subjects are in the experimental condition they will do better than when they are in the control condition. Now suppose that 19 subjects actually do better in the experimental condition than the control, while the reverse is true for the other 7. Is this difference reliable? The sign test allows an answer to this question with no more information about what the actual scores were. Under the null hypothesis we might expect 13 subjects to perform better in the experimental condition and 13 in the control. The sign test allows us to compute the exact probability that the null hypothesis is false when there are 19 cases in the predicted direction but also 7 reversals or exceptions. It turns out that the null hypothesis can be rejected in this case with a .014 confidence level (one-tailed); with a nondirectional prediction, p equals .028 (two-tailed). Once again we cannot delve into the details of how this is computed, but in Statistical Table A–3 we present the a levels (one-tailed) for cases of sample sizes from 3 to 42 when there are x number of exceptions to the predicted hypothesis. So, for example, when there are 16 subjects in the experiment (remember, in both conditions) and 13 show the predicted pattern of results while 3 exhibit reversals, we can reject the null hypothesis at the .011 level of confidence (one-tailed).

The sign test uses very little of the information from an experiment, just whether or not the subjects performed better or worse in one condition than another. For the sign test it does not matter whether the difference in performance is great or small; the direction of the difference is all that matters. The sign test therefore wastes much of the information gathered in an experiment and is not a very powerful statistical test. The Wilcoxon signed-ranks test is like the sign test in that it is used in situations where the same (or matched) subjects are employed in two conditions and the direction of the difference is taken into account, but in the Wilcoxon test the size of the difference is taken into account, too. For this reason it is also called the *sized sign test.* The Wilcoxon test is more powerful than the sign test. An example of how the Wilcoxon signed-ranks test is used is in Box 9–3.

In Boxes 9–4 and 9–5 we present the corresponding *t* tests for the analyses presented in the previous two boxes. The *t* test is a parametric test, which means that we assume that the underlying distributions are roughly normal in shape. Furthermore, the *t* test and other parametric tests were designed to be used on data that is at least interval in nature (see Chapter 2 on measurement scales). The U test and the sign test require only ordinal data. The computational formulae for the *t* tests should not blind you to the fact that the *t* tests are essentially based on *z* scores having to do with the standard error of the difference between means. So, even if the computational formulae appear unusual at first, the underlying logic is the same as that discussed earlier in this chapter.

Box 9–3 **Calculation of the Wilcoxon Signed-Ranks Test**

Imagine an experiment has just been performed testing whether or not Professor Humboldt von Widget's memory course, "How to Constipate Your Mind by Remembering Everything," really works. A group of 30 subjects is tested by presenting them with 50 words to be remembered. Then the subjects are randomly separated into two groups, and a check indicates that the groups do not differ reliably in the mean number of words recalled. The experimental group is given Professor von Widget's three week course while the control is not. Then all 30 subjects are tested again on another 50 word list. The controls show no improvement from one list to another, and the question we ask here is whether or not the experimental subjects' memories were reliably improved. (Note: We could—and should— also evaluate performance of experimental subjects on the second test to that of controls. The Mann-Whitney test is appropriate for this comparison. Do you know why?) We employ the Wilcoxon signed-ranks test to assess whether or not the experimental subjects improved reliably from the first test to the second.

Step 1. Place the data in a table such as that below where both scores for each subject (before and after the memory course) are paired together. Find and record the difference between the pairs.

Mean number of words recalled

Subject	Before	After	Difference	Rank
1	11	17	+ 6	14
2	18	16	− 2	5.5
3	9	21	+12	15
4	15	16	+ 1	2.5
5	14	17	+3	8.5
6	12	15	+ 3	8.5
7	17	16	− 1	2.5
8	16	17	+ 1	2.5
9	15	20	+ 5	13
10	19	16	− 3	8.5
11	12	13	+ 1	2.5
12	16	14	−2	5.5
13	10	14	+ 4	11.5
14	17	20	+ 3	8.5
15	6	10	+ 4	11.5
	$\bar{x} =$	$\bar{x} =$		
	13.80	16.07		

Step 2. Rank the values of the differences according to size beginning with the smallest. *Ignore the sign.* Use the absolute values of the numbers. For tied ranks, assign each the mean value of the ranks. (See the right-hand column above.)

Step 3. Add the ranks for all the difference values that are negative (5.5 + 2.5 + 8.5 + 5.5 = 22.0) and positive (14 + 15 + 2.5 + 8.5 + 8.5 + 2.5 + 13 + 2.5 + 11.5 + 8.5 + 11.5 = 98.0). These are the signed-rank values.

Step 4. Take the signed rank value that is smallest (22 in this case) and go to Table A–4. Look up the number of pairs of observations (listed as *n* on the left). There are 15 in this case. Then look at the number under the desired level of significance. Since the direction of the outcome was predicted in this case (we expected the memory course to help rather than hurt recall of words), let us choose the value under the .025 level of significance for a one-tailed test. This value is 25. If the smaller of the two values from the experiment is *below* the appropriate value in the table, then the result is reliable. Since 22 is below 25, we can conclude that Professor von Widget's course really did help memory for words.

Note: Remember that the controls showed no improvement in performance from one test to the other. This is a crucial bit of information, for otherwise we could not rule out two plausible competing hypotheses. One is that the improvement on the second list was simply due to practice on the first, and the other is that the second list was easier than the first. Actually, if Professor von Widget's course were as effective as numerous memory courses currently on the market, results from an actual experiment would show (and have shown) more spectacular improvement than the hypothetical results here. Memory improvement courses, all of which embody the same few principles, really work for objective materials such as word lists.

Box 9–4

Calculation of a Between-Subjects *t* Test

Hypothetical experimental data previously discussed (see Box 9–2). The calculation formula is:

$$t = \frac{\bar{X}_1 - \bar{X}_2}{\sqrt{\left[\dfrac{\Sigma X_1^2 - \dfrac{(\Sigma X_1)^2}{N_1} + \Sigma X_2^2 - \dfrac{(\Sigma X_2)^2}{N_2}}{N_1 + N_2 - 2}\right]\left[\dfrac{1}{N_1} + \dfrac{1}{N_2}\right]}}$$

$\bar{X}_1$ = mean of group 1 ΣX_1^2 = sum of squared scores in group

$\bar{X}_2$ = mean of group 2 ΣX_2^2 = sum of squared scores in group

N_1 = number of scores in group 1 $(\Sigma X_1)^2$ = square of group 1 sum

N_2 = number of scores in group 2 $(\Sigma X_2)^2$ = square of group 2 sum

Control (placebo)				Experimental (LSD)			
X	X^2	X	X^2	X	X^2	X	X^2
9	81	13	169	9	81	17	289
10	100	14	196	13	169	18	324
11	121	14	196	13	169	18	324
11	121	14	196	14	196	18	324
12	144	15	225	14	196	18	324
12	144	15	225	15	225	19	361
12	144	16	256	16	256	19	361
13	169	17	289	16	356	20	400
13	169	18	324	16	356	22	484
13	169	20	400	17	289	26	676

$\Sigma X = 272$ $\Sigma X^2 = 3838$ $\Sigma X = 338$ $\Sigma X^2 = 5960$

$\bar{X} = 13.60$ $\bar{X} = 16.90$

Step 1. After calculating ΣX, ΣX^2, and $\overline{X}$ for each group (by the way, there is no need to rank order your data), you need to calculate $(\Sigma X)^2/N$ for each group: $(272)^2/20 = 3699.20$ and $(338)^2/20 = 5712.20$. Then you need to determine $\Sigma X^2 - (\Sigma X)^2/N$ for each group: $3838 - 3699.2 = 138.8$ and $5960 - 5712.2 = 247.8$.

Step 2. Now add the two group figures you obtained in the last step: $247.8 + 138.8$, and divide this sum by $N_1 + N_2 - 2$: $386.6/38 = 10.17$.

Step 3. The quotient obtained in step two (10.17) is multiplied by

$$\left[\frac{1}{N_1} + \frac{1}{N_2}\right](10.17)(2/20) = 1.02.$$

Step 4. We now take the square root of the product obtained in step 3: $\sqrt{1.02} = 1.01$.

Step 5. Find the absolute difference between the mean scores of the two groups (just subtract one from the other and ignore the sign): $16.90 - 13.60 = 3.30$.

Step 6. $t =$ the difference between means (step 5) divided by the results of step 4: $3.30/1.01 = 3.27$. So, our $t = 3.27$. To evaluate this look in the tabled values of t in Table A–5 (page 314). We enter this table with the number of degrees of freedom (*df*) in our experiment, which means the number of scores that are free to vary. For a between-subjects t the degrees of freedom are $N_1 + N_2 - 2$, in this case $df = 38$. For $p = .05$ and $df = 38$, the critical value of t is 2.04 in our table (always take the next lowest *df* to figure the critical value). Since our obtained t exceeds the critical value, we can reject the hypothesis that our two gave the same running scores; that is, LSD had an effect on the behavior of our subjects.

Calculation of a Within-Subjects *t* Test

Box 9–5

The hypothetical data is from Professor Widget's experiment (see Box 9–3). The computational formula for the within-subject t test is as follows:

$$t = \sqrt{\frac{N - 1}{[N\Sigma D^2/(\Sigma D)^2] - 1}} \qquad \textbf{(9–7)}$$

where $N =$ number of subjects; $D =$ difference in the scores of a given subject (or matched subject pair) in the two conditions

Mean Number of Words Recalled

Subject	Before	After	Difference	D^2
1	11	17	+ 6	36
2	18	16	− 2	4
3	9	21	+12	144
4	15	16	+ 1	1
5	14	17	+ 3	9
6	12	15	+ 3	9
7	17	16	− 1	1
8	16	17	+ 1	1
9	15	20	+ 5	25
10	19	16	− 3	9
11	12	13	+ 1	1
12	16	14	− 2	4
13	10	14	+ 4	16
14	17	20	+ 3	9
15	6	10	+ 4	16
	$\overline{X} = 13.80$	$\overline{X} = 16.07$	$\Sigma D = 35$	$\Sigma D^2 = 285$
			$(\Sigma D)^2 = 1225$	

Step 1. After you arrange the scores for each subject in pairs as above, record the difference between each pair and then square each of these difference scores.

Step 2. Add the difference scores across subjects, which gives you ΣD, then square this sum to get $(\Sigma D)^2$: D = 35; and $(\Sigma D)^2 = 1225$.

Step 3. Calculate the sum of the squared difference scores to get $\Sigma D^2 = 285$.

Step 4. Multiply ΣD^2 (step 3) by the number of subjects: 285 X 15 = 4275.

Step 5. Divide the product found in step 5 by $(\Sigma D)^2$: 4275/1225 = 3.49 and then subtract 1 from the result: 3.49 − 1 = 2.49.

Step 6. Divide the number of subjects less 1 (N − 1) by the result of step 5: 14/2.49 = 5.62.

Step 7. $t = \sqrt{5.62} = 2.37$.

Step 8. In order to evaluate t compare it to the critical values shown in Table A–5 on page 314. Enter the table with N − 1 *df,* and for this study *df* = 14. With *df* = 14 the critical value of t is 2.145 for p = .05. Since the obtained t exceeds the critical value, we can conclude that von Widget's course really did affect memory for words.

The Analysis of Variance

Most psychological research has progressed beyond the stage where there are only two conditions, an experimental and a control, that are compared to one another. It is typical for researchers to employ more than two conditions in psychological research. Rather than only varying the presence or absence of some independent variable, it is more important and useful to vary systematically the magnitude of the independent variable. In our example of the effects of LSD on running speed of rats, it may be quite useful to vary the amount of LSD administered to the rats. Perhaps effects are different at low dosages than at high ones. We could not discover this from the two-group design where one group received LSD in some amount and the other did not. In order to evaluate the results of such an experiment with multiple groups, it is necessary to employ the analysis of variance, in particular *simple analysis of variance.* Simple analysis of variance is used in situations where one factor or independent variable (such as amount of LSD) is varied systematically. Thus it is also called one-factor analysis of variance.

Often researchers are interested in more complex situations than varying one factor. In particular, they may be interested in situations where two or more factors are varied simultaneously. In these complex or multifactor experimental designs, the analysis of variance is also appropriate, but it is more complex. In this section we introduce you to the logic of simple and multifactor analysis of variance (abbreviated ANOVA), though of course we cannot delve into it in all its complexity.

Simple Analysis of Variance. At the heart of the analysis of variance procedure is, as you might suspect from the name, a comparison of variance estimates. We have already discussed the concept of variance and its estimation from one particular sample of observations. You should refer back to the section on measures of dispersion in Chapter 6 if the concept of variance is hazy to you at this point. As a quick review, recall that the equation for the unbiased estimate of the population variance is

$$\hat{S}^2 = \frac{\Sigma(x - \bar{x})^2}{n - 1} \tag{9-8}$$

and that when the deviation of scores from the mean is large, the variance will be great. Similarly when the deviations from the mean are small the variance will be small.

In the analysis of variance two independent estimates of variance are obtained. One is based on the variability *between* the different experimental groups—how much means of the different groups vary from one another. Actually the variance is computed as to how much the individual group means differ from the overall mean of all scores in the experiment. The greater the difference among the means of the groups, the greater will be the between-groups variance. The other estimate of variance is the *within-groups variance.* This is the concept that we have already discussed in considering estimates of variance from individual samples, but now we are concerned with finding an estimate of within-groups variance that is representative of all the individual groups, so we take the mean of the variances of these groups. The within-groups variance gives us an estimate of how much subjects in the groups differ from one another (or the mean of the group). In short, two variance estimates are obtained, one for the variance within groups and one for the variance between groups. Now what good does this do?

The basic logic of testing to see whether or not the scores of the different groups or conditions are reliably different is as follows. The null hypothesis is that all the subjects in the various conditions are drawn from the same underlying population; the experimental variable had no effect. If the null hypothesis were true and all the scores in the different groups came from the same population, then the between-groups variance should be the same as the within-groups variance. That is, the means from the different groups should vary from one another no more nor less than do the scores within the groups. In order to reject the null hypothesis, then, the means of the different groups must vary from one another more than the scores vary within the groups. The greater the variance (differences) between the groups of the experiment, the more likely the independent variable is to have had an effect, especially if the within-groups variance is low.

The person who originated this logic was the eminent British statistician R. A. Fisher, and the test is referred to as an *F*-test in his honor. The *F*-test is simply a ratio of the between-groups variance estimate to the within-groups variance estimate, so

$$F = \frac{\text{between-groups variance}}{\text{within-groups variance}} \qquad \textbf{(9-9)}$$

According to the logic outlined above, the *F*-ratio under the null hypothesis should be 1.00, because the between-groups variance should be the same as the within-groups variance. The greater the between-groups variance is than the within-groups variance and, consequently, the greater the *F*-ratio is than 1.00, the more confident we can be in rejecting the null hypothesis. Exactly how much greater the *F*-ratio must be than 1.00 depends on the *degrees of freedom* in the experiment, or how free the measures are to vary. This depends both on the number of groups or conditions in the eperiment and on the number of observations in each group. The greater the number of degrees of freedom, the smaller need be the value of the F-ratio to be judged a reliable effect, as you can see from examining Statistical Table A-6. You should follow the computational example in Box 9–6 carefully to gain a feel for the analysis of variance.

Computing Simple Analysis of Variance: One Variable—Between Subjects

Box 9–6

This ANOVA is often called a *one-way* ANOVA because there is only *one* independent variable. Imagine you have just performed an experiment testing the effects of LSD on how fast rats run, but that there were three levels of LSD administered, rather than only two as in our earlier example. Ten rats received no LSD, ten more received a small amount, and yet a third group received a great amount. (The small sample sizes are unrealistic for an actual experiment, but will serve to illustrate the method here.) Thus the experiment employs a between-subjects design where amount of LSD (none, small, large) is the independent variable and running time is the dependent variable. First calculate the sum of the scores (ΣX) and the sum of the squared values of the scores (ΣX^2).

	Amount of LSD		
	None	Small	Large
	13	17	26
	11	15	20
	14	16	29
	18	20	31
	12	13	17
	14	19	25
	10	18	26
	13	17	23
	16	19	25
	12	21	27
$\Sigma X =$	133	175	249
$\overline{X} =$	13.30	17.50	24.90
$\Sigma X^2 =$	1819	3115	6351
$\Sigma\Sigma X = 557$	$\Sigma\Sigma X^2 = 11285$		

A basic quantity in calculation of analysis of variance is the *sum of squares,* which is an abbreviated form for the term *sum of squared deviations from the mean.* If you look back to Equation 6–3 (or Box 9–1), which defines the variance of a sample, you will see that the sum of squares is the numerator. There are actually three sum of squares values of interest. First, the total sum of squares (SS_{total}), which is defined as the sum of the squared deviations of the individual scores from the grand mean or the mean of all the scores in all groups in the experiment. Second, the sum of squares between groups ($SS_{between}$), which is defined as the sum of the squared deviations of the group means from the grand mean. Third, the sum of squares within groups (SS_{within}) is the mean of the sum of the squared deviations of the individual scores within groups or conditions from the group means. It turns out that $SS_{total} = SS_{between} + SS_{within}$, so that in practice only two sums of squares need be calculated and the third can be found by subtraction.

These sums of squares could be calculated by taking the deviations from the appropriate means, squaring them, and then finding the sum, but such a method would take much time and labor. Fortunately there are computational formulas which allow the calculations to be done more easily, especially if the values of ΣX and ΣX^2 have been found for each group, as in the present data. The formula for finding the total sum of squares is

$$SS_{total} = \Sigma\Sigma X^2 - \frac{T^2}{N} \qquad \textbf{(9–10)}$$

where $\Sigma\Sigma X^2$ means that each score within each group is squared (X^2) and all these squared values are added together, so ΣX^2. There are two separate summation signs, one for summing the squared values within groups and one for then summing these ΣX^2 across the different groups. The T is for the total of all scores and N here is the total number of scores in the experiment. So SS_{total} in our example is calculated in the following way:

$$SS_{total} = \Sigma\Sigma X^2 - \frac{T^2}{N}$$

$$SS_{total} = 1819 + 3115 + 6351 - \frac{(133 + 175 + 249)^2}{30}$$

$$SS_{total} = 11{,}285 - \frac{310{,}249}{30}$$

$$SS_{total} = 11{,}285 - 10{,}341.63$$

$$SS_{total} = 943.37$$

The between-groups sum of squares is calculated with the following formula:

$$SS_{between} = \Sigma\frac{(\Sigma X)^2}{n} - \frac{T^2}{N} \qquad \textbf{(9–11)}$$

The first part of the formula means that the sum of the values for each group is squared and then divided by the number of observations on which it is based or $(\Sigma X)^2/n$; then these values are summed across groups, so $\Sigma (\Sigma X)^2/n$. The second part of the formula is the same as for the SS_{total}:

$$SS_{between} = \Sigma \frac{(\Sigma X)^2}{n} - \frac{T^2}{N}$$

$$SS_{between} = \frac{17{,}689}{10} + \frac{30{,}625}{10} + \frac{62{,}001}{10} - 10{,}341.63$$

$$SS_{between} = 11{,}031.50 - 10{,}341.63$$

$$SS_{between} = 689.87$$

The sum of squares within groups can be found by subtracting $SS_{between}$ from SS_{total}, so $SS_{within} = 943.37 - 689.87 = 253.50$. But as a check it is also worthwhile to compute it directly. This is done by computing an SS_{total} as in Equation 9–10 for each group and summing all these sums of squares for the individual groups. Unless you have made an error, this quantity should equal SS_{within} obtained by subtraction. Note that

$$\frac{(\Sigma\Sigma X)^2}{N} \text{ or } \frac{T^2}{N}$$

is called the correction term because it is taken out of most SS.

After we have obtained the various sums of squares, it is convenient to construct an analysis of variance table such as that shown below. In the far left column appears the Source of Variance, or Source. Keep in mind that there are two primary sources of variance we are interested in comparing—between-groups and within-groups.

In the next column are the number of degrees of freedom *(df)*. These can be thought of as the number of scores that are free to vary given that the total is fixed. For the degrees of freedom between groups, if the overall total is fixed, all groups are free to vary except one. So the between-groups *df* is the number of groups minus one. In our example, then, it is $3 - 1 = 2$. The within-groups *df* is equal to the total number of scores minus the number of groups, because there is one score in each group that cannot vary if the group total is fixed. So within-groups *df* is $30 - 3 = 27$. The total *df* = between-groups *df* + within-groups *df*.

The third column is for the sum of squares *(SS)*, which have already been calculated. The fourth column is for the *mean squares,* which are found by dividing the *SS* for each row by the *df*. Each mean square is an estimate of the population variance if the null hypothesis is true. But if the independent variable had an effect, the between-groups mean square should be larger than the within-groups mean square.

As already discussed in the text, these two values are compared by computing an *F* ratio, which is found by dividing the $MS_{between}$ by the MS_{within}. Once the *F* value is calculated, it is necessary to determine whether or not the value reaches an acceptable level of statistical significance. By looking in Statistical Table A–6, we can see that for 2 and 26 degrees of freedom (the closest we can get to 2 and 27), an *F* value of 9.12 is needed for the .001 level of significance. Our *F* value surpasses 9.12, so we can conclude that the groups varied reliably in running speed due to variation in the independent variable—amount of LSD injected.

Source	df	SS	MS	F	p
Between-groups	2	689.87	344.94	36.73	<.001
Within-groups	27	253.50	9.39		
Total	29	943.37			

Note: If you compute analyses of variance yourself with the aid of a calculator you must guard against errors. If you ever come up with a negative sum of squares within-groups (by subtracting $SS_{between}$ from SS_{total}), you will know you screwed up. You cannot have a negative sum of squares. You should compute SS_{within} both by subtraction and directly, anyway, as a check. One common error is to confuse ΣX^2 (square each number and then sum the squares) with $(\Sigma X)^2$, which is the square of the total of the scores.

If the simple analysis of variance indicates that there is reliable variation among the conditions of an experiment, this still does not tell us all we would like to know. In particular, it is still of great interest to know which of the individual conditions vary among themselves. This is especially important in cases where independent variable manipulation is qualitative in nature. *Quantitative* variation of an independent variable refers to the case where the quantity of an independent variable is manipulated (for example, amount of LSD), while *qualitative* variation is the case of conditions that vary but not in some easily specified quantitative manner. An example of qualitative variation is an instructional manipulation where the different conditions vary in the instructions that are given at the beginning of the experiment. In such cases it is not enough simply to say that the conditions vary reliably from one another. It is of interest to know which particular conditions differ. To answer this question follow-up tests to the simple analysis of variance are needed. In follow-up tests (generally called *post hoc* tests) the conditions of the experiment are taken two at a time and compared to see which pairs are reliably different. There is a great variety of statistical tests that can be used for this purpose. One could perform analyses of variance on groups taken as pairs, which is equivalent to performing *t* tests, but usually other tests are performed. These include the Newman-Keuls test, the Scheffé test, Duncan's multiple range test, Tukey's HSD (Honestly Significant Differences) test, and Dunnett's test. These vary in their assumptions and their power. You should consult statistical texts when you need to use a follow-up test.

Follow-up tests are also used when manipulation of the independent variable is quantitative in nature. These are called *trend tests,* but we will not discuss them further here.

Within-Subjects (Treatments X Subjects) ANOVA—One Variable (One-way ANOVA)   Box 9–7

We could have conducted the previous three-level LSD study with a within-subject design rather than with a between-subject design. Of course, we would have counterbalanced the order of administering dosages across subjects. Let us assume that we used nine subjects in our within-subjects LSD study: three subjects received the dose order None-Large-Small; three received the doses in the Small-None-Large order; and the final three subjects were dosed in the order Large-Small-None. After each dose of LSD, the rats' running time in the straight alley was recorded. We could analyze the effects of order by a two-factor, within-subjects ANOVA (see Box 9–10), but for the purposes of this illustration, we will ignore the effects of treatment order.

In a within-subjects ANOVA we need to calculate the following kinds of variability:

SSTotal—This is the variation about the mean of all the scores. SSTotal is the sum of the remaining sums of squares.

SSTreatment—This is the difference among the treatment conditions and is calculated like SSBetween in the previous ANOVA.

SSSubjects—This estimates the differences among individuals in our experiment and is used to calculate the next SS.

SSError or *SSTreatment X Subject*—This represents the random variability that would occur in the scores of the same individuals in the same conditions. This interaction gives the ANOVA the name

Treatments X Subjects. Usually, this SS is called *error variance,* and it is the denominator of the *F* ratio of the treatment effect.

We will use the hypothetical data from the first nine subjects of the LSD study shown in Box 9–6. We will assume the ordering of treatments as mentioned above. You should set up your data table as below, so that the scores for each subject are in a row. Leave room in your table so that a given subject's total score summed across treatments can appear in the table. You might also want to leave room for the squares of the scores and the squares of the subjects' totals.

Running Times

Subject	None	Amount of LSD Small	Large	Subject Total	Subject Total Squared
1	13	17	26	56	3136
2	11	15	20	46	2116
3	14	16	29	59	3481
4	18	20	31	69	4761
5	12	13	17	42	1764
6	14	19	25	58	3364
7	10	18	26	54	2916
8	13	17	23	53	2809
9	16	19	25	60	3600
$\Sigma X =$ 121		154	222	497	
$\Sigma X^2 =$ 1675		2674	5622		27497

$\Sigma\Sigma X = 497$ $\Sigma\Sigma X^2 = 9971$ (1675 + 2674 + 5622)

Step 1. When you calculate $\Sigma\Sigma X$ by adding the three treatment totals (121 + 154 + 222), you can check your accuracy by adding up the subject totals, the sum of which should equal $\Sigma\Sigma X$. Calculate ΣX^2 for each treatment, $\Sigma\Sigma X^2$, and the sum of the squares of the subject totals (last column).

Step 2. Calculation of the correction term, *C.*

$C = (\Sigma\Sigma X)^2/N$, where $N =$ the number of scores in the table (9 subjects X 3 scores for each subject)
= $497^2/27$
= 247009/27
= 9148.48

Step 3. SSTotal = $\Sigma\Sigma X^2$ – Step 2
= 9971 – 9148.48
= 822.52

Step 4. SSTreatments = SSDose

SSDose = This is calculated by summing the squares of the treatment totals, dividing that sum

by the number of scores in each
treatment, and then subtracting C (Step 2).

$$\text{SSDose} = \frac{121^2 + 154^2 + 222^2}{9} - \text{Step 2}$$

$$= 87419/9 - \text{Step 2}$$
$$= 9737.89 - 9148.48$$
$$= 589.41$$

Step 5. SSSubject = Sum of the squared subject totals (final
column in the table) divided by the number
of scores per subject (3) minus C.
$$= 27947/3 - \text{Step 2}$$
$$= 9315.67 - 9148.48$$
$$= 167.19$$

Step 6. SSError = SSTotal − SSDose − SSSubject
$$= \text{Step 3} - \text{Step 4} - \text{Step 5}$$
$$= 822.52 - 589.41 - 167.19$$
$$= 65.92$$

Step 7. Determination of *df.*

$$df\,\text{Total} = \#\text{ scores} - 1 = 26$$
$$df\,\text{Dose} = \#\text{ treatments} - 1 = 2$$
$$df\,\text{Subject} = \#\text{ subjects} - 1 = 8$$
$$df\,\text{Error} = (df\text{Dose})\,(df\text{Subject}) = 16$$

Step 8. Determination of MS

$$\text{MSDose} = \text{SSDose}/df\,\text{Dose} = 589.41/2 = 294.71$$
$$\text{MSError} = \text{SSError}/df\,\text{Error} = 65.92/16 = 4.12$$

Step 9. $F = \text{MSDose}/\text{MSError} = 294.71/4.12 = 71.53$

Step 10. Summary Table

Source	SS	df	MS	F
Subjects	167.19	8		
Dose	589.41	2	294.71	71.53
Error	65.92	16	4.12	
Total	822.52	26		

We determine the significance of the F ratio by entering Table A–6
(p. 315) with 2 and 16 degrees of freedom. Since our obtained F
greatly exceeds those needed for significance with 2 and 16 *df,* we
can conclude that dose level of LSD influenced the running times of
our rats.

Multifactor Analysis of Variance. A frustrating aspect to the study of behavior is that there are hardly ever any simple or one-factor explanations. Even the simplest behaviors studied in laboratory situations turn out to be affected by multiple factors. In order to discover these multiple determinants of behavior and how they interact, it is necessary to perform experiments in which more than one factor is varied simultaneously. The appropriate procedure for analyzing results of such experiments is *multifactor analysis of variance.* This may involve analysis of experiments where any number of factors is involved, but in practice it is rare to find more than four variables of interest manipulated simultaneously. When two factors are involved, the analysis is referred to as two-way ANOVA; when three factors are involved, it is a three-way ANOVA, and so on.

The importance of such complex designs involving more than one factor is that they allow the experimenter to assess how different factors may *interact* to produce an experimental result. Recall that an interaction occurs when the effect of one experimental variable is affected by the level of the other experimental variable (see Chapter 8). If we performed a 2 X 2 experiment (this refers to two different factors with two different levels of each factor) on interpersonal attraction involving sex of the subject (male versus female) and sex of the experimental confederate who the subject was to evaluate, we might discover an interaction effect. If how close the subject stood to the confederate were one of the dependent variables, then we might find that male subjects tend to stand closer to female confederates and female subjects stand closer to the male confederates. This is an example of an interaction. There is no simple generalization as to how close male or female subjects will stand to a confederate in an experiment; it depends on the sex of the confederate.

When performing a complex analysis of variance, we find out what effect each factor has separately in the experiment—these are called *main effects*—and also how the variables affect one another, which are called *interaction effects,* or simply *interactions.* If women tended to stand closer to the confederate than did men regardless of the sex of the confederate, this would be a main effect of sex of subject on interpersonal distance. And, again, an interaction would be the different effect of sex of subject depending on sex of the confederate.

In the following three boxes, we present some "recipes" for complex ANOVAs. We have refrained from presenting much of the logic behind these tests because of space limitations. However, you should find the examples useful in analyzing your own results even if you have not had a formal course in statistics. The experiments discussed in the next three boxes were also examined in Chapter 8.

Calculation of a 2 X 2 ANOVA on the Data from the Unpublished Memory Experiment Reported in Chapter 8 (see Table 8–1).

Box 9–8

	High Imagery Words		Low Imagery Words	
	Rote Rehearsal	Elaborative Rehearsal	Rote Rehearsal	Elaborative Rehearsal
	5	8	4	7
	7	8	1	6
	6	9	5	3
	4	7	6	3
	4	10	4	5
	9	10	3	6
	7	8	4	2
	5	9	4	4
	5	8	5	5
	6	9	3	4
$\Sigma X =$	58	86	39	45
$\Sigma X_2 =$	358	748	169	225

$\Sigma X^2 = (358 + \ldots + 225) = 1500 \quad \Sigma\Sigma X = 228$

Step 1. Square the grand sum ($\Sigma\Sigma X = 228$) and divide by the total number of scores (40). $(\Sigma\Sigma X)^2/N = (228)^2/40 = 1299.6$. This is the correction term.

Step 2. SSTotal $= \Sigma\Sigma X^2 - (\Sigma\Sigma X)^2/N$. Subtract the results of Step 1 from 1500. SSTotal $= 200.4$.

Step 3. SSImagery. Get the sum of all scores in each imagery condition, square each sum, then divide each sum by the number of scores yielding each sum, add the two quotients, and then subtract the results of Step 1 from the last sum.

$$\text{SSImagery} = (58 + 36)^2/20 + (39 + 45)^2/20 - \text{Step 1}$$

$$= \frac{144^2 + 84^2}{20} - 1299.6$$

$$= 1389.6 - 1299.6$$
$$= 90$$

Step 4. SSRehearsal. This is calculated in the same manner as Step 3, except you base your calculations on the grand sum of each type of rehearsal.

$$\text{SSRehearsal} = \frac{(86 + 45)^2 + (58 + 39)^2}{20} - \textit{Step 1}$$

$$= 1328.5 - 1299.6$$
$$= 28.9$$

Step 5. SSRehearsal X Imagery. Square each group sum and add the squares. Then divide each sum by the number of scores in each sum. From this last result you subtract the SSImagery (Step 3), SSRehearsal (Step 4), and Step 1.

$$\text{SSI X R} = \frac{58^2 + 86^2 + 39^2 + 45^2}{10} - \text{Step 1} - \text{Step 3} - \text{Step 4}$$

$$= 14306/10 - 1299.6 - 90 - 28.9$$
$$= 12.1$$

Step 6. SSError. Subtract each of your treatments SS from SSTotal.

$$\text{SSError} = 200.4 - 90 - 28.9 - 12.1$$
$$= 69.4$$

Step 7. Determining degrees of freedom.

dfTotal $=$ the number of measures less one $(40 - 1) = 39$
dfImagery $=$ number of levels of Imagery less one $(2 - 1) = 1$
dfRehearsal $=$ number of levels of rehearsal less one $(2 - 1) = 1$
dfI X R $= df$Imagery X dfRehearsal $(1 \text{ X } 1) = 1$
dfError $= df$Total $- df$Imagery $- df$Rehearsal $- df$I X R $(39 - 1 - 1 - 1) = 36$

Step 8. Summary table. Calculate mean squares (MS) by dividing SS by the number of *df.*

The *F* ratios are then calculated by dividing the treatment MS by the MSError.

Summary Table of a 2 X 2 ANOVA

Source	SS	df	MS	F	p
Imagery	90.	1	90.	46.6	<.05
Rehearsal	28.9	1	28.9	15.0	<.05
Imagery X Rehearsal	12.1	1	12.1	6.3	<.05
Error	69.4	36	1.9		

Step 9. To determine the significance of the *F* ratio, enter Table A–6 on page 315 with the *df* for the numerator (in this case it is always 1), and with the *df* for the denominator (*df*Error), which is 36, for any effect you are interested in.

We can conclude that Imagery and Rehearsal both influenced recall. But we should note that the effects of imagery are dependent upon the type of rehearsal (that is, we obtained an interaction).

Calculation of a 2 X 2 X 2 ANOVA on the Data from the Unpublished Memory Experiment in Chapter 8 (see Table 8–2)

Box 9–9

This ANOVA is highly similar to the 2 X 2 shown in Box 9–8, except that there is one more variable and there are two more interaction effects to worry about. Remember, this is really the entire experiment that was abstracted as a 2 X 2.

	Two Presentations				One Presentation		
High Imagery Words		Low Imagery Words		High Imagery Words		Low Imagery Words	
Rote Rehearsal	Elab. Rehearsal	Rote Rehearsal	Elab. Rehearsal	Rote Rehearsal	Elab. Rehearsal	Rote Rehearsal	Elab. Rehearsal
5	8	4	7	5	6	1	5
7	8	1	6	4	8	4	7
6	9	5	3	3	7	2	5
4	7	6	3	4	8	3	5
4	10	4	5	2	8	4	4
9	10	3	6	2	5	1	4
7	8	4	2	6	9	2	1
5	9	4	4	4	7	2	5
5	8	5	5	1	8	1	3
6	9	3	4	4	9	1	6

$\Sigma X = 58$, 86, 39, 45, 35, 75, 21, 45

$\Sigma X^2 = 358$, 748, 169, 225, 143, 577, 57, 227

$$\Sigma\Sigma X^2 = 2504 \qquad \Sigma\Sigma X = 404$$

Step 1. The correction term $= (\Sigma\Sigma X)^2/N = (404)^2/80 = 2040.2$

Step 2. SSTotal $= \Sigma\Sigma X^2 -$ Step 1 $= 2504 - 2040.2 = 463.8$

Step 3. SSImagery $= \dfrac{(58 + 86 + 35 + 75)^2 + (39 + 45 + 21 + 45)^2}{40}$ $-$ Step 1

$= 87016/40 - 2040.2$
$= 135.2$

Step 4. SSRehearsal $= \dfrac{(86 + 45 + 75 + 45)^2 + (58 + 39 + 35 + 21)^2}{40}$ $-$ Step 1

$= 86410/40 - 2040.2$
$= 120.1$

Step 5. SSPresentations. Calculated the same ways as the other main effects, but your calculations are based on the grand sums for each number of presentations.

$$\text{SSPresentations} = \frac{(58 + 86 + 39 + 45)^2 + (35 + 75 + 21 + 45)^2}{40}$$
$$- \text{ Step 1}$$

$$= 82690/40 - 2040.2$$
$$= 33.8$$

Step 6. Calculation of the SS I X R. In general, when you calculate an interaction between two of three (or more) variables, you get condition sums that ignore the variable that you are not at the moment interested in. So, you would get the sum of all High Imagery subjects who used Rote Rehearsal, regardless of the number of presentations, then get the sum for High Imagery and Elaborative Rehearsal, regardless of the number of presentations, and so on.

$$\text{SSI X R} = \frac{(86 + 75)^2 + (58 + 35)^2 + (45 + 45)^2 + (39 + 21)^2}{20}$$
$$- \text{ Step 1} - \text{Step 3} - \text{Step 4}$$

$$= 46270/20 - 2040.2 - 135.2 - 120.1$$
$$= 18.0$$

Note: In calculating the interaction of any two factors, you subtract out the main effects associated with them as well as subtracting the correction term. Be sure you note this in the calculation of the next interaction.

Step 7. $\text{SSI X P} = \dfrac{(58+86)^2 + (39+45)^2 + (35+75)^2 + (21+45)^2}{20}$
$$- \text{ Step 1} - \text{Step 3} - \text{Step 5}$$

$$= 44248/20 - 2040.2 - 135.2 - 33.8$$
$$= 3.2$$

Step 8. $\text{SSR X P} = \dfrac{(58+39)^2 + (86+45)^2 + (35+21)^2 + (75+45)^2}{20}$
$$- \text{ Step 1} - \text{Step 4} - \text{Step 5}$$

$$= 44106/20 - 2040.2 - 120.1 - 18.0$$
$$= 11.2$$

Step 9. SSI X R X P. In calculating the three-factor interaction, square the sum of each group, get the sums of these squares, divide by the number of scores in each group, and then from this quotient you subtract all of the treatment SSs that you have calculated. *Do not,* however, subtract SSTotal.

$$\text{SSI X R X P} = \frac{58^2 + 86^2 + \ldots + 21^2 + 45^2}{10} - \text{Steps 1, 3, 4, 5, 6,}$$
$$7, 8$$

$$= 2362.2 - 2040.2 - 135.2 - 120.1 - 33.8 - 18 - 3.2$$
$$- 11.2$$
$$= .5$$

Step 10. SSError = SSTotal – Steps 3, 4, 5, 6, 7, 8, and 9
$$= 463.8 \text{ (Step 2)} - 135.2 - 120.1 - 33.8 - 18$$
$$- 3.2 - 11.2 - .5$$
$$= 141.8$$

Note: In calculating SSError, the correction term (Step 1) is not subtracted

Step 11. Calculate *df*. These are calculated in the same way as in a 2 X 2 ANOVA. In this example there are a total of 80 measures, so *df* Total = 79 and *df* Error = *df* Total – *df*s for Imagery, Rehearsal, Presentations, I X R, I X P, R X P, and I X R X P.

Step 12. Summary Table. MS and *F* ratios are calculated in the same way that they are in a 2 X 2 ANOVA.

Source	SS	df	MS	F	p
Imagery	135.2	1	135.2	75.1	.05
Rehearsal	120.1	1	120.1	66.7	.05
Presentations	33.8	1	33.8	18.8	.05
I X R	18.0	1	18.0	10.0	.05
I X P	3.2	1	3.2	1.8	n/s
R X P	11.2	1	11.2	6.2	.05
I X R X P	0.5	1	0.5	—	n/s
Error	141.8	72	1.8		

Notes. It is customary to not report the numerical value of an *F* ratio less than one. n/s = not significant.

Step 13. Significance is determined by entering Table A–6 (p. 315) with the numerator *df* and the denominator *df* (*df* Error = 72) for a particular effect. As in our example of the 2 X 2 ANOVA the numerator *df* is always 1 for this experiment.

All of our variables influenced recall, but we should be careful in noting that the effects of imagery are dependent upon the types of rehearsal, and also that the effect of type of rehearsal is dependent upon the number of presentations.

Box 9–10

Factorial ANOVA with Repeated Measures (Within-Subject)

In a within-subjects ANOVA we need to calculate both column (treatment) and row (subject) totals, because subjects are serving as their own control condition. In fact, our error variance is estimated by the interaction of subjects within treatments (see Box 9–7). Arrange your data table so that the scores of a single subject are in a row, and it is usually a good idea to leave room so that treatment totals for a single may be placed in the same table. We will analyze the data from Experiment I by Elmes and Bjork (1975) that is shown in Figure 8–5. The individual subjects total recall scores are tabled below.

Subject	Rote Rehearsal Retention Interval 2 sec	12 sec	Elaborate Rehearsal Retention Interval 2 sec	12 sec	Subject Total	Rehearsal Total Rote	Elab.	Retention Total 2 sec	12 se
1	15	3	11	11	40	18	22	26	14
2	20	15	19	18	72	35	37	39	33
3	18	2	18	19	57	20	37	36	21
4	15	13	16	15	59	28	31	31	28
5	10	1	17	12	40	11	29	27	13
6	14	5	16	13	48	19	29	30	18
7	17	6	19	18	60	23	37	36	24
8	19	12	16	19	66	31	35	35	31
9	11	4	9	12	36	15	21	20	16
10	17	10	14	7	48	27	21	31	17
11	18	11	18	10	57	29	28	36	21
12	18	4	20	19	61	22	39	38	23
13	16	9	19	18	62	25	37	35	27
14	18	6	19	17	60	24	36	37	23
15	10	5	10	7	32	15	17	20	12
16	16	5	19	18	58	21	37	35	23

$\Sigma X = $ 252 111   260 233   856   363 493   512 344

$\Sigma X^2 = $ 4114 1033   4408 3669   47776   24820   24910

$\Sigma \Sigma X = $ 856 $\Sigma \Sigma X^2 = $ 13224

Step 1. Determine the total score/subject (row) and total score/treatment combination (column). Find each subject's total score for each independent variable. The subject totals for a particular IV (for example, for subject # *1* her rehearsal totals are 18 and 22) should add up to that subject's total score (in this case 40). Determine each treatment total by adding the appropriate column sums; check your answer by also adding the subject totals for that level of the IV. For example, the Rote Rehearsal total = 252 + 111 = 363 (sum of columns 1 and 2, which is equal to the sum of Column 6).

Step 2. Determine the Correction Term (C). $C = (\Sigma\Sigma X)^2/N$, where N = the number of measures in the table. N = 16 subjects X 4 scores = 64.

$C = 856^2/64$
$ = 732736/64$
$ = 11449$

Step 3. SSTotal $= \Sigma\Sigma X^2$ – Step 2
$ = 13224 - 11449$
$ = 1775$

Step 4. SSSubjects. Square each subject's total score (Column 5), add the squares, and divide that total by the number of scores for each subject (4), then subtract the results of Step 2.

SSSubj. $= 47776/4$ – Step 2
$ = 11944 - 11449$
$ = 495$

Step 5. SSRehearsal $= (363^2 + 493^2)/32$ – Step 2
$ = 374818/32$ – Step 2
$ = 11713.06 - 11449$
$ = 264.06$

Step 6. MSRehearsal. Divide the SSRehearsal by the *df* for Rehearsal. The *df* Rehearsal = the number of levels of Rehearsal – 1.

df Rehearsal $= 2 - 1$.
MSRehearsal $= 264.06/1$
$ = 264.06$

Step 7. SSErrorRehearsal. The error term for Rehearsal is the interaction of subjects with rehearsal. Square the subject totals for each level of Rehearsal (Columns 6 and 7), add the squares, divide by the number of scores needed to get each sum (2 in this case), then subtract C (step 2), SSSubj. (Step 4), and SSRehearsal (Step 5).

$$\text{SSErrorRehearsal} = \frac{18^2 + 22^2 + \ldots + 21^2 + 37^2}{2} - \text{Steps 2, 4, and 5}$$

$ = 24820/2$ – Steps 2, 4, and 5
$ = 12410 - 11449 - 495 - 264.06$
$ = 201.94$

Step 8. MSErrorRehearsal. Divide SSErrorRehearsal by df ErrorRehearsal. $df = (\#\ \text{Subject} - 1)\ (df\ \text{Rehearsal}) = (15)\ (1)$

$$\text{MSErrorRehearsal} = 201.94/15$$
$$= 13.46$$

Step 9. F Rehearsal $=$ MSRehearsal/MSErrorRehearsal
$$= \text{Step 6/Step 8}$$
$$= 264.06/13.46$$
$$= 19.62$$

Step 10. Repeat Steps 5–9 to find the F for Retention Interval (RI)

$$\text{SSRI} = (512^2 + 344^2)/32 - \text{Step 2}$$
$$= 441.00$$
$$\text{MSRI} = 441.00/(2 - 1)$$
$$= 441.00$$

$$\text{SSErrorRI} = \frac{26^2 + 14^2 + \ldots + 35^2 + 23^2}{2} - \text{Step 2, Step 4, and}$$
$$\text{SSRI}$$
$$= 24910/2 - C - \text{SSSubj.} - \text{SSRI}$$
$$= 12455 - 11449 - 495 - 441$$
$$= 70$$

$$\text{MSErrorRI} = \text{SSErrorRI}/(15 - 1)(2 - 1)$$
$$= 70/15$$
$$= 4.67$$
$$F\text{RI} = 441.00/4.67$$
$$= 94.43$$

Step 11. SSRehearsal X RI $= \dfrac{252^2 + 111^2 + 260^2 + 233^2}{16} - C$
$$- \text{SSReh} - \text{SSRI}$$
$$= 12357.13 - 11449 - 264.06 - 441.00$$
$$= 203.07$$

Step 12. MSRehearsal X RI $= 203.07/(df\ \text{Rehearsal})(df\ \text{RI})$
$$= 203.07/1$$
$$= 203.07$$

Step 13. SSErrorRehearsal X RI. Calculate this triple interaction by subtracting all the SS you have calculated from SSTotal.

SSErrorRehearsal X RI $=$ SSTotal $-$ SSSubj. $-$ SSRehearsal $-$ SSRI
$$- \text{SSRehearsal X RI} - \text{SSErrorRehearsal} -$$
$$\text{SSErrorRI}$$
$$= 1775 - 495 - 264.06 - 441 - 203.07 -$$
$$201.94 - 70$$
$$= 99.93$$

Step 14. MSErrorRehearsal X RI = 99.93/ (#Subject – 1)
$$\qquad\qquad (X \; df\text{Rehearsal})(df\text{RI})$$
$$= 99.93/15$$
$$= 6.66$$

Step 15. F Rehearsal X RI = MSRehearsal X RI/MSErrorRehearsal
$$\qquad\qquad X \; RI$$
$$= 203.07/6.66$$
$$= 30.49$$

Step 16. Summary Table of 2 X 2 Within-Subjects ANOVA

Source	SS	df	MS	F
Subjects	495.00	15		
Rehearsal	264.06	1	264.06	19.62
Error Reh	201.94	15	13.46	
Retention Interval	441.00	1	441.00	94.43
Error RI	70.00	15	4.67	
Reh X RI	203.07	1	203.07	30.49
Error Reh X RI	99.93	15	6.66	
Total	1775.00	63		

To determine significance enter Table A-6 with the appropriate degrees of freedom for each F ratio. (In this case the $df = 1$ and 15.) We can note that both Rehearsal and Retention Interval had significant effects on recall. We should also note that the effects of type of rehearsal are dependent upon the length of the retention interval.

Summary

This chapter is concerned with ways of determining if an experimental effect is due to chance factors or due to the manipulation of the independent variable. An experimental hypothesis is tested against the null hypothesis. The experimental hypothesis is supported if the null hypothesis can be rejected on the basis of a statistical test.

There are several tests available for making inferences about differences between conditions in an experiment. Nonparametric tests (ordinal data and an unknown distribution of scores) for two-condition experiments include: the Mann-Whitney U test for a between-subjects experiment and the Wilcoxon signed-ranks test for a within-subjects experiment. The corresponding parametric tests (requiring interval or ratio data) for two-condition experiments are the between-subjects and within-subjects t tests.

When more than two conditions are examined, then an analysis of variance (ANOVA) should be used if you have interval or ratio data. The choice of a particular ANOVA depends upon the number of independent variables and the design (between-subjects or within-subjects).

The principles for choosing a particular inferential test are summarized on the facing page for this chapter.

Study and Review

Exercises

1. In a between-subjects design with 11 subjects in one group and 14 in the other, what is the *df* for *t?*

2. Describe the differences between parametric and nonparametric statistical tests.

3. Suppose we modified our LSD experiment in the following way: we did a 3 X 2 factorial experiment between-subjects—there were three levels of LSD (none, small, and large) and two levels of age (young rats and old rats). Assume that we have ten rats in each group. Set up a summary ANOVA table showing all the appropriate *df*.

4. What is wrong with the following ANOVA table?

Source	SS	df	MS	F
Subjects		14		
Condition A		2		
Error A		27		
Condition B		3		
Error B		14		
Interaction A X B		6		
Total		179		

Key Concepts

population 200
sample 200
random sampling 200
standard error of the mean 203
experimental hypothesis 205
null hypothesis 205
level of confidence 206
significance 206
alpha level 208
type I error 209
type II error 209
conservative vs. liberal tests 210

power of a test 210
directional vs. nondirectional
    hypotheses 211
one-tailed tests 211
two-tailed tests 211
nonparametric tests 212
parametric tests 212
U test 213
sign test 215
Wilcoxon test 216
t tests 218
between-subjects *t* 218

Suggested Readings

Additional information about both descriptive and inferential statistics are provided clearly and succinctly in: Thompson, J. B., and Buchanan, W. *Analyzing psychological data.* New York: Charles Scribner's Sons, 1979.

QUESTIONS TO ANSWER
WHEN INTERPRETING THE RESULTS OF RESEARCH:

Is there a scale attenuation problem?

Are there ceiling or floor effects?

Is there a regression artifact present?

Do the data provide a "true" measure of the behavior?

Does the test provide reliable data?

Has the reliability of the test been determined by: test-retest method, parallel forms, or the split-half technique?

Are the experimental results reliable?

Has the experiment been replicated directly? Have conceptual or systematic replications been undertaken?

Have the results and concepts been validated by converging operations?

Do the results of several converging observations eliminate alternative explanations of the results?

Pitfalls in Interpreting the Results of Research

10

After you have collected and analyzed your data, you are in a position to interpret them. The purpose of this chapter is to help you understand some of the pitfalls that impede correct interpretation of your data. We will consider problems associated with the interpretation of both specific results and results from a connected series of studies. Your data, even if collected and statistically analyzed correctly, may be difficult to interpret if performance is extremely good or extremely bad (the scale attenuation problem). Often, your subject's "true" score or performance differs from the data you have collected, which means that a regression artifact has occurred. Have you obtained reliable results—would you find the same effect if the research were replicated? Are your data valid—do several results converge upon an understanding of a concept? Solutions to these problems are suggested.

Overview

Scale Attenuation

The problem.   The first topic we are considering here is important, but often overlooked in psychological research. The general problem is how to interpret performance on some dependent variable in an experiment when performance is either very nearly perfect (near the "ceiling" of the scale) or very nearly lacking altogether (near the "floor"). These effects are called *scale attenuation effects* (or, more commonly, ceiling and floor effects), and we will begin our discussion with a humorous example.

Suppose two obese men decided to make a bet as to who could lose the greatest amount of weight in a certain amount of time. One man looked much heavier than the other, but neither was sure what he actually weighed, since they both made a point of avoiding scales at all cost. The scale they decided to use for the bet was a common bathroom scale that runs from 0–300 pounds. On the day they were to begin their weight loss programs, each man weighed himself while the other watched and, to their great surprise, both men weighed in at exactly the same value, 300 pounds. So despite the fact of their different sizes, these two men decided that they were beginning their bet at equal weights.

Interpreting Specific Results

The problem here is one of ceiling effects in the scale of measurement. The weight range of the bathroom scale simply did not go high enough to record the actual weight of these men. Let us imagine that one actually weighed 300 and the other 350, if their weights had been taken by a scale with a greater range. After six months of their weight loss program, let us further suppose, both men had actually lost 100 pounds. They both reweighed themselves at this point and discovered that one now weighed 200 pounds and the other 250. Since they believed that they both had started from the same weight (300), they reached the erroneous conclusion that the person who presently weighed 200 had won the bet.

Unfortunately, scale attenuation effects in research may not be as transparent as the ceiling effect in our contrived weight-loss example. However, since scale attenuation can lead to wildly erroneous conclusions, we think it is important for you to know what to look for in your own research or in a journal report of someone else's work. Not only should you be wary of the scale used to measure behavior (as above), you should also consider the task imposed on the subjects participating in the project. For example, suppose you devised a memory experiment that involved recalling phone numbers. The people in your experiment had to study a typical seven-digit phone number for one minute and then had to dial that number on a telephone. What you would probably find is that all of your subjects did fine; in fact, they all remembered the numbers perfectly. What does that tell you? If a task is too easy (or too difficult), differences in behavior will not appear. Whenever you examine research results you should ask yourself the following: "Are the limits on performance I observe legitimate ones, or are they due to limits imposed by the measurement scale or the task used to assess behavior?"

The Eyes Have It: Scarborough's Experiment. Let us now consider the results of an experiment that contains a scale attenuation problem. Scarborough (1972) was interested in the question of modality differences in retention. Do we remember information better if it comes through our eyes or through our ears? Is information better remembered if it is presented to both the ears and the eyes simultaneously than if it is presented to only one or the other? If you are interested in this problem, and the answers have both theoretical and practical importance, you may study the question as presented in Chapter 11. For now we will consider Scarborough's analysis of the problem.

In Scarborough's (1972) experiment, all subjects received 36 consonant trigrams presented for .7 second in the Brown-Peterson technique (see Chapter 8). There were three groups of six subjects that differed in the method in which the trigrams were presented. One group of subjects *saw* the trigrams presented (visual only condition), one group of subjects *heard* the trigrams presented (auditory only), and a third group of subjects both saw and heard the trigrams (visual + auditory). Presentation time was carefully controlled by having the trigrams presented over a tape recorder or a tachistoscope, a device for quickly exposing and removing visual information. One second after presentation of the trigram, subjects heard a three-digit number, except in one condition where subjects were requested to recall the trigram immediately (the zero second retention interval condition). Subjects in each condition were required to retain the letters during retention intervals of 0, 3, 6, 9, 12, or 18 seconds. Once the three-digit number was presented, subjects were required to count backwards by threes aloud at the rate of one count per second in time with a metronome. At the end of the retention interval the metronome stopped and two green lights came on, signalling the ten-second recall period. So each trial consisted of a warning signal (two yellow lights and a tone) indicating that the trigram was about to be displayed, presentation of the trigram, presentation of the three-digit number (with the exception noted above), the retention interval during which the subjects counted backwards by threes, and finally the recall period. This procedure was repeated 36 times (six trials at each of the six retention intervals in a counterbalanced order) with different trigrams. In summary, three between-subjects conditions (visual only, auditory only, visual + auditory) were combined with six within-subjects conditions (retention intervals of 0, 3, 6, 9, 12, or 18 seconds) in the experiment.

The results of Scarborough's experiment are reproduced in Figure 10–1, where the percentage of times a trigram was correctly reported is plotted as a function of retention interval. It is quite apparent from Figure 10–1, and the statistics Scarborough reports support this, that subjects who received only visual presentation of the trigrams generally recalled them a greater percentage of the time than did subjects who received only auditory presentation. Furthermore, receiving information in both modalities simultaneously did not produce any better recall than presenting the information only visually, the percentage correct at each retention interval is roughly the same for visual only and visual + auditory subjects. So far so good. But what else can we conclude from Figure 10–1? In particular, can we conclude anything about the rates of forgetting for information that is presented auditorily and visually? Is the rate of forgetting the same or different in the two cases? Did you ask yourself about the source of limitation on performance?

Scarborough was quite careful on this score. Although the auditory only and visual only functions appear to diverge increasingly as the retention interval becomes longer, he did not draw the conclusion that the rate of forgetting is greater for information presented through the ears than through the eyes. However, consider what Massaro (1975) has to say about this experiment in his textbook: "The figure shows that the curves intercept the *Y* ordinate at roughly the same point and diverge

Figure 10–1

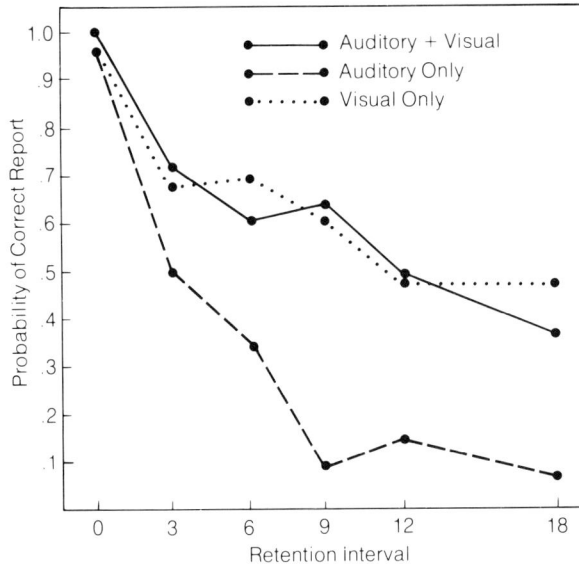

The probability of correctly recalling a stimulus trigram as a function of the three presentation conditions and the duration of the counting task. Notice that (a) visual presentation is generally superior to auditory presentation, and (b) simultaneous auditory and visual presentation is no better than only visual presentation (Scarborough. 1972).

significantly. The intercept value at zero sec. provides a measure of the original perception and storage of the stimuli, since it measures how much information the subject has immediately after the presentation of the stimuli, when no forgetting has taken place. The rate of forgetting can be determined from the slopes of the forgetting functions. According to this analysis, Figure 10–1 shows that the items presented auditorily are forgotten much faster than the items presented visually (Massaro, 1975, pp. 530–531). Unfortunately, this conclusion must be called into question. We have the same problem that our fat men had: our scale at the ceiling is not sensitive enough. Performance at the zero second retention interval is very nearly perfect in all conditions. When performance is perfect it is impossible to tell whether or not there are any "real" differences among conditions because of scale attenuation, in this case a ceiling effect. If the scale of the dependent measure were really "long" enough, it might show differences between auditory and visual presentation even at the zero second retention interval. So Massaro's conclusion that the rate of forgetting is greater for auditory than visual presentation cannot be accepted on the basis of the argument we just quoted, because the assumption of equivalent performance at the zero second retention interval may not be correct. There is no better way for us to know the rate of forgetting in the two conditions than there is for our fat men to know the rate of weight loss in judging who won their bet. In neither case can we assume equivalent initial scores before the measurement loss begins.

Possible solution. How can we avoid misinterpretation after the data are collected? (We might have considered using an additional dependent variable, such as time to respond, but the experiment has been completed. Response or, more commonly, reaction time might have "spread" out the scale by showing faster times for better learned trigrams.)

One way to avoid this problem in Scarborough's experiment would be to ignore the data points at the zero second retention interval and ask whether or not the rate of forgetting is greater between 3 and 18 seconds for auditory than for visual presentation. This could be done by computing an interaction between presentation and retention interval over the range of 3 to 18 seconds, but by simply inspecting Figure 10–1 you can get some idea as to whether the auditory only and visual only points are diverging increasingly. They are between 3 and 9 seconds, but after that the difference between them remains constant. However, this lack of an increasingly larger difference over the last three points may be due to a floor effect in the auditory only condition, since performance is so poor, especially on the last point (only 7 percent or 8 percent correct). One must be very careful in interpreting data when there are ceiling or floor effects present. A prudent investigator would hesitate to draw any conclusion from the data in Figure 10–1 about rates of forgetting, which is just what Scarborough did. But we should also note that over the retention intervals where there are neither ceiling nor floor effects (3, 6, and 9 seconds), there seems to be greater forgetting with auditory than with visual presentation.

You might be interested in knowing that Scarborough's finding that visual only results in better recall than does auditory only is the reverse of what most investigators have found. This problem and modality effects in general are discussed in Chapter 11.

Regression Artifacts

A serious problem in many areas of research is known as *statistical regression to the mean,* or the *regression artifact.* The word *artifact* in this context refers to an effect that occurred during an investigation that was unwanted (so, it is a synonym for confounding factor), and *regression* means to go back to the mean or "true" score. You can best appreciate this unwanted phenomenon by allowing yourself to become a victim of it. Try the following exercise, proceeding through the steps as given:

1. Roll six dice on a table in front of you.

2. Place the three dice showing the lowest numbers on the left, and the three dice showing the highest numbers on the right. In case of ties, randomly assign the dice to the two groups.

3. Compute and record the mean number-per-die for each group of three dice.

4. Raise both hands over your head and loudly proclaim, "Improve in the name of SCIENCE."

5. Roll the three low-scoring dice and compute a new mean number-per-die for the low group.

6. Roll the three high-scoring dice and compute a new mean number-per-die for the high group.

7. Compare the pre- and post-treatment scores for both groups of dice. Combine your data with that of your classmates, if possible.

On the average, the above experiment will produce an increase in the performance of the low group and a decrease in the performance of the high group. You might be tempted to conclude that invoking the name of SCIENCE has a beneficial effect on underachieving dice, but that overachieving dice require more individualized attention to maintain their outstanding performance. Such conclusions, however, fail to consider the effects of *regression to the mean*. This regression artifact reflects the tendency for many types of measures to yield values close to their mean. You know that the roll of a fair die can yield values from 1 to 6, but that the average value from many rolls will be about 3.5. The likelihood of the average of three dice being close to 3.5 is higher than the likelihood of this average being close to 1 or 6. Thus, when you select three dice that give you a low average and then roll them again, they will tend to yield a higher average value (a value closer to the mean of 3.5). In the same way, the three dice in the high group should yield a lower value when rolled again.

What does all this have to do with psychological research? You are well aware by now of the fact that accurate measurement lies at the heart of assessing the effects of a variable. Whenever there is a measurement error, such as the regression artifact, there is also the possibility of wrongly concluding that some sort of change has occurred or has failed to occur. While this statement may appear less than profound to you, a number of psychological studies have been faulted for failing to take adequate account of its truth.

Quasi-experimental designs (see Chapter 7), like the dice exercise, are particularly susceptible to bias due to the regression artifact. In such studies, you will remember, subjects are not assigned to treatment and control groups on a random basis, but they are matched on some factor or factors (our dice were matched on their value). We have already noted in Chapter 7 that matching on the appropriate dimension may be extremely difficult. In fact, our groups may have been taken from populations that differed on an important dimension prior to the study, or they may have come from the same population and we have matched subjects within groups on an irrelevant variable. So, our observations may result from statistical regression to the population mean rather than from our experimental manipulations.

Perhaps another example, closer to home, may help here. Suppose that you are an *A* student and that your neighbor is a *C* student, although you both have similar backgrounds. On one particular assignment you both receive a *B*. In an effort to improve, your neighbor then decides to attend a series of help sessions. Your instructor decides to evaluate the effectiveness of the help sessions by comparing the future grades of help session students with future grades of nonhelp session students who are similar in background and received the same grades on the previous assignment. You are selected as the matched student to be compared to your friend. On your next assignment, you receive an *A–*, while your friend receives a *C+*. Should the instructor conclude that the help sessions are harmful because your friend went from a *B* to a *C+*, while you went from a *B* to an *A–?* Probably not, since, just like our low- and high-scoring dice, both of you regressed toward your mean grades. The effect on grades is probably not a true treatment effect, but rather a regression artifact caused by the fact that you and your friend were not truly equivalent students. Unlike invoking SCIENCE, the help sessions may have actually benefited your friend since the grade after the sessions (*C+*) was higher than the usual grade of *C*. If "true" *B* students had been randomly assigned to help session or nonhelp session groups, and then compared on grades on the second assignment, accurate assessment of the effect of help sessions on students' grades could have been obtained.

In general terms, the reason for the phenomenon of regression to the mean is that all psychological measures are subject to a certain amount of unreliability. With any measure that is not perfectly reliable, the group of subjects obtaining the highest scores contains not only those who really belong in the highest category, but also others who were placed in this category due to chance errors of measurement (recall our dice example). On a retest these chance measurement errors will not necessarily occur in the same direction; they will usually regress toward the true score or population mean. Similarly, a group selected for poor performance on an original test will tend to average higher on a retest, just as was the case with our underachieving dice.

Regression in Compensatory Education. The importance of regression artifacts such as the above in quasi-experimental studies of education has been the subject of recent debate. One influential study of the effects of the Head Start program of the 1960s (Cicirelli et al., 1969) has received particular attention. In this study, called the Westinghouse-Ohio study, children completing their Head Start experience were randomly selected for evaluation. A control population of children from the same area, supposedly eligible for the program but who had not attended, was then defined. Control children were selected at random to be matched with experimental children on the basis of sex, racial-ethnic group measurement, and kindergarten attendance. After the final selection of experimental and control subjects, additional measures of socio-economic status, demographic status, and attitude were compiled and compared for the two groups. Differences were reported to be slight. Measures of experimental (Head Start) and control (no Head Start) children's academic achievement and potential were then computed and compared. The general conclusion from this large study was that Head Start was not effective in removing the effects of poverty and social disadvantage.

Other psychologists (Campbell and Erlebacher, 1970a) were quick to criticize this study on several grounds. First, they pointed out that the results of the study were undoubtedly due partially to regression artifacts. Worse, the magnitude of the artifacts could not be estimated, casting doubt over the entire set of findings.

What is the basic problem? Can you see why the matching of subjects may not have been effective? Cicirelli et al. laudably tried to match the sample of disadvantaged children who had been in the Head Start program with others from the same area who had not been in the program. The differences between the two groups later should be due to the program. Right? Not necessarily. It's right only if the two samples came from the same underlying population distributions, and this is unlikely.

What is more likely in studies such as this is that the two populations differ with the disadvantaged "treatment" children coming from a population that is poorer in ability than the "control" children. The "treatment" children are usually preselected to be from a disadvantaged background (which is why they were included in the program), while the "controls" who are not in the program might be from a different population that is greater in ability (a nonequivalent control group). The basic problem is that subjects are not randomly assigned to conditions, so the researchers must try to match control subjects with experimental subjects. In order to match to samples from these different populations it will then be necessary to select children *above* the population mean for the disadvantaged treatment group and *below* the population mean for the control group. But when this is done the dreaded regression artifact will always be introduced. When each group is retested, the performance of the individuals will tend to regress to the mean of the group; in other words, the disadvantaged group will tend to perform worse in this example, and the control group will tend to perform better.

This regression to the mean will happen in the absence of any treatment being given (you don't really believe that chanting SCIENCE could possibly have any real effect, do you?) and despite matching. The matching effect is the same as that in the previous example of the grades of the superior student increasing to $A-$ from B and the other's decreasing from B to $C+$ when the two students were erroneously matched as B students. Since we already expect a difference between groups (favoring the control) in this situation, due to regression to the mean, how do we evaluate the outcome of our study? Cicirelli et al. found no difference between groups. Since we might expect the treatment (Head Start) group to actually be worse due to regression, does this mean they actually improved due to Head Start?

It is impossible to answer this question because in the Westinghouse-Ohio evaluation of Head Start the direction or magnitude of regression artifacts could not be assessed. In the preceding paragraph we were making reasonable assumptions concerning regression artifacts in this type of study. But the conclusion that Head Start had no effect could not strictly be drawn from the Westinghouse-Ohio study. More properly, one can come to no conclusion on the basis of that study since it is not known how regression artifacts affected the results.

In general, then, regression artifacts of a difficult to estimate magnitude are highly probable in this type of study, and this fact is acknowledged by most researchers. Why then, would such studies be conducted, particularly when important political, economic, and social decisions will be based on their results? This question was raised by both Campbell and Erlebacher (1970a, b) and by Cicirelli and his supporters (Cicirelli, 1970; Evans and Schiller, 1970). Their answers were quite different and represent the type of issue that frequently confronts scientists, but that science can never resolve. Campbell and Erlebacher (1970a) proposed that bad information was worse than no information at all; that if properly controlled experiments could not be performed, then no data should be gathered. On the other side of the issue, Evans and Schiller replied, "This position fails to understand that every program *will* be evaluated by the most arbitrary, anecdotal, partisan, and subjective means" (p. 220). Campbell and Erlebacher concurred, but stated that " . . . we judge it fundamentally misleading to lend the prestige of science to any report in a situation where no scientific evaluation is possible" (1970b, p. 224). As a final solution they proposed that a commission "composed of experts who are not yet partisans in this controversy" be convened to decide the matter.

Possible Solutions.   This issue may not be decidable on strictly rational grounds, but we can all agree that a research study should be conducted according to the best scientific procedures available. After the fact, of course, we are not able to interpret the results of a quasi-experimental study in which there are substantial and unknown regression artifacts. The question becomes, how could the Westinghouse-Ohio study have been done appropriately? The best way would have been to randomly assign participants to either the no-treatment or treatment conditions. There is no substitute for random assignment for eliminating confounding factors (that is, there is no substitute for doing a true experiment). But it seems unfair to give half the children who seek the help of a remedial program no training whatsoever. Of course, there is no guarantee at the outset that the program would do them any good; that is what the study is designed to discover. The same issue occurs in medical research when a control group with a disease is given a placebo rather than a treatment drug. The argument could be made in both cases that in the long run more people will be aided by careful research into the effectiveness of treatments than may be harmed because treatment is withheld. Unfortunately, the issue is not quite that simple. In the case of medical research, for example, preliminary testing of an antiencephalitis drug showed that 72 percent of the patients receiving the drug survived the disease to lead normal lives, but only 30 percent of the control group, who received a placebo, survived (Katz, 1979). Is such a toll necessary for effective research design in drug development?

There are other solutions to the regression problem besides random assignment. One would be to randomly assign all the children to different groups and put them in different programs to pit the effectiveness of the programs against one another. The problem here is that we do not have a no-treatment baseline, and if the programs turn out to be equally effective, one could not know if any of them were better than no program at all.

Interpreting Patterns of Research

The problems of scale attenuation and regression artifacts focus on the results of a particular piece of research. The topics we want to examine now are concerned with interpreting patterns of research. No single observation can stand alone for long. When we are confronted with the results of psychological research, we must always ask whether they are reliable and valid. In Chapter 2 there was a brief discussion of the reliability and validity of data. Here we will expand the discussion of these topics so you can grasp the importance of determining if a particular result displays regularity and if a particular datum "fits" with other, related observations.

Reliability and Replication

Suppose you have been hired to assess presidential preferences in the United States. Your job is to find out who the people seem to prefer for president in the upcoming election. After you have developed a survey, you take a random sample of the people in the United States. What sorts of things would make you confident of the results of your survey? In the first place, we can be more confident that the results accurately reflect the attitudes of the population if our sample consists of 100,000 people rather than only 100 (see Chapter 9). Secondly, we should expect a second random sample to yield a similar result (assuming that one of the major candidates has not committed a gross moral or legal transgression between the two surveys). Large numbers of observations and a repeatable result are two key factors to insure reliability. In general terms, we should always try to maximize the number of observations we obtain, and we should devise our research so that we can determine if our results are consistent over time.

Test Reliability.   Psychological traits, such as intelligence or various abilities, are difficult to measure. Because of this, we may have a difficult time determining if our measuring devices yield reliable data. We may not know whether small changes in assessment over time reflect real changes (the person's intelligence declined) or whether there is some measurement error. For many psychological traits, it is reasonable to make the assumption that there will be little short-term variability in the underlying ability (barring injury or pathology). So, we would like to have testing devices that yield similar scores from one day to the next or one week to the next. Large changes, say in intelligence, over a short period of time could be attributed to measurement error, indicating unreliability in our test. However, a reliable device should yield similar scores on two occasions. This procedure, giving the same test twice in succession over a short time interval, is used to determine what is called the *test-retest reliability* of a measure. It is generally expressed as a correlation between first and second scores obtained by a large sample of subjects.

A slightly different procedure may be used to avoid problems such as specific practice or carry-over effects. This procedure is giving alternate or *parallel forms* of the test on the two testing occasions. Again, if correlations between the first and and second scores are high, then good reliability of the tests is indicated. Also, the equivalence of the two forms of the test may be determined in this way.

A third procedure may be used to evaluate reliability with a single test presentation. This is known as the *split-half technique* and involves dividing the test items into two arbitrary groups and correlating the scores obtained in the two halves of the test. If correlation is high, the test reliability is confirmed. In addition, the equivalence of the test items is established.

Modern tests of intelligence and other psychological traits are usually found to yield quite high test-retest reliabilities. In the case of intelligence, reliability is usually very high, with correlations on the order of .95. If you are planning to use an established test of some sort in your own research, the *Mental Measurements Yearbook* or the administration manual for the test usually contain information about the reliability of the test. Obviously, if you are developing your own test, it might be prudent to use one of the procedures mentioned above to obtain an estimate of reliability.

Experimental Reliability: Replication.   The basic issue with regard to reliability of experimental results is simply this: if an experiment were repeated, would the results come out the second time in the same way they did the first? Obviously repeatability is a crucial topic in psychological research, for an experimental outcome may be worthless if we cannot have reasonable certainty that the results from it are reliable. Since it is usually impossible to conduct the same study twice on the same subjects (with the possible exception of some small-n work), we usually repeat an experiment with a different sample of subjects. If the results of the two experiments are similar, then we can be confident that we have demonstrated reliability.

Many psychologists find *experimental reliability* more convincing than statistical reliability (see Chapter 9), since a statistically reliable finding in a single experiment may be the result of a set of accidental circumstances that favor one condition over another. We emphasize that the results of any particular experiment are to be viewed against the background of others on the same issue. If a phenomenon is not repeatable, we are likely to find out rather rapidly. *Replication,* a synonym for "copy" or "reproduction," is the term usually used to describe experimental reliability, and we will now consider an example of replication in the context of a series of famous experiments conducted by Luchins (1942).

Luchins' Einstellung (Set) Experiments.   Abraham S. Luchins was interested in the following: "Several problems, all solvable by one somewhat complex procedure, are presented in succession. If afterwards a similar task is given which can be solved by a more direct and simpler method, will the individual be blinded to this more direct possibility?" During the solution of the early problems, the subject may be said to construct a set way, or *set,* to solve the problems. After the problems are changed so that the set way no longer is the most efficient method of problem solution, will people hang on to it or will they recognize the more efficient method? The German word for set is *Einstellung,* and it is obvious that our everyday problem-solving frequently involves an Einstellung: we try our habitual ways of attacking a particular problem even though we may have more efficient procedures that are readily available to us.

Luchins usually used the water jar problem in his experiments. People are given two or three jars of varying capacity and are supposed to figure out how to obtain a required amount of water by performing arithmetical operations on the volumes the jars would hold. The basic 11 problems appear in Table 10–1. To illustrate the Einstellung effect, solve all 11 problems in order before continuing.

In Luchins' first study, the first problem served as an illustration of the task. The appropriate solution is to take the larger jar (29) and subtract the smaller jar (3) three times to get the desired amount (20). Subjects next solved problems 2–6, which may be considered set-establishing problems since they all are most easily solved by the same method of solution. In each case the solution is to take the largest jar (always the middle one), subtract the first jar once, and finally subtract the last jar twice. If we label the jars A, B, and C from left to right, then the set the subjects developed for problems 2–6 can be represented as $B - A - 2C$.

Besides the experimental or Einstellung group we have been discussing, there were two others. One group, a control of sorts, simply began with problems 7 and 8 to see how they would solve them with no induced set solution. Another group was treated in the same manner as the Einstellung group, except that before problem 7 each subject wrote "Don't be blind" on the response sheet "to make you aware of the fact that you must be cautious; you must watch out and see that you do not act foolishly while solving the subsequent problems." So, it is apparent that the primary dependent variable was the number of subjects using the Einstellung solution ($B - A - 2C$) on problems 7 and 8, even though problems 7 and 8 had much more efficient and direct solutions ($A - C$ for 7 and $A + C$ for 8). The results were that none of the control subjects used the inefficient solution in solving problems

---

The water jar problems Luchins used in his Einstellung experiments. **Table 10–1**

Problem	A	Given the following empty jars as measures B	C	Obtain the required amount of water
1	29	3		20
2	21	127	3	100
3	14	163	25	99
4	18	43	10	5
5	9	42	6	21
6	20	59	4	31
7	23	49	3	20
8	15	39	3	18
9	28	76	3	25
10	18	48	4	22
11	14	36	8	6

7 and 8, 81 percent of the Einstellung subjects used the inefficient solution on 7 and 8, and the "Don't be blind" warning reduced the use of the Einstellung solution to about 55 percent. Furthermore, after doing problem 9, which cannot be solved via the set-inducing method, 63 percent of the Einstellung subjects continued with the old solution on problems 10 and 11, while only 30 percent of the "Don't be blind" subjects reverted to the set solution.

How reliable are the results from this experiment? Luchins' work was published before the use of statistical tests was common in psychological research, so statistical tests to establish reliability were not performed. However, such tests were largely unnecessary in this case, since Luchins provided us with evidence that his results could be replicated in other experiments. Many experiments are included in the original report, and the results are in general agreement with the Einstellung results outlined above. Altogether, Luchins tested over 9000 subjects in his original studies. As noted previously, experimental reliability or replication is an exceptionally convincing way to demonstrate the reliability of a phenomenon—the Einstellung effect is a reliable one.

We may identify three types of replication attempts: *direct replication, systematic replication,* and *conceptual replication. Direct replication* is simply repeating an experiment as closely as possible with as few changes as possible in the method. Luchins replicated his original experiment several times with only slight changes in the subject population tested; such experiments constitute cases of direct replication.

A more interesting type of replication is *systematic replication.* In systematic replications one attempts to change all sorts of factors that the investigator considers irrelevant to the phenomenon of interest. If the phenomenon is not illusory, it will survive these changes. So, for example, in a systematic replication of Luchins' experiments, one might vary the nature of the problems so that the set involves a different rule (or several different rules), vary the instructions, vary the type of subjects used, and so on. The Einstellung effect should be robust across all of these manipulations. If it is not, then we have found that variables previously thought to be irrelevant are actually important, and this is crucial knowledge.

In a *conceptual replication* one attempts to replicate a phenomenon or concept, but in an entirely different way. Luchins also examined other tasks besides the water jar problem to establish the Einstellung phenomenon in diverse situations. He used series of geometry problems, words hidden in letters, and paper mazes. In each case subjects solved several problems that had a unique solution before they came to the critical problems that could be solved either by the old Einstellung solution or by a much more simple and direct solution. Just as in the water jar experiments, subjects usually used the old, circuitous solution and ignored the more efficient solution. These experiments constitute conceptual replications of the concept of Einstellung.

You should note the following carefully: the problem of reliability of results is interwoven with the problem of generality and validity. As we progress from direct to systematic to conceptual replication, we not only show reliability, we also show increasing validity. Are we studying something that is not only really "there," but is it something that ties in with or is related to our knowledge of other psychological phenomena in a reasonable way? A conceptual replication is closely related to our next topic, converging operations, which are procedures that validate a hypothetical construct used to explain behavior by eliminating alternative explanations.

Converging Operations

Suppose that Luchins had conducted just the one experiment outlined in Table 10–1. What sorts of conclusions could he have drawn from his results (assume, too, that he directly replicated the study so that he knew his results were reliable)? Can he legitimately conclude that Einstellung caused the results? Without some independent evidence to the contrary, he could have said that the results were due to a "water-jar effect" or to a "$B - A - 2C$ effect" rather than an Einstellung effect. This is because each of these concepts was part of the one experiment, and each is a reasonable cause of the results. By doing systematic and conceptual replications, Luchins ruled out the alternative hypotheses and made the concept of Einstellung a reasonable explanation of the rigidity seen in many problem-solving situations.

In other words, the results of experiments that had different rules and different problems converged on the Einstellung hypothesis by systematically eliminating alternative hypotheses. *Converging operations,* then, are a set of two or more operations that eliminate alternate concepts that might explain a set of experimental results. The importance of converging operations in psychological research was initially emphasized in a landmark paper by Garner, Hake, and Eriksen (1956). They noted that converging operations are necessary to validate operationally defined constructs (see Chapter 2) as well as experimental results. Because converging operations are crucial to an understanding of psychological research and psychological theorizing, we will consider two more examples of converging operations at work.

Stroop effect: input or output?   Before the discussion continues, we want you to try a simple experiment. All you need are some index cards, colored markers, and a watch with a second hand or, even better, a stop watch. Take sixteen index cards and, using your markers, write the name of the color in its color—that is, with a green marker write GREEN, and so on. If you have eight markers, each color will be repeated twice. If you only have four markers, repeat each color four times. Take another sixteen index cards and write color names that do not correspond to the ink—that is with a green marker write RED, and so on. Your stimuli are now completed. Pick one of your two decks and, for each card, name the color of the ink. Time how long it takes you to go through all sixteen cards. Do the same for the other deck. Were you faster for the deck that had compatible color names and inks?

If you tried this experiment, you probably found that responding to mismatches between ink colors and color names was slower than when they were compatible. Furthermore, you should have noticed mistakes, stuttering, and hesitation in the incompatible condition. A variation of this frustrating demonstration experiment was first done by Stroop (1935), and the *Stroop effect* refers to the increase in time required to name the ink color when the ink and color names do not match.

The Stroop effect is a highly reliable one; the question is, what causes the Stroop effect? One possibility is that it is due to the input or perceptual aspects of the task. Stroop and others have found that reading is usually faster than naming; therefore, the perceptual argument is that reading color words inhibits the perception of the ink color. An alternative hypothesis is that output (the subject's responses) is affected and not perception. The output notion goes like this: after the subject has perceived both the ink color and the color word, there is response competition when two different color names are elicited—one by the ink and another by the word. On the basis of Stroop's original work, we have no way of deciding between these two hypotheses. Which is important—the perceptual system or the response system?

A simple but clever experiment was conducted by Egeth, Blecker, and Kamlet (1969) to answer this question by using converging operations. Three important conditions from one of their studies are shown in Figure 10–2. The control or baseline condition is shown at the top of this figure ("Neutral Condition"). Subjects saw two color patches with a neutral symbol (XXXX) imbedded in them. The two color patches were either the same color or they were of different colors. An important factor in this study is that instead of responding with color names, the subjects responded SAME when the two patches matched and DIFFERENT when the colors of the two patches were different.

The crucial conditions of the experiment are illustrated in the next rows. As in the baseline condition, the subject responded SAME or DIFFERENT on the basis of the colors of the two patches. In the Perceptual Inhibition Condition, color words appeared in the color patches, and on a given trial the same color word appeared in both boxes. Both color patches could be the same and match the color word (a SAME trial) or the color patches could be different, with only one patch matching the names (a DIFFERENT trial). Egeth et al. reasoned that there should not be any response competition in the Perceptual Inhibition Condition because the responses SAME and DIFFERENT should not compete with the various responses to the color names. The prediction is that if the Perceptual Inhibition Condition leads to slower responding

Figure 10–2

	Response	Symbols in Colors		Color of Patches
Neutral Condition	Same	XXXX	XXXX	both patches red
	Different	XXXX	XXXX	one patch red, one blue
Perceptual Inhibition	Same	RED	RED	both patches red
Condition	Different	RED	RED	one patch red, one blue
Response Competition	Same	SAME	SAME	both patches red
Condition	Different	SAME	SAME	one patch red, one blue

An outline of some of the conditions in the work by Egeth, Blecker, and Kamlet (1969). In all three conditions, subjects responded SAME when there was agreement among the stimuli and DIFFERENT when there was a mismatch. Subjects saw two colored patches on each trial and responded on the basis of the colors. The Neutral Condition served as a control by having neutral symbols (XXXX) imbedded in colored patches. Color names were in the patches in the Perceptual Inhibition Condition—the color names should inhibit the perception of the colors. SAME or DIFFERENT appeared in the patches in the Response Competition Condition—reading the response SAME in different colored patches should inhibit the correct response of DIFFERENT. The Stroop effect occurred in the Response Competition Condition but not in the Perceptual Inhibition Condition.

than the neutral condition, then the Stroop Effect is due to perceptual inhibition and not due to response competition. In the Perceptual Inhibition Condition, Egeth et al. found that the Stroop effect disappeared: responding was about as fast as in the control condition.

So far so good. We seem to have eliminated one alternative as an explanation of the Stroop effect. Now for a converging operation that will bring back the Stroop effect and identify the processes involved. To accomplish this Egeth and his co-workers used the condition outlined at the bottom of Figure 10–2. As was true of the other two conditions, the subjects responded SAME and DIFFERENT in the Response Competition Condition. However, in the Response Competition Condition the words SAME or DIFFERENT appeared in the color patches rather than neutral symbols or color names. Egeth et al. reasoned that if response competition is important, then mismatches between SAME or DIFFERENT and the stimulus information should result in slower responding than in the Neutral Condition. That is, if conflict among responses causes the Stroop effect, then responding should be slower in the Response Competition condition than in the Neutral Condition. This is exactly what they found. The Stroop effect returned: now the responses SAME and DIFFERENT took longer when they conflicted with the response in the stimulus. Recall that the identical response words did not produce a Stroop effect in the Perceptual Inhibition Condition. Thus, the converging operations removed the perceptual process as an alternative explanation for the results leaving us to conclude that a response process accounts for the Stroop effect. Other studies on the Stroop phenomenon also lead to the conclusion that response competition is an important contributing factor to Stroop interference (see Keele, 1973, for an excellent review).

Personal Space. The concept of personal space implies that you are surrounded by an invisible bubble designed to protect you from a wide variety of social encroachments. How do psychologists know that such a bubble exists? Since it cannot be directly sensed by vision, smell, touch, etc., the concept must be indirectly evaluated. The next two experiments demonstrate that there is a personal space bubble by using two different kinds of spatial invasion, both of which yield similar results.

It is ironic that the personal space bubble that helps you to maintain privacy is best studied by invasions that violate the privacy it affords. A simple experiment conducted by August Kinzel (1970) shows one operation that defines personal space. Kinzel was interested in the personal space bubbles surrounding violent and nonviolent prisoners. Thus one independent variable—more precisely a subject variable (see Chapter 7), since it was not manipulated—in his study was classification of prisoners as violent (having inflicted physical injury to another person) or not. Each prisoner stood in the center of an empty room 20 feet wide and 20 feet long. The experimenter then approached from one of eight directions (the second independent variable) until the prisoner said "stop" because the experimenter was too close. The dependent variable was the distance between prisoner and experimenter when the prisoner said "stop." If there is no personal space bubble, the experimenter should be able to walk right up to the prisoner (distance = 0). Control variables were the room itself and the experimenter who was the same person throughout the experiment. Results of this experiment are shown in Figure 10–3. It is clear that violent prisoners have larger personal space bubbles than nonviolent prisoners.

This experiment may not have convinced you entirely that there really is a personal space bubble. A concept based only upon a single experiment is just a restatement of that particular experimental finding. In Kinzel's experiment you may feel that there is something strange

Figure 10–3

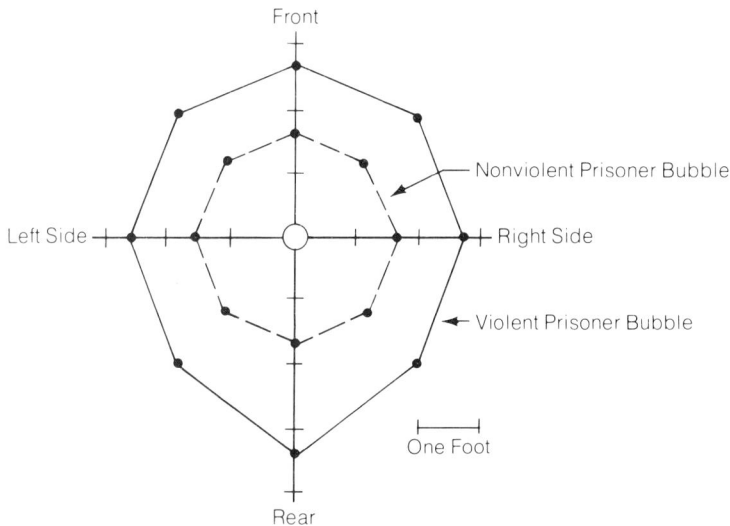

Looking down on the personal space bubble of violent and nonviolent prisoners (after Kinzel, 1970).

about a person walking right up to you without saying anything. Certainly if this happened to you on the street you would think it unusual, to say the least. The next experiment avoids this potential difficulty.

In order to avoid actively invading someone's personal space bubble, Barefoot, Hoople, and McClay (1972) gave subjects the opportunity to invade the experimenter's bubble. The experimenter sat near a water fountain and pretended to read a book. Anyone getting a drink of water had to invade the experimenter's personal space. The independent variable was the distance between the experimenter and the water fountain. This could be either one foot, five feet, or ten feet. This last distance is large enough so that it exceeds the bounds of the experimenter's personal space and thus is a control condition. A confederate kept track of the number of persons passing by the fountain in each of the three experimental conditions. The dependent variable was the percentage of passers-by who drank from the fountain. When the experimenter was one foot away only 10 percent drank; five feet away 18 percent drank. Finally, at a distance of ten feet 22 percent drank from the fountain.

These results agree with those of the active invasion paradigm used by Kinzel. The single concept of a personal space bubble explains findings of both experiments. Hence, the experiments provide converging operations supporting the personal space concept.

The examples of converging operations we have just detailed are actually rather simple, because only a small number of experiments was needed to provide validity and generality. In actual practice, many concepts and phenomena require a considerable amount of independent evidence before they can be considered as valid.

We also should not be complacent about our understanding of the Stroop effect and the concept of personal space. As is true of any concept, additional research is likely to refine our knowledge about personal space and the Stroop effect. For example, there may be tasks involving incompatible stimuli and responses that place exceptional demands on our perceptual system. So, some kinds of Stroop phenomena could result from both input and output effects. In a similar fashion, future research may show that the size of the personal space bubble differs in active and passive situations: your bubble may be smaller when someone invades it than when you enter the personal space of another person.

It seems fitting to end this section and this chapter with a reminder from one of the greatest scientists, Sir Isaac Newton: "Knowledge is gained bit by bit."

Summary

Several pitfalls may make it difficult for you to interpret the results of your research. Some of these pitfalls pose particular problems in any single research project, and others make it difficult to interpret patterns of research. Scale attenuation and regression artifacts can lead to the misinterpretation of the results of a specific project, while replications (reliability) and converging operations (validity) are important for interpreting patterns of research. Scale attenuation refers to an inability to observe differences in thought and behavior because performance is either too good (a ceiling effect) or too poor (a floor effect). The scale must be spread out or the task modified in order to handle the attenuation problem. Regression to the mean is likely to occur whenever subject variables are included in a project. The regression artifact refers to the tendency for the subject's behavior to drift toward his or her "true" mean performance. Random assignment (a random groups design) is the best way to guard against regression artifacts. An experiment that can be replicated is a reliable one, as is a test whose results are consistent. The three types of replications are: direct, systematic, and conceptual. Test reliability can be determined via the split-half method, using alternate forms of the test, or simply repeating the test again (test-retest method). Converging operations are several independent operations that validate the meaning of constructs. The necessity for converging operations demands that scientific research on a problem be varied and extensive.

Exercises

1. Here is another design problem for you. Reread the description of Luchins' first experiment that is outlined in Table 10–1. There seem to be several problems with that study; see if you can pinpoint two or three of them. As a hint, consider the following questions: Did Luchins use an appropriate control group—if not, what should be the control condition? Are there points in the study that require counterbalancing? What additional dependent variables might have been informative?

2. Examine the figures and tables in several recent journal articles. From this examination see if you can discover any ceiling or floor effects. If you find any, and it may take a while, read the article to see if the investigator was aware of the scale attenuation problem. Can the problem be rectified?

3. Pinpointing regression artifacts may be difficult. However, you might find it worthwhile to examine several assessment-type studies that use subject variables in an attempt to discover a regression problem. If you find evidence for a regression artifact, see if you can determine why the study was published anyway. Remember our discussion of medical research and the difficulty of random assignment. Try these two journals: *Journal of Educational Psychology* and the *Journal of Applied Psychology.*

4. Find an example of each type of replication in recent journals. You may not find any examples of direct replication, and yet Barber (1976) has asserted that direct replications are crucial to the advancement of psychology. Why is it the case that direct replications rarely appear in the literature?

5. More often than not, good examples of converging operations can be found in a single journal article. Papers by Paivio, Mayer, and Thios and D'Agostino listed in the suggested readings offer evidence for converging operations at work. You might take a look at these articles.

Key Concepts

scale attenuation effects 243
ceiling effects 243
floor effects 243
statistical regression
   to the mean 247
regression artifact 247
test-retest reliability 253
parallel forms reliability 253
split-half reliability 253
experimental reliability 254

Einstellung 254
replication 254
direct replication 256
systematic replication 256
conceptual replication 257
converging operations 257
validity 257
Stroop effect 258
personal space 260

Suggested Readings

The following three articles illustrate both reliability and converging operations. Read them carefully. They are available in the book *Readings in Experimental Psychology* by Elmes (Chicago: Rand McNally, 1978): Mayer, R. E. Problem-solving performance with task overload: effects of self-pacing and trait anxiety. *Bulletin of the Psychonomic Society,* 1977, 9:283–86; Paivio, A. Perceptual comparisons through the mind's eye. *Memory and Cognition,* 1975, 3:635–47; Thios, S. J., & D'Agostino, P. R. Effects of repetition as a function of study-phase retrieval. *Journal of Verbal Learning and Verbal Behavior,* 1976, 15:529–36.

Purposes of research

Provide explanatory data base

Test theories

Replicate and extend previous results

Curiosity

Sources of research ideas

Experts

Journal articles

Textbooks

Curiosity

Practical problems

Nuts and bolts of research

Get the idea

Formulate a testable hypothesis

Review the pertinent literature

Design the project

Collect the data

Ontogeny of a Research Project

11

In biology, ontogeny refers to the life history of an organism. So in this chapter we will discuss the growth and development of a typical research project. This is essentially a how-to-do-it chapter, in which we discuss the purpose of research, where ideas come from, important resources in psychology, and formulating and testing hypotheses.

Overview

As noted at the beginning of this book, the general aim of psychological research is to find out why people think and act as they do. Up to this point we have emphasized particular methods and problems associated with this fundamental question. Now we want to consider some general aspects of the research process in some detail.

Purposes of Research

You may conduct a research project for any one of several good reasons. Ignoring the possibility that you are doing projects solely because of a course requirement, let us consider some purposes behind attempts to answer the fundamental question. *Most basic research is performed to provide the data base for explanations of behavior and to test theories.* With a sufficient data base, derived from the research procedures we have discussed, well-planned experiments (so-called critical experiments) are conducted. These experiments try to pit two theories that make different predictions against each other. One outcome favors Theory A and the other Theory B. Thus, in principle, the experiment will determine which theory to reject and which to keep. In practice, these critical experiments do not work out so well since supporters of the rejected theory are ingenious in thinking up explanations to discredit the unfavorable interpretation of the experiment. For example, two major explanations of forgetting are that (1) items decay or fade out over time just the way an incandescent light bulb fades when the electricity is turned off, or (2) items never fade, but they interfere with each other, causing confusion. A simple critical experiment would vary the time between successive items, holding the number of items constant (Waugh and Norman, 1965). Memory should be worse with longer times according to trace decay, since there is more time for the item to fade out. However, since the number of items is the same for all conditions, interference theory predicts no differences in forgetting. When this experiment is performed there is no difference, which would seem to reject the trace decay explanation. However, trace decay theorists argue that the extra time between items allows people to rehearse—that is, repeat the items to themselves—which prevents forgetting. So, if you accept the latter interpretation, our critical experiment is no longer so critical with regard to these two theories. Therefore, the argument about these two theories is still undecided on the basis of this experiment.

A second general purpose of research is to replicate and extend previous findings. Since we have discussed replication in detail in Chapter 10, we will simply note here that a single observation or experiment by itself is far less convincing than a series of related studies. A network of results provides generality and will converge on an explanation of the phenomenon in question. In this fundamental sense, psychological research is a never-ending (and exciting) enterprise.

You may conduct psychological research simply because you are curious. While your intuitions and general knowledge may lead to important research, frequently a project is undertaken just to see what happens. We call this "what-if" research. Students in laboratory courses often come up with what-if experiments since these projects require no knowledge of theory or the existing data base and can be formulated on the basis of their own personal experience and observations. The main objection to a what-if experiment is its inefficiency. If, as is often the case, nothing much happens—say, the independent variable has no effect—not much is gained from the experiment. But if nothing much happens in a careful experiment where a theory predicts that something will happen, the null results can still be useful. We must admit to having tried what-if experiments. Most of them did not work, but they were fun. Our advice is to check with your instructor before trying a what-if project. More often than not, your instructor can probably give you an estimate of the odds of your coming up with firm results or may even know the results of a similar study that has already been performed. In the latter instance, you would then be able to examine the existing data base.

Getting the Idea

After reading the previous section, the thought may have occurred to you that you are still no better off with regard to undertaking your research project. Where do research ideas come from? We mentioned the rather obvious tactic of asking your instructor about what-if research projects. You should seek out a consultant, and within a particular course, your instructor is the obvious choice. Beyond a particular course, on the other hand, you may try to seek advice from someone whose competence or interest matches what you are interested in doing.

Don't be afraid to try and get help this way. Many faculty members are only too happy to discuss research with you. If you have read an interesting journal article, you can even try writing (or telephoning, if you are brave) the author whose article created your initial interest.

Ideas frequently come from reading journal articles. If you read in the critical fashion outlined in Chapter 3, stopping after each section to quickly write down answers to the checklist questions, you will soon have a longer list of possible experiments than you could perform. Every difference of opinion between you and the author leads to a potential experiment. In order to keep track of ideas generated from your critical reading of journals (textbooks are another source), you should keep records of your research ideas. Most psychologists have some sort of index file containing information about the articles they have read. On your file cards you should have several kinds of information: authors' names, journals, and article titles; information about the procedure and results; and your checklist questions and answers. It is probably best to supplement your article file with a file of research ideas. Most psychologists keep a file of such ideas, and you should too. Write down the reference that started you thinking and a short description of your idea for a project. Many people write down the date the idea occurred, and it is quite interesting to go back through your files to see how your thinking about some topic has changed over time.

As your idea file gets larger because each article you read suggests at least one additional project to you, you are now confronted with another problem. At first an idea for any project was cause for celebration. Later the problem becomes one of deciding which of several ideas in your file should be tried. Some potential ideas will be eliminated because you do not have access to specialized equipment or special subject populations. Others will be too complicated or take too long to carry out. After paring your list down, you probably still may have more than one alternative. Assuming each idea is equally practical and feasible, given your resources, our advice is to tackle the project you think would be most fun.

At this point we would like to remind you of our discussion of curiosity and serendipity in Chapter 1. Psychological research is interesting, exciting, and often has important outcomes. In order for lady luck to influence your research, you have to do research (follow up on your idea file), and you have to be prepared to do a good job.

Many students are unsure about what journals and other resources they should examine to obtain research ideas. We have prepared Table 11–1 to help you along. You will notice that there are several general sources of information as well as journals with particular topical emphases. Perhaps the most important general resource is the *Psychological Abstracts,* which contains brief abstracts of articles from almost all journals publishing psychological research. After you have found abstracts of interest in the *Abstracts,* you can then read the entire article or send a note to the author, requesting a reprint of the article or additional information. The other resources listed in Table 11–1 have a variety of purposes, and we recommend that you try to familiarize yourself with each of the general purpose resources and as many of the research journals as seem to be of interest to you. Note that we have included only a small number of research journals in the table, but the ones we have included are among the most widely read ones in psychological research. Others emphasizing education, clinical problems, sociology, law, and industrial concerns can be ferreted out of your school's library.

We have tried to design this text to be a source of some research projects. If you have been conscientious about answering the design-related questions that appear at the end of most chapters, the germ of a good research project may be lurking in one or more of your answers. Most of the design questions have been based on actual research, so it is apparent that even "experts" goof up from time to time. There is no reason why you cannot profit from the mistakes of others. Another source of ideas are the research problems in the *Nuts and Bolts* section of this chapter. We have worked through a couple of problem areas with the assumption that you could pose and attempt to answer your own hypotheses about these topics.

The last source of research ideas we wish to mention might be called the *"itch" of research.* Some particular practical problem is bothering you, and you seem to need an answer to help you solve a problem. How can I study more effectively? Why are my roommates such conforming jerks? How can I become a better public speaker? These and related practical concerns are often important goads to good research. In order to tackle such problems adequately, however, you will probably have to seek the help of a consultant and also examine the relevant data base. Most of the things that have bugged you have probably bothered someone else. So, you should review the literature, beginning with the *Psychological Abstracts,* relevant to your problem. If you are lucky, you may not have to do much research before a solution is forthcoming. However, we would like to warn you that reasonable solutions to practical problems often take a considerable amount of investigation before a resolution is possible. This slow progress is one of the things that keeps applied researchers in business.

Nuts and Bolts of Research

You have a problem or idea you want to investigate; what next? Well, you simply formulate a testable hypothesis, review the literature, design the project, and then collect the data. Sounds easy doesn't it—it isn't. One thing we have noticed (and you may have too, by now) is that

Some Important Resources for Psychological Research		**Table 11-1**
Topic Area	*Title of Resource*	*Comment*
Article Titles	*Current Contents*	several specialty areas
Author Citations	*Science Citation Index*	
Article Abstracts	*Biological Abstracts*	
	Ergonomics Abstracts	
	Index Medicus	
	Psychological Abstracts	
Review Articles	*American Psychologist*	
	Annual Review of Psychology	book with chapter length reviews
	Journal of Experimental Psychology: General	contains original experiments
	Psychological Bulletin	
	Psychological Review	often contains original studies
Laboratory Experiments	*American Journal of Psychology*	
	Animal Learning and Behavior	some field studies
	Behavior Research Methods & Instrumentation	notes on apparatus and computers
	Bulletin of the Psychonomic Society	
	Canadian Journal of Psychology	
	Cognitive Psychology	
	Journal of Comparative and Physiological Psychology	some field studies
	Journal of Experimental Child Psychology	
	Journal of Experimental Psychology: Animal Behavior Processes	some field studies
	Journal of Experimental Psychology: Human Learning & Memory	
	Journal of Experimental Psychology: Human Perception & Performance	
	Journal of Experimental Social Psychology	
	Journal of the Experimental Analysis of Behavior	small-*n* experiments
	Journal of Verbal Learning and Verbal Behavior	
	Learning and Motivation	
	Memory & Cognition	
	Perception & Psychophysics	
	Physiological Psychology	
	Quarterly Journal of Experimental Psychology	
Various Research Methods	*Behavior Therapy*	case histories, small-*n*
	Child Development	
	Developmental Psychology	
	Developmental Psychobiology	
	Journal of Abnormal Psychology	
	Journal of Applied Behavioral Analysis	small-*n*
	Journal of Applied Psychology	
	Journal of Educational Psychology	
	Journal of Personality and Social Psychology	
	Perceptual and Motor Skills	
	Psychological Reports	

students eventually can generate some very interesting ideas for research but get bogged down when they try to actually investigate their problem. The biggest stumbling block seems to be the development of a testable hypothesis and the *general* research plan that goes with the hypothesis. In this section, we work through a couple of problems to show you how people with some experience develop a research project. Two things should be noted: (1) we may have made some inappropriate choices in our analysis of these problems, so you should be alert for the possibility of taking alternative routes to a solution; and (2) we have deliberately not included all possible research hypotheses associated with these questions, because we want you to think up some of your own.

Dear Folks: I Can't Study . . .

Problem. Where you live is rather noisy, and your grades are not as good as you would like them to be. You are convinced (or, you are trying to convince others such as your parents) that the reason your academic performance is not as good as expected is because of the overall noise level of your college residence. Can you demonstrate that noise level inhibits adequate academic work? There are several potential research hypotheses here, and how the hypotheses are posed will determine, in part, your general research plan.

Hypothesis 1. *Students who live in noisy dormitories have lower grade averages than do students who live in quiet dorms.* Since this hypothesis suggests a subject variable (where students live) instead of a true independent variable, something other than a laboratory experiment may be most appropriate. The hypothesis suggests that you determine some way of assessing "noisiness" and then relate students' grades to the noisiness level of their residence. You could use a sound-level meter to measure the average sound level. This means you would have to have a sound-level meter. If you don't have access to such a device, noise could be measured by yourself and some other "judges" by using a psychophysical scaling procedure. So, you and the judges could fill out a ten point rating scale on the extent of noise, or you could estimate the magnitude of noise by assigning a number proportional to the noise level. As an alternative you could have the occupants of a particular dorm rate the noise level. It might be best to have neighbors rate the noise level in some way.

You may have noticed that there are several difficulties that result from this general research procedure. When should we measure the noise level? If we take our measures at night, we will be catching people when they should be studying (let's assume that it is a weeknight—Monday through Thursday—because you have a pressing social engagement that prohibits data collection Friday through Sunday). On the other hand, if we just happen to hit a party or a bull session we might bias our measures. So, we will have to get more than one sample of noise level. Where should we measure the noise level? Getting several samples from all parts of an entire dorm would be very time consuming. We might have to get samples floor-by-floor or hall-by-hall (it depends on how your dorms are laid out). If we get noise samples in this way, we may want to redefine our initial hypothesis as follows: *Students living in noisy areas of a dormitory do more poorly academically than do students who live in quiet areas of that dorm.* Now we have to get some measure of academic performance, and this could pose a troublesome ethical problem. Even if you could get your school administration to agree to let you see the grade averages of the students in question, it is possible that those students don't want you to know what their averages are. If you plan to correlate noise and grade average, you need to have each student's grades. Short of breaking into administrative offices, the best thing to do would be to interview each resident, get an estimate of the grade average, and assure the individual resident that personal data will remain confidential. You would also have to make sure that you received replies from every resident in question, or you would have to devise some way to randomly sample these people. Some of the students in the quiet section might be in the library studying all the time (hence the high grades), or students in the noisy section may have no where else to go to raise cain.

If you actually do this study or one similar to it, you will probably raise more questions than you answer. Since you are using a correlational design, you will have to be careful about causal statements. Furthermore, there are several questions that remain to be considered: Why are some dorms more noisy than others? Can the noise level be controlled? Are all students equally sensitive to noise?

Hypothesis II. Let us pursue the last question. After all, your grades are suffering, but the "genius" next door plugs along despite noisy disruptions on your dorm floor. *Students are differentially disrupted by noise; those who are sensitive to noise perform more poorly than do those who are less sensitive to noise.* One way to approach this hypothesis is to develop a survey that discovers the sensitivity to noise. You have an advantage here over Hypothesis I because Weinstein (1978) has developed a reliable scale to measure individual differences in sensitivity to noise. Most of this scale is reproduced in Table 11–2, and respondents are to circle the appropriate number for each question. Questions marked with an asterisk have the answers reversed before the numerical scores are summed to get a total sensitivity score for a subject. Weinstein found that noise-sensitive students have lower scholastic aptitude (as measured by standard tests) than do students who are not particularly sensitive. Furthermore, Weinstein correlated noise sensitivity with various personality traits (as measured by other tests) and found the noise-sensitive students had a higher need for privacy than did the less sensitive students. Since Weinstein's work is correlational in nature, some interesting questions arise. Do noise-sensitive students party less than noise-insensitive students? What is the relationship between noise sensitivity and the use of stereos, radios, and TVs? What kind of student makes the most noise? What kind of noise is the most disruptive: human noise, music, continuous noise, or sudden noise, and what combinations are important?

Table 11-2 Some Items on Weinstein's Noise Sensitivity Scale

	agree strongly	maybe			disagree strongly
1. I wouldn't mind living on a noisy street if the apartment I had was nice.	1	2	3	4	5
* 2. I am more aware of noise than I used to be.	1	2	3	4	5
3. No one should mind much if someone turns up his stereo full blast once in a while.	1	2	3	4	5
* 4. At movies, whispering and crackling candy wrappers disturb me.	1	2	3	4	5
* 5. I am easily awakened by noise.	1	2	3	4	5
* 6. If it's noisy where I'm studying, I try to close the door or window or move someplace else.	1	2	3	4	5
* 7. I get annoyed when my neighbors are noisy.	1	2	3	4	5
8. I get used to most noises without difficulty.	1	2	3	4	5
* 9. Sometimes noises get on my nerves and get me irritated.	1	2	3	4	5
*10. Even music I normally like will bother me if I'm trying to concentrate.	1	2	3	4	5
11. It wouldn't bother me to hear the sound of everyday living from neighbors (footsteps, running water, etc.)	1	2	3	4	5
*12. When I want to be alone, it disturbs me to hear outside noises.	1	2	3	4	5
13. I am good at concentrating no matter what is going on around me.	1	2	3	4	5
14. In a library, I don't mind if people carry on a conversation if they do it quietly.	1	2	3	4	5
*15. There are often times when I want complete silence.	1	2	3	4	5
*16. Motorcycles ought to be required to have bigger mufflers.	1	2	3	4	5
*17. I find it hard to relax in a place that's noisy.	1	2	3	4	5
*18. I get mad at people who make noise that keeps me from falling asleep or getting work done.	1	2	3	4	5
19. I wouldn't mind living in an apartment with thin walls.	1	2	3	4	5
*20. I am sensitive to noise.	1	2	3	4	5

On the basis of these questions, the maximum sensitivity score would be 120 points. In order to derive this score, the points awarded to the subjects' answers to the questions marked with an asterisk are reversed. So, if a subject marked question 20 with a 1, this would mean that he strongly agrees with that question—he or she is sensitive. To make the scoring of that question compatible with the scoring of question 19, on which a noise-sensitive answer would be circling 5, we have to assign reverse values to the numbers chosen on question 20: 5 becomes 1, 4 becomes 2, 2 becomes 4, and 1 is changed to a 5. In Weinstein's study, the subjects were also asked about the noise conditions in their dorm. Some of the questions asked included such things as how often they had to ask neighbors to quiet down or how difficult it was to sleep.

Hypothesis III. The lengthy final question in the previous paragraph suggests several hypotheses. *The more annoying a noise is, the greater it will interfere with a complex task.* One way to approach this hypothesis is to survey the students on the degree of annoyance associated with certain types of noises and then relate this to their academic performance. In the present instance, a laboratory experiment seems preferable, and there is a substantial data base from which to work (see the end of this section for an annotated listing of references). Noises are played (music, party conversations, trucks, aircraft, and so forth) and rated for the degree of annoyance. Then the noises are presented while people engage in some task. Selecting the levels of your independent variable may be difficult. Do you want to vary it qualitatively (for example, party noise versus trucks versus silence) or quantitatively (vary the intensity of a particular noise)? If you choose the latter route, you will probably need a sound level meter so you can measure the actual intensity of the sound (you could, in the absence of a meter, have judges make preliminary scales of loudness). What task will your subjects perform? What would be a good dependent variable? If you examine the data base for this type of research, you will find that some tasks are more disrupted by noise than are others. So, a good idea would be to include at least two situations: one task that is likely to be disrupted and another that is unlikely to be disrupted. As a general hint, you might expect that tasks requiring listening would be more easily disrupted than tasks that did not require listening. After you have selected your independent and dependent variables, you have to worry about subject variables (is the hearing of the subjects equally sensitive) and your experimental design (should this be within-subjects or between-subjects). Some of the research in the data base suggests that there are carry-over effects from experiencing a particularly annoying noise. If that is the case and the issue has not been settled (see Moran and Loeb, 1977), then a between-subjects design may be more appropriate. Alternatively, you could use a within-subjects design and carefully counterbalance the order of presenting the different levels of your independent variable. If you do use a within-subjects design, you may want to assess the carry-over effects of the different levels by examining the effects of order of presenting the levels. This would mean that you would have a fairly complex within-subjects analysis of variance to perform on your results.

Hypothesis IV. The previous experiment, as is true of any single laboratory experiment, suffers from a potential lack of generality. How do we know that our independent and dependent variables are representative? Should we select additional tasks and types of noises to study? Furthermore, Hypotheses I and II are restricted in their focus, since they are primarily concerned with college students' reactions to noise. How can we add generality to our research on noise? *Residents of a noisy street will (a) move more frequently and (b) score lower on a rating scale for residential satisfaction than residents of a quiet street.* This hypothesis deals with the long-term effects of permanent residence, so it may avoid some of the problems of generalization associated with the other three hypotheses. However, there are several problems associated with doing research on Hypothesis IV. A familiar problem is how to measure sound levels. The experimenter will have to decide whether to measure sound levels only at certain times, for example, during rush hours, or to take 24-hour averages. The independent variable is not completely under the control of the experimenter. Furthermore, it may be confounded with things like income, status, population density, and so forth, since persons with lower socioeconomic status are more likely to reside on noisier streets than are higher status people who may be able to "get away from it all."

The dependent variables are not entirely satisfactory either. Even if residents desire to move more often from noisy streets, economic factors may prohibit them from accomplishing this. On the other hand, the turnover rate in an area is an objective number that can be reliably measured. The second dependent variable depends intimately upon the validity of the rating scale used to assess residential satisfaction. If you used a modification of the scale shown in Table 11–2, you could be assured of the reliability of your instrument. This scale has not been validated directly, and validation is a time-consuming activity. What can be said for the validity of the scale? In the first place, it looks as if it should measure what it is supposed to measure. That is, it seems to have *face validity*—it looks as if it should measure attitudes about noisy living conditions. In the second place, the scale results fit in fairly sensibly with the other results reported by Weinstein (1978). The scale measures some underlying psychological concept, which indicates that it has *construct validity*—we actually are measuring something to do with people's attitudes. To sum up Hypothesis IV: the price of greater ease of generalization in this study is a considerable loss of investigator control.

When we compare the four studies as solutions to the problem posed at the start of this section, it is clear that none of them is perfect. This is always true with research. No single piece of research, experiment or otherwise, can completely answer a question. The scientist is forced to focus on a more specific hypothesis, thus answering only a narrow part of the problem. This is a major source of frustration for all psychologists, since no general answers are forthcoming until many tiny pieces, each corresponding to a specific hypothesis, are put together. An environmental psychologist could easily spend an entire career trying to answer the problem of noise and its psychological effects. This converging nature of science (see Chapter 10 on converging operations) is also illustrated, in a slightly different way, in the next problem we have decided to illustrate.

References for the Effects of Noise

Broadbent, D. E. *Decision and stress.* London: Academic Press, 1971. This is a good general reference that summarizes a great deal of research on the effects of noise on behavior. The most pertinent chapter is Chapter 9.

Glass, D. C. and Singer, J. E. *Urban stress: experiments on noise and social stressors.* New York: Academic Press, 1972. This work includes more than you ever want to know about noise as a stressor. You might want to read their article in *American Scientist,* 1972, 60, 457–465, which is also reprinted in *Current trends in psychology: readings from American Scientist,* edited by I. L. Janis.

The following two articles describe some recent research on the effects of noise on behavior. The first contains experiments, the second is a correlational study:

Moran, S. L. V. and Loeb, M. Annoyance and behavioral aftereffects following interfering and noninterfering aircraft noise. *Journal of Applied Psychology,* 1977, 62:719–26.

Weinstein, N. D. Individual differences in reactions to noise: a longitudinal study in a college dormitory. *Journal of Applied Psychology,* 1978, 63:458–66.

You should examine the reference lists in these two articles for other papers that seem relevant. *Psychological Abstracts* and *Ergonomics Abstracts* may have abstracts of potentially relevant articles.

Reading Versus Listening in Memory

Problem. Just for the sake of argument, let us assume that you were intrigued by the results of Scarborough's (1972) study that were discussed in Chapter 10. You will remember that Scarborough found that short-term memory was better for visually presented trigrams than for auditorily presented trigrams, and, furthermore, he found that a combination of auditory and visual presentation resulted in no better retention than simple visual presentation. These results are interesting for at least two reasons. In the first place, we might speculate on the generality of the results. Does the same relationship hold for other types of materials (for example, prose or textbook information) and other tasks (for example, memory over longer periods or with different dependent variables)? In order to answer these questions, we will first have to examine the data base and then go into the laboratory. The second reason that

Scarborough's data are interesting is that they suggest some important practical implications. For example, it might not be too bold an extension to argue that auditory presentation, such as lecturing, is not as efficient a way to present material as is visual presentation, such as textbook material. Your suspicions about those deadly lectures have been confirmed in the psychological laboratory!

If you check with your instructor on this problem, or if you go into the literature on your own, what you will find is a vast number of articles concerned with the problem of modality effects on memory. *Modality* refers to the sensory system (eyes, ears, skin, etc.) that is affected during presentation. Another thing you will find (and we are going to tell you, so don't go read all the articles yet) is that there are some puzzling inconsistencies. In immediate recall, auditory presentation leads to much better retention of the most recent items than does visual presentation (an extensive review is provided by Penney, 1975). This is the reverse of what Scarborough found. Why? A second major inconsistency is that memory for large amounts of information over longer periods of time than that studied by Scarborough generally shows little influence of presentation modality. Sometimes there is a slight benefit in favor of auditory presentation, but this is inconsistent and sometimes reversed. Why?

Hypothesis I. Let us first examine the discrepancy between Scarborough's results and the data from numerous other short-term memory experiments. One possibility is that there was simply something wrong with his experiment. Perhaps an unintentional confounding of some sort led him to an erroneous conclusion. For example, maybe subjects in the visual only condition were simply better than those in the other conditions, because subject assignment was not random. This sort of thing is the first possibility that should be checked whenever a finding is unusual in some way. But it seems unlikely in this case that there was any simple confounding. The experiment was carefully done, the differences were rather large and statistically reliable. We have to search harder for an answer.

One very likely possibility is the nature of the distractor activity that Scarborough used between presentation and recall, that is, counting backwards from the three-digit number out loud. If we assume that there are separate auditory and visual short-term memory systems, it could be that the auditory nature of the counting task in Scarborough's experiment produced greater interference for items presented auditorily than for those presented visually. Since this is interference occurring after presentation of the material to be remembered, we call it *retroactive interference.* In general, retroactive interference refers to the disrupting effect of a second task on the retention of a first task. It would be very interesting to perform an experiment where visual or auditory presentation of stimuli was followed by a distractor task that was either visual or auditory in nature. If the retroactive interference interpretation of Scarborough's experiment is accurate, *one would expect auditory presentation to be better than visual with a visual distractor task, but for the reverse to be the case (as Scarborough found) with an auditory distractor task.*

Most of the methodological considerations seem straightforward— all we need to do is mimic Scarborough's study and include conditions with a visual distractor task. However, there are some crucial questions that need to be considered. Can we guarantee that the only difference between the auditory and visual distractor tasks is their modality of presentation? If the two tasks differ in their ease or in how long they take to accomplish, then we have added an important confounding to our study. We might be able to have our visual distraction involve the visual presentation of a three-digit number and have the subject write down the successive subtractions by threes. But if the writing and verbal response requirements lead to markedly different numbers of subtractions during any given retention interval, then it could be argued that any observed differences in retention were due to the amount of distracting activity and not the modality of distracting activity. This confounding of modality with amount of activity would be particularly damaging to any conclusion about the absolute amount of forgetting. Since we are predicting an interaction between the effects of modality of presentation and modality of distraction, we could still obtain some valuable information from our study, as long as we ignored the absolute levels of recall. So, we might want to use a slightly different kind of distracting activity. One that occurred to us would be to have some people hear digits and repeat them aloud, while others would see digits and write them down. You might have to do some preliminary or "pilot" work to determine what is a good rate for presenting the digits either visually or auditorily. You would have to find a rate that led to equivalent performance on the repeating task regardless of the modality used.

Another problem to consider is: How closely should Scarborough's original study be replicated? Should we include six retention intervals? Should we have a visual + auditory group? If we have the latter group, what kind of distracting task should be used? Answers to these questions will probably lead to other questions about design: Should I use a complete within-subjects design rather than the mixed design used by Scarborough? How should I counterbalance my materials (digits and trigrams) across conditions?

Experiments more complex than the one we have been considering seem to support the retroactive interference hypothesis. Hopkins, Edwards, and Cook (1973) showed that an auditory filler task disrupted the retention of words presented auditorily more than it did for words presented visually. Hopkins et al. also found the expected reverse effect when the filler task was visual. Another experiment (Elliot and Strawhorn, 1976) compared auditory and visual short-term memory following either silent or vocalized distractor activity. Vocalization disrupted retention more for the auditorily presented digits only after at least a ten-second retention interval. So, Elliot and Strawhorn obtained an interaction very similar to the one found by Scarborough (see Chapter 10).

Whenever an experimental result, such as Scarborough's, does not generalize, noting this fact is only the first step. The real problem is in finding out why. Scientists often tend to disbelieve exceptions to firmly held beliefs, at least until the exception has been replicated enough times to be made salient. It is always uncomfortable to have to change one's mind, but one way science sometimes progresses by leaps is when an empirical exception causes us to throw out or greatly modify our theory. So failures of generalization are not necessarily to be lamented; they can be great opportunities.

Hypothesis II.   Recently, Kintsch and Kozminsky (1977) had subjects either read or listen to 4–5 page stories. After a story was finished, the subjects had to write a summary of 80 words or less. They used this procedure to examine the effects of modality of presentation on prose recall because earlier work (King, 1968; Kintsch et al., 1975) that had used shorter texts and a more straightforward test procedure requiring recall of the entire text, found little difference between auditory and visual presentation. Kintsch and Kozminsky wanted to use a difficult task because, "When subjects listen to a story, they must rely completely on their memory. When they read it, they can go back to the text and check points about which they are uncertain. In order to maximize this contrast between reading and listening, such checking of the text was permitted even while subjects wrote their summaries (p. 491)." A comparison of the content of the summaries, both in terms of accuracy and idiosyncratic inclusions, revealed little difference due to modality of presentation.

When reading and listening times are equated, summaries following listening will be more accurate than summaries following reading. Two factors led to this hypothesis: (1) the numerous results reported by Penney (1975) suggest that auditory presentation is best at least for small amounts of information retained over short intervals of time—why should more complex retention be any different; and (2) it occurred to us that even though the subjects who read in the Kintsch and Kozminsky study had a tremendous advantage over the subjects who listened, performance was similar in the two groups, which must indicate that auditory presentation is much better than visual presentation. How do we equate reading and listening time? This is a fairly straightforward matter when consonant trigrams are the stimuli. How do you do it for a 4–5 page story? How do we minimize the "cheating" (looking back) by the subjects who read the stories?

These questions indicate that we are trying to develop an unconfounded independent variable: we want our two presentation conditions to differ on the basis of modality of presentation and nothing else. (Note that the quote from the Kintsch and Kozminsky article indicates that they were aware of the confounding of time of presentation with modality; however, their purposes were slightly different from ours.) This is a very tricky problem. Suppose we select stories that take 15 minutes to read aloud in the listening condition. In the reading condition should we also allow 15 minutes to read the passage? If so, the readers could quite likely have more actual presentation time, since most people can read silently faster than they can read aloud. Thus people who read to themselves could spend more time on the difficult material. Kintsch and Kozminsky allowed the people who read to do so naturally, which means that one of their interests was in a fundamental difference between reading and listening. Since their results were inconclusive with regard to the modality effect, we could force our subjects to read straight through the story via instructions. We also would not allow them to look at the text during the test phase. Perhaps a more precise way to equate reading and listening times and to prevent looking back would be to record the time taken to read each sentence aloud, and then present each sentence singly for reading for as long as it takes to vocalize it. Although this technique might give an advantage to very fast readers, the advantage would be much less than in the original experiment.

What about our dependent variable? Summarizing is a complex task, and Kintsch and Kozminsky had several reasons for using the summary technique. However, most students have to recall or recognize rather specific information, so we might want to use either a reproduction task (recall the entire story), a cued recall task (either fill-in-the-blank questions or more open-ended, short-answer questions), or we could use a multiple-choice recognition task. Perhaps we could use all the dependent variables mentioned and counterbalance the order of assessment across subjects. Then we could see if reading and listening differentially affect summarizing, reproduction, cued recall, and multiple-choice recognition. This ideal experiment would be very complex, and such a design would lead to a number of other questions with regard to equating the difficulty of the short-answer questions with the difficulty of the multiple-choice questions. Should we ask just simple, surface-level questions (Was _____ discussed in the third paragraph?) or more meaningful questions about the text? There are several alternative routes one could take here—which is the most interesting to you?

After you have decided upon your independent and dependent variables, there are a few other problems that must be resolved. Should you use each subject in both the reading and listening conditions, or should you use different groups of subjects in the two conditions? In general it is best to use a within-subjects design, since in that case we do not have to worry about differences between conditions being due to differences between subjects in the two conditions. So long as we counterbalance the conditions for practice effects by testing half the subjects in the read condition before the listen condition and the other half in the reverse order, there is nothing to prevent us from using the advantageous within-subjects design. Choice of a within-subjects design leads to another problem. Obviously we will have to use at least two stories to test the subjects, one in one condition and one in the other. We would have to make sure that we counterbalance passages across conditions and order so that reading and listening were examined and not the effects of a particular passage or story. We might even want to use more than two stories, since we would like to have some confidence that our results generalize to materials other than the particular ones used in this study. The issue of generalizable materials is an important one, especially since it is widely overlooked in certain types of research, with the result that statistical tests are often misapplied (see Clark, 1973).

Perhaps the final decision you have to make is to select the stories or passages. Kintsch and Kozminsky used translations of three short stories by Boccaccio that were about 2000 words long. You could use the same materials, but to enhance the generality of your experiment you might want to select passages from a magazine or book. In any event, you want to select material that is relatively unfamiliar, since we want to test what was gained during the experiment, not what was learned prior to it. Ceiling effects could arise if the material were too easy or too familiar. If subjects could answer all the questions on the multiple-choice test, for example, before the experiment started, there would be no chance for our independent variable (reading versus listening) to exert any influence over our dependent variable (recognition in this case), since we would have a ceiling effect on the test (close to 100 percent recognition).

To avoid overly familiar materials, people investigating memory for "naturalistic" prose passages have often chosen material that contains so many words and concepts foreign to the experience of the subjects that one wonders how "natural" these bizarre stories are. Furthermore, very difficult passages could lead to a floor effect. Regardless of the presentation condition (reading or listening), the material could be so complicated that no college student could be expected to answer questions about it after one reading. We should try to select stories that are by an author who is likely to be unfamiliar (as did Kintsch and

Kozminsky), or we should use passages with mostly familiar words but new information. Passages might be taken from *The Scientific American, Human Nature,* or other magazines at a similar level.

Following are some additional hypotheses on reading versus listening. We present them to you without commentary. See if you can figure out some of the problems you might encounter if you attempted to test these hypotheses. In some instances you will have to search the technical literature for the relevant data base. A good place to start would be the article by Penney (1975) or the one by Watkins, Watkins, and Crowder (1974). Both of these papers are listed in the references for this problem.

Hypothesis III. *Rate of forgetting in short-term memory will be slower for visual than auditory presentation, regardless of the type of distracting activity.* (Hint: read Thompson, J. T., and Clayton, K. N. Presentation modality, rehearsal-prevention conditions, and auditory confusions in tests of short-term memory. *Memory and Cognition,* 1974, 2:426–30.)

Hypothesis IV. *Intonation* (loudness, quality, and variation in expression) *is an important variable in determining the effectiveness of auditory presentation.*

Hypothesis V. *For the long-term memory of prose passages, combined auditory and visual presentation is better than either mode alone.*

References for Reading Versus Listening

Clark, H. H. The language-as-fixed-effect fallacy: A critique of language statistics in psychological research. *Journal of Verbal Learning and Verbal Behavior,* 1973, 12:335–59.

Elliot, L. A., and Strawhorn, R. J. Interference in short-term memory from vocalization: aural versus visual modality differences. *Journal of Experimental Psychology: Human Learning and Memory,* 1976, 2:705–11.

Hopkins, R. H., Edwards, R. E., and Cook, C. L. Presentation modality, distractor modality, and proactive interference in short-term memory. *Journal of Experimental Psychology,* 1973, 98:363–67.

King, D. J. Retention of connected meaningful material as a function of modes of presentation and recall. *Journal of Experimental Psychology,* 1968, 77:676–83. This article should provide you with some good ideas about both independent and dependent variables other than the particular ones we have just discussed.

Kintsch, W., et al. Comprehension and recall of text as a function of content variables. *Journal of Verbal Learning and Verbal Behavior,* 1975, 14:196–214. This long article contains only one study concerning modality effects, but it should be worth reading for many of the numerous methodological considerations.

Kintsch, W. and Kozminsky, E. Summarizing stories after reading and listening. *Journal of Educational Psychology,* 1977, 69:491–99. In this article you should pay close attention to the rationale behind the "natural" reading times, and you should note how the subjects' responses were scored.

Penney, C. Modality effects in short-term verbal memory. *Psychological Bulletin,* 1975, 82:68–84. This is a comprehensive review of the research concerned with modality effects in short-term memory.

Scarborough, D. L. Stimulus modality effects on forgetting in short-term memory. *Journal of Experimental Psychology,* 1972, 95:285–89.

Thompson, J. T. and Clayton, K. N. Presentation modality, rehearsal-prevention conditions, and auditory confusions in tests of short-term memory. *Memory and Cognition,* 1974, 2:426–30.

Modality effects are a "hot" topic, especially theories of how modality effects operate in short-term memory. See the *Psychological Abstracts.* A good, but difficult theoretical paper is:

Watkins, M. J., Watkins, O. C., and Crowder, R. G. The modality effect in free and serial recall as a function of phonological similarity. *Journal of Verbal Learning and Verbal Behavior,* 1974, 13:430–47.

A Final Word

Neither the practice nor the use of science is easy. The benefits that can be derived from scientific knowledge and understanding depend upon critical and well-informed citizens and scientists.

Your involvement with a career, a family, and social affairs will be partially determined by scientific findings. You must be in a position to evaluate those findings accurately and accept those that seem most reliable and valid. Unless you plan to hibernate or drop out of society in some other way, you are going to be affected by psychological research. As a citizen you will be a consumer of the results of psychological research, and we hope that the material discussed in this book will help to make you an intelligent consumer.

Some of you, we hope, will become scientists. We also hope that some of you budding scientists will focus on why people think and act as they do. We wish you future scientists good fortune. Your scientific career will be exciting, and we hope that your endeavors will be positively influenced by the principles of psychological research presented herein.

About 100 years ago, T. H. Huxley, a British scientist, said: "The chessboard is the world, the pieces are the phenomena of the universe, the rules of the game are what we call the laws of Nature. The player on the other side is hidden from us. We know that his play is always fair, just, and patient. But we also know, to our cost, that he never overlooks a mistake, or makes the smallest allowance for ignorance."

Where do research ideas originate? You can, of course, get them from your instructor or from this text. Other sources are journal articles, your own curiosity, the need for replication, and the "itch" to solve a practical problem. Most good research projects require that you understand the existing data base for your problem. After you have selected your problem, you need to review the literature and formulate a testable hypothesis before you can design your research procedure. Your procedure is determined by many practical factors in addition to the scientific and ethical ones discussed earlier in the text. **Summary**

Study and Review

Exercises

1. Comment upon the following field experiment. A researcher interested in the influence of reading versus listening on classroom learning found a sixth-grade class in Oak Hall School that emphasized individual reading in Social Studies. A sixth-grade class in Central Elementary, which was in the same school district as Oak Hall, used the more traditional lecture approach in Social Studies. Both classes were fairly large (33 in the Oak Hall class, 30 in the Central Elementary class), there was about a 50-50 split of boys and girls in each class, and both classes had experienced women teachers. At the end of the semester the researcher administered the same standardized Social Studies test to both classes. On this test, the Oak Hall class averaged 91.2 percent (a *B+* in their grading scheme), and the Central Elementary class average was 82.6 percent (a low *C*). The researcher concluded that reading about Social Studies leads to better academic performance than does listening about Social Studies.

2. Look up *aggression* in the index of the *Psychological Abstracts* and read several abstracts listed under aggression. Note how articles with various emphases are organized in the Abstracts (for example, animal aggression as opposed to clinical treatment of aggression).

Key Concepts

purposes of research 267
critical experiments 267
what-if research 268
sources of ideas 268

"itch" research 270
hypothesis testing 272
face validity 276
construct validity 276

References

American Psychological Association. *Ethical principles in the conduct of research with human participants.* 1973.

American Psychological Association. Guidelines for psychologists for the use of drugs in research. *American Psychologist,* 1972, 27:336.

American Psychological Association. Guidelines for the use of animals in school science behavior projects. *American Psychologist,* 1972, 27:337.

American Psychological Association. *Publication manual of the American Psychological Association* (2d ed.). Washington, D.C., 1974.

Annett, J. *Feedback and human behaviour.* Baltimore: Penguin, 1969.

Atkinson, R. C. Mnemotechnics and second-language learning. *American Psychologist,* 1975, 30:821–28.

Bachman, J. D. and Johnston, L. D. The freshman. *Psychology Today,* 1979, 13:78–87.

Barash, D. P. Human ethology: displacement activities in a dental office. *Psychological Reports,* 1974, 34:947–49.

Barber, T. X. *Pitfalls in human research: ten pivotal points.* New York: Pergamon, 1976.

Barefoot, J. C., Hoople, H., and McClay, D. Avoidance of an act which would violate personal space. *Psychonomic Science,* 1972, 28:205–06.

Barker, R. G. *Ecological psychology.* Stanford, Calif.: Stanford University Press, 1968.

Barker, R. G. and Wright, H. F. *One boy's day.* New York: Harper & Row, 1951.

Bartell, G. D. Group sex among the mid-Americans. *Journal of Sex Research,* 1970, 6:113–30.

Bem, D. J. and Lord, C. G. Template matching: a proposal for probing the ecological validity of experimental settings in social psychology. *Journal of Personality and Social Psychology,* 1979, 37:833–46.

Boe, R. and Winokur, S. A procedure for studying echoic control in verbal behavior. *Journal of the Experimental Analysis of Behavior,* 1978, 30:213–17.

Boring, E. G. *A history of experimental psychology.* New York: Appleton-Century-Crofts, 1950.

Boring, E. G. The nature and history of experimental control. *American Journal of Psychology,* 1954, 67:573–89.

Bower, G. H. Mental imagery and associative learning. In L. Gregg, ed., *Cognition in learning and memory.* New York: Wiley, 1972.

Broadbent, D. E. *Decision and stress.* London: Academic Press, 1971.

Brown, J. Some tests of the decay theory of immediate memory. *Quarterly Journal of Experimental Psychology,* 1958, 10:12–21.

Calfee, R. C. *Human experimental psychology.* New York: Holt, Rinehart and Winston, 1975.

Campbell, D. T. and Erlebacher, A. How regression artifacts in quasi-experimental evaluations can mistakenly make compensatory education look harmful. In J. Helmuth, ed., *Compensatory education: a national debate,* vol. 3, *Disadvantaged child.* New York: Brunner/Mazel, 1970(a).

Campbell, D. T. and Erlebacher, A. Reply to the replies. In J. Helmuth, ed., *Compensatory education: a national debate,* vol. 3, *Disadvantaged child.* New York: Brunner/Mazel, 1970(b).

Campbell, D. T. and Stanley, J. C. *Experimental and quasi-experimental designs for research.* Chicago: Rand McNally, 1963.

Carver, C. S., Coleman, A. E., and Glass, D. C. The coronary-prone behavior pattern and the suppression of fatigue on a treadmill test. *Journal of Personality and Social Psychology,* 1976, 33:460–66.

Cicirelli, V. The relevance of the regression artifact problem to the Westinghouse-Ohio evaluation of Head Start: a reply to Campbell and Erlebacher. In J. Helmuth, ed., *Compensatory education: a national debate,* vol. 3, *Disadvantaged child.* New York: Brunner/Mazel, 1970.

Cicirelli, V., et al. The impact of Head Start: an evaluation of the effects of Head Start on children's cognitive and affective development. A report presented to the Office of Economic Opportunity pursuant to Contract B89-4536, June 1969. Westinghouse Learning Corporation, Ohio University. (Distributed by Clearinghouse for Federal Scientific and Technical Information, U.S. Department of Commerce, National Bureau of Standards, Institute for Applied Technology, PB 184 328.)

Clark, H. H. The language-as-fixed-effect fallacy: a critique of language statistics in psychological research. *Journal of Verbal Learning and Verbal Behavior,* 1973, 12:335–59.

Cole, M., Gay, J., Glick, J. A., and Sharp, D. W. *The cultural context of learning and thinking.* New York: Basic Books, 1971.

Cook, T. D. and Campbell, D. T. *Quasi-experimentation: design and analysis for field settings.* Chicago: Rand McNally, 1979.

Craighead, W. E., Kazdin, A. E., and Mahoney, M. J. *Behavior modification: principles, issues, and applications.* Boston: Houghton Mifflin, 1976.

Craik, F. I. M. Age differences in human memory. In J. E. Birren and W. Schaie, eds., *Handbook of the psychology of aging.* New York: Van Nostrand Reinhold, 1977.

DeGreene, K. B., ed. *Systems psychology.* New York: McGraw-Hill, 1970.

Edwards, A. L. The relationship between the judged desirability of a trait and the probability that the trait will be endorsed. *Journal of Applied Psychology,* 1953, 37:90–93.

Edwards, A. L. *The social desirability variable in personality research.* New York: Dryden, 1957.

Egeth, H., Blecker, D. L., and Kamlet, A. S. Verbal interference in a perceptual comparison task. *Perception & Psychophysics,* 1969, 6:355–56.

Elliot, L. A. and Strawhorn, R. J. Interference in short-term memory from vocalization: aural versus visual modality differences. *Journal of Experimental Psychology: Human Learning and Memory,* 1976, 2: 705–11.

Elmes, D. G. *Readings in experimental psychology.* Chicago: Rand McNally, 1978.

Elmes, D. G. and Bjork, R. A. The interaction of encoding and rehearsal processes in the recall of repeated and nonrepeated items. *Journal of Verbal Learning and Verbal Behavior,* 1975, 14:30–42.

Elmes, D. G. and Thompson, J. B. Magnitude estimation of imagery. *Bulletin of the Psychonomic Society,* 1976, 8:343–44.

Eron, L. D., Huesman, L. R., Lefkowitz, M. M., and Walder, L. O. Does television violence cause aggression? *American Psychologist,* 1972, 27:253–63.

Evans, J. W. and Schiller, J. How preoccupation with possible regression artifacts can lead to a faulty strategy for the evaluation of social action programs: a reply to Campbell and Erlebacher. In J. Helmuth, ed., *Compensatory education: a national debate,* vol. 3, *Disadvantaged child.* New York: Brunner/Mazel, 1970.

Feingold, B. F. Hyperkinesis and learning disabilities linked to artificial food flavors and colors. *American Journal of Nursing,* 1975, 75:797–803.

Festinger, L., Riecken, H. W., and Schachter, S. *When prophecy fails.* Minneapolis: University of Minnesota Press, 1956.

Fossey, D. Living with mountain gorillas. In T. B. Allen, ed., *The marvels of animal behavior.* Washington, D.C.: National Geographic Society, 1972.

Garmezy, N. Vulnerability research and the issue of primary prevention. *American Journal of Orthopsychiatry,* 1971, 41:101–16.

Garner, W. R., Hake, H. and Eriksen, C. W. Operationism and the concept of perception. *Psychological Review,* 1956, 63:149–59.

Gescheider, G. A. *Psychophysics: method and theory.* Hillsdale, New Jersey: Lawrence Erlbaum, 1976.

Glass, D. C. and Singer, J. E. *Urban stress: experiments on noise and social stressors.* New York: Academic Press, 1972.

Graessle, O. A., Ahbel, K., and Porges, S. W. Effects of mild prenatal decompressions on growth and behavior in the rat. *Bulletin of the Psychonomic Society,* 1978, 12:329–31.

Hanson, N. R. *Patterns of discovery.* Cambridge: Cambridge University Press, 1972.

Harlow, H. F., Gluck, J. P., and Suomi, S. J. Generalization of behavioral data between nonhuman and human animals. *American Psychologist,* 1972, 27:709–16.

Hart, B. M., Allen, K. E., Buell, J. S., Harris, F. R., and Wolf, M. M. Effects of social reinforcement on operant crying. *Journal of Experimental Child Psychology,* 1964, 1:145–53.

Hebb, D. O. What psychology is about. *American Psychologist,* 1974, 29:71–79.

Helson, H. *Adaptation-level theory: an experimental and systematic approach to behavior.* New York: Harper & Row, 1964.

Hinton, W. M. Serendipity in psychology. *Virginia Journal of Science,* 1966, 17:57–64.

Homans, G. C. Group factors in worker productivity. In H. Proshansky and L. Seidenberg, eds., *Basic studies in social psychology.* New York: Holt, 1965.

Hopkins, R. H., Edwards, R. E., and Cook, C. L. Presentation modality, distractor modality, and proactive interference in short-term memory. *Journal of Experimental Psychology,* 1973, 98:363–67.

Horowitz, L. M. *Elements of statistics for psychology and education.* New York: McGraw-Hill, 1974.

Huff, D. *How to lie with statistics.* New York: Norton, 1954.

Hull, C. L. *Principles of behavior.* New York: Appleton-Century-Crofts, 1943.

Jacobson, E. *You must relax.* 5th ed. New York: McGraw-Hill, 1978.

Kantowitz, B. H. and Bartell, A. Proxemics and helping: the lost lunch technique. 1977 (unpublished paper).

Kantowitz, B. H. and Roediger, H. L. III. *Experimental psychology: understanding behavioral research.* Chicago: Rand McNally, 1978.

Katz, D. Paying the price for drug development. *Roanoke Times & World News,* February 7, 1979.

Keele, S. W. *Attention and human performance.* Pacific Palisades, Calif.: Goodyear, 1973.

Kerlinger, F. *Foundations of behavioral research.* New York: Holt, Rinehart and Winston, 1973.

King, D. J. Retention of connected meaningful material as a function of modes of presentation and recall. *Journal of Experimental Psychology,* 1968, 77:676–83.

Kintsch, W. and Kozminsky, E. Summarizing stories after reading and listening. *Journal of Educational Psychology,* 1977, 69:491–99.

Kintsch, W., Kozminsky, E., Streby, W. J., McKoon, G., and Keenan, J. M. Comprehension and recall of text as a function of content variables. *Journal of Verbal Learning and Verbal Behavior,* 1975, 14:196–214.

Kinzel, A. F. Body-buffer zone in violent prisoners. *The American Journal of Psychiatry,* 1970, 127:59–64.

Koocher, G. P. Bathroom behavior and human dignity. *Journal of Personality and Social Psychology,* 1977, 35:120–21.

Kuhn, T. S. *The structure of scientific revolutions.* Chicago: University of Chicago Press, 1962.

Leon, G. R. *Case histories of deviant behavior: a social learning analysis.* Boston: Holbrook Press, 1974.

Luchins, A. S. Mechanization in problem solving: the effect of Einstellung. *Psychological Monographs,* 1942, 54 (6):1–95. Whole No. 248.

Marx, M. H. The general nature of theory construction. In M. H. Marx, ed., *Theories in contemporary psychology.* New York: Macmillan, 1963.

Massaro, D. W. *Experimental psychology and information processing.* Chicago: Rand McNally, 1975.

McSweeny, A. J. The effects of response cost on the behavior of a million persons: charging for directory assistance in Cincinnati. *Journal of Applied Behavior Analysis,* 1978, 11:47–51.

Medawar, P. B. *Induction and intuition in scientific thought.* London: Methuen, 1969.

Middlemist, R. D., Knowles, E. S., and Matter, C. F. Personal space invasions in the lavatory: suggestive evidence for arousal. *Journal of Personality and Social Psychology,* 1976, 33:541–46.

Middlemist, R. D., Knowles, E. S., and Matter, C. F. What to do and what to report: a reply to Koocher. *Journal of Personality and Social Psychology,* 1977, 35:122–24.

Milgram, S. Behavioral study of obedience. *Journal of Abnormal and Social Psychology,* 1963, 67:371–78.

Mill, J. S. *A system of logic.* London: Longmans Green, 1930 (originally published in 1843).

Miller, D. B. Roles of naturalistic observation in comparative psychology. *American Psychologist,* 1977, 32:211–19.

Miller, G. A., Galanter, E., and Pribram, K. H. *Plans and the structure of behavior.* New York: Holt, Rinehart & Winston, 1960.

Mitroff, I. and Kilmann, R. H. On evaluating scientific research: the contribution of the psychology of science. *Technological Forecasting and Social Change,* 1975, 8:163–74.

Moran, S. L. V., and Loeb, M. Annoyance and behavioral aftereffects following interfering and noninterfering aircraft noise. *Journal of Applied Psychology,* 1977, 62:719–26.

Morin, R. E. and Grant, D. A. Learning and performance of a keypressing task as a function of the degree of spatial stimulus-response correspondence. *Journal of Experimental Psychology,* 1954, 49:39–47.

Natsoulas, T. What are perceptual reports about? *Psychological Bulletin,* 1967, 67:249–72.

NIH Guide for grants and contracts (NIH 4206), No. 7, June 14, 1971.

Notterman, J. M. and Mintz, D. E. *Dynamics of response.* New York: Wiley, 1965.

Orne, M. T. On the social psychology of the psychological experiment: with particular reference to demand characteristics and their implications. *American Psychologist,* 1962, 17:776–83.

Orne, M. T. Demand characteristics and the concept of quasi-controls.

In R. Rosenthal and R. L. Rosnow, eds., *Artifact in behavioral research.* New York: Academic Press, 1969.

Orne, M. T. and Evans, T. J. Social control in the psychological experiment: antisocial behavior and hypnosis. *Journal of Personality and Social Psychology,* 1965, 1:189–200.

Parducci, A. The relativism of absolute judgments. *Scientific American,* 1968, 219:84–90.

Parsons, H. M. What happened at Hawthorne? *Science* 1974, 183:922–31.

Peirce, C. S. The fixation of belief. *Popular Science Monthly,* 1877, 12:1–15. Reprinted in E. C. Moore, ed., *Charles S. Peirce: the essential writings.* New York: Harper & Row, 1972.

Penney, C. Modality effects in short-term verbal memory. *Psychological Bulletin,* 1975, 82:68–84.

Peterson, L. R. and Peterson, M. J. Short-term retention of individual items. *Journal of Experimental Psychology,* 1959, 58:193–98.

Plotkin, W. B. The alpha experience revisited: biofeedback in the transformation of psychological state. *Psychological Bulletin,* 1979, 86:1132–48.

Richman, C. L., Mitchell, D. B., and Reznick, J. S. Mental travel: some reservations. *Journal of Experimental Psychology: Human Perception and Performance,* 1979, 5:13–18.

Rose, T. L. The functional relationship between artificial food colors and hyperactivity. *Journal of Applied Behavior Analysis,* 1978, 11:439–46.

Rosnow, R. L. and Rosenthal, R. Volunteer effects in behavioral research. In *New directions in psychology 4.* New York: Holt, Rinehart and Winston, 1970.

Rowland, L. W. Will hypnotized persons try to harm themselves or others? *Journal of Abnormal and Social Psychology,* 1939, 34:114–17.

Scarborough, D. L. Stimulus modality effects on forgetting in short-term memory. *Journal of Experimental Psychology,* 1972, 95:285–89.

Schaie, K. W. Quasi-experimental designs in the psychology of aging. In J. E. Birren and K. W. Schaie, eds., *Handbook of the psychology of aging.* New York: Van Nostrand, 1977.

Scott, W. A. and Wertheimer, M. *Introduction to psychological research.* New York: Wiley, 1962.

Sidman, M. *Tactics of scientific research.* New York: Basic Books, 1960.

Skinner, B. F. *The behavior of organisms: an experimental analysis.* New York: Appleton-Century-Crofts, 1938.

Skinner, B. F. A case history in scientific method. *American Psychologist,* 1956, 11:221–33.

Spreen, O. and Schulz, R. W. Parameters of abstraction, meaningfulness, and pronunciability for 329 nouns. *Journal of Verbal Learning and Verbal Behavior,* 1966, 5:459–68.

Squire, L. R. and Slater, P. C. Forgetting in very long-term memory as assessed by an improved questionnaire technique. *Journal of Experimental Psychology: Human Learning and Memory,* 1975, 1:50–54.

Sternberg, R. J. *Writing the psychology paper.* New York: Barron's, 1978.

Stroop, J. R. Studies of interference in serial verbal reactions. *Journal of Experimental Psychology,* 1935, 18:643–62.

Suppes, P. and Zinnes, J. L. Basic measurement theory. In R. Luce, R. Brush, and E. Galanter, eds., *Handbook of mathematical psychology,* vol. 1. New York: Wiley, 1963.

Thompson, J. B. and Buchanan, W. *Analyzing psychological data.* New York: Charles Scribner's Sons, 1979.

Thompson, J. T. and Clayton, K. N. Presentation modality, rehearsal-prevention conditions, and auditory confusions in tests of short-term memory. *Memory & Cognition,* 1974, 2:426–30.

Tversky, B. and Teiffer, E. Development of strategies for recall and recognition. *Developmental Psychology,* 1976, 12:406–10.

Underwood, B. J. Individual differences as a crucible in theory construction. *American Psychologist,* 1975, 30:128–34.

Uttal, W. R. *The psychobiology of mind.* Hillsdale, NJ: Lawrence Erlbaum Associates, 1978.

Walters, C., Shurley, J. T., and Parsons, O. A. Differences in male and female responses to underwater sensory deprivation: an exploratory study. *Journal of Nervous and Mental Disease,* 1962, 135:302–10.

Warren, R. M. Are loudness judgments based on distance estimates? *Journal of the Acoustical Society of America,* 1963, 35:613–14.

Watkins, M. J., Watkins, O. C., and Crowder, R. G. The modality effect in free and serial recall as a function of phonological similarity. *Journal of Verbal Learning and Verbal Behavior,* 1974, 13:430–47.

Waugh, N. C. and Norman, D. A. Primary memory. *Psychological Review,* 1965, 72:89–104.

Webb, E. J., Campbell, D. T., Schwartz, R. D., and Sechrist, L. *Unobtrusive measures: nonreactive research in the social sciences.* Chicago: Rand McNally, 1966, 1981.

Weinstein, N. D. Individual differences in reactions to noise: a longitudinal study in a college dormitory. *Journal of Applied Psychology,* 1978, 63:458–66.

Weinstock, S. Acquisition and extinction of a partially reinforced running response at a 24-hour intertrial interval. *Journal of Experimental Psychology,* 1958, 56:151–58.

Welford, A. T. *Skilled performance: perceptual and motor skills.* Glenview, Ill.: Scott Foresman, 1976.

Wohwill, J. F. Methodology and research strategy in the study of developmental change. In L. R. Goulet and P. B. Baltes, eds., *Life-span developmental psychology: research and theory.* New York: Academic Press, 1970.

Young, P. C. Antisocial uses of hypnosis. In L. M. LeCron, ed., *Experimental hypnosis.* New York: MacMillan, 1952.

Zajonc, R. B. and Markus, N. Birth order and intellectual development. *Psychological Review,* 1975, 82:74–88.

Glossary

ABA and ABAB Designs. see reversal design

ABBA counterbalancing. intrasubject counterbalancing in which treatments or conditions A and B are administered in the ABBA or BAAB order

Abscissa. the horizontal axis (or x-axis) in a graph

Adaptation level. a source of difficulty in psychophysical studies resulting from the context or reference level surrounding a given psychophysical judgment

Alpha level. see significance level

Analysis of variance. a statistical test appropriate for analyzing reliability from experiments with any number of levels on one or more independent variables

Anthropomorphizing. attributing human characteristics or emotions, such as happiness, to animals

APA format. the journal article format specified by the American Psychological Association (APA)

A priori method. according to Peirce, a way of fixing belief due to the reasonableness of the event (see method of tenacity, method of authority, and empirical)

Balanced Latin square. counterbalancing scheme in which each condition is preceded and followed equally often by every other condition

Baseline. the "normal" or typical behavior used as a standard of comparison in an experiment

Between group variance. a measure of the dispersion among groups in an experiment

Between-subject design. an experimental design in which each subject is tested under only one level of each independent variable

Carry-over effect. relatively permanent effect that testing subjects in one condition has on their later behavior in another condition

Case study. intensive investigation of a particular instance, or case, of some behavior; does not allow inferences of cause and effect, but is merely descriptive

Ceiling effect. see scale attenuation

Central tendency. descriptive statistics indicating the center of a distribution of scores; see mean, median, and mode

Cohorts. the people (and society in general) living at the time a given individual is developing; a potential confound when age is a subject variable that may be likened to the "generation gap"

Conceptual replication. attempt to demonstrate an experimental phenomenon with an entirely new paradigm or set of experimental conditions (see converging operations)

Confidence level. see significance level

Confounding. simultaneous variation of a second variable with an independent variable of interest so that any effect on the dependent variable cannot be attributed with certainty to the independent variable; inherent in correlational research

Continuous reinforcement. schedule of reinforcement in which a reward follows every time the appropriate behavior is emitted

Control variable. a potential independent variable that is held constant in an experiment

Converging operations. a set of related lines of investigation that all bolster a common conclusion

Correlation. a measure of the extent to which two variables are related, not necessarily causally

Correlation coefficient. a number that can vary from –1.00 to +1.00 and indicates the degree of relation between two variables

Counterbalancing. refers to any technique used to vary systematically the order of conditions in an experiment to distribute the effects of time of testing (e.g., practice and fatigue) so they are not confounded with conditions

Criterion. an independent means of determining the validity of an observation, experiment, or judgment

Critical experiments. experiments designed to test the predictions of two or more theories

Cross-lagged panel correlation. calculating several correlation coefficients across time on the same participants in order to increase the internal validity of correlational research

Cross-over interaction. when the effect of one independent variable on a dependent variable reverses at different levels of a second independent variable

Cross-sectional studies. taking a large sample of the population of various ages at one time and testing them (contrast with longitudinal studies)

Cross-sequential design. a quasi-experimental design used when age is a subject variable to try to control for cohort and time of testing effects; involves testing several different age groups at several different time periods (see longitudinal method and cross-sectional method)

Data. the scores obtained on a dependent variable

Deception. a research technique in which the participant is mislead about some aspect of the project; may be unethical (see double blind)

Deduction. reasoning from the general to the particular

Degrees of freedom. the number of values free to vary if the total number of values and their sum are fixed

Demand characteristics. those cues available to subjects in an experiment that may enable them to determine the purpose of the experiment, or what is expected by the experimenter

Dependent variable. the variable measured and recorded by the experimenter

Description. a determination of the quantity (frequency, magnitude) of behavior resulting from observation, case study, survey, and testing methods

Descriptive statistics. methods of organizing and summarizing data

Determinism. fundamental tenet of science that asserts that there are knowable causes of an event in contrast to *in*determinate (unknowable) causes; implies that events are lawful (follow rules)

Deviant case analysis. investigation of similar cases that differ in outcome in an attempt to specify the reasons for the different outcomes

Directional/nondirectional statistical tests. see one- and two-tailed tests

Direct measurement. the observer applies his/her scale in assigning numbers (see indirect measurement)

Direct replication. repeating an experiment as closely as possible to determine whether or not the same results will be obtained

Dispersion. the amount of spread in a distribution of scores

Distribution. a set of values of a variable

Double blind. experimental technique in which neither the subject nor the experimenter knows which subjects are in which treatment conditions

Ecological validity. the extent to which a research setting matches the environment of the problem under investigation; a threat to the external validity of experiments

Einstellung. see set

Empirical.   relying upon or derived from observation or experiment

Ethology.   the systematic study of behavior; usually animal behavior in natural settings

Experiment.   the systematic manipulation of some environment in order to observe the effect of this manipulation upon behavior; a particular comparison is produced

Experimental control.   holding constant extraneous variables in an experiment so that any effect on the dependent variable can be attributed to manipulation of the independent variable

Explanation.   a causal statement about why or when a particular event occurs resulting from experimental methods (see method of differences)

Ex post facto.   literally, from after the fact; refers to conditions in an experiment that are not determined prior to the experiment, but only after some manipulation has occurred naturally

External validity.   refers to the generality of research; externally valid research is representative of "real life" and does not distort the question under investigation

Face validity.   when a measuring instrument intuitively seems to measure what it is supposed to measure

Factorial design.   an experimental design in which each level of every independent variable occurs with all levels of the other independent variable

Field research.   research conducted in natural settings where subjects typically do not know that they are in an experiment

Floor effect.   see scale attenuation

Forced-choice tests.   tests in which the participant must select between two or more statements; often used to control response styles

F ratio.   a ratio of between-groups variance to within-groups variance; forms the basis of the analysis of variance

Frequency distribution.   a set of scores arranged in order along a distribution indicating the number of times each score occurs

Frequency polygon.   a frequency distribution in which the height of the curve indicates the frequency of scores (see histogram)

Functional theory.   a combination of inductive and deductive approaches that stresses data and explanation about equally

Fundamental question.   why do people think and act as they do?

Generality of results.   the issue of whether or not a particular experimental result will be obtained under different circumstances, such as with a different subject population or in a different experimental setting

Hawthorne effect.   refers to conditions where performance in an experiment is affected by the knowledge of participants that they are in an experiment; see demand characteristics

Heterogeneous.   dissimilar

Higher order interaction.   interaction effects involving more than two independent variables in multifactor experiments

Histogram.   a frequency distribution in which the height of bars in the graph indicates the frequency of a class of scores; also called a bar graph

Homogeneous.   similar

Hypothesis.   a testable statement that offers a predicted relationship between dependent and independent variables

Independent variable.   the variable manipulated by the experimenter

Indirect measurement.   the observer limits judgments to a small set of categories in order to scale the attribute in question (contrast with direct measurement)

Induction.   reasoning from the particular to the general

Inferential statistics.   procedures for determining the reliability and generality of a particular experimental finding

Interaction.   an experimental result that occurs when the levels of one independent variable are differentially affected by the levels of other independent variables

Internal validity.   allows straightforward statements about causality; experiments are usually internally valid because the Method of Differences is employed

Interrupted time series design.   a quasi-experiment that involves examination of a naturally occurring treatment on the behavior of a large number of participants

Introspection.   literally, looking within; a way of obtaining subjective reports from observers (see phenomenological report)

"Itch" research.   a research project whose origin is the need to solve a particular practical problem

Knowability in science.   events are discoverable (see determinism)

Lawfulness.   events are regular, following rules (see determinism)

Longitudinal studies.   testing one group of people repeatedly as they age (contrast with cross-sectional studies)

Magnitude estimation.   observers assign numbers to attribute usually without restriction except that the numbers be assigned proportionately to the judged magnitude (a ratio scale)

Main effect.   when the effect of one independent variable is the same at all levels of another independent variable

Matched groups design. experimental design in which subjects are matched on some variable assumed to be correlated with the dependent variable and then randomly assigned to conditions

Matching. see subject variables and matched group design

Mean. measure of central tendency; the sum of all the scores divided by the number of scores

Measurement. the systematic assignment of numbers to objects or attributes of objects

Measurement scales. in order of increasing power: nominal, ordinal, interval, and ratio

Median. measure of central tendency; the middle score of a distribution, or the one that divides a distribution in half

Method of Agreement. asserts that if event A is always followed by result X, then A is the likely cause of X (see method of differences)

Method of Authority. a method of fixing belief in which an authority's word is taken on faith (contrast with empirical)

Method of Concomitant Variation. a method of determining causality that involves the joint use of the Methods of Agreement and Differences

Method of Differences. according to J. S. Mill if X always follows A and *not* X always follows *not A,* then A surely causes X

Method of Tenacity. a way of fixing belief involving a steadfast adherence to a particular belief, regardless of contrary arguments (see empirical)

Mixed design. an experimental design that contains both between-subjects and within-subjects manipulations of the independent variables

Modality effect. different effects on retention often produced by visual and auditory presentation; auditory presentation usually produces better memory for the last few items in a series than does visual presentation

Mode. measure of central tendency; the most frequent score

Model. an analogical theory in which a psychological process is asserted to be similar to some other process; e.g., memory works like a computer

Modulus. an anchor point sometimes used in the method of magnitude estimation to indicate an average value of the dimension

Monotonic relationship. relationship between two variables in which an increase on one variable is accompanied by a consistent increase or decrease on the other variable

Motivated forgetting. distortions of past events reported retrospectively, due to the emotional nature of those events

Naturalistic observation. description of naturally occurring events without intervention on the part of the investigator

Nonequivalent control group. in quasi-experiments a control group that is not determined by random assignment but is usually selected after the fact and is supposed to be equivalent to the naturally treated group

Nonreactive. term to describe observations that are not influenced by the presence of the investigator; nonreactive methods are also referred to as unobtrusive

Normal distribution. one producing a symmetric bell-shaped curve

Nonparametric statistics. statistical tests that do not make any assumptions about the underlying distribution of scores; ordinarily require just ordinal-level data (see parametric statistics)

Null hypothesis. states that the independent variable will have no effect on the dependent variable

Null result. an experimental outcome where the dependent variable was not influenced by the independent variable

Observational methods. research techniques based on simply observing behavior without trying to manipulate it experimentally

One-shot case study. (see case study) a quasi-experiment in which the behavior of a single individual is studied and "explained" in terms of life events (see also deviant case analysis)

One-tailed test. test that places the rejection area at one end of a distribution

Operational definition. a definition of a concept in terms of the operations that must be performed to demonstrate the concept

Ordinate. the vertical axis (or y-axis) in a graph

Parallel forms. two alternative forms of a test

Parametric statistics. statistical tests that make assumptions about the distribution of scores (e.g., normally distributed); require interval or ratio data

Parsimony. a good, powerful theory should explain many events with few statements or explanatory concepts; thus, refers to simplicity

Participant observer technique. an observation procedure in which the observer participates with those being observed; e.g., living with gorillas in the wild

Personal space. the "invisible bubble" surrounding a person

Phenomenological report. subject's description of his or her own behavior or state of mind; also called subjective report

Placebo effect. improvement often shown in drug effectiveness studies where patients believe they have received a drug although they actually received an inert substance

Population. the total set of potential observations from which a sample is drawn

Power (of a statistical test). the probability of rejecting the null hypothesis in a statistical test when it is in fact false

Precision. a good theory should be precise in its predictions

Prediction. a specification of relationships resulting from correlational methods (see method of agreement); also one aim of a theory

Psychometrics. the judged specification of psychological attributes that do not have a known physical dimension; e.g., friendliness

Psychophysics. judgment of stimuli along a known physical dimension; e.g., the perceived brightness of lights of different intensities

Quasi-experiment. an experiment in which the independent variable occurs naturally and is not under direct control of the experimenter (see ex post facto research)

Random groups design. when subjects are randomly assigned to conditions in a between-subjects design

Randomized blocks. a counterbalancing technique in which the treatment orders are randomized in successive blocks (groups) of presenting those conditions

Range. descriptive measure of dispersion; the difference between the largest and smallest score in a distribution, plus one

Rating technique. a measurement procedure in which observers arrange the attributes in question into groups or categories along some continuum (see indirect measurement)

Reactive. term to describe observations that are influenced by (or may be, in part, a reaction to) the detected presence of the investigator

Reification. incorrectly making real a hypothetical (theoretical) concept

Regression artifacts. an artifact in the measurement of change on a variable when groups of subjects who scored at the extremes on the variable are tested again (see regression to the mean)

Regression to the mean. tendency for extreme measures on some variable to be closer to the group mean when remeasured, due to unreliability of measurement

Reliability. refers to the repeatability of an experimental result; inferential statistics provide an estimation of how likely it is that a finding is repeatable; also refers to the consistency of a test or measuring instrument determined by computing a correlation between scores obtained by subjects taking the test twice (test-retest reliability), or taking two different parallel forms of the test, or scores obtained on each half of the test (split-half reliability)

Repeated measures design. several measures are taken on the same subject, such as several learning trials or numerous psychophysical judgments; a type of within-subject experiment

Replication. the repetition of an earlier experiment to duplicate (and perhaps extend) its findings (also see systematic replication)

Reproduceability. see reliability

Researcher bias. deliberate or inadvertent bias in which data is misanalyzed or participants are differentially treated over and above any planned differences in treatment

Response acquiescence. a habitual way of responding on tests that involves frequently responding "yes" (see response styles)

Response deviation. a habitual way of responding on tests that involves frequently responding "no" (see response styles)

Response styles. habitual ways of responding on a test that are independent of the particular test item; see response deviation, response acquiescence, and social desirability

Retroactive interference. forgetting of material produced by learning of subsequent material

Retrospective report. in case studies when the person has to report on events that occurred in the distant past; subject to ordinary and motivated forgetting

Reversability. an assumption made in research that the characteristics of different populations and species of subjects have the same underlying processes; the behavioral "equation" can be determined from the behavior that is observed

Reversal (ABA) design. small-n design in which a subject's behavior is measured under a baseline (A) condition, then an experimental treatment is applied during the B phase and any changes in behavior are observed; finally, the original baseline (A) conditions are reinstituted to ensure that the experimental treatment was responsible for any observed change during the B phase

Sample. observations selected from a population

Scale attenuation effects. difficulties in interpreting results when performance on the dependent variable is either nearly perfect (a ceiling effect) or nearly lacking altogether (a floor effect)

Scatter diagrams. a graphical relationship indicating degree of correlation between two variables made by plotting the scores of individuals on two variables

Self-correction. science is self-correcting because it relies on public, empirical observation; old beliefs are discarded if they do not fit the empirical data

Serendipitous pattern. "luck" or chance observations that may prove valuable in scientific discovery; a good scientist is alert for serendipitous findings

Set. the effect of expectancy on cognition; for example, if the people solve problems in one particular way, they will often approach new problems in the same set way even when the original strategy is no longer effective

Shadowing task. a form of dichotic listening where the listener is required to repeat aloud (shadow) the message presented in one ear as it occurs

Significance level. probability that an experimental finding is due to chance, or random fluctuation, operating in the data

Simulated experiment. a fake experiment in which subjects are told to simulate the behavior of real subjects in a particular experiment; also called a thought experiment

Skewed distribution. a nonsymmetrical distribution

Small-*n* design. research design utilizing a small number of subjects

Social desirability. a habitual way of responding on tests that involves making socially desirable responses (see response styles)

Split-half reliability. determining reliability of a test by dividing the test items into two arbitrary groups and correlating the scores obtained on the two halves of the test

Standard deviation. descriptive measure of dispersion; square root of the sum of squared deviations of each score from the mean divided by the number of scores

Standard error of the mean. the standard deviation of the distribution of sample means

Standard scores. also called z scores; differences between individual scores and the mean score expressed in units of standard deviations

Stroop effect. difficulty in naming the color of an object when the color conflicts with the name of the object (when the word "blue" is printed in red ink)

Subject representativeness. determination of generality of results across different subject populations

Subject variable. some characteristics of people that can be measured or described, but cannot be varied experimentally (e.g. height, weight, sex, I.Q., etc.)

Subjective report. see phenomenological report

Sum of Squares (SS). sum of the squared scores used to calculate effects via analysis of variance

Survey research. technique of obtaining a limited amount of information from a large number of people, usually through random sampling

Systematic replication. repeating an experiment while varying numerous factors considered to be irrelevant to the phenomenon to see if it will survive these changes

Template matching. a procedure involving a match between the behavior in a research setting and the behavior in "real life"; a way to determine the ecological validity of research

Testability. a good theory needs to be capable of disproof

Test-retest reliability. giving the same test twice in succession over a short interval to see if the scores are stable, or reliable; generally expressed as a correlation between scores on the tests

Thought experiment. see simulated experiment

Time-lag design. a quasi-experimental design used when age is a subject variable in order to control time of testing effects; subjects of a particular age (e.g., 19 year olds) are tested at different time periods

Treatment X treatment X subjects design. a within-subjects factorial design with two independent variables

Truncated range. a problem in interpreting low correlations; the amount of dispersion (or range) of scores on one variable may be small, thus leading to the low correlation found

t tests. parametric tests for testing differences between two groups

Two-tailed test. test that places the rejection area at both ends of a distribution

Type 1 error. probability that the null hypothesis is rejected when it is in fact true; equals the significance level

Type 2 error. failure to reject the null hypothesis when it is in fact false

Unobtrusive methods. see nonreactive

Variable representativeness. determination of generality of results across different manipulations of an independent variable or different dependent variables

Variance. measure of dispersion; the standard deviation squared

What if experiment. an experiment performed to see what might happen rather than to test a specific hypothesis

Within-group variance. a measure of the dispersion among subjects in the same group in an experiment

Within-subject design. an experimental design in which each subject is tested under more than one level of the independent variable

Appendix: Statistical Tables

Table A–1

Proportions of Area Under the Normal Curve

How to Use Table A–1: The values in Table A–1 represent the proportion of areas in the standard normal curve, which has a mean of 0, a standard deviation of 1.00, and a total area equal to 1.00. To use Table A the raw score must first be transformed into a z score. Column A represents the z score, Column B represents the distance between the mean of the standard normal distribution (0) and the z score, and Column C represents the proportion of area beyond a given z.

(A) z	(B) area between mean and z	(C) area beyond z	(A) z	(B) area between mean and z	(C) area beyond z	(A) z	(B) area between mean and z	(C) area beyond z
0.00	.0000	.5000	0.55	.2088	.2912	1.10	.3643	.1357
0.01	.0040	.4960	0.56	.2123	.2877	1.11	.3665	.1335
0.02	.0080	.4920	0.57	.2157	.2843	1.12	.3686	.1314
0.03	.0120	.4880	0.58	.2190	.2810	1.13	.3708	.1292
0.04	.0160	.4840	0.59	.2224	.2776	1.14	.3729	.1271
0.05	.0199	.4801	0.60	.2257	.2743	1.15	.3749	.1251
0.06	.0239	.4761	0.61	.2291	.2709	1.16	.3770	.1230
0.07	.0279	.4721	0.62	.2324	.2676	1.17	.3790	.1210
0.08	.0319	.4681	0.63	.2357	.2643	1.18	.3810	.1190
0.09	.0359	.4641	0.64	.2389	.2611	1.19	.3830	.1170
0.10	.0398	.4602	0.65	.2422	.2578	1.20	.3849	.1151
0.11	.0438	.4562	0.66	.2454	.2546	1.21	.3869	.1131
0.12	.0478	.4522	0.67	.2486	.2514	1.22	.3888	.1112
0.13	.0517	.4483	0.68	.2517	.2483	1.23	.3907	.1093
0.14	.0557	.4443	0.69	.2549	.2451	1.24	.3925	.1075
0.15	.0596	.4404	0.70	.2580	.2420	1.25	.3944	.1056
0.16	.0636	.4364	0.71	.2611	.2389	1.26	.3962	.1038
0.17	.0675	.4325	0.72	.2642	.2358	1.27	.3980	.1020
0.18	.0714	.4286	0.73	.2673	.2327	1.28	.3997	.1003
0.19	.0753	.4247	0.74	.2704	.2296	1.29	.4015	.0985
0.20	.0793	.4207	0.75	.2734	.2266	1.30	.4032	.0968
0.21	.0832	.4168	0.76	.2764	.2236	1.31	.4049	.0951
0.22	.0871	.4129	0.77	.2794	.2206	1.32	.4066	.0934
0.23	.0910	.4090	0.78	.2823	.2177	1.33	.4082	.0918
0.24	.0948	.4052	0.79	.2852	.2148	1.34	.4099	.0901
0.25	.0987	.4013	0.80	.2881	.2119	1.35	.4115	.0885
0.26	.1026	.3974	0.81	.2910	.2090	1.36	.4131	.0869
0.27	.1064	.3936	0.82	.2939	.2061	1.37	.4147	.0853
0.28	.1103	.3897	0.83	.2967	.2033	1.38	.4162	.0838
0.29	.1141	.3859	0.84	.2995	.2005	1.39	.4177	.0823
0.30	.1179	.3821	0.85	.3023	.1977	1.40	.4192	.0808
0.31	.1217	.3783	0.86	.3051	.1949	1.41	.4207	.0793
0.32	.1255	.3745	0.87	.3078	.1922	1.42	.4222	.0778
0.33	.1293	.3707	0.88	.3106	.1894	1.43	.4236	.0764
0.34	.1331	.3669	0.89	.3133	.1867	1.44	.4251	.0749

Table A–1 *(Continued)*

(A) z	(B) area between mean and z	(C) area beyond z	(A) z	(B) area between mean and z	(C) area beyond z	(A) z	(B) area between mean and z	(C) area beyond z
0.35	.1368	.3632	0.90	.3159	.1841	1.45	.4265	.0735
0.36	.1406	.3594	0.91	.3186	.1814	1.46	.4279	.0721
0.37	.1443	.3557	0.92	.3212	.1788	1.47	.4292	.0708
0.38	.1480	.3520	0.93	.3238	.1762	1.48	.4306	.0694
0.39	.1517	.3483	0.94	.3264	.1736	1.49	.4319	.0681
0.40	.1554	.3446	0.95	.3289	.1711	1.50	.4332	.0668
0.41	.1591	.3409	0.96	.3315	.1685	1.51	.4345	.0655
0.42	.1628	.3372	0.97	.3340	.1660	1.52	.4357	.0643
0.43	.1664	.3336	0.98	.3365	.1635	1.53	.4370	.0630
0.44	.1700	.3300	0.99	.3389	.1611	1.54	.4382	.0618
0.45	.1736	.3264	1.00	.3413	.1587	1.55	.4394	.0606
0.46	.1772	.3228	1.01	.3438	.1562	1.56	.4406	.0594
0.47	.1808	.3192	1.02	.3461	.1539	1.57	.4418	.0582
0.48	.1844	.3156	1.03	.3485	.1515	1.58	.4429	.0571
0.49	.1879	.3121	1.04	.3508	.1492	1.59	.4441	.0559
0.50	.1915	.3085	1.05	.3531	.1469	1.60	.4452	.0548
0.51	.1950	.3050	1.06	.3554	.1446	1.61	.4463	.0537
0.52	.1985	.3015	1.07	.3577	.1423	1.62	.4474	.0526
0.53	.2019	.2981	1.08	.3599	.1401	1.63	.4484	.0516
0.54	.2054	.2946	1.09	.3621	.1379	1.64	.4495	.0505
1.65	.4505	.0495	2.22	.4868	.0132	2.79	.4974	.0026
1.66	.4515	.0485	2.23	.4871	.0129	2.80	.4974	.0026
1.67	.4525	.0475	2.24	.4875	.0125	2.81	.4975	.0025
1.68	.4535	.0465	2.25	.4878	.0122	2.82	.4976	.0024
1.69	.4545	.0455	2.26	.4881	.0119	2.83	.4977	.0023
1.70	.4554	.0446	2.27	.4884	.0116	2.84	.4977	.0023
1.71	.4564	.0436	2.28	.4887	.0113	2.85	.4978	.0022
i.72	.4573	.0427	2.29	.4890	.0110	2.86	.4979	.0021
1.73	.4582	.0418	2.30	.4893	.0107	2.87	.4979	.0021
1.74	.4591	.0409	2.31	.4896	.0104	2.88	.4980	.0020
1.75	.4599	.0401	2.32	.4898	.0102	2.89	.4981	.0019
1.76	.4608	.0392	2.33	.4901	.0099	2.90	.4981	.0019
1.77	.4616	.0384	2.34	.4904	.0096	2.91	.4982	.0018
1.78	.4625	.0375	2.35	.4906	.0094	2.92	.4982	.0018
1.79	.4633	.0367	2.36	.4909	.0091	2.93	.4983	.0017
1.80	.4641	.0359	2.37	.4911	.0089	2.94	.4984	.0016
1.81	.4649	.0351	2.38	.4913	.0087	2.95	.4984	.0016
1.82	.4656	.0344	2.39	.4916	.0084	2.96	.4985	.0015
1.83	.4664	.0336	2.40	.4918	.0082	2.97	.4985	.0015
1.84	.4671	.0329	2.41	.4920	.0080	2.98	.4986	.0014

Table A–1 *(Continued)*

(A) z	(B) area between mean and z	(C) area beyond z	(A) z	(B) area between mean and z	(C) area beyond z	(A) z	(B) area between mean and z	(C) area beyond z
1.85	.4678	.0322	2.42	.4922	.0078	2.99	.4986	.0014
1.86	.4686	.0314	2.43	.4925	.0075	3.00	.4987	.0013
1.87	.4693	.0307	2.44	.4927	.0073	3.01	.4987	.0013
1.88	.4699	.0301	2.45	.4929	.0071	3.02	.4987	.0013
1.89	.4706	.0294	2.46	.4931	.0069	3.03	.4988	.0012
1.90	.4713	.0287	2.47	.4932	.0068	3.04	.4988	.0012
1.91	.4719	.0281	2.48	.4934	.0066	3.05	.4989	.0011
1.92	.4726	.0274	2.49	.4936	.0064	3.06	.4989	.0011
1.93	.4732	.0268	2.50	.4938	.0062	3.07	.4989	.0011
1.94	.4738	.0262	2.51	.4940	.0060	3.08	.4990	.0010
1.95	.4744	.0256	2.52	.4941	.0059	3.09	.4990	.0010
1.96	.4750	.0250	2.53	.4943	.0057	3.10	.4990	.0010
1.97	.4756	.0244	2.54	.4945	.0055	3.11	.4991	.0009
1.98	.4761	.0239	2.55	.4946	.0054	3.12	.4991	.0009
1.99	.4767	.0233	2.56	.4948	.0052	3.13	.4991	.0009
2.00	.4772	.0228	2.57	.4949	.0051	3.14	.4992	.0008
2.01	.4778	.0222	2.58	.4951	.0049	3.15	.4992	.0008
2.02	.4783	.0217	2.59	.4952	.0048	3.16	.4992	.0008
2.03	.4788	.0212	2.60	.4953	.0047	3.17	.4992	.0008
2.04	.4793	.0207	2.61	.4955	.0045	3.18	.4993	.0007
2.05	.4798	.0202	2.62	.4956	.0044	3.19	.4993	.0007
2.06	.4803	.0197	2.63	.4957	.0043	3.20	.4993	.0007
2.07	.4808	.0192	2.64	.4959	.0041	3.21	.4993	.0007
2.08	.4812	.0188	2.65	.4960	.0040	3.22	.4994	.0006
2.09	.4817	.0183	2.66	.4961	.0039	3.23	.4994	.0006
2.10	.4821	.0179	2.67	.4962	.0038	3.24	.4994	.0006
2.11	.4826	.0174	2.68	.4963	.0037	3.25	.4994	.0006
2.12	.4830	.0170	2.69	.4964	.0036	3.30	.4995	.0005
2.13	.4834	.0166	2.70	.4965	.0035	3.35	.4996	.0004
2.14	.4838	.0162	2.71	.4966	.0034	3.40	.4997	.0003
2.15	.4842	.0158	2.72	.4967	.0033	3.45	.4997	.0003
2.16	.4846	.0154	2.73	.4968	.0032	3.50	.4998	.0002
2.17	.4850	.0150	2.74	.4969	.0031	3.60	.4998	.0002
2.18	.4854	.0146	2.75	.4970	.0030	3.70	.4999	.0001
2.19	.4857	.0143	2.76	.4971	.0029	3.80	.4999	.0001
2.20	.4861	.0139	2.77	.4972	.0028	3.90	.49995	.00005
2.21	.4864	.0136	2.78	.4973	.0027	4.00	.49997	.00003

Critical Values of the *U* Statistic of the Mann-Whitney Test

To use these tables, first decide what level of significance you want with either a one- or two-tailed test. For example, if you want p = .05, two-tailed, use (*c*). Then locate the number of cases or measures (*n*) in both groups in the particular subtable you have chosen. The U value you have calculated must be *less* than that at the appropriate place in the table. For example, if you had 18 subjects in each group of an experiment, and calculated U = 90, then you could conclude that the null hypothesis can be rejected because the critical U value with groups of these sizes is 99 (see subtable *c*).

(*a*) Critical Values of *U* for a One-Tailed Test at .001 or for a Two-Tailed Test at .002

n_1 \ n_2	9	10	11	12	13	14	15	16	17	18	19	20
1												
2												
3									0	0	0	0
4		0	0	0	1	1	1	2	2	3	3	3
5	1	1	2	2	3	3	4	5	5	6	7	7
6	2	3	4	4	5	6	7	8	9	10	11	12
7	3	5	6	7	8	9	10	11	13	14	15	16
8	5	6	8	9	11	12	14	15	17	18	20	21
9	7	8	10	12	14	15	17	19	21	23	25	26
10	8	10	12	14	17	19	21	23	25	27	29	32
11	10	12	15	17	20	22	24	27	29	32	34	37
12	12	14	17	20	23	25	28	31	34	37	40	42
13	14	17	20	23	26	29	32	35	38	42	45	48
14	15	19	22	25	29	32	36	39	43	46	50	54
15	17	21	24	28	32	36	40	43	47	51	55	59
16	19	23	27	31	35	39	43	48	52	56	60	65
17	21	25	29	34	38	43	47	52	57	61	66	70
18	23	27	32	37	42	46	51	56	61	66	71	76
19	25	29	34	40	45	50	55	60	66	71	77	82
20	26	32	37	42	48	54	59	65	70	76	82	88

Table A–2 *(Continued)*

(b) Critical Values of U for a One-Tailed Test at .01 or for a Two-Tailed Test at .02

n_1 \ n_2	9	10	11	12	13	14	15	16	17	18	19	20
1												
2					0	0	0	0	0	0	1	1
3	1	1	1	2	2	2	3	3	4	4	4	5
4	3	3	4	5	5	6	7	7	8	9	9	10
5	5	6	7	8	9	10	11	12	13	14	15	16
6	7	8	9	11	12	13	15	16	18	19	20	22
7	9	11	12	14	16	17	19	21	23	24	26	28
8	11	13	15	17	20	22	24	26	28	30	32	34
9	14	16	18	21	23	26	28	31	33	36	38	40
10	16	19	22	24	27	30	33	36	38	41	44	47
11	18	22	25	28	31	34	37	41	44	47	50	53
12	21	24	28	31	35	38	42	46	49	53	56	60
13	23	27	31	35	39	43	47	51	55	59	63	67
14	26	30	34	38	43	47	51	56	60	65	69	73
15	28	33	37	42	47	51	56	61	66	70	75	80
16	31	36	41	46	51	56	61	66	71	76	82	87
17	33	38	44	49	55	60	66	71	77	82	88	93
18	36	41	47	53	59	65	70	76	82	88	94	100
19	38	44	50	56	63	69	75	82	88	94	101	107
20	40	47	53	60	67	73	80	87	93	100	107	114

(c) Critical Values of U for a One-Tailed Test at .025 or for a Two-Tailed Test at .05

n_1 \ n_2	9	10	11	12	13	14	15	16	17	18	19	20
1												
2	0	0	1	1	1	1	1	1	2	2	2	2
3	2	3	3	4	4	5	5	6	6	7	7	8
4	4	5	6	7	8	9	10	11	11	12	13	13
5	7	8	9	11	12	13	14	15	17	18	19	20
6	10	11	13	14	16	17	19	21	22	24	25	27
7	12	14	16	18	20	22	24	26	28	30	32	34
8	15	17	19	22	24	26	29	31	34	36	38	41
9	17	20	23	26	28	31	34	37	39	42	45	48
10	20	23	26	29	33	36	39	42	45	48	52	55
11	23	26	30	33	37	40	44	47	51	55	58	62
12	26	29	33	37	41	45	49	53	57	61	65	69
13	28	33	37	41	45	50	54	59	63	67	72	76
14	31	36	40	45	50	55	59	64	67	74	78	83
15	34	39	44	49	54	59	64	70	75	80	85	90
16	37	42	47	53	59	64	70	75	81	86	92	98
17	39	45	51	57	63	67	75	81	87	93	99	105
18	42	48	55	61	67	74	80	86	93	99	106·	112
19	45	52	58	65	72	78	85	92	99	106	113	119
20	48	55	62	69	76	83	90	98	105	112	119	127

(*d*) Critical Values of *U* for a One-Tailed Test at .05 or for a Two-Tailed Test at .10

n_1 \ n_2	9	10	11	12	13	14	15	16	17	18	19	20
1											0	0
2	1	1	1	2	2	2	3	3	3	4	4	4
3	3	4	5	5	6	7	7	8	9	9	10	11
4	6	7	8	9	10	11	12	14	15	16	17	18
5	9	11	12	13	15	16	18	19	20	22	23	25
6	12	14	16	17	19	21	23	25	26	28	30	32
7	15	17	19	21	24	26	28	30	33	35	37	39
8	18	20	23	26	28	31	33	36	39	41	44	47
9	21	24	27	30	33	36	39	42	45	48	51	54
10	24	27	31	34	37	41	44	48	51	55	58	62
11	27	31	34	38	42	46	50	54	57	61	65	69
12	30	34	38	42	47	51	55	60	64	68	72	77
13	33	37	42	47	51	56	61	65	70	75	80	84
14	36	41	46	51	56	61	66	71	77	82	87	92
15	39	44	50	55	61	66	72	77	83	88	94	100
16	42	48	54	60	65	71	77	83	89	95	101	107
17	45	51	57	64	70	77	83	89	96	102	109	115
18	48	55	61	68	75	82	88	95	102	109	116	123
19	51	58	65	72	80	87	94	101	109	116	123	130
20	54	62	69	77	84	92	100	107	115	123	130	138

SOURCE: Adapted from Tables 1, 3, 5, and 7 of D. Aube, "Extended Tables for the Mann-Whitney Statistic," *Bulletin of the Institute of Educational Research at Indiana University*, 1953, 1, No. 2. From S. Siegel, *Nonparametric Statistics for the Behavior Sciences*. New York: McGraw-Hill Book Company, 1956. Reprinted by permission of the Institute of Educational Research and McGraw-Hill Book Company.

Table A–3 **Distribution for the Sign Test**

Alpha levels of the sign test for pairs of observations ranging from 3 to 41 x denotes the number of exceptions (the number of times the difference between conditions is in the unexpected direction), while the p level indicates the probability that that number of exceptions could occur by chance. If there are 28 paired observations and 20 are ordered in the expected direction, while only 8 are exceptions, the probability that this could occur by chance is .018.

x	p	x	p	x	p	x	p	x	p	x	p
n = 3		*n* = 12		*n* = 19		*n* = 25		*n* = 31		*n* = 37	
0	.125	1	.003	3	.002	5	.002	7	.002	10	.004
n = 4		2	.019	4	.010	6	.007	8	.005	11	.010
0	.062	3	.073	5	.032	7	.022	9	.015	12	.024
1	.312	4	.194	6	.084	8	.051	10	.035	13	.049
n = 5		*n* = 13		7	.180	9	.115	11	.075	14	.094
0	.031	1	.002	*n* = 20		10	.212	12	.141	15	.162
1	.188	2	.011	3	.001	*n* = 26		*n* = 32		*n* = 38	
n = 6		3	.016	4	.006	6	.005	8	.004	10	.003
0	.016	4	.133	5	.021	7	.014	9	.010	11	.007
1	.109	*n* = 14		6	.058	8	.038	10	.025	12	.017
2	.344	1	.001	7	.132	9	.084	11	.055	13	.036
n = 7		2	.006	*n* = 21		10	.163	12	.108	14	.072
0	.008	3	.029	4	.004	*n* = 27		13	.189	15	.128
1	.062	4	.090	5	.013	6	.003	*n* = 33		*n* = 39	
2	.227	5	.212	6	.039	7	.010	8	.002	11	.005
n = 8		*n* = 15		7	.095	8	.026	9	.007	12	.012
0	.004	1	.000	8	.192	9	.061	10	.018	13	.027
1	.035	2	.004	*n* = 22		10	.124	11	.040	14	.054
2	.145	3	.018	4	.002	11	.221	12	.081	15	.100
n = 9		4	.059	5	.008	*n* = 28		13	.148	16	.168
0	.002	5	.151	6	.026	6	.002	*n* = 34		*n* = 40	
1	.020	*n* = 16		7	.067	7	.006	9	.005	11	.003
2	.090	2	.002	8	.143	8	.018	10	.012	12	.008
3	.254	3	.011	*n* = 23		9	.044	11	.029	13	.019
n = 10		4	.038	4	.001	10	.092	12	.061	14	.040
0	.001	5	.105	5	.005	11	.172	13	.115	15	.077
1	.011	6	.227	6	.017	*n* = 29		14	.196	16	.134
2	.055	*n* = 17		7	.047	7	.004	*n* = 35		*n* = 41	
3	.172	2	.001	8	.105	8	.012	9	.003	11	.002
n = 11		3	.006	9	.202	9	.031	10	.008	12	.006
0	.000	4	.025	*n* = 24		10	.068	11	.020	13	.014
1	.006	5	.072	5	.008	11	.132	12	.045	14	.030
2	.033	6	.166	6	.011	*n* = 30		13	.088	15	.059
3	.113	*n* = 18		7	.032	7	.003	14	.155	16	.106
4	.274	3	.004	8	.076	8	.008	*n* = 36		17	.174
		4	.015	9	.154	9	.021	9	.002	*n* = 42	
		5	.048			10	.049	10	.006	12	.004
		6	.119			11	.100	11	.014	13	.010
		7	.240			12	.181	12	.033	14	.022
								13	.066	15	.044
								14	.121	16	.082
								15	.203	17	.140

Critical Values of Wilcoxon's *T* Statistic for the Matched-Pairs Signed-Ranks Test

In using this table, first locate the number of *pairs* of scores in the *n* column. The critical values for several levels of significance are listed in the columns to the right. For example, if *n* were 15 and the computed value 19, it would be concluded that since 19 is less than 25, the difference between conditions is significant beyond the .02 level of significance for a two-tailed test.

	Level of significance for one-tailed test		
	.025	.01	.005
	Level of significance for two-tailed test		
n	.05	.02	.01
6	1	—	—
7	2	0	—
8	4	2	0
9	6	3	2
10	8	5	3
11	11	7	5
12	14	10	7
13	17	13	10
14	21	16	13
15	25	20	16
16	30	24	19
17	35	28	23
18	40	33	28
19	46	38	32
20	52	43	37
21	59	49	43
22	66	56	49
23	73	62	55
24	81	69	61
25	90	77	68

Note that *n* is the number of matched pairs.

SOURCE: Adapted from Table I of F. Wilcoxon, *Some Rapid Approximate Statistical Procedures*, (Rev. ed.) New York: American Cyanamid Company, 1964. Taken from S. Siegel, *Nonparametric Statistics for the Behavioral Sciences*. New York: McGraw-Hill Book Company, 1956. Reprinted by permission of the American Cyanamid Company and McGraw-Hill Book Company.

Table A–5

Critical Values of *t*

To find the appropriate value of *t,* read across the row that contains the number of degrees of freedom in your experiment. The columns are determined by the level of significance you have chosen. The value of *t* you obtain must be *greater* than that in the table to be significant. For example, with $df = 15$ and $p = .05$ (two-tailed test), your *t* value must be greater than 2.131.

	Level of significance for one-tailed test					
	.10	.05	.025	.01	.055	.0005
	Level of significance for two-tailed test					
df	.20	.10	.05	.02	.01	.001
1	3.078	6.314	12.706	31.821	63.657	636.619
2	1.886	2.920	4.303	6.965	9.925	31.598
3	1.638	2.353	3.182	4.541	5.841	12.941
4	1.533	2.132	2.776	3.747	4.604	8.610
5	1.476	2.015	2.571	3.365	4.032	6.859
6	1.440	1.943	2.447	3.143	3.707	5.959
7	1.415	1.895	2.365	2.998	3.449	5.405
8	1.397	1.860	2.306	2.896	3.355	5.041
9	1.383	1.833	2.262	2.821	3.250	4.781
10	1.372	1.812	2.228	2.764	3.169	4.587
11	1.363	1.796	2.201	2.718	3.106	4.437
12	1.356	1.782	2.179	2.681	3.055	4.318
13	1.350	1.771	2.160	2.650	3.012	4.221
14	1.345	1.761	2.145	2.624	2.977	4.140
15	1.341	1.753	2.131	2.602	2.947	4.073
16	1.337	1.746	2.120	2.583	2.921	4.015
17	1.333	1.740	2.110	2.567	2.898	3.965
18	1.330	1.734	2.101	2.552	2.878	3.922
19	1.328	1.729	2.093	2.539	2.861	3.883
20	1.325	1.725	2.086	2.528	2.845	3.850
21	1.323	1.721	2.080	2.518	2.831	3.819
22	1.321	1.717	2.074	2.508	2.819	3.792
23	1.319	1.714	2.069	2.500	2.807	3.767
24	1.318	1.711	2.064	2.492	2.797	3.745
25	1.316	1.708	2.060	2.485	2.787	3.725
26	1.315	1.706	2.056	2.479	2.779	3.707
27	1.314	1.703	2.052	2.473	2.771	3.690
28	1.313	1.701	2.048	2.467	2.763	3.674
29	1.311	1.699	2.045	2.462	2.756	3.659
30	1.310	1.697	2.042	2.457	2.750	3.646
40	1.303	1.684	2.021	2.423	2.704	3.551
60	1.296	1.671	2.000	2.390	2.660	3.460
120	1.289	1.658	1.980	2.358	2.617	3.373
∞	1.282	1.645	1.960	2.326	2.576	3.291

Source: Taken from Table III of R. A. Fisher and F. Yates, "Statistical Tables for Biological, Agricultural and Medical Research," 6th ed. Oliver and Boyd, Edinburgh, 1963. Reproduced by permission of the authors and publishers.

Critical Values of the *F* Distribution

Find the location of appropriate values in table by looking up the degrees of freedom in the numerator and denominator of the *F*-ratio. After you have decided on the level of significance desired, the obtained *F*-ratio must be *greater* than that in the table. For example, with $p = .05$. and 10 *df* in the numerator and 28 in the denominator, your *F* value must be greater than 2.19 to be reliable.

df for denom.	α	1	2	3	4	5	6	7	8	9
	.25	2.02	2.28	2.36	2.39	2.41	2.42	2.43	2.44	2.44
	.10	5.54	5.46	5.39	5.34	5.31	5.28	5.27	5.25	5.24
	.05	10.1	9.55	9.28	9.12	9.01	8.94	8.89	8.85	8.81
3	.025	17.4	16.0	15.4	15.1	14.9	14.7	14.6	14.5	14.5
	.01	34.1	30.8	29.5	28.7	28.2	27.9	27.7	27.5	27.4
	.001	167	148	141	137	135	133	132	131	130
	.25	1.81	2.00	2.05	2.06	2.07	2.08	2.08	2.08	2.08
	.10	4.54	4.32	4.19	4.11	4.05	4.01	3.98	3.95	3.94
	.05	7.71	6.94	6.59	6.39	6.26	6.16	6.09	6.04	6.00
4	.025	12.2	10.6	9.98	9.60	9.36	9.20	9.07	8.98	8.90
	.01	21.2	18.0	16.7	16.0	15.5	15.2	15.0	14.8	14.7
	.001	74.1	61.2	56.2	53.4	51.7	50.5	49.7	49.0	48.5
	.25	1.69	1.85	1.88	1.89	1.89	1.89	1.89	1.89	1.89
	.10	4.06	3.78	3.62	3.52	3.45	3.40	3.37	3.34	3.32
	.05	6.61	5.79	5.41	5.19	5.05	4.95	4.88	4.82	4.77
5	.025	10.0	8.43	7.76	7.39	7.15	6.98	6.85	6.76	6.68
	.01	16.3	13.3	12.1	11.4	11.0	10.7	10.5	10.3	10.2
	.001	47.2	37.1	33.2	31.1	29.8	28.8	28.2	27.6	27.2
	.25	1.62	1.76	1.78	1.79	1.79	1.78	1.78	1.78	1.77
	.10	3.78	3.46	3.29	3.18	3.11	3.05	3.01	2.98	2.96
	.05	5.99	5.14	4.76	4.53	4.39	4.28	4.21	4.15	4.10
6	.025	8.81	7.26	6.60	6.23	5.99	5.82	5.70	5.60	5.52
	.01	13.8	10.9	9.78	9.15	8.75	8.47	8.26	8.10	7.98
	.001	35.5	27.0	23.7	21.9	20.8	20.0	19.5	19.0	18.7
	.25	1.57	1.70	1.72	1.72	1.71	1.71	1.70	1.70	1.69
	.10	3.59	3.26	3.07	2.96	2.88	2.83	2.78	2.75	2.72
	.05	5.59	4.74	4.35	4.12	3.97	3.87	3.79	3.73	3.68
7	.025	8.07	6.54	5.89	5.52	5.29	5.12	4.99	4.90	4.82
	.01	12.2	9.55	8.45	7.85	7.46	7.19	6.99	6.84	6.72
	.001	29.2	21.7	18.8	17.2	16.2	15.5	15.0	14.6	14.3
	.25	1.54	1.66	1.67	1.66	1.66	1.65	1.64	1.64	1.63
	.10	3.46	3.11	2.92	2.81	2.73	2.67	2.62	2.59	2.56
	.05	5.32	4.46	4.07	3.84	3.69	3.58	3.50	3.44	3.39
8	.025	7.57	6.06	5.42	5.05	4.82	4.65	4.53	4.43	4.36
	.01	11.3	8.65	7.59	7.01	6.63	6.37	6.18	6.03	5.91
	.001	25.4	18.5	15.8	14.4	13.5	12.9	12.4	12.0	11.8
	.25	1.51	1.62	1.63	1.63	1.62	1.61	1.60	1.60	1.59
	.10	3.36	3.01	2.81	2.69	2.61	2.55	2.51	2.47	2.44
	.05	5.12	4.26	3.86	3.63	3.48	3.37	3.29	3.23	3.18
9	.025	7.21	5.71	5.08	4.72	4.48	4.32	4.20	4.10	4.03
	.01	10.6	8.02	6.99	6.42	6.06	5.80	5.61	5.47	5.35
	.001	22.9	16.4	13.9	12.6	11.7	11.1	10.7	10.4	10.1

Table A–6 *(Continued)*

df for denom.	\multicolumn{9}{c}{df for numerator}
	10	12	15	20	24	30	40	60	∞
	2.44	2.45	2.46	2.46	2.46	2.47	2.47	2.47	2.47
	5.23	5.22	5.20	5.18	5.18	5.17	5.16	5.15	5.13
	8.79	8.74	8.70	8.66	8.64	8.62	8.59	8.57	8.53
3	14.4	14.3	14.2	14.2	14.1	14.1	14.0	14.0	13.9
	27.2	27.0	26.9	26.7	26.6	26.5	26.4	26.3	26.1
	129	128	127	126	126	125	125	124	124
	2.08	2.08	2.08	2.08	2.08	2.08	2.08	2.08	2.08
	3.92	3.90	3.87	3.84	3.83	3.82	3.80	3.79	3.76
	5.96	5.91	5.86	5.80	5.77	5.75	5.72	5.69	5.63
4	8.84	8.75	8.66	8.56	8.51	8.46	8.41	8.36	8.26
	14.6	14.4	14.2	14.0	13.9	13.8	13.8	13.6	13.5
	48.0	47.4	46.8	46.1	45.8	45.4	45.1	44.8	44.0
	1.89	1.89	1.89	1.88	1.88	1.88	1.88	1.87	1.87
	3.30	3.27	3.24	3.21	3.19	3.17	3.16	3.14	3.10
	4.74	4.68	4.62	4.56	4.53	4.50	4.46	4.43	4.36
5	6.62	6.52	6.43	6.33	6.28	6.23	6.18	6.12	6.02
	10.0	9.89	9.72	9.55	9.47	9.38	9.29	9.20	9.02
	26.9	26.4	25.9	25.4	25.1	24.9	24.6	24.3	23.8
	1.77	1.77	1.76	1.76	1.75	1.75	1.75	1.74	1.74
	2.94	2.90	2.87	2.84	2.82	2.80	2.78	2.76	2.72
	4.06	4.00	3.94	3.87	3.84	3.81	3.77	3.74	3.67
6	5.46	5.37	5.27	5.17	5.12	5.07	5.01	4.96	4.85
	7.87	7.72	7.56	7.40	7.31	7.23	7.14	7.06	6.88
	18.4	18.0	17.6	17.1	16.9	16.7	16.4	16.2	15.8
	1.69	1.68	1.68	1.67	1.67	1.66	1.66	1.65	1.65
	2.70	2.67	2.63	2.59	2.58	2.56	2.54	2.51	2.47
	3.64	3.57	3.51	3.44	3.41	3.38	3.34	3.30	3.23
7	4.76	4.67	4.57	4.47	4.42	4.36	4.31	4.25	4.14
	6.62	6.47	6.31	6.16	6.07	5.99	5.91	5.82	5.65
	14.1	13.7	13.3	12.9	12.7	12.5	12.3	12.1	11.7
	1.63	1.62	1.62	1.61	1.60	1.60	1.59	1.59	1.58
	2.54	2.50	2.46	2.42	2.40	2.38	2.36	2.34	2.29
	3.35	3.28	3.22	3.15	3.12	3.08	3.04	3.01	2.93
8	4.30	4.20	4.10	4.00	3.95	3.89	3.84	3.78	3.67
	5.81	5.67	5.52	5.36	5.28	5.20	5.12	5.03	4.86
	11.5	11.2	10.8	10.5	10.3	10.1	9.92	9.73	9.33
	1.59	1.58	1.57	1.56	1.56	1.55	1.54	1.54	1.53
	2.42	2.38	2.34	2.30	2.28	2.25	2.23	2.21	2.16
	3.14	3.07	3.01	2.94	2.90	2.86	2.83	2.79	2.71
9	3.96	3.87	3.77	3.67	3.61	3.56	3.51	3.45	3.33
	5.26	5.11	4.96	4.81	4.73	4.65	4.57	4.48	4.31
	9.89	9.57	9.24	8.90	8.72	8.55	8.37	8.19	7.81

df for denom.	α	1	2	3	4	5	6	7	8	9
					df for numerator					
	.25	1.49	1.60	1.60	1.59	1.59	1.58	1.57	1.56	1.56
	.10	3.29	2.92	2.73	2.61	2.52	2.46	2.41	2.38	2.35
	.05	4.96	4.10	3.71	3.48	3.33	3.22	3.14	3.07	3.02
10	.025	6.94	5.46	4.83	4.47	4.24	4.07	3.95	3.85	3.78
	.01	10.0	7.56	6.55	5.99	5.64	5.39	5.20	5.06	4.94
	.001	21.0	14.9	12.6	11.3	10.5	9.92	9.52	9.20	8.96
	.25	1.47	1.58	1.58	1.57	1.56	1.55	1.54	1.53	1.53
	.10	3.23	2.86	2.66	2.54	2.45	2.39	2.34	2.30	2.27
	.05	4.84	3.98	3.59	3.36	3.20	3.09	3.01	2.95	2.90
11	.025	6.72	5.26	4.63	4.28	4.04	3.88	3.76	3.66	3.59
	.01	9.65	7.21	6.22	5.67	5.32	5.07	4.89	4.74	4.63
	.001	19.7	13.8	11.6	10.4	9.58	9.05	8.66	8.35	8.12
	.25	1.46	1.56	1.56	1.55	1.54	1.53	1.52	1.51	1.51
	.10	3.18	2.81	2.61	2.48	2.39	2.33	2.28	2.24	2.21
	.05	4.75	3.89	3.49	3.26	3.11	3.00	2.91	2.85	2.80
12	.025	6.55	5.10	4.47	4.12	3.89	3.73	3.61	3.51	3.44
	.01	9.33	6.93	5.95	5.41	5.06	4.82	4.64	4.50	4.39
	.001	18.6	13.0	10.8	9.63	8.89	8.38	8.00	7.71	7.48
	.25	1.45	1.55	1.55	1.53	1.52	1.51	1.50	1.49	1.49
	.10	3.14	2.76	2.56	2.43	2.35	2.28	2.23	2.20	2.16
	.05	4.67	3.81	3.41	3.18	3.03	2.92	2.83	2.77	2.71
13	.025	6.41	4.97	4.35	4.00	3.77	3.60	3.48	3.39	3.31
	.01	9.07	6.70	5.74	5.21	4.86	4.62	4.44	4.30	4.19
	.001	17.8	12.3	10.2	9.07	8.35	7.86	7.49	7.21	6.98
	.25	1.44	1.53	1.53	1.52	1.51	1.50	1.49	1.48	1.47
	.10	3.10	2.73	2.52	2.39	2.31	2.24	2.19	2.15	2.12
	.05	4.60	3.74	3.34	3.11	2.96	2.85	2.76	2.70	2.65
14	.025	6.30	4.86	4.24	3.89	3.66	3.50	3.38	3.29	3.21
	.01	8.86	6.51	5.56	5.04	4.69	4.46	4.28	4.14	4.03
	.001	17.1	11.8	9.73	8.62	7.92	7.43	7.08	6.80	6.58
	.25	1.43	1.52	1.52	1.51	1.49	1.48	1.47	1.46	1.46
	.10	3.07	2.70	2.49	2.36	2.27	2.21	2.16	2.12	2.09
	.05	4.54	3.68	3.29	3.06	2.90	2.79	2.71	2.64	2.59
15	.025	6.20	4.77	4.15	3.80	3.58	3.41	3.29	3.20	3.12
	.01	8.68	6.36	5.42	4.89	4.56	4.32	4.14	4.00	3.89
	.001	16.6	11.3	9.34	8.25	7.57	7.09	6.74	6.47	6.26
	.25	1.42	1.51	1.51	1.50	1.48	1.47	1.46	1.45	1.44
	.10	3.05	2.67	2.46	2.33	2.24	2.18	2.13	2.09	2.06
	.05	4.49	3.63	3.24	3.01	2.85	2.74	2.66	2.59	2.54
16	.025	6.12	4.69	4.08	3.73	3.50	3.34	3.22	3.12	3.05
	.01	8.53	6.23	5.29	4.77	4.44	4.20	4.03	3.89	3.78
	.001	16.1	11.0	9.00	7.94	7.27	6.81	6.46	6.19	5.98
	.25	1.42	1.51	1.50	1.49	1.47	1.46	1.45	1.44	1.43
	.10	3.03	2.64	2.44	2.31	2.22	2.15	2.10	2.06	2.03
	.05	4.45	3.59	3.20	2.96	2.81	2.70	2.61	2.55	2.49
17	.025	6.04	4.62	4.01	3.66	3.44	3.28	3.16	3.06	2.98
	.01	8.40	6.11	5.18	4.67	4.34	4.10	3.93	3.79	3.68
	.001	15.7	10.7	8.73	7.68	7.02	6.56	6.22	5.96	5.75

Table A–6 *(Continued)*

df for denom.	df for numerator								
	10	12	15	20	24	30	40	60	∞
	1.55	1.54	1.53	1.52	1.52	1.51	1.51	1.50	1.48
	2.32	2.28	2.24	2.20	2.18	2.16	2.13	2.11	2.06
	2.98	2.91	2.85	2.77	2.74	2.70	2.66	2.62	2.54
10	3.72	3.62	3.52	3.42	3.37	3.31	3.26	3.20	3.08
	4.85	4.71	4.56	4.41	4.33	4.25	4.17	4.08	3.91
	8.75	8.45	8.13	7.80	7.64	7.47	7.30	7.12	6.76
	1.52	1.51	1.50	1.49	1.49	1.48	1.47	1.47	1.45
	2.25	2.21	2.17	2.12	2.10	2.08	2.05	2.03	1.97
	2.85	2.79	2.72	2.65	2.61	2.57	2.53	2.49	2.40
11	3.53	3.43	3.33	3.23	3.17	3.12	3.06	3.00	2.88
	4.54	4.40	4.25	4.10	4.02	3.94	3.86	3.78	3.60
	7.92	7.63	7.32	7.01	6.85	6.68	6.52	6.35	6.00
	1.50	1.49	1.48	1.47	1.46	1.45	1.45	1.44	1.42
	2.19	2.15	2.10	2.06	2.04	2.01	1.99	1.96	1.90
	2.75	2.69	2.62	2.54	2.51	2.47	2.43	2.38	2.30
12	3.37	3.28	3.18	3.07	3.02	2.96	2.91	2.85	2.72
	4.30	4.16	4.01	3.86	3.78	3.70	3.62	3.54	3.36
	7.29	7.00	6.71	6.40	6.25	6.09	5.93	5.76	5.42
	1.48	1.47	1.46	1.45	1.44	1.43	1.42	1.42	1.40
	2.14	2.10	2.05	2.01	1.98	1.96	1.93	1.90	1.85
	2.67	2.60	2.53	2.46	2.42	2.38	2.34	2.30	2.21
13	3.25	3.15	3.05	2.95	2.89	2.84	2.78	2.72	2.60
	4.10	3.96	3.82	3.66	3.59	3.51	3.43	3.34	3.17
	6.80	6.52	6.23	5.93	5.78	5.63	5.47	5.30	4.97
	1.46	1.45	1.44	1.43	1.42	1.41	1.41	1.40	1.38
	2.10	2.05	2.01	1.96	1.94	1.91	1.89	1.86	1.80
	2.60	2.53	2.46	2.39	2.35	2.31	2.27	2.22	2.13
14	3.15	3.05	2.95	2.84	2.79	2.73	2.67	2.61	2.49
	3.94	3.80	3.66	3.51	3.43	3.35	3.27	3.18	3.00
	6.40	6.13	5.85	5.56	5.41	5.25	5.10	4.94	4.60
	1.45	1.44	1.43	1.41	1.41	1.40	1.39	1.38	1.36
	2.06	2.02	1.97	1.92	1.90	1.87	1.85	1.82	1.76
	2.54	2.48	2.40	2.33	2.29	2.25	2.20	2.16	2.07
15	3.06	2.96	2.86	2.76	2.70	2.64	2.59	2.52	2.40
	3.80	3.67	3.52	3.37	3.29	3.21	3.13	3.05	2.87
	6.08	5.81	5.54	5.25	5.10	4.95	4.80	4.64	4.31
	1.44	1.43	1.41	1.40	1.39	1.38	1.37	1.36	1.34
	2.03	1.99	1.94	1.89	1.87	1.84	1.81	1.78	1.72
	2.49	2.42	2.35	2.28	2.24	2.19	2.15	2.11	2.01
16	2.99	2.89	2.79	2.68	2.63	2.57	2.51	2.45	2.32
	3.69	3.55	3.41	3.26	3.18	3.10	3.02	2.93	2.75
	5.81	5.55	5.27	4.99	4.85	4.70	4.54	4.39	4.06
	1.43	1.41	1.40	1.39	1.38	1.37	1.36	1.35	1.33
	2.00	1.96	1.91	1.86	1.84	1.81	1.78	1.75	1.69
	2.45	2.38	2.31	2.23	2.19	2.15	2.10	2.06	1.96
17	2.92	2.82	2.72	2.62	2.56	2.50	2.44	2.38	2.25
	3.59	3.46	3.31	3.16	3.08	3.00	2.92	2.83	2.65
	5.58	5.32	5.05	4.78	4.63	4.48	4.33	4.18	3.85

df for denom.	α	df for numerator								
		1	2	3	4	5	6	7	8	9
	.25	1.41	1.50	1.49	1.48	1.46	1.45	1.44	1.43	1.42
	.10	3.01	2.62	2.42	2.29	2.20	2.13	2.08	2.04	2.00
	.05	4.41	3.55	3.16	2.93	2.77	2.66	2.58	2.51	2.46
18	.025	5.98	4.56	3.95	3.61	3.38	3.22	3.10	3.01	2.93
	.01	8.29	6.01	5.09	4.58	4.25	4.01	3.84	3.71	3.60
	.001	15.4	10.4	8.49	7.46	6.81	6.35	6.02	5.76	5.56
	.25	1.41	1.49	1.49	1.47	1.46	1.44	1.43	1.42	1.41
	.10	2.99	2.61	2.40	2.27	2.18	2.11	2.06	2.02	1.98
	.05	4.38	3.52	3.13	2.90	2.74	2.63	2.54	2.48	2.42
19	.025	5.92	4.51	3.90	3.56	3.33	3.17	3.05	2.96	2.88
	.01	8.18	5.93	5.01	4.50	4.17	3.94	3.77	3.63	3.52
	.001	15.1	10.2	8.28	7.26	6.62	6.18	5.85	5.59	5.39
	.25	1.40	1.49	1.48	1.47	1.45	1.44	1.43	1.42	1.41
	.10	2.97	2.59	2.38	2.25	2.16	2.09	2.04	2.00	1.96
	.05	4.35	3.49	3.10	2.87	2.71	2.60	2.51	2.45	2.39
20	.025	5.87	4.46	3.86	3.51	3.29	3.13	3.01	2.91	2.84
	.01	8.10	5.85	4.94	4.43	4.10	3.87	3.70	3.56	3.46
	.001	14.8	9.95	8.10	7.10	6.46	6.02	5.69	5.44	5.24
	.25	1.40	1.48	1.47	1.45	1.44	1.42	1.41	1.40	1.39
	.10	2.95	2.56	2.35	2.22	2.13	2.06	2.01	1.97	1.93
	.05	4.30	3.44	3.05	2.82	2.66	2.55	2.46	2.40	2.34
22	.025	5.79	4.38	3.78	3.44	3.22	3.05	2.93	2.84	2.76
	.01	7.95	5.72	4.82	4.31	3.99	3.76	3.59	3.45	3.35
	.001	14.4	9.61	7.80	6.81	6.19	5.76	5.44	5.19	4.99
	.25	1.39	1.47	1.46	1.44	1.43	1.41	1.40	1.39	1.38
	.10	2.93	2.54	2.33	2.19	2.10	2.04	1.98	1.94	1.91
	.05	4.26	3.40	3.01	2.78	2.62	2.51	2.42	2.36	2.30
24	.025	5.72	4.32	3.72	3.38	3.15	2.99	2.87	2.78	2.70
	.01	7.82	5.61	4.72	4.22	3.90	3.67	3.50	3.36	3.26
	.001	14.0	9.34	7.55	6.59	5.98	5.55	5.23	4.99	4.80
	.25	1.38	1.46	1.45	1.44	1.42	1.41	1.39	1.38	1.37
	.10	2.91	2.52	2.31	2.17	2.08	2.01	1.96	1.92	1.88
	.05	4.23	3.37	2.98	2.74	2.59	2.47	2.39	2.32	2.27
26	.025	5.66	4.27	3.67	3.33	3.10	2.94	2.82	2.73	2.65
	.01	7.72	5.53	4.64	4.14	3.82	3.59	3.42	3.29	3.18
	.001	13.7	9.12	7.36	6.41	5.80	5.38	5.07	4.83	4.64
	.25	1.38	1.46	1.45	1.43	1.41	1.40	1.39	1.38	1.37
	.10	2.89	2.50	2.29	2.16	2.06	2.00	1.94	1.90	1.87
	.05	4.20	3.34	2.95	2.71	2.56	2.45	2.36	2.29	2.24
28	.025	5.61	4.22	3.63	3.29	3.06	2.90	2.78	2.69	2.61
	.01	7.64	5.45	4.57	4.07	3.75	3.53	3.36	3.23	3.12
	.001	13.5	8.93	7.19	6.25	5.66	5.24	4.93	4.69	4.50
	.25	1.38	1.45	1.44	1.42	1.41	1.39	1.38	1.37	1.36
	.10	2.88	2.49	2.28	2.14	2.05	1.98	1.93	1.88	1.85
	.05	4.17	3.32	2.92	2.69	2.53	2.42	2.33	2.27	2.21
30	.025	5.57	4.18	3.59	3.25	3.03	2.87	2.75	2.65	2.57
	.01	7.56	5.39	4.51	4.02	3.70	3.47	3.30	3.17	3.07
	.001	13.3	8.77	7.05	6.12	5.53	5.12	4.82	4.58	4.39

Table A–6 *(Continued)*

df for denom.	10	12	15	20	24	30	40	60	∞
					df for numerator				
	1.42	1.40	1.39	1.38	1.37	1.36	1.35	1.34	1.32
	1.98	1.93	1.89	1.84	1.81	1.78	1.75	1.72	1.66
	2.41	2.34	2.27	2.19	2.15	2.11	2.06	2.02	1.92
18	2.87	2.77	2.67	2.56	2.50	2.44	2.38	2.32	2.19
	3.51	3.37	3.23	3.08	3.00	2.92	2.84	2.75	2.57
	5.39	5.13	4.87	4.59	4.45	4.30	4.15	4.00	3.67
	1.41	1.40	1.38	1.37	1.36	1.35	1.34	1.33	1.30
	1.96	1.91	1.86	1.81	1.79	1.76	1.73	1.70	1.63
	2.38	2.31	2.23	2.16	2.11	2.07	2.03	1.98	1.88
19	2.82	2.72	2.62	2.51	2.45	2.39	2.33	2.27	2.13
	3.43	3.30	3.15	3.00	2.92	2.84	2.76	2.67	2.49
	5.22	4.97	4.70	4.43	4.29	4.14	3.99	3.84	3.51
	1.40	1.39	1.37	1.36	1.35	1.34	1.33	1.32	1.29
	1.94	1.89	1.84	1.79	1.77	1.74	1.71	1.68	1.61
	2.35	2.28	2.20	2.12	2.08	2.04	1.99	1.95	1.84
20	2.77	2.68	2.57	2.46	2.41	2.35	2.29	2.22	2.09
	3.37	3.23	3.09	2.94	2.86	2.78	2.69	2.61	2.42
	5.08	4.82	4.56	4.29	4.15	4.00	3.86	3.70	3.38
	1.39	1.37	1.36	1.34	1.33	1.32	1.31	1.30	1.28
	1.90	1.86	1.81	1.76	1.73	1.70	1.67	1.64	1.57
	2.30	2.23	2.15	2.07	2.03	1.98	1.94	1.89	1.78
22	2.70	2.60	2.50	2.39	2.33	2.27	2.21	2.14	2.00
	3.26	3.12	2.98	2.83	2.75	2.67	2.58	2.50	2.31
	4.83	4.58	4.33	4.06	3.92	3.78	3.63	3.48	3.15
	1.38	1.36	1.35	1.33	1.32	1.31	1.30	1.29	1.26
	1.88	1.83	1.78	1.73	1.70	1.67	1.64	1.61	1.53
	2.25	2.18	2.11	2.03	1.98	1.94	1.89	1.84	1.73
24	2.64	2.54	2.44	2.33	2.27	2.21	2.15	2.08	1.94
	3.17	3.03	2.89	2.74	2.66	2.58	2.49	2.40	2.21
	4.64	4.39	4.14	3.87	3.74	3.59	3.45	3.29	2.97
	1.37	1.35	1.34	1.32	1.31	1.30	1.29	1.28	1.25
	1.86	1.81	1.76	1.71	1.68	1.65	1.61	1.58	1.50
	2.22	2.15	2.07	1.99	1.95	1.90	1.85	1.80	1.69
26	2.59	2.49	2.39	2.28	2.22	2.16	2.09	2.03	1.88
	3.09	2.96	2.81	2.66	2.58	2.50	2.42	2.33	2.13
	4.48	4.24	3.99	3.72	3.59	3.44	3.30	3.15	2.82
	1.36	1.34	1.33	1.31	1.30	1.29	1.28	1.27	1.24
	1.84	1.79	1.74	1.69	1.66	1.63	1.59	1.56	1.48
	2.19	2.12	2.04	1.96	1.91	1.87	1.82	1.77	1.65
28	2.55	2.45	2.34	2.23	2.17	2.11	2.05	1.98	1.83
	3.03	2.90	2.75	2.60	2.52	2.44	2.35	2.26	2.06
	4.35	4.11	3.86	3.60	3.46	3.32	3.18	3.02	2.69
	1.35	1.34	1.32	1.30	1.29	1.28	1.27	1.26	1.23
	1.82	1.77	1.72	1.67	1.64	1.61	1.57	1.54	1.46
	2.16	2.09	2.01	1.93	1.89	1.84	1.79	1.74	1.62
30	2.51	2.41	2.31	2.20	2.14	2.07	2.01	1.94	1.79
	2.98	2.84	2.70	2.55	2.47	2.39	2.30	2.21	2.01
	4.24	4.00	3.75	3.49	3.36	3.22	3.07	2.92	2.59

df for denom.	α	1	2	3	4	5	6	7	8	9
					df for numerator					
	.25	1.36	1.44	1.42	1.40	1.39	1.37	1.36	1.35	1.34
	.10	2.84	2.44	2.23	2.09	2.00	1.93	1.87	1.83	1.79
	.05	4.08	3.23	2.84	2.61	2.45	2.34	2.25	2.18	2.12
40	.025	5.42	4.05	3.46	3.13	2.90	2.74	2.62	2.53	2.45
	.01	7.31	5.18	4.31	3.83	3.51	3.29	3.12	2.99	2.89
	.001	12.6	8.25	6.60	5.70	5.13	4.73	4.44	4.21	4.02
	.25	1.35	1.42	1.41	1.38	1.37	1.35	1.33	1.32	1.31
	.10	2.79	2.39	2.18	2.04	1.95	1.87	1.82	1.77	1.74
	.05	4.00	3.15	2.76	2.53	2.37	2.25	2.17	2.10	2.04
60	.025	5.29	3.93	3.34	3.01	2.79	2.63	2.51	2.41	2.33
	.01	7.08	4.98	4.13	3.65	3.34	3.12	2.95	2.82	2.72
	.001	12.0	7.76	6.17	5.31	4.76	4.37	4.09	3.87	3.69
	.25	1.34	1.40	1.39	1.37	1.35	1.33	1.31	1.30	1.29
	.10	2.75	2.35	2.13	1.99	1.90	1.82	1.77	1.72	1.68
	.05	3.92	3.07	2.68	2.45	2.29	2.17	2.09	2.02	1.96
120	.025	5.15	3.80	3.23	2.89	2.67	2.52	2.39	2.30	2.22
	.01	6.85	4.79	3.95	3.48	3.17	2.96	2.79	2.66	2.56
	.001	11.4	7.32	5.79	4.95	4.42	4.04	3.77	3.55	3.38
	.25	1.32	1.39	1.37	1.35	1.33	1.31	1.29	1.28	1.27
	.10	2.71	2.30	2.08	1.94	1.85	1.77	1.72	1.67	1.63
	.05	3.84	3.00	2.60	2.37	2.21	2.10	2.01	1.94	1.88
∞	.025	5.02	3.69	3.12	2.79	2.57	2.41	2.29	2.19	2.11
	.01	6.63	4.61	3.78	3.32	3.02	2.80	2.64	2.51	2.41
	.001	10.8	6.91	5.42	4.62	4.10	3.74	3.47	3.27	3.10

Table A–6 *(Continued)*

df for denom.	df for numerator								
	10	12	15	20	24	30	40	60	∞
	1.33	1.31	1.30	1.28	1.26	1.25	1.24	1.22	1.19
	1.76	1.71	1.66	1.61	1.57	1.54	1.51	1.47	1.38
	2.08	2.00	1.92	1.84	1.79	1.74	1.69	1.64	1.51
40	2.39	2.29	2.18	2.07	2.01	1.94	1.88	1.80	1.64
	2.80	2.66	2.52	2.37	2.29	2.20	2.11	2.02	1.80
	3.87	3.64	3.40	3.15	3.01	2.87	2.73	2.57	2.23
	1.30	1.29	1.27	1.25	1.24	1.22	1.21	1.19	1.15
	1.71	1.66	1.60	1.54	1.51	1.48	1.44	1.40	1.29
	1.99	1.92	1.84	1.75	1.70	1.65	1.59	1.53	1.39
60	2.27	2.17	2.06	1.94	1.88	1.82	1.74	1.67	1.48
	2.63	2.50	2.35	2.20	2.12	2.03	1.94	1.84	1.60
	3.54	3.31	3.08	2.83	2.69	2.55	2.41	2.25	1.89
	1.28	1.26	1.24	1.22	1.21	1.19	1.18	1.16	1.10
	1.65	1.60	1.55	1.48	1.45	1.41	1.37	1.32	1.19
	1.91	1.83	1.75	1.66	1.61	1.55	1.50	1.43	1.25
120	2.16	2.05	1.94	1.82	1.76	1.69	1.61	1.53	1.31
	2.47	2.34	2.19	2.03	1.95	1.86	1.76	1.66	1.38
	3.24	3.02	2.78	2.53	2.40	2.26	2.11	1.95	1.54
	1.25	1.24	1.22	1.19	1.18	1.16	1.14	1.12	1.00
	1.60	1.55	1.49	1.42	1.38	1.34	1.30	1.24	1.00
	1.83	1.75	1.67	1.57	1.52	1.46	1.39	1.32	1.00
∞	2.05	1.94	1.83	1.71	1.64	1.57	1.48	1.39	1.00
	2.32	2.18	2.04	1.88	1.79	1.70	1.59	1.47	1.00
	2.96	2.74	2.51	2.27	2.13	1.99	1.84	1.66	1.00

Author Index

Subject Index

Credits

Alpha production in humans under conditions of false feedback, by Ernest Lindholm and Steven Lowry, pp. 54–61. Copyright 1978 by the Psychonomic Society. Reprinted by permission.

Table 4-1, p. 78. Copyright 1965 by the American Psychological Association. Reprinted by permission.

Table 4-4, p. 93. Reprinted courtesy of the National Institutes of Health.

Table 4-5, p. 94. Copyright 1972 by the American Psychological Association. Reprinted by permission.

Table 4-6, p. 95. Copyright 1972 by the American Psychological Association. Reprinted by permission.

Table 4-7, p. 97. Copyright 1973 by the American Psychological Association. Reprinted by permission.

Figure 8-6, p. 194. Copyright 1958 by the American Psychological Association. Used by permission.

Table 9-1 and Table 9-2, p. 203 and p. 205. From *Elements of Statistics for Psychology and Education* by L. M. Horowitz. Copyright 1974 by McGraw-Hill. Used by permission of McGraw-Hill Book Company.

Table 11-2, p. 274. Copyright 1978 by the American Psychological Association. Reprinted by permission.